The Age of Van Eyck
*The Mediterranean World
and Early Netherlandish Painting*
1430–1530

The Age of Van Eyck

The Mediterranean World and Early Netherlandish Painting 1430–1530

Till-Holger Borchert

with contributions by

Andreas Beyer
Dagmar Eichberger
Paul Huvenne
Margaret L. Koster
Philippe Lorentz
Mauro Lucco
Michael North
Paula Nuttall
Elena Parma
Jacques Paviot
José Luís Porfírio
Manfred Sellink
Pilar Silva Maroto
Joaquín Yarza Luaces

With 375 illustrations, 370 in colour

Thames & Hudson

First published on the occasion of the exhibition
Jan van Eyck, de Vlaamse Primitieven en het Zuiden,
1430–1530, held at the Groeningemuseum, Bruges,
from 15 March to 30 June 2002, as part of 'Bruges 2002
– European City of Culture'.
The exhibition was produced by 'Bruges 2002'
and organized by the Stedelijke Musea, Bruges.

First published in the United Kingdom in 2002
by Thames & Hudson Ltd, 181A High Holborn,
London WC1V 7QX

First published in hardcover in the United States
of America in 2002 by Thames & Hudson Inc.,
500 Fifth Avenue, New York, New York 10110

British Library Cataloguing-in-Publication Data
A catalogue record for this book is available from
the British Library.

Library of Congress Catalog Card Number
2001099215

ISBN 0-500-23795-6

Translation: (from the German and Dutch) Ted Alkins;
(from the French and Italian) Caroline Beamish;
(from the Spanish and Portuguese) Alayne Pullen
and Julie Martin, in association with First Edition
Translations Ltd, Cambridge, UK

Printed in Belgium

Illustrations:
Frontispiece: Jan van Eyck, *The Virgin and Child with
Saints Donatian and George and Canon Joris van der Paele*
(detail of cat. 22)
Page 226, Master of San Lorenzo della Costa,
Triptych of Saint Andrew (detail of fig. 116)

Contents

Foreword

For Bruges, 1902 was an extraordinary year in which tens of thousands of visitors descended on the city to view a highly ambitious exhibition devoted to the 'Flemish Primitives'. That ground-breaking show, a blockbuster featuring hundreds of paintings and *objets d'art*, did much to mould international public admiration for and study of Jan van Eyck and the masters who followed in his wake.

It would have been all too easy and predictable to stage some kind of pale imitation of that earlier exhibition during Bruges' year as European City of Culture. Instead, 'Bruges 2002' was keen from the outset to explore Early Netherlandish painting in a fresh, contemporary light, taking full account of the latest research. The dismantling of national frontiers and the advent of European monetary union may have influenced the desire to look to the intensive cross-border interaction that existed in fifteenth-century Europe in pursuit of an intellectual concept that has proved as challenging as it is ambitious – 'The Age of Jan van Eyck. The Mediterranean World and Early Netherlandish Painting'. The purpose of the exhibition – a collaboration between 'Bruges 2002' and the Stedelijke Musea (Municipal Museums) of Bruges – is to examine the interaction between artists in the Low Countries and the Mediterranean, and to reveal the extent to which this was a manifestation of the prevailing political, dynastic and economic relations between northern and southern Europe.

A great many people and institutions have, of course, taken part in the preparation, organization and realization of this exhibition and the accompanying catalogue. As much as we would like to, we cannot thank each of them individually for their contribution and enthusiasm. All the same, there are a number of key figures whom we must mention by name.

First of all, we are grateful to Till-Holger Borchert, who curated the exhibition and who, together with Valentin Vermeersch (Honorary Chief Curator of the Bruges Museums) and Hilde Lobelle-Caluwé (Curator of the Memlingmuseum–Sint-Janshospitaal), shaped the underlying concept and subsequently devoted two years of his life to the project. Manfred Sellink, Project Director and current Chief Curator, bore overall responsibility for the organization. The event could never have been realized without the assiduous collaboration of the research assistant Ina Verrept and of Lothar Casteleyn, Beatrijs Eemans and Véronique de Schepper, who made up the core 'exhibition cell'.

We are also grateful to all the staff of 'Bruges 2002' and the Stedelijke Musea, which co-operated in an exemplary manner in occasionally difficult and frequently hectic conditions. Our congratulations go to Peter Ruyffelaere, head of Ludion Press, and to everyone involved in the production of this book for the fine result they have achieved, while the board and volunteers of the Friends of the Municipal Museums deserve our gratitude for a contribution that was as great as we have come to expect.

Without the generosity of all the museums, art dealers and private collectors who lent the works on show, we would not, of course, have had the opportunity to write this foreword. We are all the more grateful to them, because we fully recognize that lending fragile fifteenth-century panels – almost all of which are on permanent display in their collections – is far from straightforward these days. The same goes for the financial support provided by our three sponsors, Electrabel, KBC and Randstad, without whose contribution we could never have embarked on this project in the first place.

What matters, however, to you – the visitor – is not how much effort has been expended but how fruitful it has been. We trust that you will enjoy visiting the exhibition and reading this catalogue every bit as much as we have.

Hugo De Greef
Director Bruges 2002

Patrick Moenaert
Mayor of Bruges
Chairman Bruges 2002

Preface

The desire to organize a large-scale exhibition in Bruges in 2002, devoted to the relationship between Early Netherlandish masters and painters from southern Europe, was not destined to make our lives any easier. It was no mean feat to bring together some 130 paintings from the fifteenth century – almost all of them on panel – the majority of which are pre-eminent works in their respective permanent collections. Yet, thanks to the immense effort and support of the scientific committee and the exceptional generosity of all the lenders, the exhibition has indeed been staged.

It was never the intention – even assuming that such a thing might be possible – to produce a re-run of the famous 'Flemish Primitives' exhibition, held in Bruges' Provinciaal Hof in 1902. Nevertheless, the current exhibition cannot be viewed in isolation from its illustrious predecessor, which represented one of the most significant moments in the reassessment of Early Netherlandish painting, while simultaneously providing an important stimulus to Bruges' development as a centre of cultural tourism.

The exhibition concept draws on two lines of research. First of all, we wished to explore the issue – viewed by some as outdated – of how far dynastic relations in fifteenth-century Europe influenced the international dissemination of the Flemish *ars nova*. Secondly, we were interested in how quickly and in what way Early Netherlandish painters exerted their influence on their French, Spanish, Portuguese and, of course, Italian counterparts. The relationship with Italy was addressed by the exhibition 'Il Rinascimento a Venezia e la pittura del Nord' ('Renaissance Venice and the North. Crosscurrents in the Time of Bellini, Dürer and Titian'; Venice 1999), while artistic relations between Flanders and Spain were explored by the excellent 'El Renacimiento Mediterraneo' (Madrid and Valencia 2001). Following on from the latter exhibition, but with greater emphasis on Flemish art and a wider and possibly more ambitious geographical scope, we have attempted to show that the appearance of Jan van Eyck led to a quiet but unmistakable revolution in painting, which left visible traces in southern Europe. Our goal is to illustrate that 'Eyckian revolution' and to highlight a moment in the constantly shifting interaction between North and South.

A great many other questions are, of course, also addressed in the exhibition and in the catalogue – issues of style, technique, iconography, workshop practice, economic relationships, patronage, and so forth. Some of the questions – it is to be hoped – are answered in this publication, but many others remain open. The catalogue is intended primarily as a book for the general reader, without the overwhelming scholarly pyrotechnics that have come to dominate certain other publications of this kind. This reflects our view that the academic value of this project lies in the exhibition itself. We emphatically invite everyone who sees it to test for themselves the relationships, confrontations, comparisons and interactions we propose. Lectures, gallery talks, a symposium, professional group visits and technical and scientific study outside visiting hours have all been organized with this goal in mind. The aim is for the results of this critical reflection and further research to be published in a scholarly collection in the year or so following the event. Above all, as the organizers of the exhibition, we are convinced that it ought not to represent the culmination of study but that it should form the catalyst for further, hopefully innovatory research.

What could possibly stimulate the eye and the mind more than a marvellous collection of key fifteenth-century paintings from northern and southern Europe, assembled from a single, specific angle? We hope that our selection will charm and seduce you as it has us.

Till-Holger Borchert
Exhibition Curator

Manfred Sellink
Artistic Director
Stedelijke Musea Bruges
Project Director

Introduction. Jan van Eyck's Workshop

Till-Holger Borchert

Between 1420 and 1440, a fundamentally new form of painting emerged in the Netherlands, in the work of Jan van Eyck, Robert Campin and Rogier van der Weyden. It supplanted – seemingly abruptly – the hitherto prescriptive representational conventions of the 'International Style', which still dominated the different branches of art at many of Europe's princely courts around 1400. The new painting then began to exert its influence on the production of art elsewhere in Europe, from the Iberian peninsula to the eastern borders of the Holy Roman Empire. The school that arose in the Low Countries and the neighbouring areas had no apparent predecessors. Instead of the stylized forms of expression of late-Gothic art, it set out to convey an observed or pursued reality in a 'realistic' or 'naturalistic' painting style that transcended even the high standard of the generation of artists active around 1400 at the courts of the King of France's four sons.

Many of the painters, illuminators and sculptors who worked for the Valois princes of Anjou, Berry, Burgundy and Orléans at Angers, Bourges, Dijon and Orléans had been born or at least trained in the Netherlands or adjoining regions. André Beauneveu came from Valenciennes, Claus Sluter from Haarlem and Henri Bellechose from Brabant. Jean Malouel and the Limbourg brothers – his nephews – came from Gelderland. Ypres was the native town of Melchior Broederlam, who painted the wings for the *Crucifixion* altarpiece that Philip the Bold commissioned for the Charterhouse at Champmol – one of the most important instances of pre-Eyckian Netherlandish panel painting. The presence of Netherlandish artists at the different Valois courts represented the final displacement of Paris as the leading northern European artistic metropolis of the Middle Ages and the beginning of the decentralization of French art. It is also the context to which the roots of Robert Campin and Jan and Hubert van Eyck have long been retraced.

It is, of course, a long way from Broederlam's panels to the Ghent altarpiece, which was installed in the Church of Saint John (now Saint Bavo's Cathedral) in 1432 (figs 4–5). The reference to Franco-Flemish courtly art around 1400 as a precursor of Early Netherlandish painting inevitably provides a less than satisfactory explanation for the origins of an artist like Jan van Eyck. This reflects the fact that what has survived is extremely fragmentary, with entire modes of art – murals, for instance – having now all but disappeared, while a once rich body of tapestries, panel paintings and, above all, painted canvases, has come down to us in a far from complete state.

Beyond the work destined for princely courts, virtually nothing has survived of the output of workshops in cities like Bruges, Ghent, Lille, Valenciennes and even Liège in the early fifteenth century. Nevertheless, the *Crucifixion* altarpiece, which was painted for the Bruges Tanners' Corporation in the early years of the fifteenth century (fig. 2), and the Saint Ursula shrine from Saint John's Hospital, which was produced around the same time (fig. 3), provide an impression of the range of Bruges panel painting before Van Eyck and, together with 'pre-Eyckian' book illumination, give us a rough idea of art production in Flemish cities.

Only in the case of painting in Tournai – a bishop's enclave to the west, closely linked to Flanders because of the river Scheldt – is art-historical knowledge somewhat more detailed. Rogier van der Weyden (after 1427–32) and Jacques Daret (1423/27–32) worked in Tournai at the workshop of Robert Campin (d. 1444), who was active as a panel painter, muralist, book illuminator and polychromist, and who is widely considered to have been the 'Master of Flémalle'. According to the sources, Campin, who is first referred to in 1406, was only slightly younger than Broederlam. However, the works attributed to the Master of Flémalle are crucially more progressive, in terms of the landscape and spatial conception,

fig. 4
Jan and Hubert van Eyck
Adoration of the Lamb
(The Ghent altarpiece, open)
Sint-Baafskathedraal, Ghent

fig. 5
Jan and Hubert van Eyck
Adoration of the Lamb
(The Ghent altarpiece, closed)
Sint-Baafskathedraal, Ghent

the plasticity of the figures and the naturalistic representation of everyday objects. The question is whether this work preceded that of Jan van Eyck or whether it represents a parallel development.

The latter seems more plausible. It was only recently recognized that the works that make up the Flémalle group ought actually to be attributed to several different artists and that a significant number of them – including the Flémalle panels (Städelsches Kunstinstitut, Frankfurt) after which the group is named and the famous Merode altarpiece (The Cloisters, New York) – actually appear to be early works by Rogier van der Weyden, who was employed in Campin's workshop. Other panels – including the *Betrothal of the Virgin* and the *Annunciation* (both Prado, Madrid) – are, by contrast, probably the work of Jacques Daret, who also painted the 1434 Madonna cycle from the Church of Saint-Vaast at Arras (fig. 79).

All this prompts a number of questions regarding the structure of Campin's workshop. Although Rogier, who was appointed Brussels town painter in 1435, entered the workshop as an apprentice in 1427, he may already have completed his training elsewhere, possibly abroad. This is important, as it appears to have been the decisive influence of this 'apprentice', whose artistic origins can firmly be placed in Tournai, that caused Campin to undergo a striking evolution in the space of a few short years. His development is plain from a comparison of the *Entombment* triptych (Courtauld Institute, London), which was probably painted in the mid-1420s, and the *Annunciation* (Musées Royaux, Brussels) with the *Virgin and Child Before a Firescreen* (National Gallery, London), the *Nativity* (fig. 200), the *Virgin and Child in a Glory* (fig. 44) and the fragment with a Crucified Thief from a lost Bruges *Descent from the Cross*, the influence of which was still felt by Van der Goes. Since none of these works is dated, the precise chronology of the paintings attributed to Campin's workshop continues to be hotly disputed. However, none of the surviving works – whose influence had spread to neighbouring Flanders by the 1430s and from there, through Louis Allyncbrood (fig. 161), to as far away as Spain – is likely to have been painted before 1420.

fig. 6
Jan van Eyck
The Three Marys at the Tomb
Museum Boijmans Van Beuningen, Rotterdam

As a result, the monumental Ghent altarpiece (figs 4–5) is the first Early Netherlandish painting to be securely dated. It also functions as a crucial link between the surviving and firmly attributed work of Jan van Eyck – which was actually produced in the latter part of his career – and an entirely unknown body of early work. The inscription on the frame of the altarpiece describes Jan as the painter who completed the altarpiece, which was begun by his brother Hubert (d. 1426) – presumably Jan's senior. It also mentions the donor – Jodocus Vijd – and gives the year in which the altarpiece was completed and installed as 1432 (the final verse is a chronogram).

The open altarpiece offers a magnificent panoramic landscape in the lower register, stretching across several individual panels to cover the entire width of the painting. The landscape, which is flooded with light, includes both inhospitable, rocky zones and fertile, southern European vegetation and lush meadows. At its centre is the Adoration of the Lamb, on which converge columns of Christian warriors, judges, martyrs, hermits, pilgrims, and so on from every corner of the earth. For the first time in panel painting a convincing balance between light and

fig. 7
Jan van Eyck
Niccolò Albergati
Kunsthistorisches Museum, Vienna. Gemäldegalerie (see cat. 24)

shade is achieved, while the principle of atmospheric perspective is applied in order to create an illusion of depth in the landscape, and the cloud formations have been precisely observed as they appear in nature. In the central axis of the altarpiece, the water from the Fountain of Life described in Saint John's Revelation threatens to flow out of the painting. One can only guess at the impact that illusionism of this kind will have had on contemporaries. The upper register of the altarpiece, which displays an unprecedented realism in its rendering of robes, jewelry and musical instruments, speaks another language. The presentation of this divine realm weighs heavily on the paradisiacal world landscape below. At its centre is a monumental Deisis group, with angels on either side and the first humans – Adam and Eve after the Fall – shown as near-life-sized nude figures on the extreme left and right respectively.

A different approach is adopted in the closed wings, where the mood of the donor figures and the saints shown in niches is clearly differentiated from that of the Annunciation scene set above them in a room in a tower. This shift, which also conveys different hierarchies, enables the polyptych to communicate a complex visual salvation programme through painting – the satisfactory interpretation of which poses a significant challenge to art historians.

Yet this is nothing compared to the as yet unanswered question of which elements of the painting are attributable to Hubert and which to Jan van Eyck. Settling this issue would, of course, tell us a great deal about Jan's artistic origins. Sadly, there is no other work apart from the Ghent altarpiece that can be firmly ascribed to Hubert van Eyck.

Art historians were long convinced that the two brothers could not have practised a common workshop style, even though this would not have been unusual for the period. There is no firm evidence to support the otherwise plausible hypothesis that Jan was trained by Hubert and that both brothers – who were born in the Meuse region – were employed at the court of the Prince-Bishop of Liège before going their separate ways. The first documentary reference to the brothers does not occur until the 1420s. Jan van Eyck was employed between 1422 and 1425 as court painter to John of Bavaria, Count of Holland and former

Prince-Bishop of Liège (until 1418). Jan and his assistants produced a number of unspecified works at the Count's residence in The Hague. Immediately after John's death, Jan entered the service of Duke Philip the Good of Burgundy in May 1425. In August of that year, the Duke commanded him to leave Bruges, to which he had fled from the politically unstable The Hague, and to settle in Lille as Philip's *valet de chambre*. Between 1426 and 1429, he made several journeys on the Duke's behalf to 'certain distant regions', which took him to Spain, Portugal and – presumably via Italy – to the Holy Land. The rich, southern vegetation in the Ghent altarpiece appears to reflect these travel experiences, as does the astonishingly detailed rendering of Jerusalem in several of Van Eyck's paintings (fig. 6).

Meanwhile, Master 'Lubrecht van Heyke' – possibly the 'Magister Hubertus pictor', who reportedly supplied a painting for the Church of Our Lady in Tongeren in 1409 – was active in the mid-1420s in Ghent, where he produced two designs for the City Council. He was paid for this work in 1425, while his assistants received a gratuity from the magistracy. 'Master Hubrecht' was also commissioned by Robert Poortier to work on an altarpiece, the elements of which will probably still have been in the workshop in 1426, the year of Hubert's death. No doubt the Ghent altarpiece was also left unfinished, although it is likely that some of Hubert's assistants continued to run the workshop after 1426, and that they also completed the altarpieces. Jan van Eyck, by contrast, travelled almost constantly in this period, and so it will only have been after returning from Portugal, where he had been part of the mission to prepare for the wedding of Philip the Good and Isabella of Portugal (1428–29), that he was able to switch his attention to the Ghent altarpiece. There are also documentary references to a third brother, Lambert van Eyck, who appears in the ducal accounts in 1430/31, a year before Jan settled in Bruges once and for all. It was Lambert who saw to it in 1442 that Jan's remains were re-interred in Bruges Cathedral following his death in 1441.

Even if it is difficult to imagine when examining Jan van Eyck's work, all the evidence suggests that the

fig. 8
Petrus Christus
Saint Anthony and a Donor
Statens Museum for Kunst,
Copenhagen (see cat. 11)

paintings he produced in the final decade of his life were done within a workshop employing several artists. Nor is he likely to have completed the Ghent altarpiece alone. He is sure to have turned to the highly qualified members of his brother's workshop, and might even have brought in other assistants too, some of whom may have been working with him since his days in The Hague, and who will have perfectly mastered his technique.

The presence of these assistants in Bruges is confirmed by the fact that they are reported as receiving gifts of money from both the city magistrates and the Duke himself during visits to the workshop. Lambert van Eyck, who already belonged to his brother's entourage in The Hague and who was responsible, together with Jan's widow Margaret, for running and eventually dissolving the Bruges workshop after 1441, may have played an important part in its production. A sixteenth-century document attributes a portrait of Jacqueline of Bavaria to Lambert, painted in 1432.

Until recently, art historians tended to steer clear of the issue of the structure and personnel of the Van Eyck workshop. The literature focused instead on other questions, such as the stylistic evolution, chronology and interpretation of this complex body of work. What is more, Jan van Eyck's putative assistants are only detectable in a few paintings and a series of miniatures attributed to the painter's closest circle or immediate followers – all of which works have, moreover, been identified in the past as early creations of Jan or as the work of Hubert van Eyck. In reality, most of the paintings in question appear to have been produced in the 1440s, suggesting that it was not until their master's death that the individual talents within his workshop were able to emerge from Jan's shadow and the collective workshop style – a pattern for which there are significant parallels in Early Netherlandish art.

Jan headed the Bruges workshop for less than a decade, from 1432 to 1441. Most of the works that we know today were produced in quick succession during that period. They consist for the most part of images of the Virgin and Child and portraits, some of which still have original frames inscribed with the

16

fig. 11
Anonymous (France)
Man with a Glass of Wine
Musée du Louvre, Paris

date and the painter's name. Several portraits also feature his motto 'ALC IXH XAN' ('as I can' or 'to the best of my ability'). This makes Van Eyck the first Netherlandish artist to state his authorship in writing. The signature, which he set out in pseudo-Greek letters, not only communicates the painter's learning and pride in his own person, but also attests to the authenticity of the ducal artist's paintings.

Yet, despite the inscribed dates, the chronology of Jan's work remains extremely problematic. The so-called *Arnolfini Wedding* (fig. 127) – the double portrait of 1434, with its marvellous interior, reminiscent of Annunciation scenes – is seemingly unparalleled in Early Netherlandish painting. The similarly conceived image of a bathing woman, which has survived through a fifteenth-century Flemish copy (fig. 126), also derives from Van Eyck. The two works provide a vague glimpse of Van Eyck's non-religious work – a largely unknown aspect of his oeuvre, the presence of which is documented in several fifteenth-century Italian collections.

Certain clues exist as to the sequence in which the portraits were painted. The likeness of a member of the Dutch Order of Saint Anthony (possibly the Count of Holland, John of Bavaria, himself), for instance, probably dates from the artist's period in The Hague (fig. 19). It is known via an excellent late fifteenth-century copy. The earliest surviving autograph portrait is the *Man in a Blue Chaperon* (fig. 219), which dates from before the completion of the Ghent altarpiece – the same period as '*Tymotheos*' (1432; fig. 223) and the *Man in a Red Turban* (1433; fig. 10). The posture of the upper body in the portrait of *Baudouin de Lannoy* (Staatliche Museen, Berlin) is very similar to that in the 'Tymotheos' painting, suggesting a date of around 1432. Lannoy, who was governor of Lille, will have commissioned the portrait from the ducal court painter to mark his elevation to the Order of the Golden Fleece in November 1431.

The Berlin Arnolfini portrait, by contrast, is usually dated to the final years of Van Eyck's life, around a decade later. The Bruges goldsmith Jan de Leeuw gazes amiably at the viewer. In this respect his portrait (Kunsthistorisches Museum, Vienna), inscribed 1436, resembles the marvellous 1433 *Man in a Red Turban*, while at the same time it looks forward to certain aspects of the artist's 1439 portrait of his wife Margaret (fig. 229). The portrait of the papal legate Niccolò Albergati (fig. 7), by contrast, is deliberately aloof. The extensively annotated sketch for it, in which Van Eyck captured the cardinal's features probably in Arras in 1435 (fig. 12), was not developed into a painted portrait until years later, in 1438. This discrepancy inevitably prompts questions regarding the criteria used to examine Van Eyck's portraits, as other likenesses may also have been done from earlier sketches by the painter who, moreover, may have adjusted their treatment depending on their purpose as either official or private portraits.

The more or less simultaneous use of differing styles by Jan van Eyck and his workshop – a practice that flatly contradicts traditional notions of linear stylistic development – is illustrated by the contrast between the large *Virgin and Child with Canon Joris van der Paele* (1436; fig. 92) and the small, miniature-like Dresden triptych (1437; fig. 115). Although the two paintings were done around the same time, their spatial and figural conception is entirely different. The ambivalent nature of these results does not provide any compelling arguments for the chronological ordering of other Marian paintings, such as the *Virgin and Child with Chancellor Nicolas Rolin* (fig. 13) and the 'Lucca Madonna' (fig. 29). And while 1439 is the documented date for Jan's later *Virgin and Child at the Fountain* (fig. 204), the dating of his masterful *Virgin and Child in a Church* (fig. 14) is still disputed. On the one hand, the gently stylized figure of the Madonna is closely linked to Franco-Flemish courtly art around 1400, while on the other, the painter brilliantly renders the complex spatial construction of a Gothic cathedral, flooded with light, simultaneously visualizing the common theological equation of the Mother of God with 'Ecclesia' – the Church – and creating one of the most exquisite and progressive interiors anywhere in Early Netherlandish painting. In other words, there are arguments in favour of both an early and a late date. The only constant is the high quality of painting. Everything else – the treatment of landscape and space, volumes and surfaces, stylization and realism – appears subordinate to the function and purpose of the image and therefore, at least in part, to the painter's intentions.

Unsurprisingly, particular problems are posed by the ordering of Van Eyck's Passion scenes, none of which is dated. The commendable hypothesis of narratively early and 'iconic' late work by Jan van Eyck is methodologically untenable. With the exception of the Ghent altarpiece and the late and entirely untypical *Saint Barbara* (fig. 1) – which is effectively a drawing – any secure reference works are lacking. It is ultimately impossible, therefore, to place a firm date on *Christ Carrying the Cross*, the original of which has been lost, and the *Three Marys at the Tomb* (fig. 6). Stylistic references to the Ghent altarpiece are not, in themselves, sufficient to prove an early dating, as Van Eyck will also have painted Passion scenes after 1432

fig. 12
Jan van Eyck
Niccolò Albergati
Preliminary drawing for fig. 7
Staatliche Kunstsammlungen, Dresden. Kupferstich-Kabinett

fig. 13
Jan van Eyck
The Virgin and Child with Chancellor Nicolas Rolin
Musée du Louvre, Paris

that did not necessarily share the same character with his surviving Madonnas. The suggestion that a small diptych linking the Crucifixion and the Last Judgment – whose attribution and dating are the subject of controversy – is an early work of Jan van Eyck is, in this respect, problematic (fig. 15). In fact, there is nothing to refute the recently posited idea, which is also supported by technical findings, that this may be a late painting by Jan van Eyck and his workshop, whose composition was reworked by Petrus Christus in Bruges around 1450 for a Spanish patron (Staatliche Museen, Berlin). Echoes of the interior of the Ghent altarpiece – in terms of both figures and landscape – do not necessarily argue in favour of chronological proximity. Rather they illustrate a specific stylistic approach that may have been motivated by content, and which differs fundamentally from the Madonnas that Jan van Eyck produced in the 1430s.

Account also has to be taken of the organization of the Van Eyck workshop and working practices there, which are unlikely to have differed too widely from those of other workshops. It too will have assembled a body of earlier model and design drawings, which could be called upon as needed, and which will have been accessible to other Bruges painters after the dissolution of the workshop, if not before. This fact could explain the apparent archaism of certain 'Eyckian apocrypha'. Evidence that the Van Eyck workshop did indeed resort to earlier model drawings from time to time is provided by the example of the 'Madonna of Jan Vos' (fig. 22), which was completed in the Bruges workshop in 1442/43 – after the master's death – and was paraphrased around the same time in Petrus Christus' 'Exeter Madonna' (Staatliche Museen, Berlin). It has long been recognized that the work is a pastiche of Eyckian motifs – the Madonna figure is based on the 1439 *Virgin and Child at the Fountain* (fig. 204), of which at least one other version is known to have been made in the workshop (fig. 208). The figure of Jan Vos, the patron who is shown dressed in the habit of a Carthusian, refers back to the donor portrait in the 'Rolin Madonna' (fig. 13), as does the marvellous panoramic landscape, which is re-used in the manner of a backdrop. The cityscape in the right background also appears to

20

derive from a lost prototype by Van Eyck. It features around roughly the same time in a miniature in the frontispiece to a manuscript of Augustine's *De civitate Dei* (Bibliothèque Royale, Brussels, Ms. 9015) which was illuminated by a painter at the Bruges workshop on behalf of Jean Chevrot, the influential Bishop of Tournai. The figure of Saint Elizabeth also seems to derive from a lost Van Eyck original, as she features reversed in a donor's portrait of Isabella of Portugal from the circle of Petrus Christus (fig. 197).

Consequently, the Madrid *Fountain of Life* (fig. 24), which was probably commissioned in the mid-fifteenth century by the King of Castile and transported to Spain, where it was often copied (fig. 23), ought not to be interpreted as a copy after a lost composition by Jan or even Hubert van Eyck, but as the work of a member of the Van Eyck workshop. This painter will have drawn on sources such as the rich body of model drawings that his late master produced for the Ghent altarpiece, combining these with great technical skill in a new pictorial invention. The somewhat old-fashioned grisaille diptych in the Louvre (fig. 25) is highly reminiscent of this master, as are the related drawings, whose physiognomies and proportions recall several figures in the *Adoration of the Lamb* altarpiece.

This recourse to earlier models, which were evidently preserved with great care, is by no means unique to the post-Eyckian Bruges workshop. Two members of the workshop turned – possibly at different times – to a now lost interior by Jan van Eyck showing a Virgin and Child before a canopy. Both appear to have used workshop drawings as their point of departure, first for the 'Ince Hall Madonna' (fig. 27) and then, around 1450, for the 'Covarrubias Madonna' (fig. 28) – largely reconstructed by restorers – which was probably the work of a German-speaking assistant.

And there is more evidence of the use of workshop designs. Jan van Eyck's image of the *Stigmatization of Saint Francis* – a composition that has survived in two high-quality versions (figs 242, 243) – also borrows the saint's upper body configuration from the kneeling donor figure in the 'Rolin Madonna' (fig. 13). It seems likely that a model drawing of the donor image remained in the Bruges workshop and was re-used for the Saint Francis composition, long after the painted

fig. 16
Petrus Christus and/or workshop of Jan van Eyck
Annunciation
The Metropolitan Museum of Art, New York. The Friedsam Collection, Bequest of Michael Friedsam

fig. 17
Jan van Eyck
Annunciation
National Gallery of Art, Washington, DC. Andrew W. Mellon Collection
(see cat. 19)

prototype had been installed in Rolin's family chapel in Autun. Both versions may have been produced in the Van Eyck workshop during Jan's life. The larger variant (fig. 242) shows corrections in the underdrawing, while the smaller version, painted on parchment (fig. 243), was mounted on a wooden board that actually came from the same tree as the supports used for the Berlin portraits of *Baudouin de Lannoy* and *Giovanni Arnolfini*.

The barren, rocky landscape of the Saint Francis scenes was regularly repeated in Italian painting until 1470, suggesting that at least one of the two works must have found its way to Italy. But echoes of the composition can also be found in paintings produced in Bruges. The rocky plateau, for instance, that appears in a donor panel by Petrus Christus (fig. 8) is a direct reference, as is the landscape in a recently discovered painting of John the Baptist (fig. 9). The latter seems to be the work of another painter from the Bruges studio, who possibly also painted the Friedsam *Annunciation* (fig. 16), and who may have been active in Petrus Christus' workshop for a while

around 1445–50, or else collaborated with Christus on some other basis.

The identification of individual workshop assistants of Jan van Eyck and the potential attribution to them of individual works are still at a very early stage. Our knowledge would be even more fragmentary, in fact, were it not for the 'Turin-Milan Hours', which once formed part of the *Très Belles Heures de Notre Dame*. This manuscript, which was broken up on several occasions, was originally commissioned by Jean, Duc de Berry, and was illuminated by artists including the Master of the Parement de Narbonne and the Limbourg brothers. The *Très Belles Heures* is a richly decorated collection of prayers and Masses that was rediscovered in the early twentieth century, first in Turin and later in Milan. The Turin fragment was photographed and published by Paul Durrieu, before being destroyed by fire in 1904. Seven years later, Georges Hulin de Loo performed a detailed stylistic analysis of both fragments – the reproduction of the Turin fragment and the Milan section (now in the Museo Civico,

23

Turin) – which were now recognized as belonging to the same original. Hulin de Loo discerned a number of illuminators who had worked on the manuscript in the decade of its production. He identified them as 'Hands A to K', stretching from the Franco-Flemish miniatures from the Berry court to followers of Van Eyck around 1440/50. The miniatures by Hands G and H have been the subject of fierce controversy ever since, as some art historians have sought to identify them as early works by Jan and/or Hubert van Eyck. One of the miniatures lost in the fire – the 'Prayer on the Shore' – contained the banner with the arms of the counties of Hainaut, Bavaria and Holland. Although the arms are shown reversed, this suggested that the manuscript might once have belonged to the Counts of Holland, William VI and later John of Bavaria, for whom the court painter Jan van Eyck and his brother Hubert may have added several highly innovative miniatures, such as the *Birth of John the Baptist* (fig. 18). The miniatures contained in the Turin-Milan Hours sensationally confirmed what the Neapolitan Pietro Summonte had written in his letter to the Venetian Marcantonio Michiel in 1524, namely that Jan van Eyck had begun his career as a book illuminator.

Art historians do not agree, however, as to whether Jan van Eyck contributed to the manuscript, and, if he did, which miniatures ought to be attributed to him and how these might be dated. Meanwhile, it has been all but ruled out that Hubert made any significant contribution to the Eyckian miniatures in question. Those scholars who do believe that the miniatures are the work of Jan van Eyck further disagree about whether the relevant works date from the earlier or later part of the artist's career. It is also argued by some that Jan painted certain of the miniatures during his time in Holland, but that others were not completed until after he had moved to Bruges.

Although the key issues relating to the Turin-Milan Hours and the more central question of Jan van Eyck's early work are still debated with great heat, study of the manuscript has posed a crucial challenge to the way we perceive Van Eyck's immediate influence.

It has become evident that several of the supposedly Eyckian miniatures are actually the work of assistants or followers who, as we found with respect to panel painting, were in the habit of harking

24

fig. 19
Assistant of Jan van Eyck
Crucifixion
Staatliche Museen zu Berlin.
Gemäldegalerie

fig. 22
Assistant of Jan van Eyck
The Virgin and Child with Saints
Barbara and Elizabeth of Hungary and
a Carthusian ('Madonna of Jan Vos')
The Frick Collection, New York

fig. 20
Anonymous copy (Veneto)
after Jan van Eyck
Crucifixion
Museo d'Arte Medievale e
Moderna, Padua (see cat. 85)

fig. 21
Assistant of Jan van Eyck
Crucifixion
Galleria Giorgio Franchetti
alla Ca' d'Oro, Venice (see cat. 34)

back to earlier models. The magnificent *Crucifixion* in the manuscript (fig. 18) is based, for instance, on the same composition – the original of which is probably lost – as a panel painting by an assistant, which was copied by a painter in Padua in the fifteenth century (figs 20, 21). The image of Thomas Aquinas probably derives from a Saint Jerome (fig. 113) completed by the Van Eyck workshop, which was once owned by the Medici in Florence and which inspired Ghirlandaio's Ognissanti frescoes (fig. 112). Other Eyckian miniatures in the manuscript have been attributed to the Master of Covarrubias, the Master of the Chevrot Saint Augustine, the Master of the Philadelphia Saint Francis and even Barthélemy d'Eyck. It will be plain from this that the miniatures in the Turin-Milan Hours have played a key role in the study of Van Eyck's workshop in Bruges and its subsequent influence.

The workshop, which probably consisted of a small number of highly specialized painters, appears to have continued to operate for several years after Jan van Eyck's death in 1441. It was probably not disbanded until the mid-1450s, when Van Eyck's widow, Margaret, sold her home in Bruges and left the city. What became of the assistants? And what of Lambert

van Eyck? They might have entered other workshops in Bruges or in neighbouring towns, or else they could have moved abroad. Jan van Eyck's reputation was well established by then throughout Europe and his work was much sought after. One wonders whether it is mere coincidence, therefore, that the earliest recorded provenance of several works that are crucial to the restitution of the Van Eyck workshop point towards the Iberian peninsula and to Italy.

Select bibliography

Flémalle / Van der Weyden: Campbell 1974; Campbell 1981; Dijkstra 1990; Van Asperen de Boer *et al.* 1992; Châtelet 1996; Kemperdick 1997; De Vos 1999.
Van Eyck – Biography and documents: Weale 1908; Duverger 1932; Duverger 1936; Duverger 1977; Van Buren 1985; Paviot 1990; Reynolds 2000.
General: Baldass 1952; Snyders 1973; Dhanens 1980; Pächt 1989; Smeyers and Stroo 1994.
Early work: Dvořák 1904; Sterling 1976; Châtelet 1981; Belting and Eichberger 1983.
Ghent altarpiece: Renders 1933; Coremans 1953; Dhanens 1965; Van Asperen de Boer 1979; Herzner 1995.
Portraits: Meiss 1952; Bauch 1963; Jansen 1988.
Interpretation: Panofsky 1953; Purtle 1982; Harbison 1990; Preimesberger 1991; Belting and Kruse 1994.
Turin-Milan Hours: Durrieu 1902 (1967); Durrieu 1903; Hulin de Loo 1911; Marrow 1968; Châtelet 1981; Châtelet 1993; König and Bartz 1994; Van Buren 1996; Smeyers 1997.
Workshop: Bruyn 1957; Ainsworth and Martens 1994; Ainsworth 1995; Buck 1995; Jones 1995; Philadelphia 1997; Turin 1998; Buck 2000; Jones 2000.

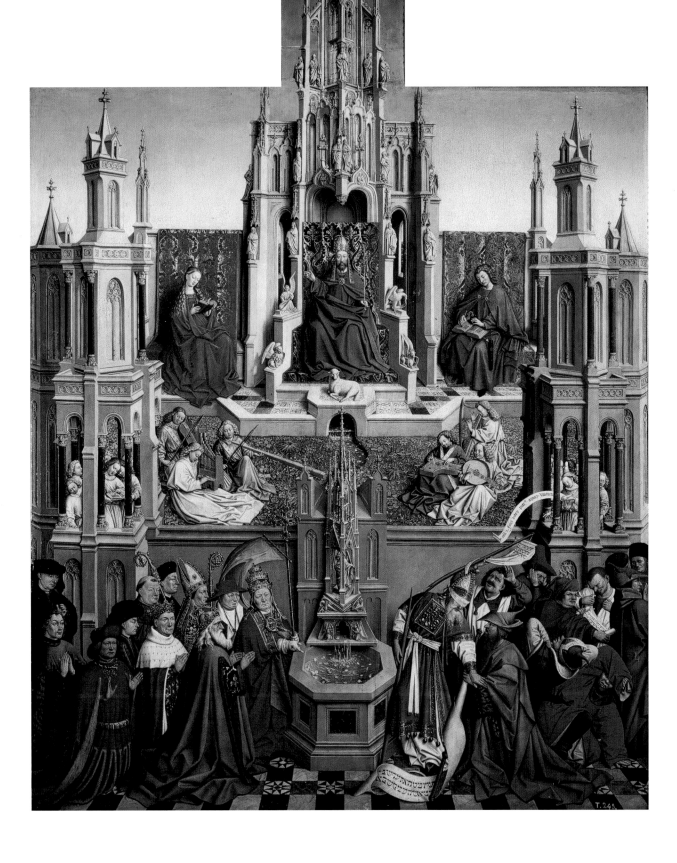

fig. 25
Assistant of Jan van Eyck
John the Baptist and *Virgin and Child*
Musée du Louvre, Paris (see cat. 33)

fig. 26
Jan van Eyck
Annunciation
Museo Thyssen-Bornemisza,
Madrid (see cat. 20)

fig. 27
Assistant of Jan van Eyck
Virgin and Child
('Ince Hall Madonna')
National Gallery of Victoria,
Melbourne (see cat. 31)

fig. 28
Master of Covarrubias
Virgin and Child
('Covarrubias Madonna')
Museo de la Colegiata de San
Cosme y Damián, Covarrubias
(Burgos) (see cat. 42)

fig. 29
Jan van Eyck
Virgin and Child ('Lucca Madonna')
Städelsches Kunstinstitut und
Städtische Galerie, Frankfurt
(see cat. 21)

fig. 30
Petrus Christus
Holy Family
Nelson-Atkins Museum of Art,
Kansas City

The Mobility of Artists.
Aspects of Cultural Transfer in Renaissance Europe
Till-Holger Borchert

Three groups were chiefly responsible for the European dissemination of the Early Netherlandish *ars nova*. The first of these were the merchants who purchased Flemish panel paintings for their own use or as merchandise for sale and export. The royal courts of Europe, meanwhile, employed their own artists, many of whom travelled around Europe on dynastic and diplomatic business. Finally, there were artists who – subject to prevailing guild rules – travelled from place to place or settled abroad. We intend to focus here on the role played by the two latter groups – court and itinerant artists.[1]

In Bruges alone, a surprising number of foreign painters were active between 1430 and 1530. Jan van Eyck, Petrus Christus, Hans Memling, Gerard David and Jan Provoost all came from outside Flanders, from such places as Holland, northern France and the Rhineland, while Ambrosius Benson came from as far away as Lombardy to settle in the Flemish commercial metropolis in 1518. A similar phenomenon is evident in European artistic centres in every period. Paris, Cologne, Antwerp, Venice, Florence, Naples, Valencia and Barcelona have all been home at one time or another to painters, illuminators and sculptors from many different countries.

Although the sources regarding the mobility of artists are meagre, and a systematic scrutiny of archive material has yet to be performed, this phenomenon undoubtedly played a crucial role in the spread of Early Netherlandish painting and the artistic influence it exerted in the fifteenth and early sixteenth centuries. As in Italy or the Iberian peninsula, it was by no means unusual in the Burgundian Netherlands and France for individual painters or sculptors to work in several places in the course of their professional lives, to settle in foreign cities or to offer their services to a variety of princely courts in the pursuit of an adequate living. War and famine will have contributed to this pattern as much as economic factors.

In the case of painters working within the guild system, the influx of non-local artists reflected a number of factors, such as the expectation of a more reliable supply of work, and citizenship and guild rules that were not unduly onerous for outsiders. The temporary relaxation or lifting of protectionist guild regulations, which customarily favoured the work of local craftsmen, served as a kind of official economic development policy that could exert an impressive influence, as was the case during Antwerp's rise as the key artistic metropolis in the Netherlands.[2]

Mobility was a necessity within the guild system, as very few journeymen had the financial wherewithal to obtain independent master status, let alone set up on their own.[3] It was all the more difficult for painters and sculptors to earn a living, as the kind of specialist workshops that required their labour for as long as demand lasted did not exist in every town. They were concentrated instead in a few cities and the distances that painters had to cover in their search were comparatively large, despite the relatively advanced infrastructure and the degree of urbanization in regions like the Burgundian Netherlands, northern Italy, northern France, the Rhineland and the Iberian coastline.[4]

Consequently, journeymen like these – referred to in the sources as *valets*, *compagnons* and *cnapen* – were crucially important.[5] In the Netherlands, where, on average, barely a third of all apprentices went on to become independent masters, their contribution in the fifteenth and early sixteenth centuries was considerable. As in Italy, most journeymen appear to have formed a mobile reserve of labour, which enabled workshops to respond flexibly to fluctuations in demand. Although a substantial proportion of journeymen were employed in the Netherlands or neighbouring regions, and a significant number enjoyed long-term employment within a given workshop, some of them were still prepared to cover considerable distances in their search for work, taking them as far as England, the Holy Roman Empire, the Baltic, southern France, Italy, Spain and Portugal. For the most part, we only know the routes followed by a few of the masters who travelled abroad or settled far from their birthplace.

The painter Joos Amman was one such itinerant artist. His artistic roots lay in the region around Lake Constance and he was influenced by the painting of Conrad Witz. An early stay in the Netherlands may have given him the opportunity to acquire first-hand knowledge of paintings produced in Robert Campin's workshop. After having been commissioned in 1445 to paint the frescoes in Constance, Joos Amman

33

travelled to Genoa, where he worked with the stonemason Jan van Brugge on behalf of Lionello and Emmanuele Grimaldi on the interior of the Dominican Convent of Santa Maria di Castello. A *Martyrdom of Saint Sebastian* produced around this time has been lost, but his monumental *Annunciation* fresco, signed 'Giusto dalla magna' and dated 1451, is one of the earliest surviving examples of northern painting in Liguria, from where the painter returned to Ravensburg in 1452. Amman's murals offer a perfect illustration of the relationship between artistic exchange and mobility.[6]

It is clear from the information on Flemish artists in Quattrocento Italy published by Müntz that Amman was by no means an exception in this respect. Flemish and northern French artists were especially active at the tapestry manufactories that were also founded all over Italy, although their paintings and designs are now largely unknown.[7]

Artists born or trained in the Netherlands or northern Europe were also active in the mid-fifteenth century on the Iberian peninsula. The Master of Sopetrán had probably been active in the circle of Rogier van der Weyden before settling around 1450–60 in Castile, where he became a successful painter. His paintings adhere closely to the formal principles of Rogier's later work, while the painting technique follows the prevailing Castilian manner. The same applies to an English (?) painter who was active in Castile a few years earlier and whose paintings also drew on Rogier van der Weyden. Jorge Inglés, as he was known, painted the Marian 'Altarpiece of Buitrago' (fig. 32) in 1455. Its famous donors' portraits closely resemble Rogier's likenesses of Nicolas Rolin and his wife on the closed wings of the *Last Judgment* in Beaune (fig. 60).[8]

Louis Allyncbrood settled in Valencia no later than 1439. The city had been a cultural melting-pot for southern Europe and the East since the fourteenth century and, from 1400 or so onwards, it also began to function as a bridgehead for Flemish painting in the Mediterranean.[9] Allyncbrood had served as *vinder* or arbitrator for the Bruges painters' guild in 1432/33 and 1436/37, from which we may infer that he was a well-established member of his profession in Flanders. He probably left Bruges during the revolt against Duke

Philip the Good (1436–38), the repercussions of which – famine, pestilence and a trade blockade – were to prove fatal to the city's prosperity. His decision to leave is likely to have reflected both economic and political considerations.[10] Although Allyncbrood died in Valencia some time before 1463, his son Joris was admitted as an independent master in the Bruges painters' corporation in 1460, suggesting that the family did not entirely sever its links with its native city. Although firm attributions have proved impossible, Post's suggested identification of Louis Allyncbrood as the Master of the Encarnación has been widely accepted. The 1445 Passion triptych from the monastery of the same name in Valencia (fig. 161) draws on the work of Robert Campin in terms of its colouring and the conception of landscape and space. The triptych has been linked to an upright Passion scene (fig. 33) which, however, seems closer to Van Eyck in terms of its landscape.[11] The Flemish influence in Valencia and the Kingdom of Aragon was almost universal from that time onwards; it may have been encouraged by the personal tastes of King Alfonso V of Aragon, who dispatched his court painter Lluís Dalmau to the Netherlands in 1431–37 and who later owned several paintings by Van Eyck.[12]

Artists from Italy and France also travelled to the Spanish kingdoms in the fifteenth century. The Florentine Dello Delli set up a workshop

fig.33
Louis Allyncbrood
Crucifixion with Passion Scenes
Former Collection of Rodríguez
Bauzá, Madrid

fig.34
Quentin Massys
*Saint John and the Three Marys
at the Tomb* (panel from the Madre
de Deus altarpiece)
Museu Nacional de Arte Antiga,
Lisbon (see cat. 41)

fig.35
Quentin Massys
Rest on the Flight into Egypt (panel
from the Madre de Deus altarpiece)
The Worcester Art Museum,
Worcester, Mass. (see cat. 41)

in Seville and Salamanca that introduced the innovations of the Tuscan Renaissance to locally based painters,[13] while the French-born Nicolas Francés was active in León.[14] Having completed his training in Ferrara, Paolo di San Leocadio settled in Valencia in 1472, along with the painters Francesco Pagano from Naples and Riccardo Quartararo from Sicily.[15] In the latter part of the fifteenth century, Isabella of Castile offered tax exemptions to encourage Netherlandish and German artists to relocate to her kingdom. The absence of unduly restrictive guild regulations, demand from the court and an increasingly prosperous élite, and the existence of large fairs, such as the one in Medina del Campo, also exerted a powerful influence on the migration process.[16]

Dynastic links between Portugal and the House of Habsburg-Burgundy grew especially close around 1500, as a result of which the former, too, became a preferred destination of Netherlandish painters. Conversely, Portuguese artists also began to appear in the North around this time. Two Portuguese painters are recorded at the Antwerp workshops of Quentin Massys and Goswyn van der Weyden. They undoubtedly contributed to the often surprisingly close links between Portuguese painting and the latest, export-oriented art produced in Antwerp, such as the carved altarpieces that the Portuguese Queen Eleanor

of Austria commissioned from the Flemish city for the monasteries and convents she founded (figs 34, 35).[17]

Francisco Henriques moved to Lisbon around 1500, probably together with other Flemish artists. He later married the daughter of Jorge Afonso, the court painter. Henriques' first major commission was the painting of the high altar at the Church of São Francisco in the royal capital Évora. He also produced designs for stained-glass windows in Évora and Sintra and, in collaboration with a variety of other artists, created a series of altarpieces in Portugal (fig. 192), before succumbing to the plague in 1518.[18] Various masters – also probably from Flanders – have been placed in his circle. The only one known by name, however, is Frey (Brother) Carlos, who entered the Hieronymite Monastery at Évora in 1517 and subsequently ran its studio. Although nothing is known of this artist's life, the monumental paintings attributed to him suggest a detailed knowledge not only of Henriques' work, but also that of Hugo van der Goes. It is possible, therefore, that the Hieronymite monk received his training in Ghent or Bruges before relocating to far-away Portugal (figs 36, 186, 191).[19]

Mutual migration between the Netherlands and France gave rise to a traditionally intensive cultural exchange between the two regions. Sculptors, illuminators and panel painters – especially from

The example of the Dipre family indicates that, in some cases, a tendency to migration ran in the blood of several generations of artists. Nicolas Dipre, who worked in Avignon, painted a Marian altarpiece around 1500 in Carpentras. All that now survives of that work are a fragment and a number of predella scenes that are indebted to the Provençal tradition (figs 37–42).[22] Nicolas' grandfather was André d'Ypres, the Master of the Paris Parliament Crucifixion (figs 81, 84; see also Lorentz's essay, pp. 67–71); his father was Colin (Nicolas) d'Amiens (the Master of Coëtivy; fig. 91), who took over André d'Ypres' Paris workshop. The latter had trained in Tournai, then moved to Amiens before settling in Paris in around 1444. The surname 'Dipre', moreover, recalls the family's roots in the Flemish cloth-making centre of Ypres – the town where Melchior Broederlam had painted the outer wings of the Passion altarpiece for the Charterhouse at Champmol near Dijon.[23] We can only guess at the extent to which the Dipre family adhered to the Flemish tradition, although Nicolas Dipre appears to have shunned it in favour of the influence of Enguerrand Quarton (fig. 85) and Barthélemy d'Eyck, painters from Laon and the Netherlands, who had settled in Aix-en-Provence around 1444.[24]

Professional prospects and family reasons are likely to have encouraged Josse Lieferinx to move to Marseilles and Aix-en-Provence in 1493. A native of the Bishopric of Cambrai, the painter appears to have relocated to southern France after training in the North. He worked in the two aforementioned towns between 1493 and 1508. Having initially been active in Marseilles, he later joined the workshop in Aix run by the Burgundian painter Jean Changenet, who later became his father-in-law. Together with the Piedmontese painter Bernardino Simondi, Lieferinx was commissioned in 1497 (the year of Simondi's death) to paint a monumental altarpiece devoted to Saint Sebastian – a key work of Provençal painting around 1500 as well as a remarkable synthesis of Netherlandish, Provençal and Italian influences (fig. 55).[25]

The knowledge of Italian art displayed by Lieferinx's work (fig. 53) suggests that he spent time in Italy, although there is no archival evidence to support this assertion. The lack of firm sources means that the Italian visits postulated with regard to northern artists are frequently contested or dismissed as pure speculation. Given that Dieric Bouts and Petrus Christus clearly understood the geometrically constructed perspective (figs 45, 94, 171) that was practised in Italy by Filippo Brunelleschi, but which remained largely unnoticed in the Netherlands, it is often argued that they must have visited Italy in person. This idea is strengthened by the fact that the work of both artists displays links with contemporary Italian painting which go beyond the purely literary mediation offered by humanist libraries in Flanders.[26]

Flanders – had been drawn to Paris and the nearby artistic centres of northern France since the fourteenth century. Some of them even served as court artists to the French Crown, the Dukes of Valois and other prominent French dynasties. The Netherlandish painter Jacob de Littemont, for instance, was a predecessor of Jean Fouquet in the service of Charles VII in Paris.[20] The *peintre ordinaire du roi*, Conrad de Vulcop, who probably came from the Bishopric of Utrecht, also worked in Paris between 1445 and 1459, as did his brother Henri, who was in the service of Queen Mary of Anjou, Charles VII's wife.[21]

figs 37–42
Nicolas Dipre
Fragments from the *Altarpiece of the Virgin* of Saint-Siffrein, Carpentras (?)
(see cat. 69)

Crucifixion. The Detroit Institute of Art
Joachim and Anne. Musée du Louvre, Paris
Birth of the Virgin. Musée du Louvre, Paris
Presentation of the Virgin. Musée du Louvre, Paris
Marriage of the Virgin. Denver Art Museum
Adoration of the Shepherds. The Fine Art Museums of San Francisco
Adoration of the Magi. Musée départemental d'Art sacré, Pont-Saint-Esprit

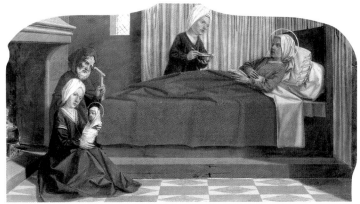

In as late as 1506, Dürer travelled from Venice to Bologna in order to be instructed in the 'heimliche Perspektive' ('mysteries of perspective'), which he considered to be one of the secrets of Italian art.[27]

The mobility of artists in the fifteenth and early sixteenth centuries ought not to be underestimated. Although visiting foreign countries could be difficult and hazardous, there was a remarkably efficient network of transport by road and sea, via which Europeans were able to exchange goods and information. Journeys to Italy and the Iberian peninsula, which became increasingly popular in the course of the sixteenth century, were already considered a calculated risk in the Quattrocento. The infrastructure was sufficiently advanced to allow pilgrimages to Santiago de Compostela and even to the Holy Land. Jerusalem and the Holy Places – visits to which are recalled in numerous fifteenth-century travel journals – were particularly expensive destinations and thus remained the preserve of the urban élite and the aristocracy.[28] Whereas Jan van Eyck's journey to the Holy Land in 1426 as an envoy of Philip the Good remains the subject of conjecture, later pilgrimages to Jerusalem are documented in the case of both Jan Provoost (fig. 56) and Jan van Scorel.[29] According to surviving accounts, the journey proceeded by road from the Low Countries to Genoa or Milan, and then on to Venice or Naples, where the pilgrims continued on their way by sea. Northern Italy alone gave Flemish artist-pilgrims plenty of opportunity to familiarize themselves with contemporary Italian painting *en route*.[30]

It is likely that only a small proportion of the journeys to Southern and Southwestern Europe undertaken by artists from the North consisted of pure pilgrimages – they also provided an opportunity for intensive artistic study and for the exchange of pictorial motifs and compositions. For his part in the rebellion against the authorities in Tournai, Robert Campin was obliged to make a pilgrimage to Saint-Gilles-du-Gard in southern France in 1429–30. Both the route taken by the painter – through Dijon, down the Rhône and back through Savoy – and the works he may have produced along the way are disputed in the literature.[31] However, the reception of Flémallesque compositions in Provençal and Piedmontese painting

around 1450 certainly argues in favour of the early presence of such paintings (figs 54, 200).[32]

We owe our knowledge of the pilgrimage that Rogier van der Weyden made to Rome in the Holy Year of 1450 to Bartolomeo Fazio. In his *De viris illustribus* (1456), the scholar stated that Rogier had taken the opportunity to admire Gentile da Fabriano's frescoes at Saint John Lateran.[33] His itinerary probably took him to Ferrara and Florence. Ciriaco d'Ancona referred in 1449 to a now lost *Deposition* by the Brussels municipal artist, which was owned at the time by Lionello d'Este in Ferrara, while in 1450 the Duke's accounts record a payment made to '*Magistro Rogiero depinctore in Bruza*'.[34] In Florence, Rogier studied Fra Angelico's *Entombment* or *Lamentation Before the Open Tomb* (fig. 96) in the predella of the recently completed Marian altarpiece in the church of the Convent of San Marco (1440). He took the composition as the basis for the *Entombment* (fig. 97) that he probably painted for Cosimo de' Medici, and which was

fig. 46
Jean Fouquet
Virgin and Child (right wing
of the 'Melun diptych')
Koninklijk Museum voor Schone
Kunsten, Antwerp (see cat. 70)

fig. 47
Jacques Daret
Portrait of a Woman
Dumbarton Oaks Research Library,
Washington, DC. House Collection
(see cat. 16)

later given a place of honour at the Villa Careggi.[35] André d'Ypres, the Master of the Paris Parliament Crucifixion, also went to Rome in 1450, the year of his death. Northern masters obviously visited Rome more frequently than has hitherto been realized.[36]

Joos van Wassenhove, who had previously worked as a painter in Antwerp, was last mentioned in Ghent in 1469 when he acted, together with Hugo van der Goes, as warrantor for the guild membership of Alexander (Sanders) Bening. He left Ghent for Rome later that year, as recorded in a bill of exchange dating from 1475. He then turns up again in 1473 as 'Giusto di Gand' in the archives of the Confraternity of Corpus Domini in Urbino, for which he painted a monumental *Communion of the Apostles* (fig. 136). Together with 'Pietro spagnolo' – the Castilian painter Pedro Berruguete, who later became court artist to the Catholic Kings – and Melozzo da Forlì, Justus of Ghent (as Joos van Wassenhove is also known) was commissioned by Federico da Montefeltro to decorate the interior of the Duke's *studiolo* in the palace at Urbino, which was home to a portrait gallery of famous philosophers, Fathers of the Church and poets.[37]

Like Van der Weyden, Jean Fouquet must also have stopped off in Florence during his journey to Rome (and possibly also in Ferrara, where he may have painted the portrait of *Gonella* [fig. 129], the famous court buffoon of the d'Este family). That he spent time in the Tuscan city is suggested by the precision with which he painted Renaissance architecture in his later manuscripts. Fouquet's visit to Rome (before 1447) is mentioned by Filarete who, in his *Trattato d'Architettura*, describes the painter, with whom he was evidently acquainted, as an excellent portraitist ('*buen maestro maxime a retrarre del naturale*').[38] It was at this time that Fouquet painted his portrait of Pope Eugenius IV, probably on behalf of the latter's protégé, Archbishop Jean Bernard of Tours. The painting was displayed at Santa Maria sopra Minerva. The artistic experience that Fouquet built up during his time in Italy was later to form the basis of a unique synthesis of Franco-Flemish realism and Italian *maniera*, which is evident in both the miniatures and panel paintings the artist produced after returning to the North.[39]

It is Fouquet who takes us beyond the realm of guild-organized painters and draws our attention to the activities and journeys undertaken by artists employed at court – artists who played a significant part in the European dissemination of Early Netherlandish art. Fouquet had not, of course, become court painter to King Charles VII at this stage, but he already boasted an influential patron in the shape of the prelate Jean Bernard, whose household and pursuit of prestige were firmly oriented towards the French royal court. Jan Gossaert's visit to Rome appears to have been undertaken for similar reasons. He arrived in the Eternal City in 1508 in the retinue of Philip of Burgundy, the later Bishop of Utrecht, and took the opportunity to produce study drawings of antique objects.[40] Scorel, too, travelled from the Low Countries to the Vatican in 1521 as part of the entourage of the newly elected Pope Adrian VI, the Utrecht-born former tutor of Charles V.[41]

The courts and residences of kings, dukes and prelates invariably acted as a magnet to painters looking for lucrative employment. Ambitious dynastic projects like the Charterhouse of Champmol near Dijon, where Philip the Bold planned to be buried, the Visconti's construction of Milan Cathedral and the foundation of the Certosa in Pavia all drew architects, sculptors and painters from all over Europe, partly for financial reasons and partly because there were not enough qualified craftsmen available at the locations in question. In this way, a whole series of innovative Netherlandish and northern French artists came to work alongside Claus Sluter, Henri Bellechose and Melchior Broederlam in and around Dijon, in the service first of Philip the Bold and then of John the Fearless. Their work had a lasting influence on art production in Burgundy and Franche-Comté. Artists employed during the building of Milan Cathedral included the Lombard sculptor and illuminator Giovannino de' Grassi and the Bruges-born illuminator Jacques Coene, who also worked for a short time in Paris and who has been identified by some scholars with the Boucicaut Master, an important precursor of the art of Jan van Eyck.[42] Coene had quit Paris in 1388 to enter the court of Juan I of Aragon.[43] Panofsky and Meiss have studied the structures of the Valois Dukes' patronage and visual representation emerging around 1400, and emphasized the key role played by Netherlandish artists in the genesis of the *ars nova*.[44]

Although fifteenth-century panel painting was subject to growing demand from institutions and the bourgeoisie, whose representational ambitions were modelled after the aristocratic ideal of *vivre noblement*,[45] princely courts, led by that of Burgundy, still employed countless painters and sculptors in the production of ephemeral but magnificent decorations. In 1454, for instance, preparations for the legendary *Banquet du Faisan* (Pheasant Banquet) drew hundreds of artists from the Netherlands and the border regions to Lille, while the celebration of the marriage of Charles

the Bold to Margaret of York in 1568 brought numerous masters and journeymen to Bruges.[46]

The rapid spread of Early Netherlandish painting across Europe also owed something to a number of important Church Councils and peace conferences. The Councils of Constance and Basle, for instance, made an important contribution to the influence that Netherlandish book illumination exerted on Upper German painting.[47] Constance (1414–15), Basle (1431–34) and Arras (where the treaty between Burgundy and France was signed in 1435) all featured painters among the retinues of kings, cardinals and papal nuncios, enabling them to enter into dialogue with one another. Jan van Eyck, for example, presumably travelled from Bruges to Arras at the order of Philip the Good in 1435 to paint the portraits of delegates to the peace congress.[48] This included a study, now in Dresden (fig. 12), for the portrait of Cardinal Niccolò Albergati (1438; fig. 7). It is also likely that Francesco Coppini, who took part as papal legate in the chapter meeting of the Golden Fleece held at Saint-Omer in 1461, came into contact there with the Picard painter Nicolas Froment. Coppini commissioned Froment to paint the triptych with the *Raising of Lazarus*, dated 1461 (now Uffizi, Florence) which came into the possession of the Medici shortly afterwards.[49] Froment then moved on to Languedoc and subsequently to Avignon, where, in 1475–76, he painted the *Burning Bush* altarpiece that can still be seen in the cathedral at Aix-en-Provence for René of Anjou and Jeanne de Laval (figs 48–49).[50]

Princely courts – which, in fifteenth-century Europe, could still be either peripatetic or residential in character – and their immediate circles, were undoubtedly one of the main reasons behind the mobility of such artists, making them a key factor within European cultural transfer. The mobility that rulers required on the part of the painters employed at court – as *valets de chambre* or otherwise – was crucial in this respect, although differences are apparent in specific cases. We have already referred to the journey to Jerusalem that Jan van Eyck appears to have undertaken on the order of the Duke of Burgundy in 1426. Yet this was not the only foreign mission that Van Eyck performed on behalf of the court. In 1427, the artist travelled by sea as part of a high-ranking Burgundian delegation to Barcelona and Valencia. The purpose of the visit was an abortive attempt to arrange a marriage with Isabella of Urguell – niece of Alfonso V – whose likeness Van Eyck painted there.[51] A year later, the court painter took part in a delegation to Portugal, which this time successfully arranged the wedding of Philip the Good and Isabella of Portugal. In both cases, Van Eyck brought with him portraits of his master. The portrait that Alfonso subsequently took to Naples was copied by Colantonio.[52] While in Portugal, Van Eyck painted two matching portraits of the Duke's wife-to-be, one of which was promptly

fig. 49
Nicolas Froment
Triptych of the Burning Bush (open)
Cathedral, Aix-en-Provence

mission, and he is recorded as having been paid the following year for another journey undertaken on the King's orders. The Valencia-born painter was also dispatched to the Netherlands in 1431 as part of the King's plans to set up a tapestry manufactory in Aragon. Together with Guillaume d'Ixelles, the King's Netherlandish tapestry-maker, Dalmau was presumably to gather know-how and recruit personnel.[57] He evidently used the opportunity to study Early Netherlandish paintings, including the Ghent altarpiece (which had probably not been finished at the time), as his *Altarpiece of the Consellers*,

fig. 48
Nicolas Froment
Triptych of the Burning Bush (closed)
Cathedral, Aix-en-Provence

dispatched to Flanders by land and the other by sea.[53] His portraits thus had even less immediate impact in Portugal than had previously been the case in Aragon – it is only in the work of Nuno Gonçalves that the influence of early Flemish portrait painting becomes an essential component (fig. 188).[54]

In later years, Emperor Maximilian I sent the painter Juan de Flandes – possibly Memling's sole pupil, Annekin Verhanneman – to Spain to paint the portraits of Joan the Mad and Juan of Aragon, who celebrated a crucially important double marriage with Philip the Handsome and Margaret of Austria in 1496.[55] Juan de Flandes so impressed Isabella of Castile that she appointed him court painter that same year, making him the third northern European artist at her court, together with the Englishman Antonio Inglés and the Bruges-trained Michel Sittow from Reval (Estonia). Isabella also employed the German architect Juan Guas and the Flemish sculptors Gil de Siloé and Egas Cueman.[56]

Alfonso V's court painter Lluis Dalmau visited Castile in 1428 as part of an Aragonese wedding

painted in 1443–45 for Barcelona City Council (fig. 153), quotes a number of motifs from Van Eyck's polyptych. Although only one other painting by Dalmau has survived (fig. 158), he is likely to have played a key part in the transmission of Early Netherlandish innovations to painters in Valencia and Barcelona such as the Master of Bonastre and Jaume Huguet (figs 157, 163).[58]

Because rulers like Philip the Good and Alfonso V availed themselves of their court painters' services as required – sending them on occasional diplomatic missions, as we have seen – the artists in question were able to set up permanent workshops, whether in Lille or Bruges, Valencia or Barcelona. René of Anjou's court artists, by contrast, were permanent members of the titular King of Jerusalem's entourage. Having secured his claim to the powerful Kingdom of Naples in 1438, 'Good King René' took up residence on the Bay in 1440, accompanied by his court painter Pierre du Billant.[59] Opinions differ as to whether Billant's stepson, the painter Barthélemy d'Eyck, who came from the Prince-Bishopric of Liège, had already joined the Angevin retinue in Naples at that time.[60] The Aix

Annunciation, which has been attributed to d'Eyck (figs 142, 146, 147), is certainly linked very closely in stylistic terms with Niccolò Colantonio's *Saint Jerome in His Study* from San Lorenzo Maggiore (fig. 148). In his famous letter to Venice in 1524, the Neapolitan humanist Pietro Summonte stated that Colantonio – Antonello da Messina's teacher – had been instructed in the new painting techniques emanating from Flanders by René himself.[61] Whatever the truth, both the painting and Summonte's dispatch indicate the extraordinarily close relations that existed between the court artists active in René's circle and locally based Neapolitan painters. René was obliged to relinquish Naples to Alfonso v of Aragon in 1442, but in the ensuing years, he continued to place great value on having court artists like Barthélemy d'Eyck work in surprisingly close proximity to him, whether he was in Aix-en-Provence or in Angers.[62]

René's Aragonese rival also brought his court artists with him following the capture of Naples. In due course, Alfonso began to attract Italian artists, such as Pisanello, Leonardo da Besozzo and Francesco Laurana to work at his Neapolitan court. Before this, however, his court painter Jaume Baçó (Jacomart), already exposed to Netherlandish art during his time in Aragon, and Baçó's colleague Juan Reixach, had come into contact, as *familiari* of the King, with the work of René's Franco-Flemish court painters, their local imitators and the rapidly growing royal collection of Early Netherlandish paintings. As a result, both had begun to incorporate the new style in their own paintings.[63]

Ferrante I was to follow the example of his natural father, Alfonso v, who had dispatched Dalmau to the Netherlands in 1431. In 1469–70 he sent Giovanni di Basilio or di Giusto from Naples to Bruges to study painting under Flemish craftsmen[64] – it must have seemed the natural choice. The Sforza in Milan displayed a similar attitude when they gave their court painter Zanetto Bugatto a kind of grant in 1460 so that he could go and train under Rogier van der Weyden. Bianca Maria Visconti seems to have been the prime mover in this instance. Although Bugatto remained in Brussels until 1463, his time with Rogier does not appear to have gone smoothly. In as early as 1461, the Milanese ambassador to the Burgundian court had to dispatch a letter to Milan seeking assistance in the settlement of a dispute that had arisen. Zanetto, the diplomat informed Milan, had promised to stop drinking…[65] Bugatto returned to the Duchy of Milan in 1463. He remained in the service of Francesco Sforza, who even sent him to the court of Louis XI of France. Characteristically, following Bugatto's death in 1476, the Duke of Milan Gian Galeazzo Sforza sought in vain to recruit a Venice-based painter whose work contained especially clear echoes of the painting of Jan van Eyck and Petrus Christus – Antonello da Messina.

The dispatch of Giovanni di Giusto and Zanetto Bugatto, and before that, the journey undertaken by Lluis Dalmau, are prominent examples of the way the active pursuit of training and retraining – especially in the context of southern European princely courts – necessitated the mobility of court artists. The fact that the art of the Burgundian Netherlands was adopted as the standard for courtly art no doubt also reflected the special status granted in royal art collections and, increasingly, in Italian art literature to the work of Jan van Eyck and Rogier van der Weyden. The situation also demonstrates that the structures of visual representation of the mighty Burgundian court, of which Netherlandish art formed an essential component, had established themselves as the model for princely courts throughout Europe. They were, moreover, to remain so long after the death of Charles the Bold heralded the decline of Burgundian power.

It is worth recalling in this connection that Filarete – in Book 24 of his *Trattato d'Architettura*, compiled at the Sforza court – cited Jean de Berry as the *exemplum* of princely patronage,[66] while Giovanni Pontano, who was employed at the court of the Kings of Naples, referred in his moral treatise *De splendore* (1493–94) to Alfonso the Magnanimous' ambition to surpass Berry as a patron of the arts. And when the same Pontano discussed Jan van Eyck's painting of Saint George, which entered Alfonso's collection at an early date, describing the artist as 'Master Johannes, the great painter of the illustrious Duke of Burgundy', his ultimate aim was to glorify the painter, his work and its owners by reference to Philip the Good.[67]

The Burgundian court was the literal heir to Jean de Berry, in that the latter's court painters entered

fig. 50
Anonymous (Northern Italy)
Saint Jerome
Pinacoteca dell'Accademia Carrara,
Bergamo (see cat. 103)

fig. 51
Jean Hey (Master of Moulins?)
Saint Victor (or Maurice?) and a Donor
Kelvingrove Art Gallery and
Museum, Glasgow (see cat. 72)

Philip the Bold's service following their patron's death. The splendour and magnificence that the Dukes of Burgundy deployed in order to express their claim to royal power – to which end they had the best artists in the Netherlands at their disposal – were unmatched anywhere in Europe, and were thus seen as worthy of imitation. And not only by the high nobility. The first step in emulating the Burgundians was to employ a Netherlandish painter or an artist who had trained in Flanders.

This may also explain why the painter Jean Hey – the Master of Moulins, who probably trained in Ghent under Hugo van der Goes – entered the service of the Bourbons and later that of their relative by marriage Charles VIII,[68] and why, following the death of Barthélemy d'Eyck, René of Anjou turned to another Netherlandish artist, Nicolas Froment, for altarpiece and portrait commissions (fig. 195).[69]

These few examples – drawn exclusively from the field of panel painting – are sufficient to illustrate just how crucial the mobility of artists was to European cultural transfer and to the spread of Netherlandish painting in the fifteenth and early sixteenth centuries. They also illustrate the active role that princely courts and court artists played in raising Burgundy, its courtly culture and hence also the art of the Low Countries into an example worthy of emulation. The dynastic networks and political alliances developed by the Burgundians and their Habsburg successors – especially in Southern and Southwestern Europe – undoubtedly contributed to the tremendous influence enjoyed by the art of Van Eyck and the 'Flemish Primitives'. To some extent, it is already possible to discern the tendencies towards institutionalization on which the state propaganda of Charles V and François I would build in later years.[70]

1 Warnke 1996.
2 Blockmans 1995, pp. 14–15; Martens 1995, p. 43.
3 Martens 1992, pp. 45–46; Martens 1995, pp. 43–44; Martens 1998, pp. 19–27.
4 Rodger 1993; Stabel 1997.
5 Campbell 1981, pp. 43–61, esp. pp. 48–50.
6 Castelnovi 1987, pp. 75–78; Algerin 1997, pp. 44–45.
7 Müntz 1895, pp. 190–96.
8 Cuttler 1968, pp. 250–51.
9 Duverger 1955, pp. 92–102; Bermejo 1980, pp. 75–77.
10 Blockmans 1995, p. 14.
11 Bermejo 1980, p. 76; Valencia 2001, pp. 29–30.
12 Pemán y Permatín 1969, pp. 50–52; Valencia 2001, pp. 26–28.
13 Panera Cuevas 1995.
14 Sánchez Cantón 1964.
15 Company 1987; Madrid and Valencia 2001, no. 85.
16 Alvarez 1998, pp. 45–61.
17 Lisbon 1959; Curvelo 1999, pp. 138–40; Weniger 1999b, p. 51.
18 Évora 1997, pp. 35–51; Weniger 1999a, pp. 125–26; Weniger 1999b, pp. 50–51.
19 Reis Santos 1940; Évora 1997, p. 182; Weniger 1999a, p. 126.
20 Schaefer 1994, pp. 277–82.
21 Sterling 1990, pp. 51–77, esp. pp. 72–75.
22 Laclotte and Thiébaut 1983, pp. 266–68; Sterling 1990, pp. 88–95, 108–12.
23 Comblen-Sonkes 1986, pp. 70–158.
24 Sterling 1983, pp. 173–80; Reynaud 1989, pp. 22–43; König 1996.
25 Sterling 1964; Laclotte and Thiébaut 1983, pp. 255–64.
26 Panofsky 1953, pp. 3–9; Collier 1983;

Ainsworth and Martens 1994, pp. 43–49; Sander 1995, pp. 161–68; Pauwels 1998, pp. 71–95.
27 Panofsky 1977, pp. 330–31; Nuremberg 1971, pp. 341–42.
28 Schauder 1993, pp. 653–75; Ohler 2000.
29 Sterling 1976, pp. 28–32; Spronk 1998, pp. 94–95; Faries 1996.
30 Heers 1978, pp. 1–17.
31 Troescher 1967, pp. 100–134; Sterling 1986, p. 21; see also Wymans 1969, pp. 381–92; Châtelet 1996, p. 29; Kemperdick 1997, p. 152.
32 Châtelet 1996, pp. 257–79.
33 Baxandall 1964, pp. 98–99.
34 Dhanens 1995, pp. 104–5.
35 Rohlmann 1994, pp. 29–40.
36 See Lorentz's essay in this book, pp. 67–71.
37 Lavalleye 1936, pp. 29–42, esp. pp. 37–38; Reynaud and Ressort 1991, pp. 84–122; Comblen-Sonkes and Lorentz 1995, pp. 81–180; Silva Maroto 1998, pp. 84–122.
38 Von Oettingen 1890, p. 307; Schaefer 1994, p. 345 n. 9; see also Clancy 1998, p. 123 n. 1; for the *Gonella* portrait, see Pächt 1974, pp. 31–88.
39 Wescher 1947, pp. 25–41; Avril and Reynaud 1993, pp. 130–48.
40 Boon 1965, pp. 15–18; Dacos 1995, pp. 14–31.
41 Altringer 1998, pp. 52–53; Faries 1996.
42 Durrieu 1906a, pp. 5–22; Durrieu 1906b, pp. 401–15; Meiss 1968, pp. 60–62; Heinritz 1993, pp. 113–15.
43 Avril 2002, 67.
44 Panofsky 1953, pp. 34–129; Meiss 1967; Meiss 1968; Meiss 1974.
45 Wilson 1998, pp. 13–84.
46 Devliegher 1964, pp. 232–36; Martens 1992, pp. 79–85.

47 Van Miegroet 1986; Schauder 1991, pp. 137–45.
48 Paviot 1990, p. 90.
49 Spears Grayson 1976, pp. 49–52; Rohlmann 1994, pp. 49–52.
50 Sterling 1981; Laclotte and Thiébaut 1983, pp. 241–48; Robin 1985, pp. 137–41, 211–14.
51 Pemán y Permatín 1969, pp. 33–34; Sterling 1976, pp. 33–34; Jolly 1976, p. 260, no. 3.
52 Jolly 1976, pp. 83–84.
53 Pemán y Permatín 1969, pp. 52–56; Paviot 1990, pp. 87–88.
54 Abrantes and Vandevivere 1994.
55 Vandevivere 1985, pp. 10–13; Wiesflecker 1971–86, II, pp. 27–43.
56 Yarza Luaces 1993; Alvarez 1998, pp. 49–50.
57 Marinesco 1959, pp. 33–48; Simonson Fuchs 1982, pp. 48–52; Valencia 2001, pp. 20–28.
58 See Yarza Luaces' essay in this book, pp. 129–33.
59 Robin 1985; Châtelet 1998, p. 203.
60 Reynaud 1989, pp. 21–43, esp. pp. 25–27; Thiébaut 1993, pp. 28–39; König 1996, pp. 95–96; Châtelet 1998, pp. 199–220, esp. p. 215.
61 Van Asperen de Boer 1997, pp. 99–102.
62 König 1996, pp. 95–96; Châtelet 1998, pp. 200–218.
63 Bologna 1977; Valencia 2001, pp. 31–45.
64 Warnke 1996, p. 137; Strehlke 1998, p. 55.
65 Dhanens 1995, pp. 111, 114; De Vos 1999, pp. 63–64.
66 Canfield 1995, p. 37.
67 *Ibid.*
68 Lorentz and Regond 1990; Lorentz 1994, pp. 116–18; see also Châtelet 2001.
69 Robin 1985, pp. 78–82.
70 Scheller 1999, pp. 195–242; Burke 1999.

fig. 52
Josse Lieferinx
Abraham and the Angels
Denver Art Museum (see cat. 76)

fig. 53
Antonello da Messina
Abraham and the Angels (fragment)
Museo della Magna Grecia, Reggio
di Calabria (see cat. 86)

fig. 54
Anonymous (Savoy?)
*Nativity with Saint Jerome, a Pope
(Saint Gregory?) and a Praying
Cardinal*
Kelvingrove Art Gallery and
Museum, Glasgow (see cat. 63)

fig. 55
Josse Lieferinx
Pilgrims at the Tomb of Saint Sebastian
Galleria Nazionale di Palazzo
Barberini, Rome (see cat. 77)

fig. 56
Jan Provoost
Crucifixion
Stedelijke Musea,
Groeningemuseum, Bruges
(see cat. 54)

fig. 58
Bartolomé Bermejo
Death of the Virgin
Staatliche Museen zu Berlin.
Gemäldegalerie (see cat. 110)

fig. 57
Hugo van der Goes
Death of the Virgin
Stedelijke Musea,
Groeningemuseum, Bruges
(see cat. 39)

fig. 59
Juan de Nalda
Death of the Virgin
Musée des Beaux-Arts, Lyons

fig. 60
Rogier van der Weyden
Polyptych of the Last Judgment (open)
Musée de l'Hôtel-Dieu, Beaune

fig. 61
Rogier van der Weyden
Polyptych of the Last Judgment (closed)
Musée de l'Hôtel-Dieu, Beaune

Art Markets
Michael North

Demand for art grew steadily throughout Europe from the waning of the Middle Ages onwards. The pattern emerged in Italy in the fourteenth century before reaching its peak in the Netherlands in the seventeenth century, with paintings adorning the walls of every other home. Burgeoning demand for art served to alter the function and social status of paintings, sculptures, illuminated books and other art objects. In the fifteenth century, the nobility and Church forfeited their hitherto almost exclusive role as patrons of the arts, as members of the burgher class increasingly began to commission works for their own use. Some of them acted as art dealers and collectors, while a few also became active as craftsmen themselves.[1] This essay on the development of an art market explores issues of supply and demand in relation to works of art, together with the factors that underpinned the process as a whole.

The development of an art market

Before offering an account of its historical development, we first have to define what we mean by 'art market'. An art market differs from the situation in which art is chiefly or exclusively produced on commission in that the prices charged for works of art are wholly determined by the forces of supply and demand. Artists working for such a market produce their work on behalf of an anonymous clientele rather than, as was previously the case, for a specific patron with whom they would have reached a prior contractual agreement regarding the theme of the painting, the materials to be used, the size, the price, and so forth.[2] As for the customers in this market, they were now able to purchase paintings at the artist's workshop as finished products, without having to order them in advance or pay a deposit.

Taking this definition as our basis, the first signs of an art market began to emerge in Italy in the fourteenth century. Demand for statues of the Virgin, Crucifixions and images of John the Baptist had grown very strong, while the prescriptive power of pictorial tradition had resulted in a high degree of standardization. Together, these two factors enabled artists' workshops to produce works before a specific buyer had been found, safe in the knowledge that this

would happen. A number of merchants, including the celebrated Francesco Datini, traded in images of this kind, as recorded in the unique business correspondence that survives in the Datini archive in Prato. Datini's company had branches in cities such as Paris and Avignon, which placed orders with the firm's headquarters in Florence. On 10 July 1373, for instance, an order is recorded for a 'Painting of Our Lady on a gold background with two wings. Wooden socle with ornaments and foliage, attractively and painstakingly carved so as to create the desired impression. The painting should have good, attractive and plentiful figures by the best local master. Christ on the Cross or Our Lady should appear in the centre, depending on what you can find. I don't mind either way, provided that the figures are large and splendid – the best and most attractive that you can get hold of for five or no more than six florins. Also an image of the Virgin on a gold ground – similar but a little smaller. About four florins maximum. I need them for customers who set great store by paintings like this.'[3]

It is evident here that works of art were regularly being purchased as finished products in northern Italy in the fifteenth century. The type of paintings bought at fairs tended to be of lower quality or copies. Such work was relatively inexpensive and fairs provided the opportunity to reach a wider clientele and to meet a widespread demand for religious images. Many merchants appear to have specialized in a particularly lucrative trade, which at first drew the customers for its costly paintings from the courts of Renaissance princes but also from the patrician nobles of the northern Italian cities.[4] Important and extremely valuable works of art were offered for sale by agents and middlemen on either side of the Alps: in 1444/45, for instance, a Valencian merchant called Gregori bought a painting of Saint George by Jan van Eyck – *'lo gran pintor del illustre duch de Burgunya'* – at auction in Bruges. The work appears to have been purchased on behalf of King Alfonso V, to whom it was shipped in Naples.[5]

There was also growing demand in Italy at this time for 'antiquities' – a trade stimulated by the growth of humanism, and one that paralleled the growth of a 'European' art market of the kind we have just described. Trading in antiquities included fragments of inscriptions, statuettes, terracottas,

fig. 62
Domenico Ghirlandaio
(after Memling)
Christ Crowned with Thorns
Philadelphia Museum of Art.
The John G. Johnson Collection
(see cat. 99)

53

carved gems, and Greek and Roman coins. Like paintings and engravings, these were classified as *artificialia*, and hence as works of art.[6] Antiquities of this kind were much sought-after by Italian courts, where they decorated the *studioli* of princes and potentates, often accompanied by rare Early Netherlandish panel paintings.[7]

There is evidence in the Netherlands, too, of production for an art market in the course of the fifteenth century. The situation in Bruges – the most important artistic centre north of the Alps – illustrates the extraordinary conditions for artistic creativity that existed in Flanders. It was founded on steadily increasing demand for works of art, especially illuminated manuscripts and panel paintings. Patrons of the celebrated Bruges panel painters included the Burgundian court, wealthy local merchants, the foreign business community and an unusually broad and prosperous burgher class.

The influence of the Burgundian court on local art production ought not to be overstated – the Dukes only visited Bruges intermittently and they commissioned prestigious works from painters and sculptors from all over the Burgundian territories. The majority of commissions in Bruges actually came from locally based religious confraternities, which brought together members of the nobility, the merchant class, entrepreneurs and socially privileged craftsmen.[8] The patrons of Hans Memling included foreign merchants, especially Italians, followed by prominent local citizens and confraternities (fig. 239). The same appears to have applied to Petrus Christus, whose work had found its way to southern Italy and the Iberian peninsula (fig. 125) by as early as the fifteenth century. Even the clientele of the court artist Jan van Eyck included members of Bruges-based merchant communities, such as the Arnolfini, who originally came from Lucca,[9] and the Giustiniani and Lomellini of Genoa (figs 115, 127).[10]

Art functioned as a key expression of social prestige for local and foreign merchants in Bruges and for the confraternities in which the craft élite banded together.[11] Similar motives appear to have prompted Angelo Tani and Tommaso Portinari – both representatives of the Medici bank in Bruges – to commission altarpieces from Hans

Memling and Hugo van der Goes to adorn chapels in their homeland (figs 76, 107).[12]

At the same time, art was also developing into an export commodity in fifteenth-century Bruges. An expanding and hence guild-regulated art market can be identified around 1450. The paintings it offered were relatively cheap canvases on popular themes, aimed at customers of more modest means.[13] Canvas paintings or *panni* of this kind turn up as often in Italian estate inventories as they do in Flemish wills. It is clear that they were systematically exported to the South – to Spain and Italy – where their mixture of worldly and religious subjects adorned many a citizen's walls.

Traditional fairs of the kind that were held in Bruges and Antwerp also became an increasingly important focus for the trade in art, especially since the customary guild restrictions were lifted for the period of the annual fair, which had the effect of attracting suppliers from outside the region. In as early as 1438, the Spanish traveller Pero Tafur noted that *todo lo de pintura* was available for purchase at a Franciscan friary during Antwerp's annual fair.[14]

fig. 63
Hans Memling
Christ Crowned with Thorns
Galleria di Palazzo Bianco, Genoa
(see cat. 51)

fig. 64
Hans Memling
The Virgin Mary
Private collection, United Kingdom
(see cat. 52)

fig. 65
Giovanni Bellini
Pietà
Pinacoteca dell'Accademia
Carrara, Bergamo

fig. 66
Petrus Christus
Christ as the Man of Sorrows
Birmingham Museums and Art
Gallery (see cat. 10)

fig. 67
Master of Osma
*Christ Crowned with Thorns
(Ecce Homo)*
Los Angeles County Museum of
Art. Gift of Dr and Mrs Herbert T.
Kalmus (see cat. 120)

The other chief product offered on this developing art market was contemporary graphic work. A case in point is Albrecht Dürer, whose prints were sold both through middlemen and on his own behalf on the increasingly important international market for woodcuts and copper engravings. In the process, his famous 'AD' monogram came to function as a kind of trademark. When it came to paintings, however, Dürer worked exclusively to commission on behalf of patrons from Germany and beyond. More than half of his paintings were commissioned by patrons outside Nuremberg, including emperors, electors and merchants in Breslau, Frankfurt and Venice. When Dürer exhibited a triptych at the Frankfurt annual fair, it was not with a view to selling it, but in order to win new commissions.[20]

The first signs of the development of an art market were also apparent on the Iberian peninsula. The process was encouraged there by the lack of strict guild restrictions in both northern and central Spain and by the tax exemptions that were first granted by Isabella of Castile to foreign artists – especially from the Netherlands and Germany – to encourage them to settle in Spain. The fair at Medina del Campo offered Flemish tapestries and sculpture, along with German books, woodcuts, canvases and panel paintings. The principal customers for such works were members of the Castilian court, the administrative class, the aristocracy and an aspirational burgher class.[21] Sales of Flemish works of art in Spain must have been immense: the Bruges-born sculptor Guyot de Beaugrant, who worked on the monumental chimney piece of the Hall of the Brugse Vrije (Liberty of Bruges), moved in 1522 to Bilbao, where he became a successful importer of Flemish paintings. He immediately ordered several dozen identical compositions from the Bruges artist Adriaen Provoost, which he was plainly confident of selling on.[22]

A number of conditions had to be met before the market could assert itself once and for all. The cost of producing a work of art had, for instance, to be low enough to allow an artist to manage without large advances. Demand for art, meanwhile, had to be sufficiently strong to ensure continuous sales, and prices had to be high enough to cover the cost of the artist's materials, plus the day-to-day needs of his

In 1448, an agent of Giovanni de' Medici, who was instructed to acquire tapestries to decorate his master's home, reported back to Florence on the items available at the same fair. And just under two decades later, in 1466, Tommaso Portinari notified his superiors of the purchase of a work of art, also at the fair in Antwerp.[15] The *pandts* established in monastery courtyards for the duration of the annual fair were destined to become the nucleus of permanent art markets in Bruges and, above all, in Antwerp.[16]

Antwerp's artistic output in the late fifteenth and early sixteenth centuries consisted primarily of the export of carved altarpieces with wings, produced in workshops at which a clear division of labour was applied. The market was destined to collapse, however, with the advent of the Reformation.[17] A thriving trade in antiquities of Italian provenance can be identified in Germany – especially the upper part. Firms based in Upper Germany shipped items from Venice to Augsburg and Nuremberg, and later to the courts of German princes.[18] In the late sixteenth and seventeenth centuries in particular, agents from Augsburg such as Philipp Hainhofer supplied a great many German courts between Munich and Stettin.[19]

family. These were the conditions that prevailed in the Golden Age of the Dutch Republic, when 70,000 paintings were produced and sold every year, and demand for art spread for the first time to the population at large.[23]

Painters sold their work to customers who visited their workshops or counters, gave them away in lotteries or sold them at auction. They used paintings to pay off their debts to landlords and traders, and they turned to the art trade – from pedlars to established art dealers – to market their artistic output. For the majority of painters, however, the most important clients were art dealers, whose existence was first made possible by the expansion of the art market.

Demand for art

In addition to issues of supply and intermediaries, any study of the art market also has to take account of demand. The key questions in this instance are who collected what kind of work and why? The culture of collecting, too, is rooted in the Renaissance period. Any self-respecting Italian humanist would set up a *studiolo*, in which he would display statuettes and busts, store his coins, carved gems and books – which also served as material for his work – and adorn the walls with *imagines* of famous individuals.[24] The collection that Margaret of Austria assembled at her palace in Mechelen (Malines) featured objects of this nature, together with a gallery of ancestral portraits and paintings by celebrated masters, including Van Eyck, Van der Weyden, Memling and Juan de Flandes.[25]

fig. 68
Anonymous (Netherlands)
Crucifixion with Saints
Gallinat-Bank AG, Essen (see cat. 2)

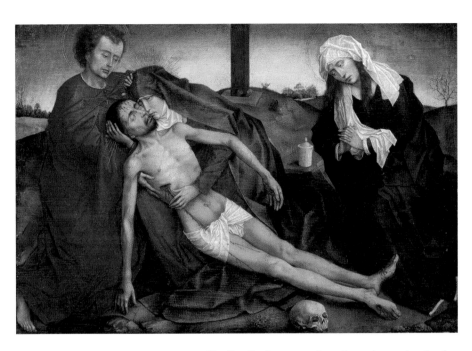

Similar displays were also adopted over time by the high bourgeoisie, primarily for reasons of prestige, and were refined as required. Meanwhile, paintings became increasingly important as interior objects. Painting was frequently used in fifteenth-century homes to decorate beds, chests and panelling, whereas in the course of the sixteenth and seventeenth centuries, it gradually assumed its own, autonomous status as wall decoration. Frames became more elaborate and costly, while the form and content of the painting grew more varied. The number of paintings per household increased. Wealthy citizens of Florence possessed dozens, if not hundreds, of works of art. Piero Guicciardini, for instance, owned 230 paintings and 165 sculptures in 1626, which he displayed in three separate rooms. Just how widespread paintings were in Italian society is illustrated by texts explaining to the uninitiated how best to hang and take care of works of art.[26]

German humanists' collections and the way they were displayed also followed the Italian example. The 1597 inventory of the Peutinger collection, for instance, describes three rooms, whose walls were decorated with paintings, prints, weapons and other ornaments. The collection's antiquities consisted of coins, statuettes and small bronzes, which were displayed on shelves. Four bronze heads stood on the mantelpiece, while 'twenty old, round emperors' heads' were displayed on a wall in the hallway.[27] The merchant and banker Raymund Fugger had a similar collection. His study was decorated with paintings from the Cranach workshop and from Italy, together with antiquities and 'curiosities', making it less a humanist workplace than a personal refuge or expression of individual prestige.[28]

Basilius Amerbach, by contrast, had a gallery added to his house, in which he hung 49 paintings, including Holbein's *Portrait of a Family* (1528) and Altdorfer's *Resurrection* (1527; Kunstmuseum, Basle). The coins and Renaissance medals were kept in special display cabinets. The quality of the Amerbach collection is remarkable, including as it did 160 drawings by Urs Graf, 56 drawings and two sketchbooks by Hans Holbein the Elder, 104 by Holbein the Younger and 84 drawings and two sketchbooks by Niklaus Deutsch.[29]

The collection founded by Paulus von Praun was even more extensive. Its substantial body of paintings, for instance, took in the Roman, Venetian, Florentine, Bolognese, Netherlandish and, above all, German schools (Dürer, Cranach, Pencz, Schäuffelein, Wolgemut, Beham and Amberger). The same tradition was represented by more than a thousand drawings and around five thousand engravings. The collection also boasted an important group of bronze and marble sculptures, terracottas, more than 1,100 stone carvings and almost four thousand coins and medals.[30]

Insofar as it is possible to reconstruct early collections, wealthy citizens elsewhere in Germany – in Cologne, for instance – owned paintings and furniture,[31] as did their counterparts in the seventeenth-century Netherlands. Netherlandish collections differed from those in Germany, however, in terms of both quantity and quality. The number of paintings was greater, and their themes also differed. I have described this long-standing, post-medieval process elsewhere as the 'secularization of taste'.[32]

In the late Middle Ages, people traditionally purchased panel paintings with religious themes – especially images of the Virgin and the saints – for private devotional use. Under the influence of the Reformation, the function of art and the tastes of the people who bought it changed in the course of the sixteenth century throughout Europe. Paintings ceased to be bought primarily for devotional purposes, and were now also chosen with a view to decorating the home and providing pleasure. As the element of enjoyment gained ground, the choice of artistic themes also began to develop, with allegorical and mythological themes first appearing alongside and then gradually displacing religious scenes.

The post-medieval secularization of taste began in the final phase of the Renaissance, as paintings and hence particular contemporary artists, became 'collectable'. The example of Hermann Weinsberg in Cologne illustrates how far the process had advanced by the mid-sixteenth century. Although Weinsberg expressed his traditional piety by endowing an altarpiece in the Church of Saint James, at home he combined an image of the Virgin and family portraits with naked goddesses (Fortuna), legendary figures (Lucretia) and pagan heroes (Marsilius and Agrippa).[33]

This trend is confirmed by Paulus von Praun's art collection and by that of Octavian Secundus Fugger – the grandson of Raymund Fugger. Although religious subjects continued to make up a third of these collections, portraits of famous individuals, mythological works, allegories, landscapes, and animal and plant paintings together formed a much more substantial body of work.[34] This evolution towards worldly themes peaked in the Netherlandish art collections of the seventeenth century, which stood out for their high proportion of non-religious themes: landscapes, still lifes and genre scenes were the most popular, while religious themes, together

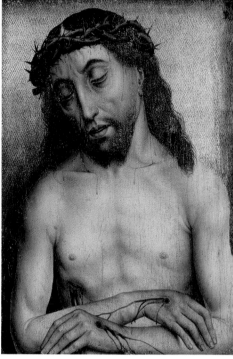

with allegorical and mythological motifs, were pushed increasingly into the background.

Traditional hierarchies of taste began to totter in the eighteenth century under the influence of Netherlandish painters and paintings – an influence that also extended to France, England and Germany. As a result, landscapes and genre scenes gradually replaced history paintings in public favour.[35] A prerequisite for this development was a broad supply of paintings – something that was increasingly provided by both the art trade and local schools of painting.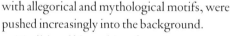

fig. 70
Workshop of Simon Marmion (?)
Mater Dolorosa and *Christ as the Man of Sorrows*
Stedelijke Musea,
Groeningemuseum, Bruges
(see cat. 81)

1 Roeck 1991.
2 Schöne 1938; Berg Sobré 1989, pp. 267–337.
3 Origo 1985, p. 33.
4 Burke 1984, pp. 110–14; Hochman 1992, pp. 87–91.
5 Weiss 1956, pp. 11, 15; Campbell 1976, p. 197.
6 Goldthwaite 1993, p. 247; Favaretto 1990.
7 Rohlmann 1994, pp. 99–103, 124.
8 Martens 1992.
9 Campbell 1998, pp. 174–211, esp. pp. 192–201; Campbell 2000, pp. 7–24.
10 Neidhart and Schölzel 2000, pp. 27–28.
11 Blockmans 1996, p. 24.
12 Rohlmann 1994, pp. 41–65.
13 Martens 1998, pp. 19–27.
14 Tafur 1986, pp. 251ff.

15 Rohlmann 1994, p. 23; De Roover 1988, p. 206.
16 Wilson 1983, pp. 476–79; Ewing 1990, pp. 558–84.
17 Jacobs 1989, pp. 207–29; Montias 1993, pp. 1541–63; Campbell 1976, pp. 188–98; Wilson 1983, pp. 476–80.
18 Lieb 1958, p. 48; von Busch 1973, pp. 87ff.; Pieper 1999; Backmann 1997, pp. 173–97.
19 Volk-Knüttel 1980, pp. 83–128; Gobiet 1984; Doering 1896; for Hainhofer, see Roeck 1991, pp. 9–53.
20 Schmid 1996, pp. 47–67; for Cranach, see Grimm, Erichsen and Brockhoff 1994.
21 Alvarez 1998, pp. 45–59.
22 Martens 1998a, p. 54.

23 Montias 1990, p. 70.
24 Von Busch 1973, pp. 83ff.
25 Eichberger and Beaven 1995, pp. 224–48; Eichberger 2000.
26 Goldthwaite 1993, pp. 232–34.
27 Von Busch 1973, pp. 64ff.
28 Ibid., pp. 85ff.
29 Ackermann 1985, pp. 63ff.
30 Weber 1983, pp. 163–75.
31 Schmid 1991, pp. 69–130.
32 North 1995, pp. 289–93.
33 Schmid 1991, p. 111.
34 Weber 1983, p. 169; Lieb 1980, pp. 68–85.
35 North 2001, pp. 123–32.

fig. 73
Dieric Bouts and
Hugo van der Goes
Martyrdom of Saint Hippolytus
(open and closed)
Stedelijke Musea,
Groeningemuseum, Bruges
(see cat. 7)

fig. 74
Hans Memling
Triptych of Saint Christopher
('Moreel triptych', open
and closed)
Stedelijke Musea,
Groeningemuseum, Bruges
(see cat. 53)

fig. 75
Hans Memling
Triptych of Jan Floreins
(open and closed)
Memlingmuseum, Sint-
Janshospitaal, Bruges (see cat. 50)

fig. 76
Hans Memling
Triptych of the Last Judgment
(open and closed)
Muzeum Narodowe, Gdańsk

63

France, 'Terre d'Accueil' for Flemish Painters

Philippe Lorentz

The introduction of the public to the work of the painters active in France in the fourteenth and fifteenth centuries, in the Paris exhibition of 'French Primitives' held in 1904, was a highly praiseworthy venture on the part of the organizers. The rediscovery, however, was strongly tainted with a kind of nationalism of which Henri Bouchot, curator of prints at the Bibliothèque Nationale and linchpin of the exhibition, made himself the mouthpiece. In rejecting the theories of the Belgian historian Georges Hulin de Loo, who was interested in demonstrating 'the influence of the Van Eyck brothers on French and Provençal painting',[1] Bouchot was defending the autonomy of French painting of the late Middle Ages, in particular with regard to the painting of the former Low Countries.

A 'national' school of painting?

Any appreciation of the contribution made by Flanders to fifteenth-century French painting assumes a preliminary definition of the 'French school', or, more accurately, in the terms used by Bouchot, the 'Schools of France'. In Bouchot's opinion all territory where the French language was spoken belonged to the 'Schools of France'. 'When we speak of France, we speak of that territory where the same basic dialect was used, where artisans could understand and influence each other, and learn from each other; we do not at all mean to indicate the *present boundaries of the country in which we live*.'[2] This cultural criterion seems even more appropriate because in France, in the mid-fifteenth century, a feeling of nationhood was beginning to emerge and the idea of the correspondence between language and that nationhood was increasingly taking shape.[3]

But French was not the only language spoken in the kingdom of the *fleur-de-lis*. It had to cohabit with the *langue d'oc*, Basque, Breton and – Flemish. In fact the ancient frontier which separated France from the Holy Roman Empire, the frontier formed by the four rivers (Scheldt, Meuse, Saône and Rhône), fixed by the Treaty of Verdun (843), left the County of Flanders, west of the Scheldt, under the authority of the King of France. Tournai, the birthplace of Rogier van der Weyden, was the fourth of the *bonnes villes*

('good towns') of the Kingdom of France. It was precisely in the artistic environment of this western part of the Low Countries that a new pictorial style was to develop in the 1420s and 1430s; its principal promoters tried to capture in their paintings the space, light and forms of reality.

The artistic centres of northern France

The *ars nova* spread throughout the whole of Europe. The first region to be touched by it was the enormous, partially francophone geographical area which shared the same urban culture, dominated by trade guilds, as Dutch-speaking Flanders. It is very difficult to draw the linguistic frontier accurately because it is 'not only geographical: it varies according to usage, written and oral, … according to social categories and local, even individual, preference'.[4] Bouchot was taking liberties with historical truth when he claimed that 'Flemings speaking a Germanic language were still in the minority'. His intentions are clear: he was particularly keen to make a Frenchman of Rogier de le Pasture, who 'only became *Van der Weyden* by a posthumous annexation'. The reality is that Rogier de le Pasture became Van der Weyden because he left francophone Tournai and moved to Brussels, the capital of Brabant, where Dutch was spoken. The painter was obviously bilingual.

The principal centres of the new painting were therefore not simply neighbours of the Kingdom of France, they were an integral part of it. One might wonder whether, in the heart of this conurbation in which French and Netherlandish culture mingled so comprehensively, it would not be as useless to try and define an artistic frontier as it would be to trace on a map a genuine linguistic frontier. Most of the towns in this vast border area were linked by the same culture; this was the area to which artistic activity retreated in the 1410s and 1420s, when the political upheavals in Paris became too disturbing and the French capital was isolated after the Treaty of Troyes (1420). The experimental painters who appeared in the towns between France and Flanders were all trained in the same tradition, a tradition whose origins can be found in the art of Paris in about 1400.

At the moment when the *ars nova* appeared, the

fig. 77
Jean Hey (Master of Moulins?)
The Virgin and Child Surrounded by Angels
Musées Royaux des Beaux-Arts de Belgique, Brussels (see cat. 75)

65

artists and their work moved frequently from one centre to another in the dense network of towns dotting the Southern Netherlands and the north of France. The innovations made in the pioneering workshops of the painters of Tournai spread rapidly to the south-west of the region. Immediately after completing his official apprenticeship in Tournai (1427–32), Jacques Daret, a colleague of Rogier van der Weyden in the studio of Robert Campin, established himself in the nearby town of Arras, although maintaining a close relationship with

which produced, according to them, 'an art that was distinct … from the Flemish art of the neighbouring region, and which was in close contact with French art'.[6] On the other hand the panels painted by Simon Marmion are examined in the various volumes of the *Corpus de la peinture des anciens Pays-Bas méridionaux* (Corpus of Early Southern Netherlandish painting). Paradoxes of this nature should encourage us to question the validity of any method of classifying artistic production which depends too heavily on the territorial divisions of today. A more informed

fig. 78
Simon Marmion
Scenes from the Life of Saint Bertin
(left wing of the altarpiece of
Saint-Bertin Abbey, Saint-Omer)
Staatliche Museen zu Berlin.
Gemäldegalerie

fig. 79
Jacques Daret
Visitation (panel from the altarpiece
of Saint-Vaast Abbey, Arras)
Staatliche Museen zu Berlin.
Gemäldegalerie

Tournai and indeed retaining a studio there as well. Conversely, the profound changes being brought about by the artists of Tournai attracted artists from other centres, such as Amiens, at the time one of the most densely populated towns in the Kingdom of France. Very shortly links were forged between the painters of Amiens and Tournai. 'Maistre Andrieu d'Amiens' (André d'Ypres or Dipre, known in Amiens from 1425–26) registered as an independent master in the painters' corporation at Tournai in 1428, at the time when Rogier van der Weyden and Jacques Daret were working with Robert Campin. André d'Ypres did not return to Amiens until about 1441, although there is evidence of familiarity with the paintings produced by the artists of Tournai in the capital of Picardy from as early as about 1435.[5]

The itinerary and the work of another artist from Amiens, Simon Marmion, illustrate the problems encountered by historians attempting to pin a 'nationality' on to the artists from this frontier region. Is Simon Marmion, the author of the *Saint Bertin* altarpiece (fig. 78) and a contemporary of Dieric Bouts, a French artist or an artist from the Low Countries? He trained in Amiens and worked for the municipality there from 1449 to 1451 before migrating to Valenciennes, part of the Empire, where his name is first mentioned in 1458 and where his career (and his life) ended in 1489. Both Amiens and Valenciennes are in present-day France. In their remarkable exhibition of illuminated manuscripts in France (1440–1520), François Avril and Nicole Reynaud included this painter and illuminator who came from a region

appreciation of historical geography should furnish us with a better comprehension of the artistic mix existing within regions which, although often complex, present an evident cultural unity.

The diffusion of the *ars nova* beyond its birthplace in the northern marches was encouraged by the end of the Hundred Years' War. Greater security on the roads permitted large numbers of painters from the Low Countries to travel to France again. The gradual return to peace began with a separate peace treaty concluded in Arras in 1435 between the King of France and the Duke of Burgundy, Philip the Good, prince of the *fleur-de-lis* and ruler of the Low Countries, who abandoned his alliance with the English in exchange for Picardy. A large number of diplomats were present at the congress culminating in this treaty. One of them was Cardinal-Legate Niccolò Albergati, who displayed an early fondness for the new painting when he eagerly set out on a visit to the Abbey of Saint-Vaast to see the painted wings of the *Altarpiece of the Virgin*, just completed by Jacques Daret (1433–35; fig. 79). The prelate also had his portrait made by Jan van Eyck, who was also present in Arras (fig. 7).[7]

With Albergati, one of the principal authors of the Peace of Arras was Nicolas Rolin, a Burgundian. His position as chancellor led this eminent character to travel constantly between Burgundy and the '*pays de par delà*' (the Burgundian Netherlands). Rolin had known Jan van Eyck since the painter had entered the service of Philip the Good (1425). He commissioned from him the celebrated *Virgin and Child with Chancellor Rolin* (fig. 13), which in about 1435 was

fig. 80
Master of Saint-Jean-de-Luze
*Diptych of Hugues de Rabutin
and Jeanne de Montaigu*
Musée des Beaux-Arts, Dijon
(see cat. 82)

in Autun, in the Church of Notre-Dame-du-Châtel. From an artistic point of view, Burgundy's fate was exactly the same as the fate of the towns of Picardy because of the particular configuration of the lands ruled by Duke Philip. When he brought Flemish works of art into his ducal foundations he was simply pursuing the tradition established at the end of the fourteenth century by his grandfather Philip the Bold. Jan van Eyck's Washington *Annunciation* (fig. 17) is a fragment of a triptych which was probably destined for a sanctuary in Burgundy (perhaps the Charterhouse of Champmol).

In the mid-1430s, the rest of the Kingdom of France was still artistically isolated from the Low Countries. The diffusion of the *ars nova* was linked to the gradual return to peace between 1435 and 1453. It was not until the middle of the century, however, that painters arrived in large numbers from the Netherlands, taking over from the ones who had come at the end of the fourteenth century or at the very beginning of the fifteenth. Barthélemy d'Eyck, Enguerrand Quarton, Coppin Delf, Jacob de Littemont, Conrad and Henri de Vulcop, André d'Ypres, Colin d'Amiens, Nicolas Froment and Jean Hey succeeded André Beauneveu, Jean de Bruges,

Jean de Beaumetz, Jacquemart de Hesdin, Jean Malouel and the Limbourg brothers. These representatives of the linear, mannered style had come to seek the fountain-head of art in Paris. Their colleagues who arrived in the middle and the second half of the fifteenth century, on the other hand, brought the new painting with them – as evidenced by the installation of André d'Ypres in Paris.

André d'Ypres, the Master of the Crucifixion of the Paris Parliament (or Master of Dreux Budé)

In 1436 Charles VII recaptured the major city of his kingdom from the English. It was not until the Truce of Tours, however, in 1444, that Paris became a vibrant commercial city again, open for business particularly with the North. Works of art imported from the Low Countries could be found for sale there from about 1450. A shrewd collector like René of Anjou procured some large pictures of the Passion '*faiz en Flandre*' ('made in Flanders'), and did business with the painters Henri de Vulcop and Jacob de Littemont, both of Netherlandish origin. The existence of this trade bears witness to the change in taste that was beginning to take place in the French capital. As far

fig. 81
Master of the Paris Parliament
Crucifixion or Master of Dreux
Budé (André d'Ypres)
Crucifixion of the Parliament of Paris
Musée du Louvre, Paris

as painting was concerned, Parisian horizons had hitherto been limited to the products of painters from the studio of the Master of Bedford, such as the Master of Dunois – although Flemish models did reach them to a limited degree.[8] The time was ripe, therefore, for enterprising northern artists to set up shop in Paris, where the main government departments were located: the servants of these departments constituted an interesting potential clientele. The Master of the Crucifixion of the Paris Parliament did exactly this.

Careful analysis of the painting – formerly in the Great Chamber – which the parliamentary councillors caused to be repainted in the middle of the fifteenth century (fig. 81), immediately reveals the fact that its painter was trained in Tournai.[9] A number of the motifs in the painting are borrowed from the repertory of Rogier van der Weyden and the Master of Flémalle, beginning with the figure of Christ, the principal figure in the painting. With his exaggeratedly long arms and his floating loincloth, he is reminiscent of the figures in Rogier's *Triptych of the Crucifixion* in Vienna (fig. 83) and in his large *Crucifixion* diptych in Philadelphia (fig. 82). Saint John the Baptist, with his diffident stance, pointing at the *Agnus Dei* with a powerful arm, recalls the Precursor

presenting the Franciscan friar Heinrich Werl on one of the two panels of the altarpiece painted at his request, attributed to the Master of Flémalle and dated 1438. The heavily modelled religious figures in the foreground, wrapped in their heavy cloaks and looking rather like polychrome statues, derive directly from the Master of Flémalle; they echo the sculptural *Virgin Suckling the Child* and *Saint Veronica* from the so-called 'Flémalle altarpiece', now in Frankfurt.

The sources of the Master of the Parliament Crucifixion, to be found in the work of the Master of Flémalle and Rogier van der Weyden, bring us instantly back to Tournai. Convinced that the painting was the work of a 'Netherlandish itinerant artist who left Paris after completing the commission he undertook for the Parliament', Charles Sterling in 1941 suggested the name of an artist from Tournai who fitted the description.[10] His identification of the painter with Louis le Duc, who became a free-master at Tournai in 1453, is based mainly on the absence of any mention of this artist in documents relating to Tournai between 1453 and 1456, the period during which the Parliament *Crucifixion* was assumed to have been painted. Our present knowledge of Tournai archives is based on material published before 1940, the year when they were destroyed by the bombing of the city. We know too little, in fact, to assume that Louis le Duc really did leave the city for the duration of these three years. In addition, we shall see that work on the *Crucifixion* started some years before Louis le Duc was made a free-master (1453), and this chronology therefore definitively excludes the painter from Tournai from any involvement in its execution.

Far from being a nomadic artist, the Master of the Crucifixion of the Paris Parliament was well settled in Paris. The existence of a *Crucifixion* triptych (fig. 84), painted for the important public servant Dreux Budé,

that he is the father of Nicolas (or 'Colin') d'Ypres, called 'd'Amiens'. It seems therefore that the latter was the Master of Coëtivy, an identification corroborated by the discovery of a documented work by Colin d'Amiens, a sculpture of the *Entombment*, executed in 1495–96, after the model made by this artist, and designed for the chapel of the château of Admiral Louis Malet de Graville in Malesherbes (Loiret).[12] The Malesherbes *Entombment* has many features in common with the *Raising of Lazarus*, a panel by the Master of Coëtivy now in the Louvre (fig. 91).

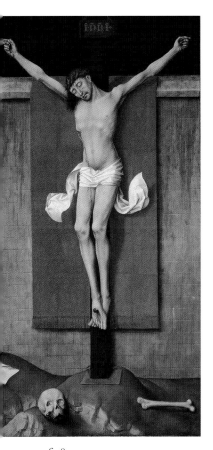

fig. 82
Rogier van der Weyden
Diptych of the Crucifixion
Philadelphia Museum of Art.
The John G. Johnson Collection

fig. 83
Rogier van der Weyden
Triptych of the Crucifixion
Kunsthistorisches Museum,
Vienna. Gemäldegalerie

'*notaire et secrétaire*' (lawyer) to King Charles VII and usher in chancery, whose career ended in about 1450, allows us to situate the activity of the painter in the French capital more securely.[11] Nicole Reynaud has considerably enlarged the group of works attributable to the 'Master of Dreux Budé' by ascribing some of the stained-glass windows in the nave of the Church of Saint-Séverin to him – a further indication that his activity in Paris was more than just transient – as well as some miniatures. These are so close in style to those by a painter and illuminator who was active in Paris during the second half of the fifteenth century, the Master of Coëtivy, that a certain number of them were previously attributed to the latter, himself a generation younger than the Master of Dreux Budé. Nicole Reynaud has explained this stylistic relationship by demonstrating the kinship which bound the two artists together – they were father and son. She identifies the Master of Dreux Budé as André d'Ypres, the aforementioned painter from Amiens who became a free-master in Tournai and who was resident in Paris after 1444. A deed drawn up by a notary in 1479 reveals

We have recently learned that André d'Ypres died at Mons in July 1450, while returning from a pilgrimage to Rome on the occasion of the Jubilee.[13] This information does not permit us to assume *a priori* that he is the author of the Parliament *Crucifixion*, which appears to have been painted in about 1452–54 – the date supplied by Albert Châtelet following his research in the archives of the Parliament of Paris.[14] Although the date is generally accepted by art historians, it seemed worth verifying it. Maintenance work on the premises of the Palais de la Cité, which housed the Parliament, was financed by the money made from fines imposed by the Court. In accordance with this custom, a sum amounting to nearly 300 *livres parisis* (pounds minted in Paris) was set aside for the restoration of the painting in the Great Chamber – not in 1452, as Châtelet erroneously claimed, but in February 1449.[15]

At this date, eighteen months before the death in Mons of '*Andrieu d'Ippre, peintre de Paris*', work on the painting in the Great Chamber was already under way. The picture, for which payment was not finally

made until July 1454, was probably not completed when the artist left for Rome. But André d'Ypres probably had time to lay out the composition in detail, as indicated by the elaborate underdrawing revealed by infrared reflectography.[16] Before leaving for Rome the painter must have planned the continuance of this important commission in his absence. It is reasonable to suppose that he gave this responsibility to his son, Colin d'Amiens (the Master of Coëtivy). The latter came to Paris as a young man with his father and pursued a brilliant career in the capital. The completion of the *Crucifixion* in the Parliament, composed by his father André d'Ypres, may have been his first effort as an independent master. So soon after his training with his father, Colin d'Amiens must have been perfectly capable of conforming to his father's style, and of giving the painting in the Great Chamber the final appearance expected by the people who had commissioned the work.

The circumstances of André d'Ypres' death also corroborate his identification as the author of the Parliament Crucifixion, otherwise known as the 'Master of Dreux Budé'. As we have seen, André

d'Ypres died at Mons in July 1450, on his return from a pilgrimage across the Alps to Italy. The Jubilee year of 1450 attracted flocks of pilgrims to Rome. One of these pilgrims was a painter whom André d'Ypres had known in Tournai in 1428: Rogier van der Weyden. Evidence of the presence of Rogier in the Eternal City in 1450 – 'iobelei anno' – is given by Bartolomeo Fazio in his *De viris illustribus* (1456). The precise moment in 1450 when Rogier went to Italy has been much discussed. A money order, presented in Ferrara on 15 August 1450, records the payment of 20 gold ducats to Rogier for paintings commissioned by Marchese Lionello d'Este (1441–50). This document ratifies a payment made around 15 June 1450 in the name of Lionello, by the agent of an Italian merchant in Bruges. In August, therefore, Rogier was evidently in the Low Countries.[17] The painter's Italian trip probably took place during the first six months of the year 1450. The artist must certainly have been in Rome for the beginning of the Jubilee, and may have left home in the autumn of 1449 in order to avoid crossing the Alps in the winter.[18]

Did Rogier van der Weyden return from Italy in

fig. 84
Master of the Paris Parliament Crucifixion or Master of Dreux Budé (André d'Ypres)
Triptych of the Crucifixion (reconstruction)
(left wing) *Arrest of Christ*. Collection Dr Heinrich Bischoff, Bremen
(centre) *Crucifixion*. J. Paul Getty Museum, Los Angeles
(right wing) *Resurrection*. Musée Fabre, Montpellier

the company of André d'Ypres? The two painters had known each other at least since 1428. At that date, André d'Ypres was received as a free-master in Tournai, and 'Rogelet de le Pasture' had been in the workshop of Robert Campin for more than a year. André d'Ypres died in July 1450 in Mons, returning from Rome, on the route from Paris to Brussels, where Rogier had probably returned a short while earlier. Since 1428 the two painters – one of them from Amiens and then Paris (André d'Ypres) and the other from Tournai and then Brussels (Rogier de le Pasture/van der Weyden) – had probably remained in touch. At any rate, the Parisian paintings of André d'Ypres (and in particular the 'Triptych of Dreux Budé' and the Parliament *Crucifixion*) testify to a constantly renewed familiarity with the work of Rogier van der Weyden. Everything suggests that the northern painters who went to work in France maintained their links with the homeland.

Painters at court and painters in the towns

The migration of northern artists towards the Kingdom of France is evidence of the saturation of the market in the densely populated towns of the Low Countries, where it must have been difficult to run a workshop. Many of these painters, often highly talented, left home in search of better material conditions. The period of reconstruction which followed the end of the Hundred Years' War offered plenty of employment to artists. The careers of André d'Ypres and his son Colin d'Amiens, who brought new life to the artistic landscape of Paris, are a case in point.

Many painters also hoped to enter the service of a powerful person, a position which guaranteed a fixed income (wages, often annual) yet did not prevent the artist accepting commissions from outside. Courts at the time were peripatetic, but because easel painting is not compatible with being constantly on the move, these 'court' artists often lived and worked in a town studio, in one of the cities in which the prince had a residence. In this way Jan van Eyck lived in Bruges, Jean Fouquet lived in Tours and Jean Hey, painter to the Bourbons (the 'Master of Moulins'), in Moulins. Barthélemy d'Eyck, the Master of the Aix Annunciation (fig. 142) and of René of Anjou's *Cœur d'amour épris*, seems to have been very close to King René and to have followed him in his peregrinations. In the inventory of the Château d'Angers (1471–72) a chair is listed on which the artist used to sit and work, a '*cherre à coffre et à ciel sur laquelle se siet Barthelemy pour besongner*'. This piece of furniture is situated in the '*petit retrait du roy*' ('the King's small private room'), an indication of the close friendship existing between the prince and his painter, a relation of Jan van Eyck.

Nearly one hundred years after the memorable exhibition of 'French Primitives', our knowledge of the activity of the painters in the kingdom of the *fleur-de-lis*, at the end of the century-long conflict with the English, invalidates the judgments of Henri Bouchot and declares in favour of Hulin de Loo. At the end of the day, the history of French painting in the fifteenth century is the history of a constant and progressive assimilation of the Flemish pictorial view, brought about by the many artists who came to France from the Burgundian Netherlands. If we were of a mind to denigrate the historical conclusions of the exhibition of 1904 we might describe what occurred as the 'colonization' of the main French centres of the arts by Flemish artists and Flemish painting. 🌶

1   Hulin de Loo 1904.
2   Bouchot 1904, p. 2.
3   Beaune 1991, pp. 291–99.
4   Nordman 1998, p. 459.
5   Nash 1995, pp. 428–37.
6   Avril and Reynaud 1993, pp. 11, 80–89.
7   Paviot 1990, pp. 83–93, esp. pp. 90–93.
8   Reynaud 1999, pp. 23–25.
9   Sterling 1990, pp. 36–49; Dijkstra 1997, pp. 53–59; Lorentz 1998, pp. 101–24.
10 Sterling 1941, p. 60.
11 Fredericksen 1983, pp. 183–96; Avril and Reynaud 1993, p. 53.
12 Grodecki 1996, pp. 329–42.
13 Vanwijnsberghe 2000, pp. 365–69.
14 Châtelet 1964, pp. 60–69, esp. pp. 63–64.
15 Lorentz and Comblen-Sonkes 2001 (forthcoming).
16 Lorentz 1998, pp. 101–24, esp. p. 118, ill. 16.
17 Kantorowicz 1939–40, pp. 165–80, esp. p. 179.
18 Maquet-Tombu 1951, pp. 95–104, esp. p. 99.

fig. 85
Enguerrand Quarton
Virgin and Child with Angels; *Saint John the Baptist*; *The Prophets Isaiah
and Jeremiah* (reconstruction of a diptych)
Staatliches Lindenau-Museum, Altenburg (see cat. 83); Musei Vaticani,
Vatican City (prophets)

fig. 86
Barthélemy d'Eyck
Holy Family
Cathedral Treasury,
Le Puy-en-Velay (see cat. 67)

fig. 87
Simon Marmion
Saint Jerome with a Donor
Philadelphia Museum of Art.
The John G. Johnson Collection

fig. 88
Anonymous (Southern
France/Provence)
Dionysius the Areopagite
Bonnefantenmuseum, Maastricht.
On loan from Rijksmuseum,
Amsterdam (see cat. 64)

fig. 89
Barthélemy d'Eyck
Portrait of a Man
Sammlungen des Fürsten von
Liechtenstein, Schloss Vaduz
(see cat. 66)

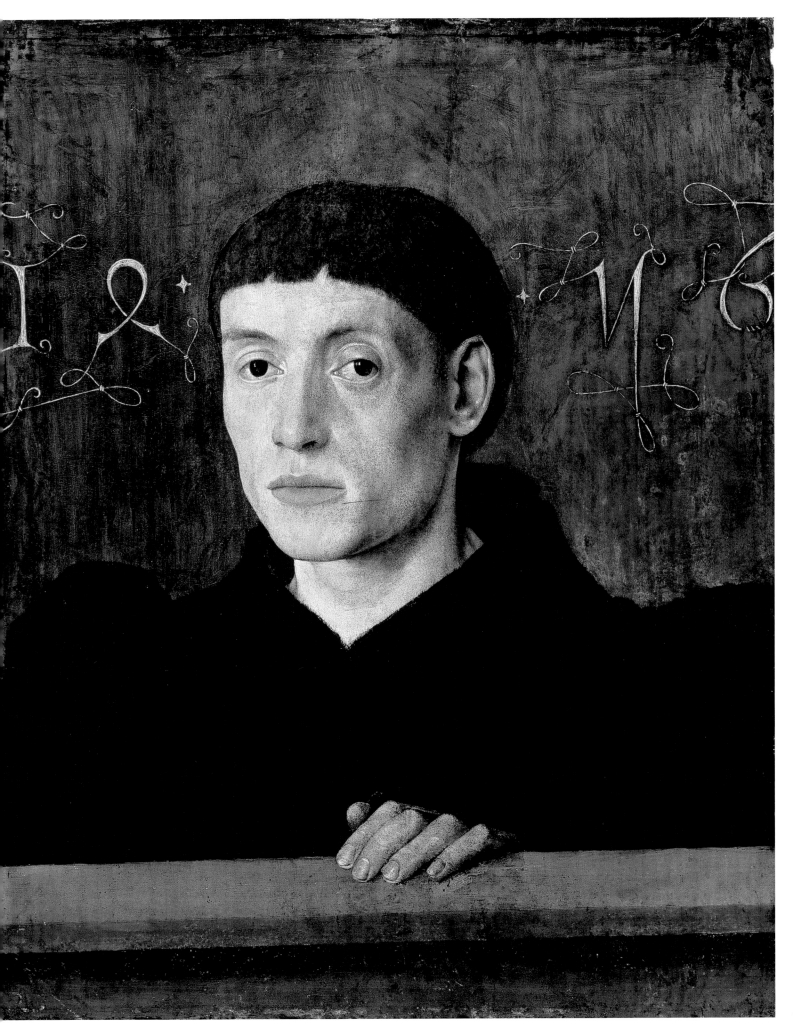

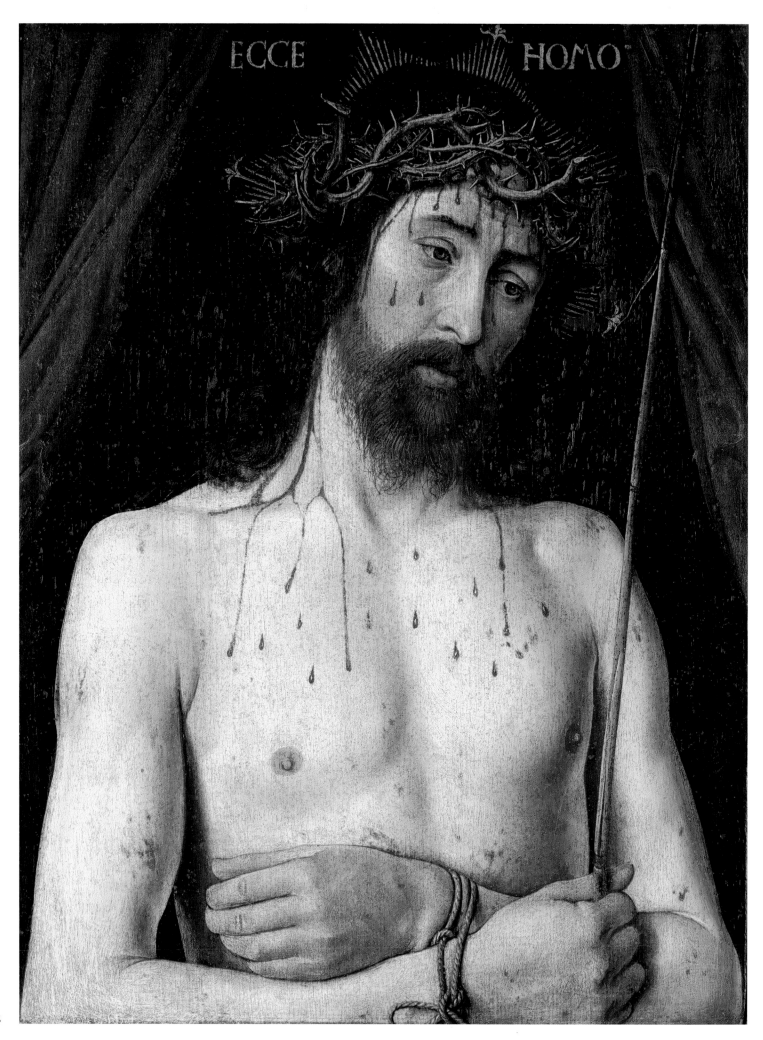

ECCE HOMO

fig. 91
Master of Coëtivy
(Colin d'Amiens?)
Raising of Lazarus
Musée du Louvre, Paris

fig. 90
Jean Hey (Master of Moulins?)
Ecce Homo
Musées Royaux des Beaux-Arts
de Belgique, Brussels (see cat. 74)

Italy and the North.
A Florentine Perspective
Margaret L. Koster

Despite recent contributions to the field, most discussions of artistic relations between Italy and the Low Countries still revolve around certain commonplaces: Jan van Eyck invented the oil technique; monumentality is Italian; detailed, mountainous landscapes are northern; use of 'correct' perspective equals modernity; Van der Weyden did/did not go to Italy; Dürer was a gentleman in Italy; and so on.[1] A reading of the evidence more open to complexity, however, can yield an illuminating picture of mutual fascination. The following essay focuses primarily on artistic exchange between Flanders and Florence.

Gombrich long ago set up a contrast between the lustre of northern painting – light as descriptive of rich, gleaming surfaces – and the Italian method of using light as an instrument in the rendering of three-dimensional form.[2] As opposed to the stark reality of Masaccio's weighty figures and their tangible architectural surroundings, the Flemish brand of naturalism was not to everyone's taste – indeed, Gombrich himself articulated the comparison with the pre-eminence of the Italians in mind. Van Eyck, he stated, was 'not in possession of the art of perspective', a technology that often was considered a benchmark for a good painter. Therefore, we read that the floor of Van Eyck's 'Van der Paele Madonna' (fig. 92) slopes and that the forms are less secure in space. 'We become aware of this when we look at a painting done in Florence ten years later', is his introduction to Domenico Veneziano's *Saint Lucy* altarpiece, to which we will be returning shortly.[3]

In Italy, one does find some early acknowledge-ment of Van Eyck's high stature; in 1456, Bartolomeo Fazio singled out four painters for highest praise: Jan van Eyck, Rogier van der Weyden, Pisanello and Gentile da Fabriano.[4] Fazio's international taste, encouraged by his patron (see Beyer's essay, pp. 123–24), indicates how northern and southern paintings were equally sought-after by humanists.

But that was Naples. In Florence, genuine belief in the city's artistic superiority was already developing by the fifteenth century and would soon turn into full-blown condescension towards the outside world: Anton Francesco Doni, in his *Disegno* (1549), says that the *oltramontani* have 'their brains in their hands',

a point of view famously shared by Michelangelo. Why were the Florentines often so critical in writing and yet so keen to collect or to commission Flemish pictures? Perhaps because Florentine scholars liked painters who reflected their interests – geometrical perspective, emulation of classical models – and these are not typically found in northern painting until around 1500, by which time Italy *was* setting the artistic standard. However, while the Florentine theorists were the most negative of all, perhaps due to the age-old antagonism between Neoplatonism and naturalism, Florentine artists were the most clearly influenced.[5] This is why things get confusing. Modern art history has followed the theorists. The pictorial evidence shows that Florentines loved Jan van Eyck.

In a typical survey of Italian Renaissance art Fra Angelico will most likely be presented as the father of the *sacra conversazione*, a composition of saints gathered around an enthroned Virgin and Child, as in his 'San Marco altarpiece', dated to 1437–40 (Museo di San Marco, Florence).[6] Domenico Veneziano followed suit shortly thereafter with his *Saint Lucy* altarpiece of around 1445 (fig. 93), proving that a single-panel *sacra conversazione* was an idea that took hold in the Florentine school. These two works are often seen as a harbinger of things to come. But part of the story is routinely omitted, not necessarily because of ignorance, but because art history is arbitrarily divided at a certain mountain range that marks a difference in language and custom, where a steady cross-cultural trade in art flourished. The missing link is Van Eyck's 'Van der Paele Madonna' (fig. 92). Signed and dated January 1436, it anticipates the two Italian works in its grouping of saints on a single panel.

Comparing this painting with Veneziano's altarpiece reveals that contrast now so well codified: the lustrous Van Eyck with his virtuoso display of materials, and the cool, pale Veneziano, the space described with mathematical accuracy. Veneziano's figures resemble an architectural colonnade, lacking the Fleming's surface materiality. Van Eyck produced some of the best examples of atmospheric perspective, a technique first introduced by a northern illuminator known as the Boucicaut Master. Is it possible, then, that it might have been a Netherlander who first

79

moved isolated figures of a gold-ground polyptych into an atmospheric space?

The *sacra conversazione* – a later term – evolved during the 1420s out of the multi-panelled altarpiece.[7] No surviving pictorial evidence exists in support of the presumption that unifying saints around the Virgin on a single panel was a Florentine invention. Since this composition was particularly popular in Florence in this period, discussing its development would naturally focus on Florentine painters. Despite this, Jan van Eyck's Bruges painting predates any

client.[9] Some scholars believe that this painting proves that Rogier visited Florence; only there could he have seen a *sacra conversazione* on which to base his composition,[10] they argue, thereby neglecting Van Eyck's example.

The dialogue between paintings by Rogier and Fra Angelico plays an interesting part in this story,[11] and, as usual, a part with some surprises. The Strozzi *Deposition* (Museo di San Marco, Florence) painted by Fra Angelico in the early to mid-1430s,[12] displays a remarkable similarity to Rogier's *Deposition* (Prado,

surviving Florentine example of a *sacra conversazione*; applying the Italian term itself indicates blindness to Van Eyck's prescient role.

It is easy to find other northern examples of this kind, presumably responding to Italian demand. Petrus Christus' *Virgin and Child with Saints* (fig. 94) includes Saint Francis, a popular saint in Italy. Here, too, the saints gather around the enthroned Virgin in a *sacra conversazione*. It seems that assimilating Van Eyck's style made Petrus Christus a great success abroad: of his 25 or so extant works, no fewer than eight have Italian or Spanish provenances.[8]

A *Virgin and Child with Saints* attributed to Rogier van der Weyden is known as the 'Medici Madonna' (fig. 95); the presence of the Medici saints Cosmas and Damian, the Florentine lily (*giglio*), and the *sacra conversazione* composition would suggest links with the leading Florentine family. Partly owing to the painting's absence in Medici inventories and churches, Lorne Campbell has preferred to leave the question of patronage in doubt; citing the oak panel and unexceptional quality, he considers it a workshop product made to order in Brussels for a Florentine

Madrid), dated to the same span of years.[13] How do we account for the parallels – most obviously the draped body of Christ held parallel to the picture plane and the graceful arc of his left arm? A small triptych featuring a Deposition by Rogier was in Ferrara by 1449, as witnessed by both Ciriaco d'Ancona and Fazio.[14] Illuminators might have had access to it there much earlier, initiating a wider circulation of Rogier's composition in miniatures. Fra Angelico's monastery had an excellent library, full of both spiritual and visual sources of inspiration. But in the final analysis, we cannot be sure which came first, the northern or southern example.

Rogier's *Entombment* and Fra Angelico's version of this subject in his 'San Marco altarpiece' are also undeniably related (figs 96, 97). Since Fra Angelico's predella panel predates Rogier's painting by some twenty years, it presumably provided the Brussels painter with a model.[15] Rogier's work was painted on oak and therefore apparently was produced in his workshop to be shipped to Florence, where oak was not available. His *Entombment* was recorded in the Medici inventories of 1482 and 1492 at the Villa

fig. 93
Domenico Veneziano
Altarpiece of Saint Lucy
Galleria degli Uffizi, Florence

fig. 94
Petrus Christus
The Virgin and Child Enthroned Between Saints Francis and Jerome
Städelsches Kunstinstitut und Städtische Galerie, Frankfurt

fig. 95
Rogier van der Weyden
and workshop
The Virgin and Child with Four Saints
('Medici Madonna')
Städelsches Kunstinstitut und
Städtische Galerie, Frankfurt

fig. 96
Fra Angelico
Entombment
Bayerische Staatsgemälde-
sammlungen, Alte Pinakothek,
Munich. Wittelsbacher
Ausgleichsfonds

Careggi, which occasionally led to the conclusion
that Rogier was commissioned by the Medici to copy
Fra Angelico's *Entombment.*

Certain details cast doubt on this hypothesis,
however. Because of the early date of Fra Angelico's
composition, his 'carpet of vegetation' supposedly
provides an argument for the idea that Rogier was the
copyist,[16] although the simplified forms of the Tuscan
artist make Rogier's rendering of the foliage appear
all the more ambitious. Netherlandish painters and
tapestry designers routinely rendered vegetation in
vivid detail. Flemish artists of Van Eyck's generation
created the prototype for numerous mountain
landscapes in the backgrounds of Italian paintings.
All the more surprising, therefore, is the perception
that Rogier's trees could 'only be explained in terms
of a direct knowledge of Florentine painting'.[17] What
about Ghirlandaio's contemporaries in Florence, who
borrowed city and landscape motifs from this very
Entombment by Rogier?[18] Is it possible that such
features were regarded as Florentine precisely because
they were assiduously copied from Netherlandish
pictures filling Florentine collections?[19] Clearly, both
Rogier's and Fra Angelico's *Entombment*s are related
beyond coincidence. But is it impossible that both
Rogier and Fra Angelico were drawing inspiration
from a lost northern prototype?

Fra Angelico's interest in Netherlandish painting
was both progressive, because it was new (only
Filippo Lippi was equally fascinated by it in the 1430s),
and profound, because it was motivated by faith.

Imbued with immediacy and spiritual significance,
his works at San Marco suggest links to the *Devotio
Moderna*, a form of piety which took root in the
Netherlands, and as such to ideas that inspired
contemporary northern artists. Fra Angelico himself
was a monk, and it is therefore not implausible that
his art was related to religious imagery of the cultural
environment of Geert Groote and Thomas à Kempis.
These certainly found a readership at San Marco,
a learned community supported by the Medici. The
devout in Florence – and among them Fra Angelico –
were drawn to Netherlandish pictures as much as
were the secular merchants.[20]

Is there a reason for the popularity of Flemish

fig. 97
Rogier van der Weyden
Entombment
Galleria degli Uffizi, Florence

fig. 98
Antonello da Messina
Crucifixion
Koninklijk Museum voor Schone
Kunsten, Antwerp

fig. 99
Fra Angelico
Holy Face
Museo Civico Giovanni Fattori,
Livorno (see cat. 84)

fig. 100
Copy after Jan van Eyck
Portrait of Christ
Stedelijke Musea,
Groeningemuseum, Bruges
(see cat. 37)

fig. 101
Antonello da Messina
Ecce Homo
Collegio Alberoni, Piacenza

Memling at the time of his wedding are produced in the same tradition of portraiture as Rogier's or Van Eyck's princely likenesses.

Saint Jerome, the Crucifixion and the Holy Face: the demand for these bedrock themes was astonishingly high throughout Europe, and Van Eyck provided ground-breaking models for all three. Through these channels, his innovation spread – a clear illustration of the way popular types aid in the migration of images. The popularity of Jerome, patron saint of scholars, with humanists contributed to the success many artists had in reprising the Eyckian *Saint Jerome*. The one documented in the Medici collection at the death of Lorenzo the Magnificent (fig. 113) may have been a prototype (there are interpretations by Ghirlandaio [fig. 112], Antonello [fig. 111], Pizzolo). A Van Eyck *Crucifixion* with a spectacular mountainous landscape (Metropolitan Museum of Art, New York) provided the blueprint for derivative works made all over the Mediterranean. It has become almost impossible to attribute some of them, based as they are on copies of copies of copies (some examples by Witz, Christus, Colantonio, Jacopo Bellini, Mantegna, Antonello).

And it was Van Eyck's arresting transformation of the Holy Face from generalized type to portrait[21] that led to painstaking repetitions of the strangely recognizable likeness (variations by Christus, Bouts, Fra Angelico [fig. 99], Mantegna, Antonello, Giovanni Bellini, Memling, Botticelli). Ancient workshop copies of Van Eyck's prototype still survive.

The similarities that link North and South in the rendering of the Holy Face indicate a liberal transference of imagery and religious practice; the *Vera Icon* was a much-favoured *Andachtsbild* and indulgence image, which surely accounts for the large numbers of them. A surviving letter from 1460 demonstrates the extent to which appreciation of Netherlandish devotional pictures had spread: Alessandra Macinghi Strozzi, writing from Florence to her son in Bruges, encouraged him to send her some pictures so that she could capitalize on the brisk local business in Flemish art. But she would not part with her 'Holy Face': *'El Volto santo serberò, che è una divota figura e bella'*.[22]

Works by Van Eyck must have been copied into Florentine studio pattern books. There are two extant

(particularly Bruges) painting in Florence and the other major Italian city-states? Since Warburg there have been efforts to link the mentalities of Italian merchants with those of the northern artists they collected – a pairing of pictorial and fiscal realism. In a sense, both embody practices and talents which have to do with accounting for the world as it really is. This was Burckhardt's Florence: the culture of the individual, where entrepreneurial innovation led the way to modernity – not true, say, of the courtly milieu of Urbino or Ferrara. In some ways, Bruges had the same kind of mercantile society, and its artists were accustomed to satisfying merchants. It seems logical, too, that the same desire for success in world markets that spurred on Bruges businessmen would also be instilled in its painters. On the other hand, Jan van Eyck was a court painter and those lucky enough to own his works often belonged to the aristocracy. The countless derivations of Eyckian models must to some degree reflect the ensuing demands of a burgeoning middle class with upper class pretensions. The portraits ordered by Tommaso Portinari, manager of the Medici bank in Bruges, from

fig. 103
Jacobello di Antonello
Virgin and Child
Pinacoteca dell'Accademia Carrara,
Bergamo (see cat. 103)

fig. 104
Filippo Lippi
Virgin and Child
('Tarquinia Madonna')
Galleria Nazionale di Palazzo
Barberini, Rome

versions of the *Stigmatization of Saint Francis* attributed
to Jan van Eyck, now in Turin and Philadelphia
(figs 242, 243), that influenced painters throughout the
Mediterranean.[23] Botticelli, Verrocchio and Leonardo
copied large sections of the rocky terrain from
this Eyckian composition so closely that it must have
been available in Florence in one form or another.[24]
Memling's *Portrait of a Young Man* (fig. 239) provided a
sliver of a landscape with trees for the background of a
Virgin and Child most recently attributed to Domenico
Ghirlandaio, while the whole composition inspired
Perugino's presumed *Self-Portrait* (fig. 237).[25]

The Florentine Filippo Lippi, who worked in the
Veneto as well, displays an early taste for the Eyckian
style. His 'Tarquinia Madonna' of 1437 (fig. 104) is
strikingly close to the idea of the 'typical' Flemish
painting: the use of a domestic interior setting for the
Virgin, a landscape seen through a window at the left,
a glass vase filled with water, attention to marbles,
jewels and rich material, and particularly a sense of the
room's atmosphere. Some of these features come from
local Tuscan sources.[26] Domestic Marian interiors
were common in Siena long before Van Eyck, as
revealed by Duccio's *Annunciation* from the *Maestà*
or works by the Lorenzetti. It has also been shown
that the affinity of Lippi's faces of the Virgin to
Netherlandish types reflects a common heritage in
the International Style of the fourteenth century.[27]
The idea of a mutual development out of a cross-
cultural style is convincing.[28] Nevertheless, Lippi
seems to have known Eyckian painting.

The 'Tarquinia Madonna''s *cartellino* signifies
another parallel.[29] Van Eyck made a habit of inscribing
his works on a *trompe-l'œil* surface, often on a painted
frame on the picture plane at the lower edge. Many
Venetian painters took up the practice of including
a *cartellino* with a signature; this was particularly the
case with artists showing other signs of Eyckianism:
Antonello, Jacometto, the Bellini, Mantegna, and
so on into the next century. But strictly speaking, an
Eyckian model for the 'Tarquinia Madonna' cannot be
cited. The idea of an internationalism that continued
through the fifteenth century seems evident, and with
the new century came an increase in individual talents
motivated to display their own powers of invention
and technical prowess. These qualities, along with

the large numbers of lost paintings, make sources hard to trace.

Among the most frequently discussed Early Netherlandish works made for an Italian patron is probably Hugo van der Goes' 'Portinari altarpiece' (fig. 107).[30] Commissioned by Tommaso Portinari, the triptych was to adorn the family chapel in the church of the largest hospital in Florence, Santa Maria Nuova. Until documents were published proving its arrival in Florence in May 1483, unverifiable speculation had often been devoted to its influence on indigenous Florentine altarpieces.[31] Hugo's shepherds rushing in as a group from the right wing is the most frequently noted feature in commentaries. The similar arrangement of figures in Ghirlandaio's 'Sassetti altarpiece' (fig. 105) was painted just a few years later (1485). Leonardo, Botticelli, Filippino Lippi and Piero di Cosimo have all been signalled as painters who responded to the Flemish altarpiece, on display in what had been the chapel of the painter's guild until 1450, then with frescoes by Castagno and Veneziano.[32]

Undoubtedly Ghirlandaio and his contemporaries were stimulated by Hugo's work, but he was revisiting a tradition already established in Florentine painting. Alesso Baldovinetti's *Nativity* (1466) has its own group of shepherds entering from the right side of the large fresco at SS. Annunziata (a few blocks from Santa Maria Nuova) and was a highly visible example which preceded Hugo's work. Other Florentines like Agnolo Gaddi and Taddeo di Bartolo had already painted such 'naturalistic' shepherds entering the scene at right. Illuminations by Monte di Giovanni dated 1474–76 from the Santa Maria Nuova collection display a strong relationship to the Portinari altarpiece's shepherds as well, years before the painting's arrival in Florence.[33] A Netherlandish flavour in this illuminator's style may be attributed to the large number of Flemish works of art donated to Santa Maria Nuova Hospital by the Portinari family over the years.

The point is that by the time the 'Portinari altarpiece' had arrived on the scene, many Netherlandish features had been assimilated by the Florentine school already. A large-scale variation on the background of Van Eyck's 'Rolin Madonna' (fig. 13) may be found in Antonio and Pietro Pollaiuolo's *Saint Sebastian* (National Gallery, London), completed by

1475. But Pollaiuolo could have been thinking of works by earlier Florentine artists, such as Baldovinetti's *Nativity*, or Veneziano's *Epiphany* tondo, with its serpentine river landscape.

Not that the expansive landscape and down-to-earth shepherds were only a Florentine phenomenon. Mantegna's *Adoration of the Shepherds* (fig. 108), dated as early as 1450, also includes these features. Mantegna was exposed to the sophisticated tastes of the humanists in Padua, at the learned court of Mantua, and in Venice, where he must have gone frequently to visit his wife's family, the Bellini. In Mantegna a generation of Venetian painters found their leader. The repercussions of his interest in the International Style had a tremendous effect on Renaissance painting of the Veneto region.

The reason for the commission of Ghirlandaio's *Nativity* in fact may have been friendly competitiveness. It had been commissioned by one of Tommaso Portinari's most loyal associates – his former colleague in the Medici bank partnership, Francesco Sassetti.[34] It is possible that Sassetti specifically requested a work based on Portinari's, wanting to be the first to have the next best thing to Hugo's masterpiece. In another clear case of emulation, Sassetti had Ghirlandaio paint a fresco cycle featuring portraits of prominent members of the Medici circle, similar to the one the Portinari had at Santa Maria Nuova since the 1450s.[35]

The frescoes in the Portinari chapel, where Hugo's altarpiece stood, were especially admired by Vasari because they were painted in oil – at least that is what he believed. They are gone now so we cannot be sure. Although the truth is that it was probably a mixture of media, as was typical for the period, the Portinari were a family known for having things in the latest fashion. The technique of the Netherlanders was another reason for the desirability of their paintings. While Cennino Cennini's advice on the subject of oleous binders is well known, Alberti and Filarete also suggested their use. Filarete's *Trattato d'Architettura* (c. 1460–64), written in humanist dialogue form, provides early acknowledgment of northern proficiency in the use of oils. He may have been fishing around in the dark for the details, but he was right about the names of the artists and even the kind of oil they used:

fig. 105
Domenico Ghirlandaio
Adoration of the Shepherds
Santa Trinità, Florence.
Sassetti Chapel

In Germany they work well in this technique, especially Maestro Giovanni da Bruggia and Maestro Ruggieri, who have both worked excellently in these oil colours. 'Tell me how one works in oil. What oil is it?' 'It is linseed oil.' 'Isn't it very dark?' 'Yes, but it can be lightened. I do not know how except that it is put in an amoretto. Let it stand for a good time and it will clarify. It is true that they say there is another way to do it quicker. Let us leave this.' [36]

Thus as early as the 1460s, northerners were acknowledged in Italy as masters of the oil technique. And thus the myth was born. But although the common assumption was then and still remains that these artists painted with pure oil, Early Netherlandish painters – Jan van Eyck, Petrus Christus and Robert Campin to name a few proven examples – used tempera layers underneath oil glazes.[37] The fact is that painters on both sides of the Alps used a combination of media. In fifteenth-century Italy, artists applied mixed media in two ways: oil glazes layered over tempera underpainting, or egg and oil blended together (*tempera grassa* in Italian) – tempera with more body or viscosity.[38] As with the appropriation of northern motifs in their paintings, so went the gradual shift to the oil technique – subtly, through stages of local development, so that very soon after the time of Van Eyck these characteristics were transformed from 'northern' to fully 'Italian'.

1 Venice 1999, pp. 52–53.
2 Gombrich 1976, pp. 19–35, esp. p. 20; Castelfranchi Vegas 1983, p. 38.
3 Gombrich 1976, p. 20.
4 Baxandall 1971, p. 110.
5 Roberts 1987, pp. 470–72.
6 Hood 1993, p. 102 and n. 13.
7 Shearman 1992, pp. 94–95, 98.
8 Bazin 1952, p. 196.
9 De Vos 1999, pp. 317–20; Campbell 1990, pp. 577–78; Campbell, lecture, Courtauld Institute of Art, London, autumn 1991.
10 De Vos 1999, p. 317.
11 Jolly 1981, pp. 113–26.
12 Hood 1993, p. 86.
13 De Vos 1999, pp. 185–86.
14 Jolly 1976, pp. 360–61, docs 31–32.

15 De Vos 1999, pp. 330–34.
16 Ibid., p. 330.
17 Ibid., p. 332.
18 Ibid., p. 334, n. 3.
19 Rohlmann 1994.
20 Nuttall 1992, pp. 70–77.
21 Koerner 1993, pp. 80–126.
22 Papini and Lanciano 1914, 58.
23 Madrid and Valencia 2001, no. 28; Koster 2001, pp. 317–23.
24 Panhans 1974, pp. 188–98.
25 Campbell 1981, pp. 674–76; New York 1998, no. 28.
26 Ruda 1984, p. 211; Ruda 1993, pp. 90–101, 126–33.
27 Ruda 1993, p. 128.
28 Ibid., p. 132.

29 For the opposite view, see Ruda 1993, p. 128.
30 Koster 2000.
31 Hatfield Strens 1968, pp. 315–19.
32 Knapp 1917, pp. 194–210; Salmi 1922, pp. 223–27.
33 Garzelli 1984, pp. 323, 327.
34 De Roover 1963, pp. 334, 344, 365.
35 Vasari (Bettarini ed.), I, p. 359–60.
36 Filarete (Spencer ed.), I, p. 311.
37 Bosshard 1992, pp. 4–11; Fronek 1995, pp. 175–80; Billinge, Campbell et al. 1987, p. 94.
38 For this information, I am grateful to Chris McGlinchey of the Museum of Modern Art, New York.

fig. 106
Filippo Lippi
Triptych of the Virgin (reconstruction)
(centre) *Virgin and Child*. The
Metropolitan Museum of Art, New
York. Jules S. Bache Collection
(wings) *Church Fathers*. Galleria
dell'Accademia, Turin

fig. 107
Hugo van der Goes
Triptych of the Adoration of the
Shepherds ('Portinari triptych')
Galleria degli Uffizi, Florence

fig. 108
Andrea Mantegna
Adoration of the Shepherds
The Metropolitan Museum of Art,
New York

Genoa – Gateway to the South
Elena Parma

Over the past twenty or so years the painting of the Low Countries has been the subject of intense scrutiny. Two particular aspects of it have been singled out to complete and elucidate the work done by earlier researchers: its technical aspects, and the economic and commercial developments in the production and sale of works of art. The activities of the workshops, in which auxiliary cartoons and other methods were used to transfer individual details of the image, have directed the attention of art historians towards the organization of work, to the various types of commission and the methods of marketing luxury goods. As we know, the courts, and in particular the Burgundian court – the model for other European, especially Italian, courts – favoured the most valuable objects. But although, as a rule, they preferred tapestries, gold and silverware and illuminated manuscripts to paintings, they did show a keen interest in portraits and, to a lesser extent, devotional paintings.

Bruges was home to large communities of foreigners, including an Italian community divided into *nationes* according to which town or region the immigrants came from: Florence, Lucca, Venice, Lombardy, Genoa. These Italians monopolized commerce and banking, and could often be found in important positions in the city administration and at court. They constituted one of the major channels through which northern painting was imported at an early date into Italy[1] and was appreciated there – as we learn from the writings of Filarete, Ciriaco d'Ancona and Bartolomeo Fazio.[2]

The rich bourgeoisie that was emerging was eager to imitate the court, and the large number of painters working on canvas in Bruges,[3] although they occupied a lower rung of the professional ladder in the local painters' corporation than the panel painters, may indicate a predilection for objects that could easily be transported and used as a substitute for the more expensive tapestries. Portrait painting was not usually an end in itself at the time. Portraits inserted into paintings or, even more frequently, painted on the wings of altarpieces, appeared quite early, however, as in Jan van Eyck's 'Lomellini triptych', now lost, which was cited by Fazio. The presence of portraits of donors or patrons could be justified by the fact that they

appear in a devotional context, unlike the portraits of aristocrats, designed to communicate a completely different kind of message.[4] A famous exception is Van Eyck's double portrait of Giovanni Arnolfini and his wife (1434; fig. 127), which never travelled to Italy although Arnolfini belonged to an important family from Lucca with connections to the Della Rovere family.[5] Another surviving portrait of Arnolfini by Van Eyck passed into the collection of Ranuccio 1 Farnese, in Parma, after 1562. The prestigious choice to have one's portrait painted by one of the major masters of the Low Countries was imitated by others belonging to prominent mercantile families, including the Venetians Marco Barbarigo and Alberto Contarini, consul for his 'nation' in Bruges from 1467 to 1470.[6] Tommaso Portinari from Florence and his wife commissioned matching portraits from Memling in about 1470[7] and are also portrayed in a triptych by Hugo van der Goes (fig. 107) (1477–78) which arrived in Florence in 1483,[8] and as we know aroused the immediate appreciation of Botticelli, Ghirlandaio and Filippino Lippi. As well as combining naturalism with opulence, northern portraiture presented descriptive detail with incredible accuracy, including the most secular aspects of reality. The two small paintings, now lost, mentioned by Fazio exemplified this trait: Van Eyck's *Bathers* reflected in the mirror, which belonged to Ottaviano della Carda, and Rogier's *Woman Bathing*, observed by two smiling youths, seen by the humanist in Genoa. Fazio dwells on the use of the mirror in the first, an expedient which made it possible to see the back of the naked woman's body as well as the front, and the virtuosity displayed in the painting of the landscape with men, mountains, groves, hamlets and castles seemingly 'fifty miles distant from one another'; in the second he comments on Rogier's ability to express feelings in the faces of the young people.[9]

A third feature of northern painting, its devotional aspect, also assured its universal success in Italy. This is confirmed by numerous sources, particularly during the second half of the fifteenth century. From among the sixty paintings imported to Florence from the Low Countries by her son in 1460, Alessandra Macinghi Strozzi chose for herself a Holy Face, 'a sacred image and beautiful'.[10] Antonio de Beatis passed appreciative judgment on Van Eyck's *Adoration of the Lamb* – the 'Ghent altarpiece' – in 1517 (figs 4–5), while Vittoria Colonna's appreciation is reported by Francisco da Hollanda. Michelangelo's judgment, however, was more qualified.[11] In 1542, he accused the painters of the Low Countries of 'painting with the hand and not with the brain',[12] condemned the miscellaneous nature of their use of genres and the excessive importance given to technical mastery. Lampsonius opposed these views in a letter to Vasari, in which he grants a position of honour to landscape painting in recognition of its technical difficulties and of the experience needed to reproduce 'such elusive objects … as landscapes, trees, water, clouds, the sun's radiance, fires and so on';[13] in his *Effigies* he gives credit to Jan van Amstel for having decided that he would paint landscape well with his hand, rather than painting men and gods badly with his head.[14] By this time we have reached the mid-sixteenth century, and the give and take between the complementary cultures of northern and southern Europe has tipped (at least from an ideological point of view) in favour of Italian 'classicism'. The critical judgment of the Italians had a fundamental influence on the development of art in the Low Countries.[15] Dürer's famous visit to Venice in 1505, and the 'study' visit recorded as being made by Gossaert to Rome in 1508[16] can be considered as reliable chronological stepping-stones to the second phase, preceded in Venice in the workshop of the Bellinis, and the activity of Mantegna and Antonello, by exchanges and appropriations in both iconography and in painting technique.[17]

The taste of the private patrons, who were predominantly Italian, influenced the stylistic development of painting in Bruges in the fifteenth century and in Antwerp at the beginning of the sixteenth. Although the point of departure, in iconographic as in other respects, was Jan van Eyck, it is to artists of the following generation such as Petrus Christus that we owe the modification of the subject matter towards a stronger emotional involvement of the viewer.

The change in humanity's view of the world was probably the catalyst that brought northern and southern Europe as well as part of the Mediterranean basin together. The beginning of the fifteenth century saw the beginning of this change, brought about by an increase in voyages of discovery and by new methods of representing the inhabited world.

The Genoese humanist Bartolomeo Fazio, working in the service of King Alfonso of Naples, quotes in his *De viris illustribus* (1456) several works by Van Eyck, including 'a map of the world of circular shape which he painted for Duke Philip' ('*orbiculari forma quam Philippo Belgarum principi pinxit*').[18] Paviot[19] has demonstrated that this object, now lost, can be identified with '*une mappamonde selon la discrecion* [description] *de Tholomée*' commissioned in 1440 from

fig. 111
Antonello da Messina
Saint Jerome in His Study
National Gallery, London

fig. 112
Domenico Ghirlandaio
Saint Jerome in His Study
Fresco
Chiesa degli Ognissanti, Florence

Guillaume Hobit, who completed the work in three and a half years. Hobit, the 'astronomer', produced a three-dimensional globe, the first ever recorded, rather than a two-dimensional map. There was a Latin translation of Ptolemy's *Cosmographia* in the inventory of the library of John the Fearless,[20] drawn up in 1420, and Jean de Berry owned at least three *mappaemundi* as well as a map of the Holy Land.[21] It is not likely that Fazio saw Hobit's globe, which remained at the Burgundian court, but its fame travelled beyond the confines of the duchy. The attribution of its execution to Van Eyck only enhanced its value. Fazio's mention of it indicates that he was not unfamiliar with the work of Jan van Eyck, whom Philip the Good in 1435 described as excellent in his 'art and science'.[22] The interest in his work was increased by his travels (undertaken with great discretion) and by his presence in Portugal in 1428–29.[23] It has been suggested that, apart from the requested portrait of Isabella of Portugal, his travels were undertaken in order to check the itinerary that the European armies might take on the new crusade planned by the Duke;[24] however, the reticence surrounding the aims of these features. It was no coincidence that merchants, and in particular Italian merchants, with a personal involvement in the subject of travel – for themselves and for their merchandise – were among the first and the most important private patrons of Jan van Eyck. The majority of the paintings executed by Jan between 1430 and 1441, the year of his death, were in fact linked to Italian patrons, some of them Genoese.

Flemish works of art and Genoese patrons

Like Lucca and Venice, Genoa, a republican city without a court, provided more private than public patrons of the arts. The sole exception is represented by a consignment of tapestries ordered from Bruges in 1511 by Niccolò Doria for the stalls of the Senate, possibly to replace an older cycle.[27] This was an expensive choice, but one that had been made in other Italian cities – in Siena, for example, where from 1428 there is documentary evidence of tapestries being acquired for the Palazzo Pubblico.[28] Few northern painters are recorded in Genoa: in 1408 a *'Magister Alexander de Bruges'* is mentioned,[29] although no work has yet been associated with the name. Joos Amman of Ravensburg (fig. 31) is mentioned in 1451, and in 1477 one 'Corrado d'Alemagna'[30] painted the frescoes (now lost) in the choir of the Church of Nostra Signora della Misericordia in Taggia. It can be assumed, therefore, that any Flemish works of art present in those early days in the city or in the surrounding region of Liguria were imported. Most usually, these were devotional paintings made for private chapels located in places of worship which were open to the public and meant to communicate the power and the wealth of the donors' family. Smaller objects for private devotion or for personal enjoyment arrived in Genoa earlier or later, according to the fate of the families who had returned to their homeland. Others, frequently commissioned by Genoese patrons, never reached the city.

Several of the works of Jan van Eyck are known to have been commissioned by patrons from Genoa. The 'Lomellini triptych', recorded by Fazio as being at the court of Alfonso of Aragon in Naples, was presumably taken to Naples in 1444 on the occasion of an embassy from Genoa of which both Fazio and Lomellini were members. The triptych consisted of an *Annunciation* flanked by *Saint John the Baptist* and *Saint Jerome in His Study*; on the outside of the wings were portraits of Battista Lomellini and his wife. The painting was possibly taken to France by Federico II, King of Naples from 1496, when he went into exile in 1501, and may have been destroyed by fire in his residence in Tours in 1504.[31] The 'Lomellini triptych' was probably the first work by Van Eyck to reach Italy and had a considerable impact on both Genoese and Neapolitan painting. The panel depicting Saint Jerome probably influenced a painting by Colantonio

fig. 113
Jan van Eyck and assistant
Saint Jerome in His Study
Detroit Institute of Arts (see cat. 30)

fig. 114
Antonio da Fabriano
Saint Jerome in His Study
The Walters Art Museum,
Baltimore (see cat. 98)

journeys may easily have been part of the secrecy always surrounding map-making work carried out in Catalonia and in Portugal.

The history of the fifteenth-century *furor geographicus* is well known.[25] It documents the progressive shift from the traditional medieval view of an imaginary world to a much more accurate view based, particularly with the assistance of the cartographers responsible for the first nautical charts (portolans), on the work of Ptolemy, whose Greek manuscript arrived in Italy in about 1397, and on the information provided by the first voyages of discovery.[26] This was a mental revolution with its roots in the culture of the merchant and the navigator. The penetrating gaze of the cartographer piercing the shadows and creating order from chaos has its equivalent in a spatially organized vision of the world, thanks to the use of perspective, and in the representation of reality in microcosmic detail. Although the outcomes were different, the painting of the Low Countries and that of Italy shared these (fig. 148), and while the possibility that the latter may have inspired the painting by Antonello (fig. 111) continues to be the subject of controversy, Antonello's *Saint Jerome*, in turn, has been linked to Van Eyck's small painting (fig. 113) on the same subject. Another painting showing *Saint Jerome in His Study*, dated 1451 and signed 'Antonio da Fabriano' (fig. 114) – who is usually identified as the Antonello da Fabriano documented in Genoa in 1447–48 – has been quoted in support of the permanent presence of the 'Lomellini triptych' in Genoa.[32] The presence of Antonello da

of Giusto – Joos Amman, of whom little is known – the *Annunciation* gives evidence of familiarity with Van Eyck. This is confirmed in the fresco by the presence of architectural elements of mixed style, Gothic and Romanesque, although in a domestic rather than an ecclesiastical setting. Such architectural mixture also appears in Jan van Eyck's Washington *Annunciation* (fig. 17) and has been interpreted as a symbol of the passage from Judaism to Christianity, from the Old to the New Testament.[36] Thanks to its location, its dimensions and its accessibility, Amman's

Fabriano in Genoa in the late 1440s would anyway imply a more permanent presence in Genoa of the triptych. The 'Lomellini triptych' has also been related to the triptych with the *Annunciation* in Aix (figs 142, 146, 147), attributed – albeit not unanimously – to Barthélemy d'Eyck, who may have been in Genoa in 1438 in the entourage of René of Anjou.[33] In addition, it has been linked with the fresco of the *Annunciation* (fig. 31) by 'Giusto d'Allamagna' (1451) in the monastery of Santa Maria di Castello in Genoa. This *Annunciation*, plus the decorations on the ceiling with *Prophets* and *Sybils*, was commissioned by the brothers Emanuele and Leonello Oliva Grimaldi.[34] Although their business was not exactly international in scale, these wool merchants must have been in contact with the powerful Humpiss family of Ravensburg, whose principal agent resided in Genoa from 1449 to 1466.[35] Apart from the German origins

Annunciation constituted a continual point of reference to painters working in Genoa in the latter half of the fifteenth century.[37]

Another surviving painting by Jan, dated 1437 and signed, can be attributed to Genoese patronage. This is the 'Giustiniani triptych' (fig. 115), with the Virgin and Child in a church in the central panel, and in the right and left wings respectively Saint Catherine of Alexandria and Saint Michael presenting the kneeling donor. There is no documentary evidence of the presence in Genoa of this so-called 'Dresden triptych'. It was acquired in 1596 in Rome by Duke Vincenzo Gonzaga of Mantua. It is the only surviving triptych by Jan, and because of its small size and the refined miniature-like technique is considered to be a work intended for private devotion. Recent research has revealed the presence of two (original) coats of arms in the angles at the top of the two wings.[38] The arms on

fig. 115
Jan van Eyck
The Virgin and Child with Saints Catherine and Michael and a Donor ('Giustiniani triptych', open and closed)
Staatliche Kunstsammlungen, Dresden. Gemäldegalerie Alte Meister (see cat. 23)

relationship with Flemish painting, possibly modified by Provençal artists and by contact with Robert Campin,[43] is also endorsed by the technique. It is a well-known fact that painters on canvas constituted a large group within the artists' corporation of Bruges. The light, manageable support was favoured because the paintings were easier to transport. Not surprisingly, almost a quarter of the Flemish canvases catalogued to date have an Italian provenance.[44] According to Fazio, Rogier's *Woman Bathing*, which he saw in Genoa, was also painted on canvas. After the middle of the century, large numbers of Italian painters were working on canvas, usually in tempera – as in Botticelli's *Venus*. The destination of Donato's monumental *Crucifixion* (*c.* 1440)[45] is not clear; it may have come from the Ospedale di San Lazzaro, whose possessions were shifted between 1513 and 1518 to the new Ospedale di San Paolo in Savona.[46] This early work is an important example of the interpretation that Italian masters were beginning to give to the work of the northern painters.

Another work that seems to confirm the presence of Van Eyck's 'Giustiniani triptych' in Genoa is an altarpiece incorporating panels from an older retable in Pontremoli (fig. 109), usually attributed to the anonymous Master of the Del Monte Annunciation.[47] The middle register shows a Virgin and Child enthroned surrounded by the four Evangelists in a church interior which, although it lacks Van Eyck's ingenious spatial conception, is reminiscent of the arrangement in the Dresden triptych. Other paintings from the workshop of Jan van Eyck which may have been purchased by Genoese clients are the 'Ince Hall Madonna' (fig. 27), signed and dated 1433, which before 1619 belonged to one Luciano Costa,[48] and two paintings depicting the *Stigmatization of Saint Francis*. In his will of 1470,[49] drawn up just before he left on a pilgrimage to the Holy Land, Anselmo Adorno (Anselmus Adornes), whose roots were also in Genoa, left the two Saint Francis pictures to his two daughters, both nuns, on the condition that his own portrait and that of his wife were added to the wings. The two small *Stigmatizations* by Van Eyck (figs 242, 243) can be identified with the ones in the possession of Adorno, and one of them must have been present in Florence around 1470, since parts of its idiosyncratic landscape were copied by Florentine painters.[50]

The importance of the Adornes family in Bruges in the fifteenth century is well known – Anselmus became burgomaster of Bruges in 1475 – as is their role as patrons of the arts and the continuity of their relations with their homeland.[51] Two portraits by Petrus Christus (fig. 232 and National Gallery, London) may represent Pieter Adornes, the father of Anselmus, who died in 1464.[52] Interestingly, it was the final descendant of this branch of the family, Agnes Adornes, and her husband Andrea della Costa, who commissioned the *Triptych of Saint Andrew* (fig. 116), one

the donor's side belong to the Giustiniani, a Genoese family some of whose members are recorded as living in Bruges during the fifteenth century,[39] while we also know that a man named Michele – the assumed name of the donor because of the presence of the archangel – who may have been born in Bruges (he is wearing Burgundian dress) requested permission to set up house in Genoa in 1430.[40] The *trompe-l'œil* internal frame bears a delicate inscription which came to light during restoration of the painting in 1959; this forges an important connection with a work to be found in Liguria, the *Crucifixion* signed by Donato de' Bardi (fig. 124), a painter from Pavia who was active in Genoa from 1426 to 1450 and who acted as guarantor in 1447 to Antonello da Fabriano.[41] The inscription on the painted frame harks back to the example of Van Eyck,[42] as does the limpid treatment of the light and the rocky landscape in the background, but its of the few Flemish paintings from Bruges to remain in the location for which it was originally destined; the triptych bears the inscription 'HOC OPUS FIERI FECIT ANDREAS DE COSTE ANNO 1499 BRUGIS'.[53]

Among the works commissioned by Genoese patrons but which may never have travelled to Liguria are two panels by Petrus Christus, with portraits of a Lomellini and of a Vivaldi (fig. 125) whose connection with the *Virgin and Child Enthroned Between Saints Francis and Jerome* (1457; fig. 94) has been challenged on both stylistic and iconographic grounds.[54]

The supposed presence in Liguria of the polyptych to which the 'Cagnola Madonna (fig. 121)' belonged presents an interesting case; its debt to Rogier van der Weyden is acknowledged – whether or not it is the work of Zanetto Bugatto – and it in its turn influenced the *Virgin and Child with Angels* by Niccolò Corso, whose provenance from the parish church of Le Turbie in Monte Carlo has been confirmed.[55]

Of the Ligurian artists working during the last quarter of the century the one who seems most influenced by Flemish and Flemish-Provençal painting is Ludovico Brea, a native of Nice who was active on the west coast of Italy, in Savona and Genoa. The influence is most evident in his youthful works, such as the *Ascension of Christ*, signed and dated 1483, in which the faces are elaborately distinct. In his later collaboration with Vincenzo Foppa from Brescia on the famous polyptych ordered by Giuliano Della Rovere for the Cathedral in Savona, dated 1490 and signed by both artists, Renaissance features are becoming more pronounced (fig. 117), yet he never abandoned a strong emotional content of patently devotional character, for example in his *Crucifixion* (fig. 118). Rocky outcrops framing distant crystalline landscapes, creating a recurrent expressive theme, also appear in the works of Giovanni Mazone, the most important Genoese painter of the late fifteenth century, as they do in the softer, more delicate work of Carlo Braccesco.[56]

Imports of Flemish paintings into Liguria seem to diminish in the final years of the fifteenth century, since, apart from the *Saint Andrew* triptych, the small panels with the *Martyrdom of Saint Catherine* and *Saint Agnes*, which may be connected with the *Adoration of the Magi* (Galleria Sabauda, Turin), and the polyptych of *Saint John the Evangelist* are not recorded in Genoa

fig. 116
Master of San Lorenzo della Costa
Triptych of Saint Andrew
San Lorenzo della Costa,
Santa Margherita Ligure

until the eighteenth century.[57] The causes of this may lie in the difficult circumstances in which Bruges found itself in the 1480s, which could have led to greater prudence on the part of foreign merchants in the commissioning of works of art; or it might have been the result of protests by local painters. Indeed, the earliest known version of the statutes of the Genoese painters, aimed at regulation of the market and protection of the artists, dates from 18 December 1481. Around the turn of the century, the documents record an exacerbation of the conflict between locals and *foresti*, the term used to define all those who were not born in the city, and who, according to the report of 1415, were in the majority in the early fifteenth century.[58] Stringent conditions were laid down for anyone wanting to practise their art in Genoa. In the sixteenth century an unsuccessful attempt was made to ban the import of paintings and prints from northern Europe, although these, to judge from the 1567 inventory of the contents of the *palazzo* of the late Stefano Squarciafico, were common currency by that time: the inventory lists eighteen paintings, sixteen pieces of 'tapestry with figures', two pieces of 'tapestry' and a roll of 'landscape paintings' from Flanders.[59] Of course patrons belonging to particularly rich and powerful families, like the Sauli, did not need to abide by the regulations. This was the case with the extraordinary Cervara polyptych by Gerard David (fig. 122). Its inscription – 'Hoc opus fecit fieri D.nus Vincentius Saulus MCCCCCVI die VII septembris' – recorded in the *Memorie storiche del*

fig. 117
Ludovico Brea
Virgin and Child Enthroned
Göteborgs Konstmuseum
(see cat. 92)

fig. 118
Ludovico Brea
Crucifixion
Galleria di Palazzo Bianco, Genoa

fig. 119
Ludovico Brea
Saint Peter
Galleria di Palazzo Bianco, Genoa
(see cat. 91)

Monistero… (1790), can no longer be seen since the lower part of the central panel of the *Virgin and Child Enthroned* has been cut off.[60] On the basis of archival evidence, this date (1506) is generally considered to be the date of the commissioning of the work rather than that of its completion.[61] The work was commissioned in Bruges by an unknown intermediary,[62] Vincenzo Sauli being at that time employed as 'orator' to a political delegation to Philip of Cleves, governor of the city for Louis XII, who had fled to Asti following the popular uprising in Genoa known as the revolt of the *cappette*.[63] Since the link between the panel with

the *Crucifixion*[64] and the overall structure of the polyptych had been demonstrated, recent studies have explored the iconography of the work, its theological programme and its compositional and technical aspects.[65] These studies presume direct contact between David and northern Italy and in particular with Leonardo's Milanese paintings, suggesting that one or two brief trips to Genoa may have been made first to inspect the future site of the painting,[66] and then to place it in position. While following the requests and the taste of his patron, supported in the planning of the painting by a theologian, David produced the most significant work of his whole career, which diverges from the nordic tradition in its vertical structure and fixed wings. The use of oak panels confirms its execution in Bruges, and the fact that it was painted without a frame suggests that the monumental wooden support in which the panels were to be inserted (now lost) was certainly made in Genoa.

In the case of Jan Provoost's *Annunciation* from the Church of San Colombano,[67] no documentary information related to its patron or the circumstances of its arrival in the city has yet been found. The proposed reconstruction of the painting with the two panels with *Saint Peter* and *Saint Elizabeth of Hungary* (fig. 120) – fragments of two donor wings – is now unanimously ruled out.[68] The presence of this

Cattaneo, which was installed in 1558 in a chapel of San Luca d'Albaro.[72] The polyptych with the *Lamentation* was ordered before 1525 by Niccolò Belogio, who is portrayed in the scene as was customary, for his funeral chapel in the (demolished) Church of Santa Maria della Pace (now Louvre, Paris). The rendering of descriptive detail, the limpid landscapes and the skilful portraits in all these works were bound to influence Pier Francesco Sacchi from Pavia, the leading artist working in Genoa during that time, who combined these features in his harrowing yet exquisite *Deposition* painted in 1527

fig. 120
Jan Provoost
Saint Peter and *Saint Elizabeth of Hungary*
Galleria di Palazzo Bianco, Genoa

fig. 121
Master of the Cagnola Madonna
Virgin and Child
Villa Cagnola, Gazzada (Varese)

painting *ab antiquo* and its designation for an important public space confirm the tendency of the Genoese to commission such monumental works rather than to purchase them on the open market.[69]

Between about 1515 and 1525 three large altarpieces were made by Joos van Cleve for Genoese patrons.[70] The triptych with the *Adoration of the Magi* was commissioned by Stefano Fieschi Raggio after 1517 and is the only one still in place, in the Church of San Donato[71]. Van Cleve also painted an *Adoration of the Magi* triptych (now in Dresden) for Oberto di Lazzaro

and still to be seen in the parish church of Multedo in Genoa-Pegli.[73] The final echoes of Flemish painting in Liguria are to be found in the work of Antonio Semino and the anonymous author of the panel with the *Stigmatization of Saint Francis* in Santa Maria della Cella; its wooden frame bears the date 1540.[74]

It is clear from the above observations that Genoa and the surrounding district of Liguria were one of the earliest and most constant importers of art from the Netherlands. 🐦

fig. 122
Gerard David
Altarpiece of the Abbey of Cervara
(reconstruction after
M. W. Ainsworth)
Galleria di Palazzo Bianco, Genoa;
Städelsches Kunstinstitut und
Städtische Galerie, Frankfurt;
The Metropolitan Museum of Art,
New York; Musée du Louvre, Paris

1 Castelfranchi Vegas 1983; Christiansen 1998, pp. 39–62; Nuttall 2000, pp. 169–82.
2 Torresan 1981.
3 Wolfthal 1989, pp. 6–12; Martens 1998, pp. 21–22.
4 Baxandall 1964, p. 103; Paviot 1990, pp. 87–88.
5 Campbell 1998, pp. 174–211, esp. pp. 192–98; Campbell 2000, pp. 17–24.
6 Compare Thiébault 1993, pp. 117–21; Lucco 1990, pp. 395–96.
7 De Vos 1994, no. 9; New York 1998, no. 27.
8 Hatfield Strens 1968, pp. 315–19.
9 Baxandall 1964, pp. 90–106; Baxandall 1985, pp. 124–35, 162–65.
10 Guasti 1877, 230; Rohlmann 1994, 23.
11 Dhanens 1965, pp. 102–3; Torresan 1981, pp. 55–56.
12 Barrocchi 1979, 150; Deswarte-Rosa 1997, pp. 277–94.
13 Sciolla and Volpi 2001, pp. 34–35.
14 *Ibid.*, pp. 86–87.
15 Christiansen 1998, p. 39.
16 For a summary, see Roeck 1999, pp. 47–50; Dacos 1995, pp. 14–16.
17 Stabel 1999, pp. 30–43; Roeck 1999, pp. 44–55; Nepi Scirè 1999, pp. 230–31; Simonetti 2000.
18 Baxandall 1964, pp. 90–107.
19 Paviot 1991, pp. 57–62; Reynolds 2000, p. 7.
20 Doutrepont 1906, no. 199.
21 Guiffrey 1894–96, I, Inventory A, nos 986–88; II, no. 195.
22 Stechow 1966, p. 4; Reynolds 2000, p. 2.
23 Sterling 1976, pp. 33–37; Paviot 1990, pp. 83–93.
24 Châtelet 2000, p. 74.
25 Skelton 1972.
26 Quaini 1991, pp. 257–70.
27 Alizieri 1873, II, pp. 482–83; Boccardo and Di Fabio 4 1994, p. 35.
28 Smit 1999, pp. 70–71.

29 Algeri and De Floriani 1991, p. 489.
30 *Ibid.*, p. 50.
31 Weiss 1956, p. 3.
32 Bologna 1977, pp. 82–83.
33 De Floriani 1997, pp. 27–28 and n. 45.
34 Heers 1989.
35 Heers 1983, pp. 326–27.
36 Purtle 1982, pp. 40–58.
37 Castelnovi 1987, pp. 84–95.
38 Neidhardt and Schölzel 2000, pp. 25–73.
39 Petti Balbi 1996, 92 nn. 46, 77, 78.
40 Weiss 1956, p. 2.
41 Algeri and De Floriani 1991, pp. 501–2; Strehlke 1998; Madrid and Valencia 2001, pp. 426–31.
42 Caldera (forthcoming).
43 Campbell 1974, pp. 634–46; Châtelet 1996, pp. 24–29, 354.
44 Wolfthal 1989, pp. 34, 38–91; Rohlmann 1994, pp. 17–23; Galassi 1997, p. 142.
45 Caldera (forthcoming) dates the painting to 1430–35.
46 Caldera (forthcoming).
47 Castelnovi 1987, pp. 90–95; Strehlke 1998, pp. 58, 67.
48 Madrid and Valencia 2001, p. 269.
49 Weiss 1956, p. 6; Rohlmann 1994, pp. 108–10; Philadelphia 1997; Geirnaert 2000, pp. 163–68.
50 Rohlmann 1994, pp. 105–10; Luber 1998, pp. 21–37.
51 Petti Balbi 1996, pp. 90–98; Chiavari Cattaneo Della Volta 1997; Parma 1999, pp. 90–93.
52 Ainsworth and Martens 1994, pp. 154–57; Gellman 1995, pp. 101–14; Parma 1999, p. 92.
53 Vicini, Carboni and Pedemonte (forthcoming).
54 Ainsworth and Martens 1994, pp. 131–41.
55 Boskovits 1987, pp. 351–87; Algeri and De Floriani 1991, pp. 247–51; Algeri 1998, pp. 48–49; Natale 1999, pp. 35–59; Romano 1994, p. 181; see also Ciardi 1965.
56 Castelnovi 1987, pp. 84–109; Algeri and De Floriani 1991, pp. 227–455.
57 For these works, see Natale 1982, pp. 164–65; Torre 1987, pp. 39–60; Algeri 1998, pp. 51–52; for the documents, see Fontana Amoretti 1996; Parma 1999, pp. 87–90.
58 Algeri and De Floriani 1991, pp. 62–63.
59 Parma 1999a, p. 245.
60 Biblioteca Universitaria, Genoa, Ms. B VIII 13.
61 Campbell 1991, pp. 624–25.
62 Hyde 1997, pp. 245–54.
63 Bologna 2000, p. 14.
64 Ainsworth 1998, pp. 188–90.
65 Di Fabio 1997, pp. 59–81; Ainsworth 1998, pp. 179–205.
66 Ainsworth 1998, pp. 191–201.
67 Cavelli 1997, pp. 83–84; Fontana 1998, no. 281.
68 Bruges 1998b, no. 26.
69 De Vos 1992, p. 337.
70 Scailliérez 1991; Parma 1997, pp. 42–45; Scailliérez 1997, pp. 111–25.
71 Scailliérez 1991, pp. 77–78.
72 *Ibid.*, p. 79.
73 *Ibid.*, pp. 45–76; Zanelli 1999, pp. 31–36.
74 Parma 1999a, p. 16.

fig. 123
Alvise Vivarini
Crucifixion
Musei Civici, Pesaro. Pinacoteca
(see cat. 105)

fig. 124
Donato de' Bardi
Crucifixion
Pinacoteca Civica, Savona (see cat. 89)

INRI

fig. 126
Copy after Jan van Eyck
Woman at Her Toilet
Fogg Art Museum, Harvard
University Art Museums,
Cambridge, Mass. Francis H. Burr,
Louise Haskell Daly, Alphaeus
Hyatt and William M. Prichard
Funds (see cat. 36)

fig. 125
Petrus Christus
Portraits of a Male and a Female Donor
(wings of a triptych)
National Gallery of Art,
Washington, DC. Samuel H. Kress
Collection (see cat. 12)

fig. 127
Jan van Eyck
Giovanni Arnolfini and His Wife
National Gallery, London

Burgundian Art for Italian Courts: Milan, Ferrara, Urbino

Mauro Lucco

By the 1440s, thanks to the works of art imported by rich merchants, or by the princely courts of the city-states, interest in the painting of northern Europe was widespread throughout Italy. Although many attempts have been made to examine the causes of this phenomenon in detail, it expressed itself in too many different ways to have had one single explanation. It is true, however, that in the types of court discussed in this essay, the success of northern European art was enhanced by a kind of primitive but comprehensive 'word of mouth' publicity; the continuous exchange of information on the subject ensured its 'democratic' distribution. There is very little qualitative or iconographic difference between the art acquired by merchants and that acquired by the courts, and the latter was not particularly luxurious. An excellent example is the triptych painted by Jan van Eyck for the Genoese merchant Battista Lomellini: in about 1444 it came into the possession of King Alfonso of Aragon in Naples without any alteration or variation. After all, it was considered from the outset to be fit for a king.

The enthusiastic appreciation of this art was engendered by the presence of the paintings in Italy, rather than by the arrival in Italy of painters from the North. The subject of mobility and the links and exchanges between courts is an extremely important one, and one that has never been fully explored, but in spite of this there are sparse indications to suggest that Jan van Eyck may have passed through Italy during his travels. More substantial is the evidence that Rogier van der Weyden was in Italy on the occasion of the Jubilee of 1450. The presence in Ferrara of Jean Fouquet, however, is very doubtful. In fact, except in Urbino, which will be discussed later, there are no records of northern artists in Italy until the presumed visits of Bosch to Venice in about 1494, and of Geertgen tot Sint Jans to Lombardy at about the same time.

In 1456, Bartolomeo Fazio, a humanist in the service of King Alfonso of Aragon in Naples from the mid-1440s, recorded at least two works of art, both alas now lost, which provide a worthy beginning to the series of Flemish paintings to come into the possession of the duchies of Milan, Ferrara and Urbino: one was the *Women Bathing* owned by Ottaviano della Carda, nephew and adviser to Federico da Montefeltro; the second was 'a triptych,

[which] is in the private apartments of the Lord of Ferrara: on one side can be seen Adam and Eve naked and the angel expelling them from the earthly Paradise, and here truly nothing detracts from the painting's absolute perfection; in the other is depicted an unidentified prince at prayer; in the central panel is a Deposition, with the Virgin Mary, Mary Magdalene and Joseph grieving and in tears, so lifelike that they cannot be distinguished from real people.' This was the work of '*Ruggero di Gallia*', i.e. Rogier van der Weyden, and it was seen and described on 8 July 1449 by Ciriaco d'Ancona, to whom it had been proudly shown by the Marchese Lionello d'Este himself. In his description, the great antiquarian summed up the extraordinary capacity of the artist to represent feelings through bodily postures, without any loss of dignity on the part of the protagonists, even when confronted with the most intense sadness. It was on account of this extraordinary skill that Rogier was the artist preferred above any other in Ferrara, to the extent that he held a kind of monopoly of painting in that town; things were slightly different in the surrounding areas. It seems likely that the propensity for depicting raw emotion was linked to familiarity over many years with courtly and chivalric literature in which, disguised behind elaborate metaphor, feelings and emotions were investigated, analysed, almost dissected, and systematized into codes of conduct. This propensity also harked back to the lessons learned by Lionello from the humanist Guarino Veronese, whose pupil he had been. In accordance with the ideas of Leon Battista Alberti in *De Pictura* (1435), to Guarino Veronese, one of the essential features of painting was the representation of the emotions in such a way that someone who was not present could be depicted in a painting, evoked in person as well as in sentiment.[1] Bearing this in mind, it is obvious why in the d'Este marquisate (later duchy) the portrait enjoyed particular success. The story of the competition in 1441 between Pisanello and Jacopo Bellini for the portrait of Lionello is well known (fig. 222). Nevertheless, we have no information about the date of the arrival of this kind of painting from northern Europe, apart from the fact that the double portrait, 'opening like a book and with a gilded frame', of Francesco Sforza, Duke of Milan, and

of his wife Bianca Maria Visconti, given in 1455 by the German painter Niccolò d'Alemagna to Borso d'Este, was referred to as specifically 'Flemish' in style.[2]

Lionello's humanistic education, however, is probably not sufficient to explain the strong attraction exerted by the painting of Rogier van der Weyden. In spite of the literary bias provided by his education, there is in fact no trace of his having commissioned any painting from Flanders after he acquired his title in 1441 and before his second marriage to Maria, illegitimate daughter of Alfonso of Aragon, in 1444. It is tempting to think that he was encouraged in that direction by his relations by marriage. At the time of the acquisition in 1445 by Alfonso the Magnanimous of a *Saint George* painted by Jan van Eyck, we find a similar commission sent by Lionello to Bruges requesting a painting on the same subject, by an artist who is not identified but who is assumed to be the same Rogier.[3] With regard to the triptych seen by Ciriaco d'Ancona, it has been suggested[4] that this could refer to a large payment made on 31 March 1447 for a '*pictura nobilissima*'; if this were true, the hypothesis[5] (which has been looking a little shaky for a considerable time already) that the central section of the lost triptych is identifiable with the *Entombment* (fig. 97), based on the painting of the same subject by Fra Angelico (fig. 96), would be proved completely without foundation. Fra Angelico's painting, which may have been the predella of the high altarpiece in the Church of San Marco in Florence, must date from about 1438–40; if, as Fazio reported, Rogier's sole visit to Italy was on the occasion of the Jubilee in 1450, how could he have seen this painting in 1446–47? Perhaps we should return to the theory that sketches of the painting were taken to Flanders by Florentine merchants. Further payments were made by the d'Este family to the artist in 1450 and 1451, the later of the two for two figures (now lost) possibly designed to decorate Lionello's study; the payments were made through a merchant who had business in Bruges, and they do not therefore constitute incontestable proof of the artist's presence in Ferrara. His relationship with the family continued, however, at least until 1462, when he painted the portrait of *Francesco d'Este* now in the Metropolitan Museum, New York (fig. 130). We need to remember, however, that the subject of the portrait was the illegitimate son of Lionello and that he was established at the Brussels court from 1444.[6] In addition, it might be possible that, at some moment, a replica, copy or variant of Rogier's 'Miraflores triptych' (fig. 131) was brought to Ferrara since, in Garofalo's *Holy Family* (fig. 132), the figure of Saint Joseph appears to have been based on the same figure in the left-hand panel of Rogier's work. There were at least five or six works by Rogier van der Weyden in Ferrara during the second half of the fifteenth century; it would hardly be surprising if the crystalline air, the

distant landscapes, and in particular the feelings so expressively rendered had been absorbed by the painters of Ferrara, from the mysterious Angelo 'Parrasio' Maccagnino da Siena, to Bono da Ferrara, Michele Pannonio, Cosmè Tura and the Paduan Andrea Mantegna who was at the court of Ferrara in 1449, at the exact time when Marchese Lionello showed his triptych to Ciriaco d'Ancona.

The presence in Ferrara of Jean Fouquet is completely hypothetical and is based only on the Ferrarese origin of the famous buffoon Gonella,

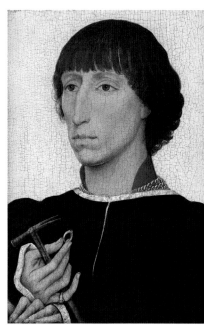

who is portrayed in the panel in the Kunsthistorisches Museum in Vienna (fig. 129). The documents used to prove the hypothesis[7] refer to a 'Johannes Bombarderius', who was lodged in the castle of Ferrara in 1441 and received payment for making some guns; the other reference is to a '*Johannes Simonis de Turana*', identified in the margin as '*pictor de Francia*' in 1446. This is too little evidence from which to construct irrefutable proof; we do not even know what Fouquet's father was called, and it would be impossible to convince oneself that he was the only painter in Tours to bear a common name like 'Jean'. What is indisputable, however – to judge by the number of copies of it that were in circulation – is that in whatever country the portrait was painted, it enjoyed great fame in Ferrara.[8]

Evidently influenced by his royal father-in-law, Lionello d'Este also had a passion for tapestries, decorative objects which at that period were very rare in Italy. Payments made to artisans working at the

fig. 131
Rogier van der Weyden
Triptych of the Virgin
(`Miraflores triptych`)
Staatliche Museen zu Berlin.
Gemäldegalerie

fig. 132
Garofalo (Benvenuto Tisi)
Holy Family
Städelsches Kunstinstitut und
Städtische Galerie, Frankfurt

court, under Borso and later under Ercole I, are frequently made out to individuals 'de Franza'. The only figure of whom there is any reliable evidence, on the basis of the tapestry in the Thyssen Collection in Madrid, executed to a design by Cosmè Tura, is Rubinetto de Franza (in fact, given his profession, it is probable that he came from the place where this particular technique of tapestry weaving originated, from Arras, at that time part of the Duchy of Burgundy); while we know that another Fleming by the name of Arnold Boeteram was established in Venice and traded in tapestries with the d'Este court. Two large tapestries depicting *Stories from the Life of Charlemagne* are listed in 1468 in an inventory of the possessions of a relative of Lionello, Sigismondo Pandolfo Malatesta of Rimini.[9]

By means of a shrewd policy of alliances, strengthened by marriages, the d'Este family was related to almost every other reigning house in Italy. The link with the Aragon princes of Naples has already been described; Niccolò III, the father of Lionello, married first Gigliola da Carrara, who belonged to a collateral branch of the ruling family of Padua, then Parasina, a member of the Malatesta family of Rimini; she was executed in 1425 for her adultery with one of Niccolò's illegitimate sons, Ugo. The third wife, Ricciarda da Saluzzo, belonged to the House of Savoy and was related to the Visconti of Milan. Lionello's first wife, Margherita, was a Gonzaga from Mantua.[10] It is very difficult to say how much the relationships between the different courts influenced the choice in artistic matters. If they are seen as part of a network, however, it is easy to realize how, for a multitude of different reasons, there were many shared tastes and fashions. In some towns in Savoy, such as Chieri, mercantile relations with northern Europe, with Bruges in particular, were traditional. From 1462, for fifteen years, the powerful Villa family ran a money-lending bank in Tournai. From the studio of Rogier van der Weyden they commissioned a triptych, now in the Abegg Foundation in Riggisberg, Switzerland.[11] In a manuscript which used to belong to Claudio Villa (now Biblioteca Reale, Turin), there is a miniature by Simon Marmion executed in Tournai in 1468.[12] In 1466 the painter Antoine de Lonhy (figs 128, 133, 138) joined the household of Amedeo IX of Savoy in Chambéry. De Lonhy trained in Burgundy in the 1440s and in 1446 is documented as being in the service of the duchy's powerful Chancellor, Nicolas Rolin, working on a stained-glass window in the Château d'Authumes.[13] After spending time in Barcelona and Toulouse in the 1450s, he settled in Avigliana in 1462 and while there he illuminated a magnificent Book of Hours for the Marchese di Saluzzo (now in the British Museum, London). For the Provana family he painted the series of paintings now in the Abbey of Novalesa. The small diptych

with the *Annunciation*, painted by Jan van Eyck in about 1435 (fig. 26),[14] probably also has a Savoy provenance. And it is also possible that even the ravishing 'Milan-Turin Hours', by Jan van Eyck and his collaborators (fig. 18), parts of which now survive in the Museo Civico in Turin, was executed for the Savoy family, since it was listed in 1713 in the library of Vittorio Amedeo II.[15]

The Swiss artist Hans Witz was working in Savoy in 1440 – although not necessarily for the Savoy family – in association with the Venetian artist Gregorio Bono. It comes as no surprise, therefore, to learn that he reappears in Milan in a document dated 11 June 1478, possibly in connection with the frescoes in Chiaravalle Milanese[16] during the period when Bona of Savoy was acting as regent for her young son Gian Galeazzo Sforza. Bona's portrait was painted in 1468 by the court's favourite painter, Zanetto Bugatto, when the young woman was in France; the beauty of the portrait (which, according to a letter written by Gian Galeazzo in 1476, 'portrayed her from life in singular perfection') brought forward the date of the marriage of the young Galeazzo Maria Sforza (assassinated eight years later), who had declared his interest in her in a letter to his mother, Bianca Maria Visconti.[17] Bianca Maria, who, as has been noted, had her portrait painted by Niccolò d'Alemagna in 1455, wrote a deferential letter to the Duke of Burgundy on 26 December 1460 requesting him to help the young Zanetto to find a place in the studio of '*Magistri Gulielmi*' in Flanders – evidently she had no first-hand knowledge of Flemish painting. In a second letter, dated May 1463, she thanked Rogier van der Weyden in Brussels for his kind welcome and for the instruction he gave to her painter.[18]

Zanetto died before March 1476, and possible plans to appoint as his substitute '*uno pictore Ceciliano*' then working in Venice, i.e. Antonello da Messina, were soon superseded by the death of the latter in 1479. The tradition of portraits *alla fiamminga* ('in the Flemish style') inaugurated by Bugatto was evidently the most popular aspect of northern painting in Milan and it seemed to be under threat. The presence of Hans Witz in Milan, therefore, in the position (although never formally described as such) of court painter seemed a confirmation rather than a defence of the continuity of the taste for the art of northern Europe, in a manner which until that time had had very few precedents: moving increasingly towards luxurious displays of wealth, a dynasty like that of the Visconti, which had recently begun aggressively to seek the limelight, also apparently set store by feudal continuity. Only two years later, with the assassination of Cicco Simonetta and the dismissal of Gian Galeazzo by his uncle Ludovico Sforza, the desire to have a great painter at court, an artist who would be able to represent the merits of the court to the outside world, and to confer legitimacy on its

fig. 133
Antoine de Lonhy
Nativity
Museum Mayer van den Bergh, Antwerp (see cat. 78)

rule, gained new strength and was rewarded by the arrival in Milan from Florence in early 1482 of Leonardo da Vinci.

Alessandro Sforza, Lord of Pesaro from 1445, belonged to a collateral branch of the Sforza family of Milan. He had spent eight months in Flanders and Burgundy, in particular in Bruges, in 1457–58, and it is probable that he brought back with him the 'Portrait of the Duke of Burgundy' (possibly Philip the Good) and a portrait of himself, both painted by Rogier van der Weyden, for the two portraits figure in an inventory of the possessions of his nephew Giovanni Sforza in 1500. The same inventory contains a mention of a portable altar in the form of a triptych, also by Rogier (fig. 139), with a *Crucifixion* and three figures;[19] this was also presumably brought back with him to Pesaro in 1458. The identification of the warrior in a cuirass on the right as Alessandro Sforza is established; the boy on the left wearing the heraldic colours of the Sforza family cannot be Rodolfo da Varano, brother of Alessandro's first wife, Costanza da Varano, as has been suggested,[20] but must be the ten-year-old son of Alessandro, Costanzo. The young lady, a little bit older than Costanzo, is therefore certainly the eldest daughter of Alessandro Sforza, Battista, who was married in 1460 to Federico da Montefeltro, and not the second wife of the Lord of Pesaro, Sveva.[21] With its wings closed, the triptych displayed the grisaille figures of Saints Jerome and George; the Saint Jerome is copied faithfully in a panel now in the Accademia Carrara in Bergamo. The saint is presented in colour, like a living person, instead of looking like a statue as he does in Brussels (fig. 50). This connection, plus the name of Sforza, and the date of the triptych (*c.* 1460) encouraged Ferdinando Bologna[22] to put forward with the utmost circumspection the name of Zanetto Bugatto for the panel in Bergamo; although this name is seldom mentioned nowadays,[23] it can still remind us of a certain historical continuity.

Urbino shared its confines with Pesaro; as mentioned earlier, Count Federico da Montefeltro (he only became Duke in 1474) married Battista Sforza in 1460, thus becoming the son-in-law of Alessandro Sforza. As such, he was well placed to see and appreciate the works of art brought back by his father-

in-law from his visit to Burgundy. During the early years of his reign, Federico was often obliged to augment his income by going to war outside Urbino, leaving the business of government in the hands of Battista and of his friend and adviser (and also nephew) Ottaviano Ubaldini della Carda; as Fazio records (1456), della Carda owned Jan van Eyck's *Women Bathing*, in which could be seen 'women of extraordinary beauty emerging from the bath with the intimate parts of their bodies – a delicate touch – veiled in soft linen; there is one woman whose face and upper part only are visible, but the back of her body is shown in a mirror so that the spectator can see the two sides of her body simultaneously. In the same painting there is an oil lamp which looks real, and an old woman apparently perspiring, a small dog lapping water, and then horses and men painted exceedingly small, mountains, woods, villages, castles, all painted with such skill that they seem to be more than fifty thousand paces distant one from the other. But there is nothing more beautiful in this painting than the mirror which reflects everything that is in the painting, as if you were looking into a real mirror' (fig. 126). Some idea of this marvellous representation of distance can be had, as has been noted,[24] in the pair of portraits of Federico and Battista Sforza, now in the Uffizi, Florence, painted by Piero della Francesca in about 1470.

It may have been the authority and the technical novelty of della Carda's painting, which the Duke must frequently have seen (Vasari's note that Jan van Eyck had sent to 'the Duke of Urbino Federico II, his stove [*la stufa*]'[25] may indicate that he became its owner), which spurred him to make a gesture which was warmly wished for by the artists, but which was without precedent in the Italy of the time. As Vespasiano da Bisticci (*c.* 1482–98) records, Federico, because he 'could not find artists to his taste in Italy, who could paint in oils, finally sent to Flanders for an accomplished artist to come to Urbino, where he made many most admirable paintings with his own hand'.[26] When and in what circumstances this happened is difficult to say. What is certain is that the result was the summoning of Joos van Wassenhove (usually known in Italy as Giusto di Gand, Justus of Ghent) to paint in Urbino. This may not in fact have necessitated a prolonged search on the far side of the

fig. 135
Pedro Berruguete
*Federico da Montefeltro
and His Son Guidobaldo*
Galleria Nazionale di Palazzo
Ducale, Urbino

Alps. Joos had probably left Ghent by 1469, possibly with a delegation from Milan which arrived in the city in June of that year, and he must have been already established in Rome by 1470.[27] The encounter with Federico da Montefeltro, who had fought with the papal armies for many years, probably took place in Rome in the early 1470s. On 12 February 1473, '*Maestro Giusti dipintor*' began receiving payments from the Confraternità del Corpus Domini, an institution which was under the direct authority of the Count – a sign that he had begun work on the altarpiece depicting the *Communion of the Apostles* (fig. 136). Paolo Uccello had painted the predella for this altarpiece in 1468, and Piero della Francesca was commissioned to paint the main picture in 1469, but turned the offer down. Work on the support was in progress in 1470–71. Joos van Wassenhove completed the entire, enormous painting by 25 October 1474, after which date he was paid 250 ducats. The sources of the composition are patently all nordic, from Ouwater to Bouts with some reference also to Hugo van der Goes, some of whose drawings may have travelled to Italy with Joos.[28] As Van Wassenhove prolonged his stay in Urbino, however, his style became more and more Italianate. Between 1474 and 1476 (the date written on the ceiling of the room), he decorated with a series of *Famous Men* the *studiolo* of Federico da Montefeltro; he may have been assisted in this by a new painter who had just arrived in Urbino,

the Spaniard Pedro Berruguete. The relationship between these two is not at all clear; the last document referring to Joos in Urbino dates from 15 June 1475, and the first and only document referring to '*Pietro Spagnolo pittore*' dates from 1477. Whether Berruguete succeeded Van Wassenhove, or collaborated with him, can be decided on stylistic grounds alone: a lead for further research is the fact that in the book held by Albertus Magnus, one of the figures in the cycle, some of the words are in Spanish. It is also very probable that the two may have collaborated on the figures of the *Arts* in the Duke's other *studiolo* in Gubbio, of which only the two panels in London survive; the panel in Hampton Court showing Federico, his son and others listening to a discourse probably belonged to another series.[29] It is possible that Berruguete's skill in reproduction was considered superior to that of any of the other painters (fig. 135), as he painted, or repainted, the hands of the Duke in the '*Pala Montefeltro*' by Piero della Francesca (fig. 137). The artist returned to Spain in 1482,[30] immediately after the death of Federico da Montefeltro. It was as if the death of the Duke had also killed off any artistic plans for the future in his magnificent court. His death also closed the period when, with surprising suddenness, the whole of Italy began to look with interest at, and often became converted to, the style and technique of the Burgundian lands.

fig. 136
Joos van Wassenhove
Communion of the Apostles
Galleria Nazionale di Palazzo
Ducale, Urbino

1 Guarino, as quoted by Baxandall 1963; Alberti 1547.
2 Campori 1870, p. 30.
3 Medica 1991, p. 314.
4 *Ibid.*
5 Winkler 1913, p. 165; Panofsky 1953, pp. 237–74.
6 Kantorowitz 1939–40, pp. 165–77.
7 Ginzburg 1996, pp. 25–39.
8 Natale 1991, pp. 22–23 n. 18.
9 Tomasini Pietramellara and Turchini 1985, p. 261.

10 Rosenberg 1997, pp. 50–53.
11 Morel 1908, pp. 223–24.
12 Passioni 1988, pp. 78–82.
13 Lorentz 1994, pp. 9–13.
14 Madrid and Valencia 2001, pp. 260–63.
15 Pettinatti 1996; Elsig 1998, pp. 27–28.
16 Romano 1994, p. 188 n. 43.
17 Malaguzzi Valeri 1902, pp. 125–36, esp. p. 128.
18 *Ibid.*, pp. 126–27.
19 Mulazzani 1971, pp. 252–53.
20 Pierce 1928, pp. 39–45.
21 Cavalieri 1990, p. 48; Madrid and Valencia

2001, p. 282.
22 Bologna 1954, pp. 45–50.
23 Madrid and Valencia 2001, pp. 281–85.
24 Castelfranchi Vegas 1983, p. 133.
25 Vasari (Milanesi ed.), I, p. 184.
26 D'Ancona and Aeschlimann 1951, p. 209.
27 Evans 1993, pp. 75–110.
28 Aronberg Lavin 1967, p. 22.
29 Evans 1993, p. 99.
30 Silva Maroto 1998, pp. 120–22.

fig. 137
Piero della Francesca
*The Virgin and Child Surrounded by
Saints and Angels* ('*Pala Montefeltro*')
Pinacoteca di Brera, Milan

fig. 138
Antoine de Lonhy
Holy Trinity
Museo Civico d'Arte Antica,
Palazzo Madama, Turin (see cat. 79)

fig. 139
Workshop of
Rogier van der Weyden
Triptych of the Crucifixion
('Sforza triptych', open and closed)
Musées Royaux des Beaux-Arts de
Belgique, Brussels (see cat. 59)

fig. 140
Rogier van der Weyden
Triptych of the Crucifixion
Abegg-Stiftung, Riggisberg

Princes, Patrons and Eclecticism. Naples and the North

Andreas Beyer

Having been identified by Giorgio Vasari as the inventor of oil painting, it is not surprising that Jan van Eyck's name became known and admired throughout Europe. Through the intermediary of Florentine merchants, who were active deep into the south, his reputation is also said to have reached the kingdom of Naples. It is typical of Vasari and his Florentine patriotism that he should present the merchants of his native city as agents of Van Eyck's breakthrough, thereby enabling Florence to share the credit for the most successful innovation in the history of painting and for Jan van Eyck's incomparable European career.

Reference to Naples in the context of an exhibition devoted to early Flemish artists – Jan van Eyck in particular – and their relationship with the Mediterranean world is as natural as it is overdue. For too long, the substantial contribution that the Neapolitan royal house made in the fifteenth century to the development of humanist culture in Europe has been pushed into the background, and the artistic achievements cultivated by the Aragonese court have too seldom found their way into the historical consciousness. Naples was a centre of European art, a place at which the great innovatory movements in the history of painting came together, especially in the second half of the Quattrocento.

However, the artistic revolution that became increasingly manifest in Naples, as elsewhere, was not wholly attributable to the immense political shift that occurred when Alfonso V of Aragon captured the kingdom in 1442. Nor did it take the Tuscan merchants that Giorgio Vasari praised so highly as heralds of Netherlandish painting for the Bay of Naples to become a key, early point of reception for art from the Low Countries. This function had already been fulfilled by the rival against whom Alfonso had battled so hard before eventually prevailing – René of Anjou, who defended the Neapolitan crown from 1435 to 1442, and actually wore it from 1438.[1] It is thanks to the wide-ranging cultural interests of 'Good King René', his familiarity with French and – involuntarily – Burgundian court culture, and his close ties with southern France (he was Count of Provence), that even before the 1440s, Naples had begun to recover from a series

of crippling wars of succession and cultural stagnation and to display a new artistic vigour. It has been frequently and correctly pointed out that these were precisely the years in which Niccolò Colantonio (*c.*1420–after 1460) received his key training, which means that one of Naples' most important early modern painters owed his development to the patronage of René of Anjou.[2] This view is supported by a letter sent by Pietro Summonte to the Venetian Marcantonio Michiel in 1524, which describes the artistic situation in fifteenth-century Naples and has become one of the most reliable and eloquent sources for the period in question. After recalling the work of Giotto and his workshop at Castel Nuovo, the letter continues: 'After that, there were no famous masters in this region – whether from outside or local men – until our Neapolitan Master Colantonio, a man who so dedicated himself to the art of painting that he would have been destined to achieve great things but for his untimely death. This prevented him from achieving the perfect rendering of antique objects that we find in the work of his pupil, Antonello da Messina – an artist with whom I assume you are acquainted.... As was customary at that time, Colantonio looked to the work of Flemish painters and to the use of colour emanating from that country. So devoted was he to them that he actually decided to move to Flanders, but King Raniero [*sic*] kept him here....'[3]

The close link that must have existed between Neapolitan painting and the North in the final years of Angevin rule is further suggested by the fact that a visit to Naples in the relevant period – around 1438 – has been proposed for the Master of the Aix Annunciation (see figs 142, 146, 147), who is probably identifiable as the later Angevin court artist Barthélemy d'Eyck (active in France around 1442–45). There is no direct archival evidence of the artist's presence in Naples – the most that can be said for certain is that the king's embroiderer and *valet*, Pierre du Billant, who was Barthélemy's stepfather, was employed at the court at that time.[4]

Because of René of Anjou's comparatively short reign, the interaction between northern and southern art did not get chance to usher in a new era of painting in Naples, and so the influence of Franco-Flemish art on the South throughout René's period largely

fig. 141
Niccolò Colantonio
Altarpiece of Saint Vincent Ferrer
(reconstruction)
Museo Nazionale di Capodimonte, Naples (see cat. 94)

fig. 142
Barthélemy d'Eyck (Master of the Aix Annunciation)
Annunciation
Sainte-Marie-Madeleine,
Aix-en-Provence (see cat. 65)

remains a matter of speculation, albeit very plausible. Tangible evidence for the period 1438–42 is confined to book illuminations,[5] more specifically the frequently cited *Santa Marta Codex*.[6] All the same, it is not unreasonable to identify a striking openness to foreign influences, a willingness to exchange and to adopt, and a penchant for the new in the period immediately prior to the Aragonese conquest. Although the characteristics of the art of Jan van Eyck, Petrus Christus, Robert Campin, Conrad Witz and Jean Fouquet must have been promulgated in Naples primarily through the intermediary of France, the foundations on which the House of Aragon and its court were to pursue an extremely vital artistic policy for the next half century had already been laid.

Niccolò Colantonio's *Saint Jerome in His Study*[7] (fig. 148) has been widely acknowledged as an outstanding work since the 1930s, and may provide the most eloquent testimony to this fruitful artistic interaction. Above all, the monumental painting is viewed as firm evidence of a lasting relationship with the namepiece of the Master of the Aix Annunciation. The character of that relationship is, however, far from clear. At one time, it was actually argued that the sparsely documented Colantonio might have been the author of both works. However, now that the anonymous Provençal master has been identified with Barthélemy d'Eyck, doubts regarding the latter's time in Naples mean that the indisputably close relationship that exists between Colantonio's *Saint Jerome* and the Aix *Annunciation* might have to be reconsidered.[8]

The painting – part of a polyptych that is now scattered across many different collections – was commissioned by Alfonso, as recalled by both his coat of arms and the fact that the iconographical programme celebrates the Franciscan rule of poverty. Alfonso the Magnanimous campaigned vigorously for the canonization of Bernardino of Siena, possibly the most important Franciscan of the fifteenth century, while the artistic policy pursued by the Aragonese court closely reflected the artistic doctrine of the mendicant orders. The different elements of the polyptych brilliantly handle both the Netherlandish-Provençal manner of painting and a contemporary stylistic and formal repertoire which derived equally from North and South. Echoes of the Valencian tradition[9] are as plain here as those of Jean Fouquet's painting style. Although one has the impression that the spirit and stylistic wealth of an entire period and continent have been distilled into the polyptych, what it really conveys is the singular mimetic talent and brilliant eclecticism that were able to flourish in a Naples hitherto debilitated by long decades of war.

Niccolò Colantonio was immensely interested in Netherlandish art and sought to emulate its style. According to Pietro Summonte, he copied numerous works of Jan van Eyck, including the portrait of Philip the Good that Alfonso brought from Aragon to Naples, and a painting of Saint George, which was located in Naples in 1445. Sadly, neither original nor copy has so far been traced.[10] The success with which Colantonio handled the new idiom and made it his own is apparent from the frequently made comparison between his *Saint Jerome* and the corresponding painting, now in Detroit, by Jan van Eyck (fig. 113). This also supports the attribution to the Neapolitan artist of a *Crucifixion* in the Thyssen Collection, Madrid, the Eyckian traits of which are brilliantly assimilated (see, for instance, the Crucifixion in Van Eyck's New York diptych [fig. 15]).[11]

Colantonio's art displays a seemingly inexhaustible elasticity. His *Descent from the Cross* (originally in San Domenico, Naples, now at the Museo di Capodimonte) offers a striking example of his stylistic pluralism. It draws equally convincingly on the influence of Petrus Christus[12] and that of a series of now lost, imported tapestries with 'Scenes from the Passion' after Rogier van der Weyden, formerly in the Castel Nuovo, Naples. At the same time, it also harks back substantially to the International Style that prevailed around 1400. Colantonio acted as a kind of medium for this artistic transfer, his constructive opportunism capable at once of meeting his patrons' wishes and of satisfying his own desire to experiment. This extraordinary adaptability is also apparent in late works, such as his *Altarpiece of Saint Vincent Ferrer* (fig. 141), in which it is manifested in what is by far the most radical translation of Eyckian landscape painting and in the simultaneous shift towards the innovations of the Italian Renaissance. The most noteworthy example of the latter is the conception of perspective, which he owed to the achievements of his contemporary Piero della Francesca, with whom he must have been at least indirectly acquainted.

The assiduousness with which Colantonio copied the Van Eycks at the Neapolitan court and sought to emulate the Netherlandish master's style attests both to Van Eyck's growing popularity and to his almost canonical status in early modern Naples. The King's activities as a collector also plainly made a considerable contribution. The primordial status that Alfonso afforded to Netherlands artists and especially to Jan van Eyck reflected the King's own background prior to his Italian conquest. When Alfonso's former humanist confidant – the poet and chancellor Giovanni Pontano – recalled in his *De Magnificentia* that one of his majesty's greatest pleasures was his ownership of a painting by Van Eyck – 'court painter to the illustrious Duke of Burgundy'[13] – he was not referring to an interest that arose after Alfonso's capture of the southern Italian kingdom, but to one rooted in the time when he still lived in Spain. The King of Aragon probably met Jan van Eyck in Valencia in 1427, when the artist came to Spain as part of a Burgundian diplomatic mission to prepare for the marriage of Philip the Good and Alfonso's niece, Isabella of Urguell.[14] It may have been on this occasion that Alfonso was able to add to his collection the Van Eyck portrait of the Duke of Burgundy that Colantonio would later copy in Naples. Even in 1444, when Alfonso acquired Jan van Eyck's *Saint George and the Dragon* on the market in Bruges – the wealth of which was attested to at the time in the travel journal of Pero Tafur – he did not do so via Florentine bankers, but through the intermediary of the Valencian merchant Juan Gregori.[15]

The tapestries with 'Scenes from the Passion' by Rogier van der Weyden that were acquired in 1456 also bear eloquent testimony to this penchant for Netherlandish art, the lasting importance of which may have been established in Italy through Alfonso.[16] The latter may also have owned other works by Rogier. Paintings by Petrus Christus have been identified in Sicily (fig. 45),[17] and the humanist author Jacopo Sannazzaro appears to have owned a work by that master.[18]

The Aragonese did not, however, entirely overlook their own roots when it came to commissioning and collecting art. Catalan, Valencian and Aragonese painters, including Jaume Baçó (Jacomart) and Juan Reixach (fig. 150), are documented at the court no later than the 1450s.[19] Meanwhile, the destruction of the fourteenth-century *Uomini famosi* cycle (ascribed to Giotto and his workshop) during the refurbishment of the Castel Nuovo might also be seen as the expression of a purposive artistic policy.[20] Whatever the case, the interests at work here appear to have been deliberately selective. Whereas the House of Aragon evidently appreciated the paintings of, for instance, Colantonio and was happy to take them over from among the booty seized from its deposed rivals, earlier evidence of the Italian art that featured so prominently at the Angevins' Neapolitan court in the fourteenth century was apparently expendable. It is evident here that the key concern for the first generation of Aragonese as they sought to establish their claim to power over the Kingdom of Naples was not to hark back to the foundations of art in the early modern era. On the contrary, their aim was to vie with courts elsewhere in Italy – and, indeed, Europe – in their cultivation of the very latest artistic forms and media.

To this end, Alfonso brought the most celebrated Italian masters of the period to his court, among them Leonardo da Besozzo and above all Pisanello, both of whom became *familiari* of the King. It is highly revealing in this respect – and it has puzzled many a student of this period – that Campanian contemporaries viewed Pisanello as the leading exponent of a humanist-inspired art. This was certainly the case with Bartolomeo Fazio, the humanist whom Alfonso appointed court historian in Naples in 1444 and who dedicated his text *De viris illustribus* to the King in 1456.[21] The treatise comprised the biographies of famous men and included a section devoted to painters ('De pictoribus'). The document provides the clearest possible expression of the equality of esteem in which the painters from different regions whom Fazio considered to be the most important of his time were held in Naples: Gentile da Fabriano ('*Gentilis Fabrianensis ingenio ad omnia pingenda habili atque accommodato fuit*'),[22] Jan van Eyck ('*Iohannes Gallicus nostri saeculi pictorum princeps iudicatus est*'),[23] Pisanello ('*Pisanus Veronensis in pingendis rerum*

formis sensibusque exprimendis ingenio prope poetico putatus est')[24] and Rogier van der Weyden (*'Rogerius Gallicus, Iohannis deiscipulus et conterraneus, multa artis suae monumenta singularia edidit'*).[25]

Fazio's failure to highlight Masaccio or other Florentine contemporaries and the way he overlooked the many residual traces of International Gothic in Pisanello and Gentile's work is puzzling. It has been plausibly attributed to the prevailing tastes within Alfonso's court, with which Fazio – the opportunist courtier – aligned himself despite the direct knowledge he must have had of other Italian centres of art. The Aragonese court appears to have adopted a kind of careless, aesthetic syncretism that enabled it to accept the contradiction between the courtly overtones of Pisanello and the unfeigned realism of Jan van Eyck.

Fazio's entry on Van Eyck's paintings includes a reference to a now lost triptych with the Annunciation in the centre panel. The wings featured images of John the Baptist and Saint Jerome in his study when open, and likenesses of the donors when closed. It is possible that the donor, the Bruges-based Genoese merchant Battista di Giorgio, who visited Naples in 1444 as part of a Genoese peace mission, took the opportunity to sell the painting to the King at a substantial profit.[26] The terms in which Alfonso's learned historian praised the work tell us a great deal about artistic tastes at the Neapolitan court: the portrait of the man 'seemed to lack only a voice, while the woman he loved was very beautiful and was painted exactly as she was, down to the minutest detail [*'ad unguem'*]. A sunbeam fell between the two, as if through a crack, which appeared entirely real [*'que verum solem putes'*].[27] As far as Fazio is concerned, therefore, it is the empirical realism that is viewed as innovative and precious and which served to inspire Alfonso's love of collecting. Writing a century later, it was the technique of oil painting – actually a chance discovery that he attributed to Van Eyck – on which Vasari would focus in his account of the Flemish painter.[28]

It is symptomatic of Aragonese eclecticism that Pisanello and Gentile da Fabriano were placed on the same level as the Flemings and that the work of Jan van Eyck appears to have enjoyed the same prestige as that of Rogier van der Weyden. Fazio describes a number of Rogier's paintings in terms that leave us in no doubt that what he most admired was their more emotional and physiognomic realism. Among the works he saw at northern Italian courts – some of which can no longer be identified – he was impressed by such things as the 'expression of pain and the tears' in a triptych in Ferrara and by figures that seemed 'so real that they were indistinguishable from actual people'.[29] This is surprising, as Rogier van der Weyden seems to us today to be a representative of International Gothic, rather than a realist in the Eyckian mould. Since no real distinction appears to have been drawn in Italy between the court painter Jan van Eyck and the Brussels municipal artist Rogier van der Weyden, nothing seems to indicate that the court's famous predilection for Netherlandish painting should be interpreted in a primarily 'bourgeois' context as was suggested by Vasari. Instead, it was no doubt both novelty and the appeal of the foreign and expensive that led to the inclusion of Netherlandish works in the royal collection.[30] This preference also had an explicitly 'private' side, as suggested by Fazio once again, who states that Van Eyck's celebrated 'Lomellini triptych' was given a place of honour in the King's private apartments at Castel Nuovo, to which only a limited number of visitors had access.[31] This might also explain why the painterly innovations were manifested in Naples no less prominently in illuminated manuscripts; the miniatures of Angiolillo Arcuccio, for instance, were meant for an equally exclusive circle of viewers.[32]

The dominant role that has long been postulated for Florence and its bourgeois urban culture in establishing the primacy of Netherlandish *ars nova* in Italian art ought to be placed in perspective. Antonello da Messina, for instance, did not bother to stop in the Tuscan city en route from Naples to the Veneto region. The spread of imported northern art in Florence can be more accurately linked with the ennoblement of the Medici family and other Florentine oligarchs that Cosimo the Elder pursued so effectively. The fixation on Florentine 'bourgeois humanism' has, however, frequently obscured the fact that Naples – not to mention the courts of Milan and Ferrara, amongst others – was ahead of Florence in this respect. In reality, what was also manifested in Florence in terms of the representational model of

fig. 145
Antonello da Messina
Crucifixion
Muzeul National de Artă
al României, Bucharest

Burgundy or the Burgundian Netherlands was an increasingly urgent desire for social advancement and recognition.[33]

It goes without saying that when Filippo Strozzi – the Medici bank's representative in Naples – sought to build up an aristocratic clientele in that city, the special gifts he distributed had an artistic and political dimension, as did every work of art that changed hands in the context of diplomatic interaction. Diomede Carafa, the humanist chancellor of both Alfonso and his son and successor Ferrante, received a number of gifts from Strozzi, including a painting by Rogier van der Weyden – said to have been an image of Saint Francis,[34] while the courtier Antonello Petrucci was given a number of Flemish tapestries.[35]

This is not, however, evidence of the export of art to the South by way of Florence. It appears instead to express an expectation that the same *Fiamminghi* ought to appear in courtiers' art collections as in the King's.

1 Beyer 2000; Ryder 1990.
2 Robin 1985; Toscano 2001, pp. 79–99.
3 Pane 1975, pp. 64–65; see Borchert and Huvenne's essay in this book, pp. 221–25.
4 Bologna 1977, pp. 53ff.; Reynaud 1989, pp. 22–47; Thiébaut 1993, pp. 28–38; König 1996; Thiébaut 1999, pp. 106–14, 993; see also Châtelet 1998.
5 Bologna 1977, pp. 70ff.; Robin 1983; Leone de Castris 1997, pp. 46–48.
6 Toscano 2001, pp. 80–81.
7 Bologna 1977, pp. 53ff.
8 *Ibid.*; Reynaud 1989; see also König 1996, pp. 91–95.
9 Toscano 2001, pp. 84–87 and n. 1.
10 Bologna 1977, pp. 91–96.
11 Compare Madrid and Valencia 2001, no. 38.
12 Leone de Castris 1997, 60.
13 Pontano 1965, pp. 117, 260; Canfield 1995, pp. 37–38; Toscano 2001, p. 98 and n. 48; Serena Romano (forthcoming).
14 For Van Eyck's journey, see Sterling 1976, pp. 28–37; for the relations between Spain and the Netherlands in the fifteenth century, see Company 1990; Yarza Luaces 1995, pp. 141ff.
15 Weiss 1956, pp. 11–13; Rohlmann 1994, 117.
16 Bologna 1977, pp. 78–79.
17 Ainsworth and Martens 1994, pp. 146, 163.
18 Sricchia Santorno 1986, pp. 29ff.
19 Filangieri 1891, p. 412.
20 See Serena Romano (forthcoming).
21 Kristeller 1965, pp. 56–74; Baxandall 1964; Baxandall 1971, pp. 91, 99, 163–71.
22 Baxandall 1971, p. 164.
23 *Ibid.*, p. 165.
24 *Ibid.*, p. 166.
25 *Ibid.*, p. 167.
26 Belting and Kruse 1994, 15.
27 See Nuttall's essay in this book, pp. 199–202.
28 See Borchert and Huvenne's essay in this book, pp. 221–25.
29 Belting and Kruse 1994, p. 16.
30 Rohlmann 1994, pp. 116–17.
31 Bologna 1977, pp. 87ff.
32 Toscano 2001, pp. 92ff.
33 Still authoritative is Warburg 1932, pp. 177–230.
34 Beyer 2000, pp. 67ff.; see also Rohlmann 1994, pp. 112–14.
35 Archivio di Stato, Florence, Strozziane V, 22, fol. 95r/v; Del Treppo 1994, pp. 483–515, esp. pp. 502, 511; Sale 1979, 13.

figs 146–147
Barthélemy d'Eyck
(Master of the Aix Annunciation)
The Prophet Isaiah and *Still Life*; *The Prophet Jeremiah*
(two fragments of the left wing and right wing of a triptych; reconstruction)
Museum Boijmans Van Beuningen, Rotterdam
(*Still Life*: on loan from Rijksmuseum, Amsterdam) (see cat. 65);
Musées Royaux des Beaux-Arts de Belgique, Brussels

fig. 148
Niccolò Colantonio
Saint Jerome in His Study
Museo Nazionale di Capodimonte,
Naples

Flanders and the Kingdom of Aragon

Joaquín Yarza Luaces

There is no doubt that the influence of northern European art was most persistent in the Kingdom of Castile. It was there that the influx of works and artists was most free-flowing and abundant, the assimilation of forms most complete, and commercial and artistic, and subsequently political, relations were most intense. None the less, documentary evidence shows that the first contacts were made with the Crown of Aragon, which included Aragon, Catalonia, Valencia and the Balearics. Although there had been commercial trading before, and the people of Valencia were represented in Bruges by merchants who were to play an important role as intermediaries, one event stands out: in 1431, before leaving for Italy, Alfonso v of Aragon sent Lluis Dalmau to Flanders to be trained there, particularly in the art of making tapestry cartoons. Dalmau had returned by 1436, but no work in Valencia has been attributed to him with any certainty, despite archival evidence of a number of valuations and commissions, including an altar frontal for the royal chapel in Játiva which dates back to 1436.

On a number of occasions the *Annunciation* from the Convent of Santo Domingo in Valencia (fig. 165) has been attributed to him, but this work has also been ascribed to the anonymous Master of Bonastre and, very recently, to Jacomart.[1] In my opinion this most unusual picture conceals two different hands. The attribution to Dalmau stems from the obvious Flemish style of the two figures and their relative positions, which are strongly reminiscent of Van Eyck's Ghent altarpiece (figs 4–5), whereas the gilded backgrounds correspond to an earlier Hispanic tradition. Whoever the artist may have been, the work was definitely made by a painter from Valencia who was familiar with the art of the Low Countries, and the available evidence for that period points to a single candidate – Dalmau. Shortly after Dalmau's return, in 1439, a painter from Bruges entered the scene – Luis Alincbrot, who was known in his native city as Allyncbrood and documented there between 1432 and 1437. He spent the rest of his life (c. 1439–63) in Spain. Two works have been attributed to him, the best known of which is the Rois de Corella *Triptych of the Crucifixion* (fig. 161), which demonstrates his knowledge of the early (?) work of Van Eyck and of the masters working with Van Eyck on the Turin section

of the *Très Belles Heures de Notre Dame* (fig. 18). Alincbrot's studio continued under his son Jorge, whom he had sent to Bruges to finish his apprenticeship and who then lived in Valencia until his death some time before 1481.[2] All of this clearly demonstrates the early date by which the Flemish influence became firmly established in the city.

However, it is assumed that Alincbrot was not the first Flemish artist to come to Spain; Jan van Eyck himself is believed to have visited the Iberian peninsula in 1427 as part of the Burgundian embassy sent to negotiate the marriage of Philip the Good and Isabella of Urgel.[3] But unlike his second (?) and more fruitful visit to Portugal, this – unsuccessful – mission is not documented, and whatever the case, it was of no artistic consequence. It is well known that Alfonso the Magnanimous had a special predilection for Flemish art and acquired a fine collection of tapestries and some important pieces by Rogier van der Weyden and, notably, by Van Eyck. We know that he purchased a triptych by Van Eyck and subsequently acquired a painting, now lost, of Saint George. The King's representative in Valencia instructed a merchant from the city living in Bruges to arrange the purchase of the painting on Alfonso's behalf shortly after the artist's death. Less well known is the fact that in 1448 Juan Reixach owned a *Stigmatization of Saint Francis* that he believed to be the work of Van Eyck and that he had purchased in Bruges. The price was not very high and it could, therefore, have been a copy. Be that as it may, a fine panel attributed to the Master of Porciúncula (fig. 156), directly inspired by the pictures of Saint Francis in the Galleria Sabauda, Turin, or in the Philadelphia Museum of Art (figs 242, 243), can be found in the Capuchin Convent in Castellón, and it has therefore been suggested that one of these may have belonged to Reixach.[4]

Meanwhile, in addition to Dalmau, Jaume Baçó, also known as Jacomart, had begun to work. He was in Valencia in 1440 when King Alfonso summoned him from Naples. He spent his whole life commuting between the two cities and died in Valencia some time after 1461. As a result of these circumstances he may have left some works unfinished that were then completed by Reixach. This has led to enormous confusion that is still far from being resolved despite

fig. 149
Jaume Huguet
The Ordination of Saint Augustine
Museu Nacional d'Art de
Catalunya, Barcelona

129

some worthy attempts to do so. Even in the case of one of the works that appeared to be autograph, the *Triptych of Saint Anne*, commissioned by the Borja family (Collegiate Church, Játiva), documents have emerged showing that an unknown Pere Reixach, possibly a relation of Juan Reixach, was paid for this. Despite the evidence, some scholars are still reluctant to reconsider the attribution to Jacomart, claiming that the commission was received and begun by him but completed and charged for by the other artist.[5] At the same time, there has been a tendency to ascribe a certain leading role and quality to Juan Reixach, despite indications that he was poorly gifted as an artist. It seems impossible that he could have been capable by himself of executing the monumental *Altarpiece of the Last Supper* from Segorbe Cathedral, where Jacomart must certainly have been involved. A *Virgin of the Annunciation* (Pinacoteca Civica, Como), previously believed to be a youthful work by Antonello de Messina, has also been attributed to Reixach.[6] Despite the many uncertainties, it is generally agreed that he was trained in the Flemish style but familiar with an environment such as Naples, where the Italian Renaissance fused with influences from the North (Colantonio).

What is certain is that throughout the fifteenth century Valencia was not only a city growing in demographic terms and gradually replacing Barcelona as the most important port in the western Mediterranean, it was also a great centre for the arts and painting in particular. Valencia was a city where the International Gothic tradition continued to a very late date, existing side by side with the Netherlandish influences and the Italian Renaissance style, imported by artists who set up their studios there, such as Nicolás Florentino, Giuliano Florentino and Paolo de San Leocadio. As a result, works that have proved difficult to ascribe, such as a *Descent from the Cross* (Museu Nacional d'Art de Catalunya, Barcelona) and a *Crucifixion* (Museo Thyssen-Bornemisza, Madrid), which for a time were believed to be Neapolitan, have recently been attributed to studios in Valencia.[7]

As a very active centre for the arts, Valencia continued to welcome artists who set up studios in the city. One such artist was Bartolomé Bermejo, perhaps the most important Spanish painter of the fifteenth century. We do not know when he arrived in Valencia but by 1468 he had finished his *Saint Michael* (National Gallery, London). Everything seems to indicate that he became established in Valencia a considerable time after Dalmau's return to the city but very close to the death of Jacomart and Alincbrot. Cordoban by birth, he travelled to the Low Countries and became the Hispanic artist who best assimilated Netherlandish painting without losing his individual style. His history, from the time of his appearance in 1468 to the last information we have about him in 1495, reflects the history of painting in the Kingdom of Aragon.

fig. 150
Jaume Huguet
'*Madonna of Vallmoll*'
Museu Nacional d'Art de
Catalunya, Barcelona

He first moved to Daroca in Aragon, where he remained for a number of years, and from there went to Saragossa where he executed the polychrome decoration of the carved *retablo mayor* in the Cathedral of La Seo on very special terms that indicate the esteem in which he was held. He returned to Valencia but spent the final years of his life in Barcelona. It was during his second period in Valencia that he received the commission from Francesco della Chiesa, a merchant from Acqui Terme, for the *Triptych of the Virgin of Montserrat* (fig. 160). In the centre panel he has placed the Virgin in a landscape bathed in an extraordinary evening light, unprecedented in Hispanic art. However, and this was not the only occasion, the painting of the wings was left in the hands of another notable artist, Rodrigo de Osona.[8]

Meanwhile in Valencia, contact with Flemish art continued but did not impede the arrival of artists from Italy. Thus, in 1494, the City Council acquired from a merchant a triptych of the *Last Judgment* (Museo de la Ciudad, Valencia, and private collection)

fig. 151
Rodrigo de Osona
Crucifixion
San Nicolao, Valencia

fig. 152
Bartolomé Bermejo
Santo Domingo de Silos
Museo Nacional del Prado, Madrid

who was familiar with the style of southern France, Naples and Palermo, produced the *Altarpiece of the Saviour* in Egea de los Caballeros (Saragossa) in 1454. The arrival of Bermejo, even if only in Daroca, a far less important town than the capital Saragossa, must have created a great impression. We know that he was there in 1470. In 1474 he worked on the *Altarpiece of Santo Domingo de Silos*, completing the central figure (fig. 152) in collaboration with Martín Bernat. He also created the *Altarpiece of Santa Engracia*, which has since been dismantled. His influence survived him and is more apparent in Martín Bernat (fig. 180) than in the Castilian Miguel Ximénez, painter to Ferdinand the Catholic.

By 1458 Tomás Giner, who won the esteem of that great patron of the arts, Dalmau de Mur, Archbishop of Tarragona and Saragossa, and of the then Infante, Ferdinand the Catholic, was also active in Aragon. The pairs of saints he created for the Archbishop's chapel in Saragossa possess a monumentality that sets them completely apart from the International Style, although they announce a concern with decorating the backgrounds with gilded *gesso* reliefs which was subsequently to become a regressive trait of painting in Aragon and Catalonia. We do not know the source of the fine *sargas* (serge fabrics) destined for the Church of Nuestra Señora del Pilar but their Flemish style is very apparent, though blended here with Castilian features. Fabrics of this kind must have been far more abundant, but the use to which they were put has resulted in their destruction.

In the second half of the fifteenth century, illuminated books did not play as important a role in Spain as they did in other European countries. However, during the reign of the Catholic Kings many cathedrals and monasteries renewed their old choirbooks with enormous illuminated codices containing historiated initials and decorative margins. As John II had not fulfilled his promise to rebuild the monastery of Santa Engracia (Saragossa), his son Ferdinand carried it out. Around 1502–4 a *scriptorium* was set up which produced a number of very fine choirbooks. According to tradition a friar known as Gilberto de Flandes was responsible for these and dedicated the whole of his long life to this work. It is clear, however, that several illuminators worked on these books. One of them displays signs of a strong Flemish influence with compositions deriving from Van Eyck and Bouts; could this be the work of the mythical Friar Gilberto?[10]

Saragossa was the principal centre of production for illuminated books, but other important centres existed such as Daroca. For a number of years Benabarre and Barbastro were also important. It was here that Pedro García of Benabarre worked and left his stamp. He was an itinerant artist who began his career in Barcelona before moving to Lérida and working for Cervera, spending his whole working

by the Brussels artist Vrancke van der Stockt, for the chapel of the City Hall, a practice common in the town halls of the Netherlands.[9] A fine and recently restored *Flagellation* (Museo de Bellas Artes, Valencia) from the circle of the same master (*c.* 1500) is an indication that northern models continued to be popular. Although Rodrigo de Osuna, whose period of activity extended well beyond 1500, was fascinated by Bermejo, he was not unaffected by Italian trends, as can be seen in his *Crucifixion* (fig. 151) of 1476.

In the Aragon region itself, with its strong tradition of International Gothic, northern innovations were slow to arrive. It was for the important figure Blasco de Grañén, who died between 1457 and 1459, that an unknown artist

fig. 153
Lluis Dalmau
Altarpiece of the Consellers
Museu Nacional d'Art de
Catalunya, Barcelona

life in Catalonia and ending it in Benabarre and
Barbastro. In Barcelona he was commissioned by
the widow of Bernat Martorell, a painter of the
International Gothic style, to complete Martorell's
unfinished commissions, an indication that García's
technique was not far removed from that style.

In Catalonia, Barcelona, unlike Valencia, was
experiencing a crisis that would culminate in civil war,
and had ceased to be the great artistic centre of former
years. However, interest in the Flemish style had been
aroused. In 1443 the *consellers* of the City Council, the
Consejo de Ciento, commissioned an altarpiece for
their chapel. The five councillors were to appear in this
piece and they commissioned the best painter they
could find to execute the work. This was Dalmau,
the artist from Valencia who had trained in the Low
Countries. The *Altarpiece of the Consellers* (fig. 153), a
piece of profound political and religious significance,[11]
shows clearly the artist's limitations and his direct
sources – Van Eyck's Ghent altarpiece (figs 4–5) and
'Van der Paele Madonna' (fig. 92). Dalmau established
himself in Barcelona and five years later produced a
painting of San Baudilio for Sant Boí de Llobregat
(fig. 158) which displays a monumentality closer to that

of the Valencia *Annunciation* (fig. 165) already referred
to and an individual style less servile to Flanders.
In 1452 he was commissioned by the Tanners' Guild
to produce what was to be his most monumental
undertaking, the *Altarpiece of Saint Augustine*, the most
sumptuous work of Catalan Gothic painting.

Dalmau died before starting work on it and the
project was taken on by Jaume Huguet, without
doubt the most important and most successful painter
in Catalonia at that time, even during the civil war
when he became painter to the pretender, Peter of
Portugal.[12] Like all Hispanic painters, he was aware
of Netherlandish art but his style consisted of many
different elements (figs 149, 154, 157). It looks as
though Catalonia was the region of the Crown
of Aragon least receptive to northern influence.
However, artists from the other side of the Pyrenees
were also present, establishing themselves in the
region on a temporary basis, including Antonio
Lonhe (Antoine de Lonhy, 1460–62), who trained
in Burgundy and derived elements from the work
of Van Eyck and Van der Weyden.[13]

It is nevertheless surprising that Bermejo, who
was held in such esteem in Saragossa, should choose

fig. 154
Jaume Huguet
Christ Carrying the Cross
Museu Frederic Marès, Barcelona

fig. 155
Bartolomé Bermejo
Pietà of Canon Luis Desplá
Cathedral, Barcelona

to come to Barcelona (*c.* 1486) at a time when the city was still recovering from the war and when the painting market was controlled by Huguet and his friends, the Vergós family. The Desplá *Pietà* (fig. 155), of around 1490, is the great painting of this period. Commissioned by the distinguished Archdeacon, its expressive capacity is as noteworthy as the realism of the faces and the quality of its almost nocturnal landscape.

In the north of the Kingdom of Aragon, anonymous artists with their own individual styles emerged, one in the Seo de Urgel, known as the Master of Urgel, and another between Gerona and Perpignan, known as the Canapost Master. The fine *Saint Jerome* (fig. 169) by the former is an important work, the style of which, although French to some extent, is essentially Flemish.

In the Balearic Islands the main centre for art was Ciutat de Palma, although there is little to note as far as the Low Countries are concerned. Two painters came to work there from outside, Pere Nisart from Nice and the Castilian Alonso Sedano. Pere Nisart was familiar with the Provençal style and perhaps through this with that of the North (*Saint George, c.* 1468).

In short, painting in the Kingdom of Aragon was varied and nourished by the area's own earlier tradition and by Italian and Flemish influences. The latter is particularly interesting although not very different from the situation in the Kingdom of Castile. On the other hand, Bermejo's painting stands out above that of any Castilian artist.

1 Madrid and Valencia 2001, no. 72; Valencia 2001, pp. 23.
2 Bermejo Martínez 1980, pp. 75–77.
3 Pemán y Pemartín 1969, pp. 29–74.
4 Valencia 2001, no. 2.

5 *Ibid.,* pp. 31–45.
6 Madrid and Valencia 2001, no. 46.
7 Madrid and Valencia 2001, nos 37–38.
8 Rebora, Rovera and Bocchiotti 1987.
9 Valencia 2001, pp. 51–52.

10 Yarza Luaces 2001, pp. 47–61.
11 Berg Sobré 1989, pp. 288–97.
12 Sureda i Pons 1994, pp. 50–89.
13 Avril 1989; Madrid and Valencia 2001, no. 79.

fig. 156
Master of Porciúncula
Stigmatization of Saint Francis
Convento de Capuchinas, Castellón
(see cat. 121)

fig. 157
Jaume Huguet
Ordination of Saint Vincent
by Bishop Valerius
Museu Nacional d'Art de
Catalunya, Barcelona (see cat. 118)

fig. 158
Lluis Dalmau
Saint Baudelius
Parish Church of Sant Baldiri, Sant
Boi de Llobregat (see cat. 113)

fig. 159
Bartolomé Bermejo
A Saint in His Study
The Art Institute of Chicago
(see cat. 109)

fig. 160
Bartolomé Bermejo
and Rodrigo de Osona
Triptych of the Virgin of Montserrat
Cathedral, Acqui Terme

fig. 161
Louis Allyncbrood
*Scenes from the Childhood
and Passion of Christ*
Museo Nacional del Prado, Madrid
(see cat. 106)

fig. 162
Master of Ávila
Triptych of the Nativity
Museo Lázaro Galdiano, Madrid

fig. 163
Bartolomé Bermejo
Pietà with Angels
Mateu Collection, Palacio de
Perelada, Gerona (see cat. 108)

Flanders and the Kingdom of Castile
Pilar Silva Maroto

Taste and patronage in fifteenth-century Castile

In the fifteenth century, in the Kingdom of Castile – which at that time included Galicia, Asturias, the Basque Country, Old Castile and New Castile, Murcia, Estremadura and Andalusia – painting displayed the influence of the new approach to representation created in the Low Countries during the 1420s. Owing to its dependence on northern European models, Castilian painting of this period became known in Spanish art history as 'Hispano-Flemish' – a term also applied to painting in the Kingdom of Aragon for that matter. As I have stated elsewhere, there is absolutely no justification for this term. Only when making deliberate copies did Hispano-Flemish painters transcribe the northern models literally; more often they transformed them to suit the tastes and wishes of those who commissioned or funded the works. They also had to conform with a particular art market, different in many respects from that of the Low Countries and from the other countries of Europe, which were subject to Netherlandish influence.[1] Furthermore, the two elements that make up the term are not in themselves appropriate. The monarchies of Castile, Aragon and Navarre continued to exist throughout the fifteenth century: as a result, there was no such thing as Spanish art per se. Nor did the 'Flemish' models that were used originate only in the Low Countries – Flanders, Brabant, Hainaut, the Prince-Bishopric of Liège and Holland – they also originated in Germany, France and, in some cases, England or even Italy. The 'Flemish' or northern aspect of Hispano-Flemish painting was, without doubt, a heterogeneous language composed of elements of very diverse origin; the same was true of the provenance of works imported and the origins of artists working in the kingdoms of Spain – in this case Castile.

To understand Castilian painting of the period – and Hispanic painting as a whole – it is important to realize that it emerged without a unified model. Throughout the fifteenth century there was a lack of stylistic definition and total freedom in the use of repertories, which were already heterogeneous in themselves as they combined elements of varying – and not exclusively pictorial – provenance. Each artist took from them what he deemed appropriate for the execution of his works, either on his own initiative or on instruction from his patron. As a result, when the Hispano-Flemish style first emerged, northern models were grafted on to the International Gothic tradition – as in the works of Jorge Inglés – or even displayed an Islamic-Mudejar influence in varying degrees. This was also the case when the influence of the Italian Renaissance began to spread, in the first place in the architectural setting, and was combined with northern or Mudejar models, as in certain works by Pedro Berruguete, including his *Virgin and Child* in the Museo Municipal of Madrid (fig. 166).[2]

In the paintings produced in the Kingdoms of Castile and Aragon during the fifteenth and early sixteenth centuries, one can identify a number of features that distinguish them from those produced by Flemish painters, or by artists from other regions influenced by the latter. These differences concern the material execution of the works and their nature and form. Hispanic painters did not paint on oak. In Castile, the preferred material was pine, and the panels were more coarsely worked and much less carefully prepared than in the Low Countries, where all this was regulated by the guilds. Nor was the same degree of perfection achieved in the execution. Instead of the Flemish oil painting technique, most Castilian painters used tempera with thin glazes of oil which did not allow the same tactile qualities to be conveyed or the same colour brilliancy to be achieved as in Flemish works. This loss of 'quality' and technical refinement was counterbalanced by the incorporation of materials that conferred 'value' in Castilian painting, and in Hispanic painting as a whole. In keeping with the taste of many patrons, the most important aspect of this was doubtless the abundance of gold, which was applied as gold leaf and sometimes also in the form of gold powder. To the gold were also added decorative patterns and any ornamental elements that might contribute to increasing the richness of the images.

Typologically speaking, the work made in the kingdoms of Spain was very different from Flemish work, too. Many of the Flemish pieces were small in scale, while the larger ones never reached the excessive proportions of certain Spanish altarpieces created for the high altars of churches such as Palencia Cathedral, where the carved and painted retable is the work of Juan de Flandes and Felipe Bigarny. In such large polyptychs, or even in somewhat smaller ones such as the altarpiece in the Alvaro de Luna chapel in Toledo Cathedral, the aim was to achieve a total impact, to leave the faithful transfixed in contemplation. The tracery of the gilded wooden frame in which the different panels were incorporated also contributed to this, as can be seen in certain retables that still remain in situ, such as those in Frómista and Villalcázar de Sirga in Palencia. According to Judith Sobré Berg,[3] the majority of these altarpieces tended towards horizontality even when their height exceeded their width. They were usually divided into horizontal tiers and vertical compartments and rested on a predella. As no emphasis was placed on highlighting their different elements, the tendency was towards a certain sameness, particularly in the arrangement of the vertical divisions, which were usually all the same width. Even where the horizontal divisions were not precisely aligned – which was not usually the case – the difference between the side panels and the slightly wider centre was barely noticeable. The resulting, rather monotonous rhythm was accentuated by the predella and also by the frame surrounding the altarpiece, which constituted a unifying element, despite the possible variations.

It seems clear that when a painter of northern origin, or one trained outside the kingdoms of Spain, was faced with a commission of this nature, he had no option but to adapt his way of painting. Using the working methods of Flemish painters, it would never have been possible to create altarpieces like those produced in Spain during this period and even less so given the very narrow time constraints that were stipulated in the contracts and the low prices paid for these works. Even if these foreign-trained artists wished to maintain a relatively high quality and employ a more careful technique (as in the case of Juan de Flandes when he accepted the commission for the Palencia Cathedral altarpiece in 1509) they had no choice but to alter their style and working method.[4] But that is not to say that Juan de Flandes – or any of the other painters who trained abroad in direct contact with Flemish painting – adopted the practices

customary in painters' studios in the Kingdoms of Castile or Aragon. In order to complete such major pieces in the limited time prescribed, the artists had to seek the collaboration of two or more fellow artists and/or of workshop assistants. Hence, the master himself would sometimes paint only the faces and hands or the more visible panels – those on the predella or the main panel in the central compartment – or else would execute those compositions that were specified in the contract to be done by the master himself.

During the fifteenth and early sixteenth centuries, there was marked difference between Castile and Aragon as far as the structure of patronage and the social background of those who imported Flemish paintings were concerned. Since the corporate element was much stronger in Aragonese society, a large proportion of the paintings commissioned or imported there were made or purchased for corporations and confraternities, particularly in Catalonia and Valencia. In Castile, on the other hand, commissions – either local or of wider importance – tended to come more from individuals, and were usually destined for religious establishments or domestic use. Moreover, in comparison with Aragon, where many paintings were paid for by brotherhoods and guilds, in Castile, a large proportion were funded by the court, the nobility and high clergy and also, as in the case of Burgos, by an urban élite that had grown wealthy through trade.

Between Flanders and Italy

The reasons why painters in the kingdoms of Spain should have embraced the new Flemish style created in the 1420s, rather than the Renaissance style developing in Italy during the same period, have frequently been discussed.[5] To the economic and political reasons – which gained in significance after 1496–97 with the double marriage between the children of the Catholic Monarchs and those of Mary of Burgundy and Maximilian of Austria – other factors must be added. There is no doubt that, compared with the paintings of the Italian Quattrocento, the northern *ars nova* represented the continuation of a tradition which artists and patrons alike considered their own. The prestige of the court

fig. 168
Filippo Lippi
Saint Jerome
Staatliches Lindenau-Museum,
Altenburg (see cat. 101)

of Burgundy and the quality and perfection of its products – in particular the most luxurious objects such as tapestries, gold and silverware, miniatures and paintings – as well as the realism of its visual arts were thought to be particularly appropriate to the representation of the sacred. Flemish artists interpreted sacred stories in a manner entirely suited to the Hispanic sensibility, integrating the various episodes into contemporary scenes of everyday life and making use of symbolic language to elevate reality wherever they saw fit. Some Castilian patrons, including John II, Henry IV, Isabella the Catholic and certain members of the nobility and high clergy, sought to acquire Flemish works, including those by the best artists. Other patrons, however, for reasons of either aesthetic preference or the destination, type or size of the work required, chose to commission works in Castile itself, from painters – foreign or Castilian – who had trained in the North or had indirect knowledge of Netherlandish art. Such commissions naturally reflected both the taste of the patron and conditions on the art market.

We have documentary evidence of a visit made by Jan van Eyck to Portugal between 1428 and 1429 as part of the embassy sent to ask the Portuguese monarch for the hand of his daughter Isabella in marriage to Philip the Good, Duke of Burgundy, whom she married in 1430. We also know that in 1429 Van Eyck made a pilgrimage to Santiago de Compostela from Portugal and visited the Castilian court, meeting King John II.[6] Unfortunately, according to the information currently available, it appears that their meeting did not lead to a direct commission by the Castilian monarch. However, we do know that John II of Castile owned the *Triptych of the Virgin* by Rogier van der Weyden (fig. 131), which he bequeathed to the monastery of Miraflores in Burgos, founded by him and intended to house his tomb.[7] Moreover, at least two Eyckian works are recorded in fifteenth-century Castile. One of these, the *Fountain of Life* or *Triumph of the Church over the Synagogue* (fig. 24), was brought to Castile between 1455 and 1459 at the latest, because we know from records of the Parral monastery in Segovia that the 'richly painted altarpiece from Flanders depicting the history of the dedication of the Church' was given to

it in 1459 by Henry IV. With regard to the other work, the *Virgin and Child* of Covarrubias (fig. 28), everything seems to indicate that, as has been suggested, it could have been produced in Castile by an artist with expert knowledge of Van Eyck's style. Of the remaining works by Van Eyck or his circle known to have a Castilian provenance, there is at present no information to corroborate the idea that they were brought to Castile during the fifteenth century.

Although there must have been other Eyckian paintings or paintings influenced by Van Eyck's work in fifteenth-century Castile, there is every indication that it was the Tournai school – that is, Campin and Van der Weyden – that initially had the greatest influence in the region. Later, particularly during the period of Isabella the Catholic, Van der Weyden's followers also influenced Castilian artists. One of these was the Master of the Legend of Saint Catherine, who produced a triptych, two panels of which – the *Virgin and Child with Saints* and the *Mass of Saint Gregory* – once formed part of the collection of Isabella the Catholic and are now kept in the Capilla Real in Granada.[8] Also during this period, the influence of the Bruges school was felt and particularly that of Memling. Isabella owned works by Memling, including the *Virgin and Child Surrounded by Angels* in the Capilla Real. In addition to these, there were other works destined for important ecclesiastical institutions such as the Benedictine monastery of Santa María la Real in Nájera, La Rioja, the main altarpiece for which was produced by the Bruges artist in around 1480. Of this altarpiece only three panels, showing Christ surrounded by musician angels, have survived (fig. 164).[9]

The lack of documentary evidence and the large number of works that have been lost make it difficult to be certain when the Flemish influence on Castilian painting began and who its first representative was. The first documented work still in Castile is the *Altarpiece of the Angels* which Iñigo López de Mendoza, Marqués de Santillana, commissioned from Jorge Inglés for the church of the hospital he had founded in Buitrago, Madrid, according to the codicil to his will drawn up in Jaén in 1455.[10] The most striking features of this altarpiece are, without doubt, the portraits of the kneeling donors (fig. 32), Mendoza and his wife

Catalina Súarez de Figueroa. These portraits are a fine example of the artist's careful technique – superior here to other works attributed to him, such as the *Saint Jerome* altarpiece from the Mejorada Convent in Olmedo (now Museo Nacional de Escultura, Valladolid). Also worth noting is his dependence on Flemish models (fig. 60), although he interprets these in his personal style, as can be seen above all in his human figures with their sad expressions and broad and strongly structured features.

The date 1455, by which time we know Jorge Inglés had produced this altarpiece, is already very late if we compare it to the activity of Lluis Dalmau, Jacomart and Alincbrot (Allyncbrood) in the Kingdom of Aragon, which is recorded from the 1430s. It seems likely that Jorge Inglés began his career some years earlier, although we cannot say exactly when. Furthermore, it is by no means certain that he was the only Hispano-Flemish painter working in Castile at that time. Although we do not know where Jorge Inglés had his studio, it is possible that, for a certain period at least, he lived in Guadalajara, part of the art centre of Toledo, which, together with Burgos and Salamanca, was one of the most important in Castile. The same may be true of another painter who worked for the Mendoza family after Jorge Inglés and who is known as the Master of Sopetrán from the panels created for the monastery of Santa María de Sopetrán in Guadalajara, founded by the Marqués de Santillana. The four panels, now in the Prado Museum, were executed in about 1460 by a painter familiar with the Tournai school,[11] as can be seen in the *Annunciation* which was clearly inspired by Van der Weyden.

Many years later, in 1488, María de Luna, wife of Don Iñigo, second Duque del Infantado, commissioned two artists we know to have been established in Guadalajara to produce an altarpiece for the chapel of her father, Alvaro de Luna, in Toledo Cathedral.[12] One of them, Juan Rodríguez de Segovia, connected with the so-called Master of the Lunas, was very familiar with Van der Weyden's models, like the Master of Sopetrán, with whom he could well have been connected. The second, Sancho de Zamora, has not been sufficiently studied but appears to be connected in some way with the Master of Santa María de la Gracia, who was active in Ávila

at the end of the fifteenth century. From the contract between the two artists and the Duquesa del Infantado – one of the few contracts surviving in Castile – we know that María de Luna asked them to execute the altarpiece with 'fine images painted according to the most elegant prescriptions of the new style … fine colours worked in oil … elegant scenes and pleasing and outlandish [i.e. Flemish] faces …'. It is clear from this document that the Duchess took great pleasure in Flemish painting. Hence her request that the altarpiece be executed 'in the modern style', following the models of the 'new art' – which is obviously what Juan Rodríguez de Segovia did in the

fig. 170
Fernando Gallego
Adoration of the Magi
Museo de Bellas Artes de Asturias,
Oviedo (see cat. 115)

fig. 171
Dieric Bouts
Virgin and Child
Capilla Real, Granada

case of the centre panel of his *Virgin and Child with Angels*, taking his inspiration from Van der Weyden's 'Durán Madonna' (Prado, Madrid), to which he also resorted in the El Muyo altarpiece in Segovia.[13]

Burgos was the centre of a style characterized by strong dependence on Flemish models, as witnessed by the work of some of the city's artists.[14] The most notable of these was Diego de la Cruz, who collaborated with Gil de Siloé to produce polychrome wooden sculptures. Supposedly of foreign origin, this painter's style has been reconstructed from the signed panel of the *Man of Sorrows*, surrounded by the Virgin and Saint John (Prado, Madrid). Among the most important works attributed to Diego de la Cruz are the *Mass of Saint Gregory* (Museu Nacional d'Art de Catalunya, Barcelona) and *Christ Among the Angels* (Colegiata de Covarrubias, Burgos), which, like the panel signed by the artist, allow us to appreciate his careful technique, his desire to give volume to the figures and his restraint in expressing the drama of the Passion.

Juan de Nalda, originally from La Rioja, who completed his training in Avignon with the Burgundian artist Jean Changenet,[15] must also have been associated with Burgos, although the majority of works ascribed to him come from Palencia. It was for the town of Palencia that the retable for the high altar of the church of the convent of Santa Clara was created, the church having been founded by the Enríquez family, who were admirals of Castile. Echoes of the artist's Provençal training, which can be detected in the four surviving panels – *Death of the Virgin* (fig. 59) and *Coronation of the Virgin* (both Musée des Beaux-Arts, Lyons); *Mass of Saint Gregory* and *Virgin of Mercy* (both Museo Arqueológico Nacional, Madrid) – give an idea of the particular nature of this artistic personality. Given the combination of Burgundian realism – derived from its master artist Changenet – and the simplification of volume characteristic of Provençal painting – the result of the period spent by Juan de Nalda in Avignon – it comes as no surprise that the two panels in the Lyons museum have been considered to be French works from the Rhône school.[16]

In Salamanca, the most notable artist was Fernando Gallego (documented 1468–1507), whose style can be reconstructed from his signed works:[17] the *Pietà with Donors* (fig. 172), the *Triptych of the Virgin of the Rose* (Cathedral, Salamanca) and the *Placing of the Chasuble on Saint Ildefonso* from the 'Cardinal Mella altarpiece' in Zamora Cathedral. In these works and in the others that have been ascribed to him, we can identify the mastery of his drawing, the characterization of his figures and the richness of his colour, despite his use of tempera. This is not the case, however, with the major altarpieces whose production necessitated collaboration of workshop assistants – these include the altarpieces of Santa María de Trujillo, the Cathedral of Ciudad Rodrigo (Tucson Museum of Art, Arizona) and the former *retablo mayor* of Zamora Cathedral, the major part of which is now found in Arcenillas, Zamora. Also worthy of note are Gallego's skilful compositions and his desire to introduce variations when executing the same theme, as can be seen in the different versions of the *Adoration of the Magi*, including those in the Museu Nacional d'Art de Catalunya in Barcelona (fig. 173) and the Museo de Bellas Artes in Oviedo (fig. 170).

In Andalusia, a greater number of documents has survived than in the rest of the Kingdom of Castile, but very few works have come down to us, most of them made in Seville. Unlike the other centres of art, the existence of signed paintings in Andalusia allows us to identify the style of certain craftsmen including, among others, Juan Sánchez de Castro, creator of the *Virgin of the Graces* in Seville Cathedral; Juan Nuñez who produced the *Pietà*, also in Seville Cathedral, and Pedro Sánchez who created the *Entombment* now in the Szepmüvészeti Múzeum, Budapest. Analysing the characteristics of these works we find that the artists lack the individuality of some of the artists already mentioned in other centres of art, such as Diego de la Cruz and Fernando Gallego or Alonso Sedano. Therefore, it is perhaps surprising to find that a work like *Saint Michael Fighting the Demons*, originally from Zafra, Badajoz, and now in the Prado Museum, was created by an unknown artist who could have been connected in some way with Seville, since Badajoz comes within its sphere of influence. The figure of the archangel is reminiscent of Eyckian models, while the forces of evil that surround him are rendered with a *horror vacui* more usually associated with sculpture.

fig. 172
Fernando Gallego
Pietà with Donors
Museo Nacional del Prado, Madrid

fig. 173
Fernando Gallego
Adoration of the Magi
Museu Nacional d'Art de
Catalunya, Barcelona (see cat. 114)

From the 1480s onwards, when Pedro Berruguete returned from Italy – he is recorded in Toledo in 1483 – the influence of the Renaissance began to be seen in Castilian painting.[18] Again, this is late in comparison with Valencia, where Paolo de San Leocadio and Francesco Pagano had been working since 1472. Berruguete's prolonged stay in Italy allowed him to assimilate the Renaissance system of representation, though he would never forget his Flemish training or his Castilian origins. When he returned to Castile, the painter from Paredes de Nava had no option but to adapt his style to meet the requirements of his patrons, who did not require that his compositions should show great technical care or originality. All that they asked of him was that he should use plenty of gold. In return, some left him free to incorporate Renaissance architecture and decorative motifs into his work, as in the *Beheading of Saint John the Baptist* from Santa María del Campo. On the other hand, he sometimes came closer to Flemish models, as in the *Annunciation* from Miraflores (fig. 174), Berruguete's most Eyckian work, no doubt because of its intended destination, since all works executed for the Burgos monastery, funded by Queen Isabella, followed northern models. Like the Flemish painters and some Italian artists, Berruguete reflected in his paintings the daily reality of Castile at that time, portraying scenes of town life, the Gothic, Renaissance and Mudejar buildings of Castile, and interiors with elements belonging to everyday life in Tierra de Campos, where he was born. This is exemplified by the heavenly scene in which some of the young women accompanying the Virgin Mary are seated on cushions in the oriental style in the panel of the *Virgin's Suitors* in the altarpiece in Santa Eulalia in Paredes de Nava. Owing to his approach of adopting Renaissance architectural or decorative motifs rather than the Italian stylistic idiom, many patrons would have found no difference between the works of Berruguete and those of Hispano-Flemish painters. Where such Renaissance elements did not appear in his works, few could identify any Italian connection in the way he rendered his figures and their postures or in his compositions and treatment of space.

One of the most studied aspects of Castilian painting of this period are the works commissioned

or purchased by Queen Isabella the Catholic, in her double role as patron and collector.[19] We know that she favoured painters with workshops in one of the Castilian centres, as epitomized by Pedro Berruguete, who worked for her or for royal religious foundations on a number of occasions. Examples include his *Saint John on Patmos*, delivered to the Alcázar in Madrid in 1499 and intended for the Capilla Real in Granada where it can still be seen, and the *Annunciation* for the monastery of Miraflores.[20] However, this was not always the case. When artists were needed to paint portraits of the monarchs and, in particular, of the royal prince and princesses at the time when the Catholic Monarchs were initiating their matrimonial policy, the commissions often went to foreign artists. The three who responded to her summons became Spain's first court artists. The first to arrive was Antonio Inglés ('the Englishman'), who came to Castile with the English embassy in March 1488 and remained at the court until September 1489. After his departure, Queen Isabella tried to obtain painters who had trained in the Low Countries, and were therefore experts in Flemish technique, to work for her. Everything seems to indicate that Michel Sittow, a native of Reval but trained in Bruges, arrived in Castile as early as 1492 and remained there until Isabella's death in 1504, at least if we are ready to accept Trizna's thesis that he is in fact the 'Melchor Alemán' who appears in documents from 1492 onwards.[21] In 1496, the Queen called upon the services of another painter, Juan de Flandes, who, like Sittow, continued to work for her until her death in 1504.[22] Immediately on his arrival in 1496, Juan de Flandes took charge of the execution of the *Altarpiece of Saint John the Baptist*, completed in 1499, for the Miraflores Monastery (fig. 245). It was probably also in 1499 that he began work on the 'Polyptych of Isabella the Catholic' (figs 175, 215–218), executed in collaboration with Michel Sittow and a third artist whom some have identified as Felipe Morras from Picardy, a painter and illuminator who entered the Queen's service in 1499.[23]

fig. 175
Juan de Flandes
Nailing to the Cross (panel from the
Altarpiece of Isabella the Catholic)
Kunsthistorisches Museum,
Vienna. Gemäldegalerie (see cat. 115)

When faced with a choice between Flanders and Italy, Queen Isabella opted firmly for Flanders, as did many Castilian patrons, both when purchasing Flemish works and when commissioning them from painters working in the Kingdom of Castile. Italian influence began to be introduced with the return of Pedro Berruguete from Italy by 1483 at the latest. His arrival and that of other painters well versed in Renaissance art who arrived in Castile after him, including Juan de Borgoña in Toledo and Alejo Fernández in Andalusia, heralded the diffusion of Italian Renaissance models, but these did not become established until the early sixteenth century, after the death of the Queen (1504). Until then, Castilian painters who had no direct knowledge of Italian art simply incorporated Renaissance architectural and decorative motifs into their works, just as had happened years before with northern art. Through the lack of stylistic definition and the heterogeneous nature of Castilian painting at the time, the new language developed in Quattrocento Italy was to be combined with the earlier Flemish idiom and the Islamic-Mudejar influence still present in the Kingdom of Castile.

1 Silva Maroto 1990, I, pp. 40–57; Silva Maroto 1993, pp. 3–21; Yarza Luaces 1992, p. 134.
2 Silva Maroto 1998, pp. 123–30, 249–51.
3 Berg Sobré 1989.
4 Vandevivere 1967; Silva Maroto 1994, pp. 578–83.
5 Brans 1952; Bemejo Martínez 1980, pp. 17–23; Silva Maroto 1990, I, pp. 17–23.
6 Pemán y Pemartín 1969.
7 Ponz 1–88, XII; De Vos 1999, no. 12.
8 Van Schoute 1966, pp. 110–22.
9 Tormo 1924, pp. 300–322; Borchert 1995, pp. 153–68; Bruges 1998, no. 8.

10 Sánchez Cantón 1917, pp. 99–100; Silva Maroto 2001, pp. 155–91, esp. pp. 181–82.
11 Carbrera and Garrido 1982, pp. 15–31.
12 Gonzalez Palencia 1929, pp. 109–22.
13 Collar de Cáceres 1986, pp. 372–78; Silva Maroto and Garrido 1993, pp. 131–33.
14 Silva Maroto 1990, passim.
15 Sterling 1973, pp. 4–19; Silva Maroto 1990, III, pp. 801–19.
16 Silva Maroto, 'La pintura castellana en tiempos de Siloe', in Gil de Siloe (forthcoming).
17 Post 1933, IV, pp. 87–147; Gaya Nuño 1958; Cabrera and Garrido 1981, pp. 27–48.

18 Silva Maroto 1998, n. 16
19 Yarza Luaces 1991, pp. 57–64; Yarza Luaces 1992, pp. 54–59; Madrid 1993; Domínguez Casas 1993.
20 Sánchez Cantón 1950, p. 166; Silva Maroto 1998, pp. 134–35.
21 Trizna 1976; Domínguez Casas 1993, pp. 120–23.
22 Vandevivere 1967; Domínguez Casas 1993, pp. 123–26; Silva Maroto 1994, pp. 578–83.
23 Yarza Luaces 1993, p. 91; Domínguez Casas 1993, p. 127; Garrido 1995, pp. 21–29.

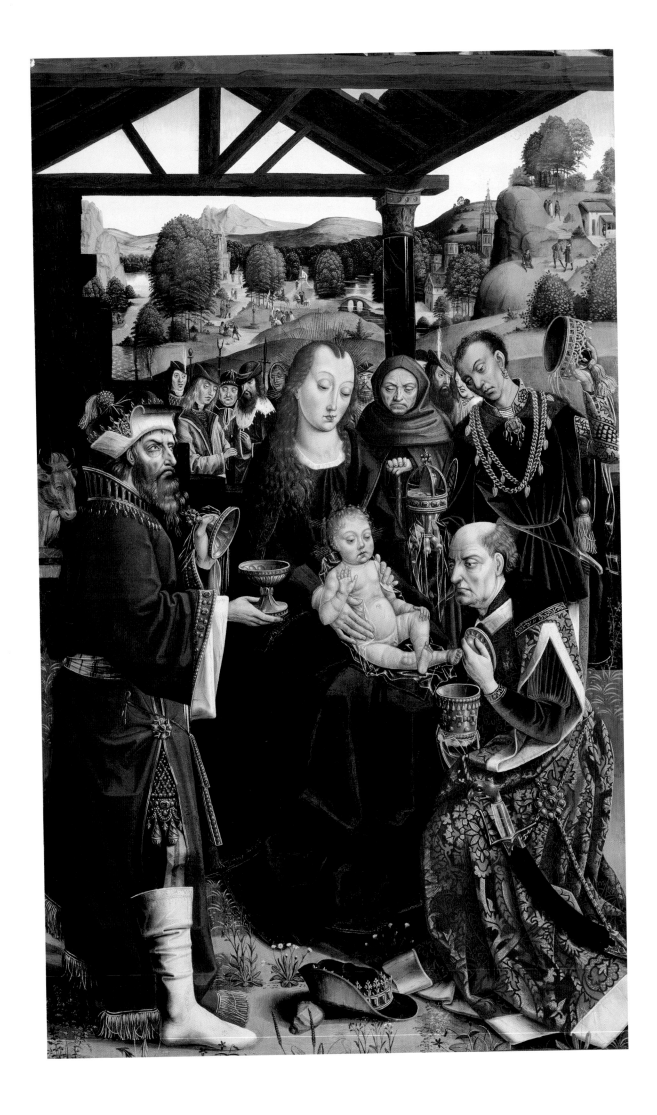

fig. 177
Spanish (?) copy after Dieric Bouts
Triptych of the Passion
Museo del Patriarca, Valencia
(see cat. 107)

fig. 176
Master of the Catholic Kings
(Diego de la Cruz?)
Adoration of the Magi
Denver Art Museum (see cat. 119)

fig. 178
Master of the Saint Lucy Legend
(Jean Hervey?)
Saint Nicholas
Stedelijke Musea,
Groeningemuseum, Bruges
(see cat. 46)

fig. 179
Master of Portillo
Saint John the Baptist Enthroned
Galería Calyus, Madrid (see cat. 122)

fig. 180
Martín Bernat
Saint Blaise
López de Aragón
collection, Madrid
(see cat. III)

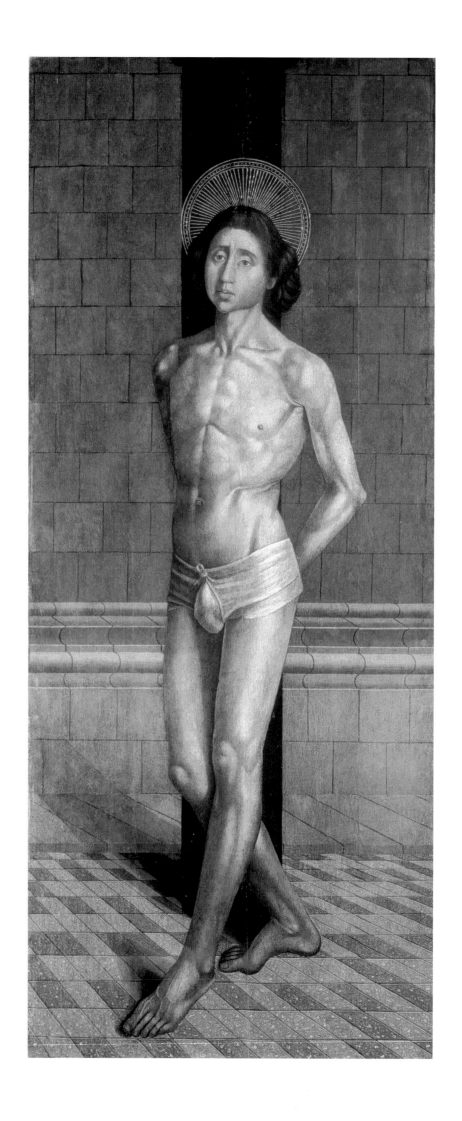

Portugal and the North

José Luis Porfírio

fig. 182
Workshop of Nuno Gonçalves
Saint Francis (?)
Museu Nacional de Arte Antiga,
Lisbon (see cat. 128)

Before it became the point of departure for great maritime voyages, Portugal was the bridge one had to cross between the Mediterranean, an enclosed sea whose coasts are never washed by the open ocean, and the Atlantic, the route linking South and North. In terms of both climate and culture, the Mediterranean and the Atlantic have helped to form this country, which is both a frontier and a connecting corridor, between the Arab culture in the South and the Christian culture in the North. When Portugal emerged as an independent state in the mid-twelfth century, its territory was divided into three cultural zones, the Portuguese and Christian Galicia in the north, the Moorish centre of mixed culture and an Arabized southern area which included Lisbon and the valley of the Tagus river.

The reconquest meant that this situation lasted only a few generations. Even before the fifteenth century the country had acquired its present configuration (apart from a few minor later adjustments), and as early as 1415 the reconquest had occupied its first African bastion, Ceuta, which passed to Spain in 1580 and has since been under Spanish political and administrative tutelage.

It was in the fifteenth century that an exceptional painting workshop emerged, created by Portuguese or by foreign artists working in Portugal. Its sudden appearance, without any known antecedents, once led me to write that 'Portuguese painting appears to have been born like Athena from the head of Zeus!' This is not such a far-fetched image, since Portuguese painting arose just like that goddess of ancient Greece – fully armed, clothed and grown to maturity. The workshop in question was centred on Lisbon, active in the second half of the fifteenth century and associated with the name of the court painter Nuno Gonçalves – a name both legendary and real – creator of the famous panels of São Vicente de Fora (fig. 188).[1] The six panels containing 58 portraits and the double figure of a deacon on the centre panels are now joined together as a polyptych in what seems to be a representation of the 'Three Estates'. This impressive retable depicting 'faces and apparel' is one of the first group portraits of European painting, gathered in a celebration whose purpose has yet to be explained. It has been the subject of contradictory interpretations

as regards the identity both of the individual portraits and of the figure of the saint presiding over the scene. As far as the latter is concerned, most interpretations suggest the martyr Saint Vincent, patron saint of the city of Lisbon. In addition to this work, two paintings on panel depicting the martyrdom of Saint Vincent (fig. 181) – the first nudes in Portuguese painting – and four others representing saints Peter, Paul, Francis (?) (fig. 182) and the local saint Teotónio,[2] constitute the surviving production of this workshop.

Although it emerged, like Portugal itself, at the junction of the influences of the North – Flanders and the Duchy of Burgundy – and the South – eastern Spain and southern France – this workshop nevertheless retained a remarkable degree of autonomy. Three basic factors make it particularly difficult to understand this fully: the absence of precedents, the extremely limited corpus and the complete lack of continuation.

Indeed, hardly anything is known of any previous paintings. What we do have are merely vestiges, usually in the form of wall paintings or stylistically insignificant works, whose dating is hypothetical. On the other hand, references to visits to Portugal of such notable artists as Van Eyck, or to such important works as the triptych (now lost) created by Rogier van der Weyden for the Batalha Monastery, do not confirm any direct link with the Gonçalves studio.[3]

From this workshop there are just twelve paintings by Nuno Gonçalves (or more precisely eleven and a half, because of one of the Saint Vincents only one section has survived), while the total body of contemporary work does not amount to fifty paintings. Of this group only an *Adoration of the Magi with Saints Francis and Anthony* (fig. 183) and a *Lamentation* (Museu Nacional de Arte Antiga, Lisbon) point to an autonomous workshop, with an original treatment of landscape and a synthetic approach comparable with that of Gonçalves' oeuvre. The remaining paintings are largely provincial works whose archaic appearance easily mislead the viewer as to their dating and which therefore do not constitute points of reference for the isolated Lisbon workshop. Slowly yet continuously this body of work has been augmented by various discoveries of important paintings from the fifteenth century, whose panels

fig. 181
Nuno Gonçalves
Saint Vincent
Museu Nacional de Arte Antiga,
Lisbon

157

fig. 183
Follower of Nuno Gonçalves
Adoration of the Magi with Saints
Francis and Anthony
Museu de Arte Sacra da Sé, Évora

fig. 184
Master of Lourinhã
Death of Saint James the Greater
Museu Nacional de Arte Antiga,
Lisbon (see cat. 131)

have been reused and overpainted at a later date. The *Adoration* in Évora is without doubt the most notable of these, particularly because it begins to lend substance to the existence of an important workshop.[4]

Finally, the school of Nuno Gonçalves disappeared as it had emerged, without antecedents or followers. In Portugal at the end of the fifteenth and beginning of the sixteenth centuries there was a profound change in taste, which may be ascribed in part to the loss of continuity when royal power was transferred from João II (1481–95) to Manuel (1495–1521), his cousin and brother-in-law.

This lack of artistic and stylistic continuity constitutes a major problem – it is the central 'mystery' surrounding the Gonçalves workshop and its most important work, the Saint Vincent panels. These comprise the most visible nucleus of a production which is believed to have lasted from 1450 to 1490, with painting of great originality in its treatment of, and emphasis on, the portrait, and also in its synthetic handling of space and its rendering of human anatomy. This humanist declaration expressed

in painting, as it might be called, was produced on the basis of broad experience; it used both the attention to reality of northern painting and the spatial awareness, albeit empirical, inspired by southern masters. This is not surprising in the Europe of the fifteenth century, it is just that in Portugal there is no obvious continuation. Historians have looked in vain for a 'missing link' which would extend the Lisbon school of painting into the following century, and in its absence have invented the legend of a tradition of portraiture in Portugal in order to provide continuity for the 58 portraits on the Lisbon panels.

By the first quarter of the sixteenth century everything had changed. There is a relative abundance of works, some Portuguese, others imported, and major commissions from the court, from prelates and from military orders can easily be related to a number of important workshops. The presence of many works and masters from the Low Countries flavours the whole production, even where the master is

fig. 186
Frey Carlos
Annunciation
Museu Nacional de Arte Antiga,
Lisbon (see cat. 127)

recognizably Portuguese, setting the tone for a complete change in which the direct influence of Flanders is accompanied by the spread of German engravings. The main workshops are those of Francisco Henriques, 'the best master of his time', a Fleming working in Évora and Lisbon (fig. 192); Frey Carlos, a Hieronymite monk, also a Fleming, working for his Order from the Espinheiro Monastery close to Évora; Jorge Afonso, Portuguese and court painter, active in Lisbon and Tomar; and the Master of Lourinhã (fig. 184), of whom very little is known apart from the fact that he apparently shared patrons with Frey Carlos.

Of these workshops, that of Frey Carlos (figs 186, 187, 191), also known as the Espinheiro school, is the most original in its combination of Flemish features, probably from its founder, with a highly unusual geometric treatment of space and figures, which seems to foreshadow the Dutch handling of space in the seventeenth century.

The presence of many painters and paintings from the North has led some historians to refer to a 'Portuguese-Flemish school of painting' which – although it certainly is difficult to separate what

is Flemish from what is Portuguese – never existed as such. For the period in question it is definitely preferable to refer to a Portuguese-Flemish generation, sparsely tinged with Germanic features.

Curiously, on the whole this was a more conservative generation, more late medieval than the previous one. When we take a closer look at the paintings from the 1490s to the 1530s, there are considerable differences from one master to another, but looking at them as a whole and comparing them with those of the generation that produced the Saint Vincent panels and even the Évora *Adoration*, we can sense that, apart from the obvious differences, a wind from the North was sweeping through Portugal. A Netherlandish wind certainly, but also one from Germany which, although it was undoubtedly less innovative, provided the basis, through the spread of engraving, for an uneven but continuous practice of painting in Portugal.

1 Abrantes and Vandevivere 1994, pp. 21–37.
2 *Ibid.*, pp. 49–57.
3 De Vos 1999, p. 364.
4 Évora 1997, pp. 79–80.

fig. 189
Master of Évora
Altarpiece of the Life of the Virgin
(reconstruction)
Museu de Évora (see cat. 130)

fig. 190
Jan Provoost
*The Virgin of Mercy with Members
of the Portuguese Royal Family*
Museu Nacional de Arte Antiga,
Lisbon (see cat. 55)

fig. 191
Frey Carlos
John the Baptist
Museu Nacional de Arte Antiga,
Lisbon (see cat. 126)

fig. 192
Francisco Henriques and workshop
Visitation
Museu de Grão Vasco, Viseu
(see cat. 129)

fig. 193
Anonymous (Bruges)
Scenes from the Passion of Christ
Museu Nacional do Azulejo, Lisbon
(see cat. 3)

Maistre Guille du Fay ~ Binchois.

Tapissier Carmen Cesaris.

Burgundy and the South

Jacques Paviot

The court of Burgundy could be said to have staged its first great celebration as a real court with the creation of the Order of the Golden Fleece at the beginning of 1430. The Order was founded in Bruges to commemorate the wedding there of Duke Philip the Good to the Infanta Isabella of Portugal in the autumn of 1429. Before that, Burgundy had been one of several French princely courts imitating the royal court of France, and the aim of the Dukes of Burgundy had been to acquire a role, if possible a leading role, at the court of the King of France. For although the Dukes of Burgundy possessed an independent court, their estates were shared between the Kingdom of France and the Holy Roman Empire and they had no personal sovereignty (except in judicial matters, and this was only valid for the northern principalities under Philip the Good's son, Duke Charles the Bold, from 1473 to 1477).

Following a tradition going back to the Frankish kings, the Duke of Burgundy, because of the division of his possessions into the *pays de par-deçà* ('lands on this side'; the Burgundian Netherlands) and *pays de par-delà* ('lands on that side'; the Duchy and County of Burgundy and adjacent territories), lived an even more nomadic life than did the other princes. Philip the Good (1419–67) maintained five different residences: Dijon, the Château of Hesdin in Artois, Lille, Bruges and Brussels. Two of these, however, were more important to him than the others: Bruges, with the *Prinsenhof* (Prince's court), and, from 1450, Brussels, with the palace of Coudenberg. Mary of Burgundy (1477–82) returned to Bruges, but Margaret of York, widow of Charles the Bold, and her grandson-in-law Philip the Handsome (1482–1506), and later Margaret of Austria (d. 1530) established themselves in Mechelen (Malines).

Pomp and circumstance, ostentation and ceremonial, nobility and grandeur to the point of megalomania: these were the guiding principles of the Dukes of Burgundy, eager to impress the world with their munificence, their power and their glory. Everything that concerned the prince's person was ordered by ceremonial. The House of Burgundy was descended from the House of France and therefore naturally followed French ceremonial – *'les Etats de France'* as it used to be called – adapting it to their own ends. We can picture the amazement of the

ambassadors of King Louis XI of France when Duke Charles the Bold received them in Saint-Omer on 15 July 1470. The Duke was seated on a throne placed on a platform with five steps leading up to it. The platform was covered with black cloth, the throne and dais with gold brocade, which, as the chronicler Georges Chastelain remarked, 'had never been the case before, whether for a king or for an emperor'. Curiously enough, unlike the procedures of the official residences which were copied, for example, in England, the Burgundian etiquette was never written down. An account of the ceremonial concerning women was given by Eleanor of Poitiers in about 1484–87, at the time of the marriage negotiations between Philip the Handsome and the Infanta Joan of Castile. The written account must have been requested by the Castilians to acquaint them with the protocol that was going to surround their princess, and was duly translated into Castilian. Their own ceremonial had already been codified by Diego de Valera in the *Ceremonial of Princes*.

'Religione, Sublimità et Apparati'. These were the three words used by the Milanese Prospero da Camogli, the envoy of the Duke of Milan, Galeazzo Sforza, to describe the impression made on him by the ceremonial of the chapter of the Order of the Golden Fleece at which he was present in Saint-Omer in 1461. The Order was modelled on the English Order of the Garter at a time when it seemed as if such orders and chivalric devices were beginning to go out of fashion, after their tremendous flowering in the second half of the fourteenth century was over. Paradoxically, the new order gave new vigour to those already in existence and brought about the creation of a number of others. The Dukes of Orléans, Brittany and Alençon were elected at the chapter of Saint-Omer in 1440. Charles of Orléans demanded that Philip the Good should receive in return his own Order of the Cape, also known as the Porcupine, which in fact was nothing more than a device. The same may have been the case with John V, Duke of Brittany, and his Order of the Ermine.

At the next chapter, held in Ghent in 1445, a king was elected for the first time: Alfonso V of Aragon and Naples. He also requested reciprocity, and Philip the Good received the Aragonese Order of the Stole and

fig. 194
Guillaume Dufaÿ and Gilles Binchois
Miniature from Martin Le Franc,
Le Champion des dames.
Bibliothèque Nationale de France,
Paris, Ms. fr. 12476, fol. 98

Garter. On the death of Alfonso the Magnanimous
in 1458 his possessions were divided up: Aragon and
Sicily went to his brother John (II), Naples to his
illegitimate son Ferrante. Both heirs were duly elected
members of the Golden Fleece, the first at the chapter
of Saint-Omer in 1461, the second at Valenciennes in
1473. In order not to be left out, Ferrante established
his own order in Naples, also called the Order of the
Ermine. Although Ferdinand II of Aragon, son of
John, and his successor, was already a member of the
Order of the Garter, he was also elected to the Order
of the Golden Fleece in Valenciennes, whereas the
fact of already being a member of an order had still
prevented Alfonso V of Portugal being elected at the
chapter of Bruges in 1468.

Possibly in order not to remain outside the
movement, King René, Duke of Anjou, Bar and
Lorraine, Count of Provence and King of Naples
from 1438 to 1442, the great enemy and one-time
prisoner of Philip the Good, created his own Order of
the Crescent in 1448. In opposition to (rather than in
competition with) the Order of the Golden Fleece,
King Louis XI of France created the Order of Saint
Michael in 1469. Not only did he take his inspiration
from the statutes of the Burgundian order, but the
members of the Order of the Golden Fleece whom
he appointed had to send their collars back.

Going on crusade was only one of the tasks allotted
to the knights of the Golden Fleece. Leading a new
crusade became the great project of Philip the Good
after 1451, although he was already thinking about it
when, in 1421 and again in 1432, he sent spies to the
Near East. His aim, to take back the Holy Land, was
somewhat vague. Pope Eugenius IV (1431–47) shared
the same dream, and it was also shared with varying
fervour by the two competitors for the Kingdom of
Naples, René of Anjou and Alfonso of Aragon, for the
King of Naples was also the titular King of Jerusalem.
Alfonso the Magnanimous was Philip the Good's
main rival with regard to crusading, but Alfonso took
malicious delight in reminding Philip that his plans
were very ill-defined, and that anyway nothing could
be done without his support – because he was a king.
This went on even after Alfonso's death in 1458:
between 1469 and 1476, Jean l'Orfèvre translated for
Charles the Bold the *Dits et faits dignes de mémoire du roi*

fig. 195
Nicolas Froment
*Diptych of René of Anjou and Jeanne
de Laval* ('Matheron diptych')
Musée du Louvre, Paris (see cat. 71)

Alphonse (*Memorable Sayings and Deeds of King Alfonso*) by Antonio Beccadelli, known as Il Panormita. The book ends with preparations for a campaign against the Turks. The Burgundians reciprocated with the celebrated Catalan chivalric romance, *Tirant lo Blanc*, by Johanot Martorell. The hero was apparently modelled on Geoffroy de Thoisy, sent by Philip the Good to fight the Mamelukes and Turks in Rhodes and Constantinople in 1441–42 and 1444–45.

The fall of Constantinople in 1453 gave a specific aim to the Burgundian scheme and to successive popes: Nicholas V (1447–55), Calixtus III (1455–58), Pius II (1458–64), Paul II (1464–71) and Sixtus IV (1471–84) all sought the support of the Duke of Burgundy in this enterprise. Philip the Good was sincere but could achieve nothing, partly because he was hindered by the King of France. His son, Charles the Bold, exploited this ideological 'capital', making promises but doing nothing; he was severely reprimanded for this by the Venetian ambassador, seconded by the ambassador of Naples, at the chapter of the Golden Fleece in Valenciennes in 1473. Although the promises made by the Burgundians might have seemed interesting, their plans were too hazy for the Italians, who were in direct contact with the Saracens and the Turks. The same could be said of the Iberian peninsula: Philip the Good expressed a wish to take part in an attack on the Kingdom of Granada, he also seems to have entered into an agreement to send a fleet of ships to the (disastrous) Tangier expedition, and he had even more nebulous proposals for a Burgundo-Portuguese expedition to conquer the Morea (1436–37).

Philip the Good made a vow to go on a crusade at the chapter of the Golden Fleece in Mons in 1451; he renewed his vow publicly during the famous *Banquet du Faisan* (Banquet of the Pheasant) in Lille, on 17 February 1454. The scene of chivalry at which this took place was taken directly from a fourteenth-century romance, *Les Vœux du Paon* (*The Vows of the Peacock*) – they could not use the same bird twice! The Lille banquet was famous for the *entremets*, a kind of mixture of scenes from chivalric romance and morality plays as depicted at a later date by Hieronymus Bosch and Pieter Bruegel. It was the final ceremonial after a series of tournaments, each followed by a banquet. The idea of holding such festivities probably did not originate at the court of Burgundy. Its source may have been the festivities accompanying the marriage by proxy of Philip the Good and Isabella of Portugal in Lisbon on 26–28 September 1429, while the *entremets* may have derived from those presented at the dinners given to celebrate the wedding of Louis of Savoy and Anne of Cyprus, at Chambéry from 7 to 11 February 1434. Jean Lefèvre de Saint-Rémy, who was king at arms (*Toison d'or*) of the Golden Fleece, had in his possession a description of the marriage celebrations in Portugal, and, with Philip the Good himself, had attended the wedding in Chambéry. The Banquet of the Pheasant was copied at least once, in Orléans on 30 September 1461 on the occasion of the solemn signing of the promise of marriage between Pierre de Beaujeu and Marie d'Orléans. The dinner was furnished with the same *entremets*, and a vow had to be pronounced over a swan, the symbol of the House of Cleves to which the mother of young Marie belonged.

The feasts held at the court of Burgundy were usually accompanied by tournaments and jousting. When the French court happened to be in Nancy in the spring of 1445, the French nobles, who spent their time sleeping, drinking and eating, had the idea of organizing jousts and tournaments, as was the custom at the Burgundian court. Charles of Anjou, Count of Maine, and John of Luxembourg, Count of Saint-Pol, took charge. The hero of the day was Jacques de Lalaing, who came from Hainaut and was a subject of Philip the Good. At the end of that year, the 'goodly knight', the 'knight without reproach' met 'Jean de Boniface', a Sicilian knight. After that he set off round Europe looking for chivalric engagements, but his renown was already so great that the various rulers prohibited any such encounter with him: this happened in 1446–47 in France, in Navarre (where the princess was Anne of Cleves, niece of Philip the Good and sister of the Duchess of Orléans), in Castile (where he did nevertheless enter the lists against Diego de Guzmán) and in Portugal.

The knight-errant was a European phenomenon which in the fifteenth century mainly involved knights from Castile and Aragon. Juan de Merlo met Pierre de Bauffremont, Seigneur of Charny, in Arras in 1435; Gutierre Quijada fought against John of Luxembourg, *Bâtard* of Saint-Pol, at Saint-Omer in 1439; Pedro Vázquez de Saavedra jousted with Pierre de Bauffremont near Dijon in 1443, then entered the service of Philip the Good and remained with him until his death in 1477.

A certain number of these encounters took place at the *pas d'armes* or tourneys which flourished simultaneously, after 1443, in the domains of Burgundy and Anjou. These consisted of jousting, accompanied by theatrical performances during which the person, or persons, organizing the tournament defended a patch of ground and let nobody through until they had engaged in armed combat. Such performances took place at the Pas de l'Arbre Charlemagne near Dijon (1443), the Pas de la Joyeuse Garde near Saumur, the Pas de la Gueule du Dragon near Chinon (1446), the Pas de la Bergère in Tarascon, the Pas de la Pèlerine near Saint-Omer (1449), the Pas de la Fontaine des Pleurs near Chalon-sur-Saône (1449–50), the Pas du Perron faé in Bruges (1463), the Pas de la Dame inconnue in Brussels (1463–64), the Pas de l'Ardre d'or in Bruges (1468) and the Pas de la Dame sauvage in Ghent (1470). The event was not Burgundian or Angevin in origin: it was adapted from a Castilian invention. The first *pas* were those held in Valladolid in 1428 and the celebrated Pas d'Honneur between León and Astorga in 1434.

When the knights were not taking part in these chivalric games in which they pretended to defend the honour of a gentle damsel in an exotic world, they could relive the same type of adventure in the romances of the period. Alongside the romances of the classic cycles – Breton, Carolingian and crusading, written in earlier centuries but still in fashion – a great number of pseudo-historical books, oriental adventure stories and biographies of crusading knights originated at the Burgundian court in the last quarter of the fifteenth century. All of them were influenced by the crusading spirit: The *Histoire d'Hélène de Constantinople* (1448), *Charles Martel* (1448) and the *Chroniques et conquêtes de Charlemagne* (1458) are attached to the Carolingian cycle; *Gillion de Trazegnies* (1454–63), *Gilles de Chin* (1456–65), *Jean d'Avesnes* (before 1469) with *La Fille du comte de Ponthieu* and *Saladin* are all crusading romances belonging to the

fig. 196
Copy after Jan van Eyck
Portrait of a Member of the Order of Saint Anthony ('Man with Carnation')
Staatliche Museen zu Berlin. Gemäldegalerie (see cat. 35)

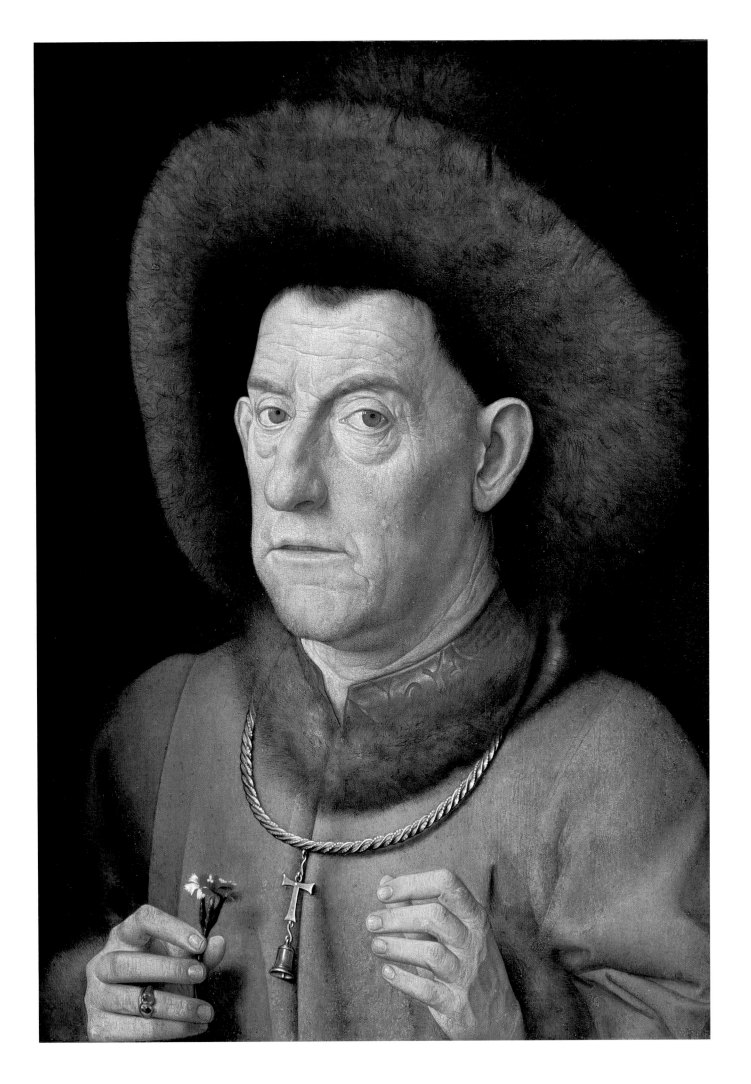

same genre as *Le Comte d'Artois* (before 1469), *Louis de Gavre* (1456–57) and *Les Trois Fils de rois* (1463). None of these seems to have travelled far. We know that Agnes of Burgundy, Duchess of Bourbon (d. 1476), had a copy of *Les Trois Fils de rois*, probably given her by her brother Philip the Good. In addition, Guy de Laval, father-in-law of René of Anjou, possessed a copy of *Baudouin de Gavre*, a variation of *Louis de Gavre* – possibly because he was Lord of Gavere in Flanders.

This kind of literature could already be found in the courts of southern France, or at any rate flourished there at the same time. At the court of Orléans (if not at the court of Burgundy) the romance of *Clériadus et Méliadice* made its appearance between 1440 and 1444; at the court of Savoy, under the influence of Anne, Duchess of Cyprus, the *Livre du gentil chevalier Philippe de Mandien* appeared in 1447–48; at Anjou came *Paris et Vienne* in 1435 and *Pierre de Provence et la belle Maguelonne* before 1453 (the latter enjoyed tremendous success in the German-speaking countries and was set to music by Johannes Brahms). Nevertheless, unlike the romances written in Italy or in the Iberian peninsula, these romances of chivalric adventures had a relatively restricted circulation and therefore produced no heirs, apart from the history of the *Trois Fils de rois* which was printed in the sixteenth century. In Florence, Andrea da Barberino (d. 1434) revived the Carolingian cycle, most notably in his *Guerino Meschino*, and the genre was continued by Luigi Pulci's *Morgante* (1460–70) and, in Calabria, by Matteo Maria Boiardo's *Orlando innamorato* (1494), whose sequel was Ariosto's *Orlando furioso* (1532). In Catalonia, *Curial e Guilfa* (*c.* 1440–60) contains a hero who has Italian origins; the King of France, the Dukes of Orléans and Burgundy, the Count of Foix and the Marquis of Montferrat all make an appearance in the romance; *Tirant lo Blanc*, mentioned above (1457), is still in the bookshops today. Finally, in Castile *Amadis of Gaul* was a continuation of the Breton cycle; its hero Amadis was to become the paragon of chivalry throughout sixteenth-century Europe and beyond.

When these heroes were not busy demonstrating their valour in enchanted or exotic realms, their time would be spent defending the honour of fair ladies. At the court of Burgundy, the 'dispute over women' was introduced in the *Champion des dames* by Martin Le

fig. 198
Anonymous (Provence)
(Pierre Vilatte?)
*Giovanni da Calabria (?) and His Wife
at Prayer and Saint Bernardino of Siena*
Musée Grobet-Labadie, Marseilles

Franc (see fig. 194), Provost of Lausanne in the service of the House of Savoy, who dedicated his book to Philip the Good (1442). The question seems to have been discussed at most length in the years between 1454 and 1465, when Isabella of Bourbon, daughter of Agnes of Burgundy, was the Countess of Charolais through her marriage with Charles, Count of Charolais, the later Duke Charles the Bold. Vasco Queimado de Vilalobos, a Portuguese courtier in the service of the Duke of Burgundy, had two books translated by his compatriot Fernando de Lucena, who was also in the service of Philip the Good: the *Triumph of Women* and the *Seat of Honour* by the Castilian Juan Rodríguez de la Cámara (or del Padron).

In fact Philip the Good's courtiers, and those of the Dauphin, Louis, son of Charles VII, who took refuge at the court of Burgundy (1456–61), revelled in the licentious aspect of relations between men and women; such encounters gave rise to the *Cent Nouvelles Nouvelles*, modelled on the *Decameron*. These stories can be compared with a contemporary Catalan piece satirizing women, although in a more moral, almost religious manner: the *Mirror* or *Book of Women* (1459) by Jaume Roig, from Valencia, doctor to Queen Maria, the wife of King Alfonso the Magnanimous.

At the court of Burgundy, as in the rest of Europe, courtiers spent their time composing poetry and songs of courtly love, a theme that was revived at the court of France by Alain Chartier's *La Belle Dame sans mercy* (1424). The poets linked to the Burgundian court, or close to it, were Pierre de Hauteville, prince of the Paris *Cour d'Amour* (d. 1448) and Achille Caulier (active *c.* 1424–41), both from Tournai, and the Burgundian Baudet Hérenc (active *c.* 1425–49); they all wrote in this vein. From the *Parlement (Tribunal) d'Amour* by Baudet Hérenc (*c.* 1425) to the *Hôpital d'Amour* by Achille Caulier (*c.* 1441), it was the norm for the Lover to end in the grave, as in Hauteville's *Confession et testament de l'Amant trépassé de deuil* (1441–47). The same themes, in particular that of the cemetery of faithful lovers and of love-lorn poets, can be found in the *Livre du Cœur d'amour épris* by René of Anjou (1457). The idea of the cemetery was taken up again by Olivier de la Marche in his *Chevalier délibéré* (1483), which marked the end of chivalry as embodied by Charles the Bold. The work was favourably received in Castile and was the bedside book of Charles V.

The tone for the most classical poetry was set for all the French courts by Charles d'Orléans and his court at Blois. The Duke had already exchanged letters on the subject with Philip the Good (who will have engaged the services of a specialist in the art) before his release from English captivity. (He had been held prisoner since the battle of Agincourt in 1415.) The debates he organized between the years 1453 and 1456, for which he probably chose the subject, gave an opportunity for poetical exchanges between the princely courts of France. At the most famous of these the poem *En la forêt de longue attente* was discussed. The debate on the theme of the *Amoureux de l'Observance* brought Georges Chastelain and Olivier de la Marche together with Vaillant, a poet from Touraine who was connected to René of Anjou. Vaillant also knew Jacques de Luxembourg (d. 1487), an important member of the Burgundian nobility who established a poetic link between the courts of Burgundy, Brittany and Anjou-Lorraine via his network of relations (he was the brother-in-law of Arthur de Richemont, Duke of Brittany in 1457–58, and of Jean d'Anjou, Duke of Calabria, then, in 1453, of Lorraine). In addition, in about 1448, Michault Taillevent, poet to Philip the Good, was in correspondence with René of Anjou's poet Pierre Chastellain.

A number of these poets were members of the *Grands Rhétoriqueurs* (Great Rhetoricians) who flourished in the fifteenth and at the beginning of the sixteenth century in the Kingdom of France and the Duchies of Burgundy, Brittany, Bourbon, Normandy and Poitou. They contributed to theory (the *Arts de seconde rhétorique*, second because they were in French not in Latin): Baudet Hérenc produced a *Doctrinal de seconde rhétorique* (1432), and Jean Molinet his important *Art de rhétorique vulgaire* (before 1492). The rhetoricians at the court of Burgundy, Georges Chastelain (d. 1474), Olivier de la Marche (d. 1502) and Jean Molinet (d. 1507), were highly influential in the French lands. Georges Chastelain was first in the service of Charles VII and joined forces with Pierre de

Brézé, whom he seems to have portrayed in the *Oultré d'amour* and whose epitaph he wrote in 1465. He wrote the *Temple de Boccace* to console Marguerite of Anjou, daughter of King René and wife of Henry VI of England. He was in correspondence with Jean Castel, Benedictine monk and chronicler of Louis XI, who was the grandson of Christine de Pisan; he also corresponded with Jean Robertet (d. 1502), who was in the service of Duke Jean II of Bourbon and, from 1469, of Louis XI, then Charles VIII. The outcome of the

fig. 199
Copy after Rogier van der Weyden
Duke Philip the Good
Stedelijke Musea,
Groeningemuseum, Bruges
(see cat. 62)

exchange of letters between Chastelain and Robertet is *Douze Dames de Rhétorique* (1463–64), written in French and in Latin verse and prose. Chastelain's influence even reached the court of Brittany via Jean Meschinot (*c.*1420–92). When Meschinot wrote his *Vingt-cinq ballades* against Louis XI, he used the last verse of the twenty-five strophes of Chastelain's *Princes* as a refrain. It is interesting to note also that in 1472 Meschinot wrote a lament on the death of the Duchess of Burgundy, Isabella of Portugal.

Georges Chastelain was the chronicler of the lives of Dukes Philip the Good and Charles the Bold. At the end of his life he was assisted in this by Jean Molinet. In about 1462 he composed a verse *Recollection des merveilles advenues en nostre temps*, describing the large and small events of his lifetime, which was completed by Jean Molinet after 1496. It is curious to note that the Portuguese historian and poet Garcia de Resende (d. 1536), who is generally thought to have been self-taught, must have owned a copy of Chastelain's *Recollection*, as in 1530–33 he used it as a model for his *Miscellania e variedade de historias, costumes, casos, e cousas que em seu tempo acontecerão*.

Having received his training from Georges Chastelain, Jean Molinet remained faithful to the House of Burgundy; he served Charles the Bold, Mary of Burgundy and Maximilian of Habsburg, their son Philip the Handsome and their daughter Margaret of Austria, Regent of the Netherlands. The life of his pupil, Jean Lemaire de Belges (d. after 1515), was less calm: he was active in the courts of various princes and princesses, spreading the rhetorical culture of Burgundy throughout the land. His patrons included Pierre de Beaujeu, Duke of Bourbon (d. 1503); Margaret, when she was Duchess of Savoy (her husband Philibert II of Savoy died in 1504); Philip the Handsome (d. 1506) (he succeeded Molinet as his chronicler); Margaret again when she was Regent of the Netherlands; and finally Anne of Brittany, Queen of France.

After Alain Chartier and his anti-curial invective (*Quadrilogue invectif*, 1422; *Dialogus familiaris amici et sodalis*, 1426–27; and *De vita curiali, c.*1427), the celebrated (and less celebrated) rhetoricians took up the matter. The most famous work on the subject is the metrical prose *Abusé en cour*, written between 1450

and 1470 and attributed by some to the court of Anjou (to King René himself), by others to the court of Burgundy (Charles de Rochefort); the success of this work persisted throughout the French lands until well into the sixteenth century, and it was imitated at the royal court by Octovien de Saint-Gelais in his *Séjour d'Honneur* (1490–94). Works like this often contained criticism of the nobility. A new definition of nobility was becoming essential, and this was the problem which occupied the court of Burgundy – late in the day – through treatises on the same subject written in Italy or in Castile and translated into French. In 1449, Jean Miélot translated for Philip the Good the *Orationes de vera nobilitate* (*Debate on True Nobility*) by Buonaccorso da Pistoia (or of Montemagno; d. 1429). Meanwhile Gonzalvo de Vargas, doctor to the Count of Charolais, the future Charles the Bold, and himself a native of the Kingdom of Sicily (he used the French form of his name, Hugues de Salve), made a French adaptation in about 1454–59 of the *Espejo de verdadera nobleza* (1444), written by the Castilian Diego de Valera who in 1449 took part in the Pas de l'Arbre d'or. At a later date, Valera wrote a *Chronique d'Espagne abrégée* which was translated into French at the beginning of the sixteenth century for Philip the Handsome, who was to inherit Castile following his marriage to Joan ('the Mad') of Castile.

The *Enseignement de la vraie noblesse* is attributed to a Flemish nobleman, Gilbert de Lannoy (d. 1482), who is also known for his didactic works: *Instruction d'un jeune prince* and the *Enseignements paternels*. The court of Burgundy was receptive to this kind of literature. The books of a southern French author, Antoine de la Sale (d. *c.* 1460), *La Salade*, written for the instruction of John of Calabria (1442–44), and *La Sale*, for the children of Louis of Luxembourg, Count of Saint-Pol (1451), enjoyed great success there. Antoine de la Sale is remembered today for his romance, *Le Petit Jean de Saintré* (1456), based on the life story of the aforementioned Jacques de Lalaing.

Having seen (by his account) a tapestry belonging to Agnes of Burgundy, Duchess of Bourbon, representing the mountains of the Lake of Pilatus and of the Sibyl in Italy, Antoine de la Sale wrote his *Paradis de la reine Sibylle* (1437), which he later integrated into *La Salade* (the legend crops up again 175 in Richard Wagner's *Tannhäuser*). Tapestries were an indispensable part of princely decoration, and the main centres of production were in the Burgundian Netherlands, in Artois, Flanders and in Tournai. They were a famous feature of the court of Burgundy and were unrolled for great feasts and ceremonies at which ambassadors and representatives of different countries could admire them. The most beautiful series of tapestries was the *History of Gideon and the Golden Fleece* (1448–52), first displayed in the chapters of the Order in The Hague (1456) and in Saint-Omer (1461), then at the marriage of Charles the Bold and Margaret of York in Bruges (1468), and at the interview between Emperor Frederick III and the Duke of Burgundy in Trier (1473). At the *Banquet du Faisan* in Lille in 1454 the walls were adorned with a *Life of Hercules*; in Saint-Omer in 1461, in the church, there were scenes from the Old and New Testaments and an *Apocalypse*. At the marriage in Bruges there featured a *Battle of Othea* woven before 1420, a *History of Clovis*, a *History of Begon, Duke of Belin* (brother of Garin le Lorrain, in the *Geste des Lorrains*), which included hunting scenes, a tapestry of *King Ahasuerus*, and in the chapel a tapestry of the *Passion*. When the Duke made his entry into Brussels in 1469 there were tapestries of *Alexander*, of *Hannibal* and of the *Valiant Knights*; in Trier there were the *Passion* and *Jason and the Golden Fleece* (!) in the church, and tapestries of *Gideon* and of *Ahasuerus* in the hall in which he met the Emperor. Other tapestries mentioned by witnesses and chroniclers included a *Sacrament*, bought in 1439–40; *Children at School*, paid for in 1445–46; the *Knight of the Swan*, acquired in 1461–62; and the *Trojan War*, commissioned in 1472 and donated by the city of Bruges in 1475–76.

Although the Dukes of Burgundy seem to have guarded their tapestries jealously, there are some examples of gifts. In 1422–23 Philip the Good acquired six tapestries of the *Life of the Virgin* to be sent as a present to Pope Martin V in order to curry favour with the pontiff for himself and for his subjects. In 1439 he included in the trousseau of his niece Agnes of Cleves, who was about to marry Charles, Prince of Viana, heir to the Kingdom of Navarre, a tapestry of a *Deer Hunt* and another entitled *The Plea for Love* (on the theme of the *Parliament of Love* by Baudet Hérenc).

In 1461–62, he gave a *Knight of the Swan* and an *Ahasuerus and Esther* to the Cardinal of Arras, Jean Jouffroy, who had been in the service of Louis XI and who finished his career at Albi. Later, in 1504, Philip the Handsome bought a tapestry 'in the manner of Portugal and the Indies', in other words depicting the discovery of India by the Portuguese, in order to present it to the ambassador of France.

The southern rulers and princes obtained supplies of tapestries from the Burgundian Netherlands and also commissioned their own. In 1434, Alfonso V of Aragon ordered from Guillaume au Vaissel, a dealer in Arras, some tapestries for his chapel and his palace in Valencia. Later, for the palace of Castel Nuovo in Naples, he appealed to Philip the Good, and made use of an agent in Flanders. He bought three very expensive tapestries of the *Passion*, after cartoons (or paintings?) by Rogier van der Weyden. Later, Peter of Portugal, King of the Catalans (1464–65), had in his possession a *History of Jephthah* which passed to Doña Juana Enriquez, mother of Ferdinand the Catholic. Her husband, John II of Aragon, owned an *Exaltation of the Holy Cross*, probably given by his son Ferdinand to the convent of the Santa Engracia at Saragossa.

The Medici took their cue from Alfonso of Aragon. In 1448 one of their agents had seen a *History of Samson* in Antwerp, but he desisted from purchasing it because it was too big and too full of corpses. Five years later, another agent bought a 'chamber' (set) on the same subject, which Giovanni de' Medici desired to present to the Lord of Faenza. The same agent, Gierozzo de' Pigli, came to Flanders with six cartoons of *Triumphs* after Petrarch, hoping to have them woven by the best master to be found there. More than half a century later, Pope Leo X, another Medici, sent a set of cartoons by Raphael to Brussels in order to have them woven into the tapestries depicting the *Acts of the Apostles*. Another example of a commission is the one given by King Alfonso V of Portugal to commemorate the capture of Arzila in Morocco (24 August 1471), of which a detailed account had arrived at the court of Burgundy.

When southern princes and rulers did not buy directly from the North, northern merchants would travel to them to offer tapestries woven in the workshops they represented. In this way, the *History of Alexander* was presented by the Grenier cousins

fig. 200
Robert Campin
Nativity
Musée des Beaux-Arts, Dijon

to Duke Francesco Sforza of Milan on 18 June 1459. It was finally sold to Duke Philip the Good on the following 30 August. In 1502, the merchant Pierre d'Enghien followed Philip the Handsome and Joan of Castile to Spain, where he sold a *Devotion of Our Lady* to the heir of Castile.

Finally, the princes and rulers of the South (and Italy is the best-known example) employed master tapestry makers from the North at their courts. Examples of this are known in Milan, Ferrara, Mantua, Florence, Correggio, Siena, Venice and Rome. The most famous case is that of Giachetto, identified as Jacquet d'Arras, who worked in Siena from 1442 to 1458, where he made a tapestry from the Lorenzetti frescoes in the Stanza della Pace in the Palazzo Pubblico. He was also in the service of Piero de' Medici in Florence and of the Pope in Rome, where he is alleged to have produced a *Coronation of Emperor Sigismund* for Eugene IV and a *History of Saint Peter* for Nicholas V.

The taste for tapestries also spread through the French territories and regions within France's sphere of influence. The case of Jean Jouffroy has already been cited. George of Saluzzo, Bishop of Lausanne (1439–61), possessed a *Justice of Trajan and Herkinbald*, after the panels by Rogier van der Weyden, now lost, in the City Hall in Brussels. Later, in about 1500, Guillaume du Breuil, Canon of Bourges and Prior of Saint-Ursin, gave to his cathedral a *Life of Saint Ursin*, apostle of Berry, while Pierre Morin, the Treasurer General, gave a *Passion* to the Church of Saint-Saturnin in Tours in 1505.

The celebrated painters of the Netherlands could be called upon to make cartoons for tapestry, but the courts of southern Europe were also fond of their paintings. Even though this subject has been widely explored, it is worth recalling a few facts. As early as 1413, Duke John the Fearless sent his portrait painted by Jean Malouel to King João I of Portugal. Later, between 1445 and 1449, Duchess Isabella of Portugal made a gift to the Royal Monastery of Batalha of a painting by Rogier van der Weyden (or from his studio), representing Philip the Good, their son Charles, Count of Charolais, and herself at prayer before a Virgin and Child enthroned. This Portuguese case seems exceptional: it is the only documented example of a painting being sent to southern Europe by the Dukes of Burgundy.

Paintings by the great masters were avidly sought after, and were acquired either by direct commission, following a gift to a prince by the owner of the work, or by purchase on the open market. John II of Castile bought a *Triptych of the Virgin* from Rogier van der Weyden and donated it to the Charterhouse of Miraflores in 1445; although it is not recorded, the

fig. 201
Master of the Portraits of Princes
Louis of Gruuthuse
Stedelijke Musea,
Groeningemuseum, Bruges
(see cat. 43)

fig. 202
Rogier van der Weyden
Anthony, 'Grand Bâtard de Bourgogne'
Private collection (see cat. 58)

same procedure will have been followed in the case of Rogier's *Triptych of Saint John the Baptist* (Staatliche Museen, Berlin). Memling, too, enjoyed a certain celebrity in Castile, as witnessed by the portrait of the ambassador to the court of Burgundy, Francisco de Rojas (fig. 220), the altarpiece of Nájera (fig. 164), the triptych with the *Adoration of the Magi* (now Prado, Madrid) and the paintings in the possession of Queen Isabella the Catholic – a *Virgin and Child Enthroned* and a *Descent from the Cross* diptych (both Capilla Real, Granada).

Alfonso V of Aragon had a *Saint George* by Van Eyck (now lost) bought in Bruges and shipped to Valencia in 1444–45, which he later took with him to Naples. In Naples he also owned Van Eyck's 'Lomellini triptych' and an *Adoration of the Magi*, plus three *Passion* tapestries after Van der Weyden. At a later date, the poet Sannazzaro owned a small *Christ in Majesty* by Petrus Christus. The 'Lomellini triptych' came from Battista di Giorgio (?) Lomellini, a Genoese, who had had it painted in Bruges. It comprised an *Annunciation*, and on the wings Saint John the Baptist and Saint Jerome. In Genoa a *Woman Bathing* by Rogier van der Weyden could also be seen, while the portable Marian triptych by Van Eyck (fig. 115), depicting the Virgin and Child enthroned in the centre and Saint Michael presenting the donor and Saint Catherine on the wings, must have come to Genoa when the Giustiniani family acquired it. In similar fashion, triptychs of the *Annunciation* (Louvre, Paris) and the *Crucifixion* (fig. 140), painted for the De Villa family who were bankers in Flanders, were recorded in Piedmont (Chieri?). A 'Patron and His Agent' by Van Eyck was in Milan in the early sixteenth century, and in Pesaro Alessandro Sforza had brought back three Van der Weydens from his visit to the Low Countries in 1457–58: portraits of Philip the Good and of himself '*in due occhi*' (in three-quarter view) and a triptych of the *Crucifixion* (fig. 139).

Venetian collectors of the early sixteenth century, such as Cardinal Grimani in Venice and Pietro Bembo in Padua, possessed paintings by Memling, and Grimani also owned a portrait of Isabella of Portugal by Van der Weyden. The d'Este family in Ferrara owned a *Lamentation* by Van der Weyden, with Adam and Eve expelled from Paradise on one of its wings,

and the portrait of the illegitimate Francesco d'Este, who had been brought up with Charles the Bold. In Urbino the Montefeltro family were the proud owners of Van Eyck's '*Stufa*' or *Women Bathing* (see cat. 36).

By the end of the fifteenth century the greatest number of paintings from the Low Countries were concentrated in Florence: a 'Head of a French Lady' by Petrus Christus; the *Virgin and Child with Four Saints* (fig. 95) and an *Entombment* (fig. 97), both commissioned from Roger van der Weyden by the Medici family; the *Adoration of the Shepherds* triptych by Hugo van der Goes, commissioned by Tommaso Portinari (fig. 107), and paintings by Memling also commissioned by the Portinari family: the portraits of Tommaso and his wife Maria Baroncelli (now Metropolitan Museum, New York), the *Panorama of the Passion* (Galleria Sabauda, Turin), the *Triptych of Benedetto Portinari* (now Staatliche Museen, Berlin, and Uffizi, Florence) and finally a *Virgin and Child Enthroned with Two Angels* (Uffizi, Florence). The *Triptych of the Last Judgment* painted for Angelo Tani and Caterina Tanagli never arrived in Florence – it was seized by pirates from Danzig (Gdańsk). Finally, Italian patrons such as the Rapondi and Arnolfini families may have commissioned Jan van Eyck's 'Lucca Madonna' (fig. 29).

The infatuation with northern painting in the Mediterranean was such that princes and rulers sent painters to be trained in the North, or welcomed northern painters to their courts, before the local artists had had time to integrate the lessons of Early Netherlandish masters into their work. In 1431 Alfonso V sent Lluís Dalmau to Flanders to perfect his skills. The result can be seen particularly clearly in his *Altarpiece of the Consellers* in Barcelona (1443–45; fig. 153), which is strongly influenced by Van Eyck's Ghent altarpiece and 'Van der Paele Madonna' (figs 4–5, 92). Conversely, Louis Allyncbrood, who was active in Bruges between 1432 and 1439 and then moved to Valencia, where he is mentioned (as Luis Alincbrot) until 1460–63, painted in the manner of Van Eyck. At the end of the century, in 1496, Queen Isabella of Castile took into her service '*Juan Flamenco*' or Juan de Flandes. After the death of the Queen in 1504, the artist worked in Salamanca, then from 1509 until his death in 1519 in the Cathedral of Palencia.

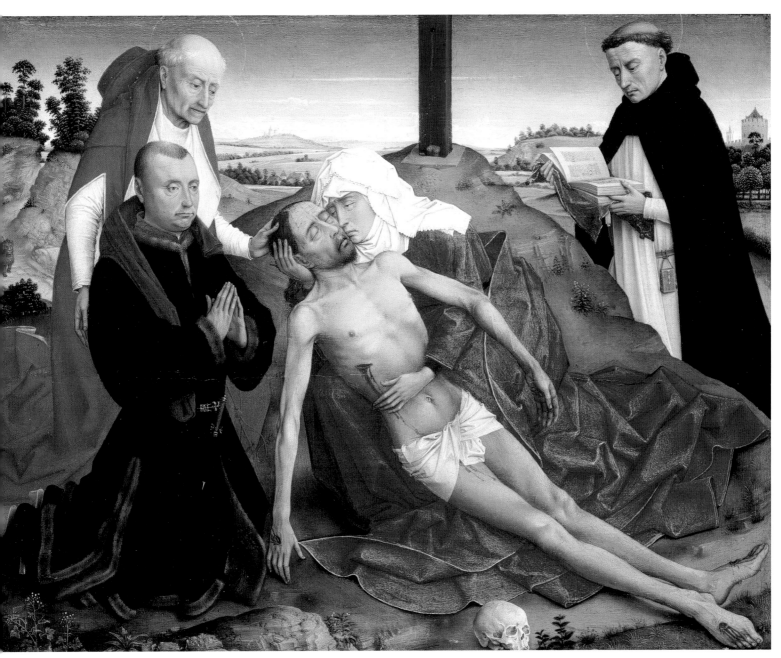

fig. 203
Workshop of
Rogier van der Weyden
Pietà
National Gallery, London

The same phenomenon is observable in Italy. In 1460, the Duchess of Milan, Bianca Maria Visconti, wrote to Philip the Good to ask him to recommend her young painter Zanetto Bugatto to Rogier van der Weyden. In spite of various difficulties, Bugatto stayed two years with the master in Brussels, and afterwards the Duchess thanked Van der Weyden personally for the instruction he gave to her painter. Justus of Ghent (Joos van Wassenhove), who was active in Antwerp in 1460, then in Ghent from 1464 to 1469, left for Italy, where he was in the service of Federico da Montefeltro from 1473 to 1475.

The situation in France was very similar to that in Spain and Italy. Before 1444, King René (of Anjou) took into his service Barthélemy d'Eyck, probably a relative of Jan van Eyck, whose activity as a painter is documented until 1451. In the same year King René acquired in Paris three large paintings of the Passion painted in Flanders. Cardinal Jean Rolin, Bishop of Autun, son of Nicolas, Philip the Good's Chancellor, commissioned at least one work from a northern painter, Jean Hey, and invited him to come to Burgundy. Jean Hey later entered the service of the Duke of Bourbon.

By this time Spanish and Italian painters had begun to absorb the lessons of the northern masters. We need only think of, in Portugal, Nuno Gonçalves; in France, Jean Fouquet; in Naples, Colantonio and, above all, Antonello da Messina, who was to take the message to the north of Italy, to Venice, where he was received by Giovanni Bellini. In Arezzo and Urbino, and in the other centres in which he worked, Piero della Francesca had already integrated northern elements into his work. It should be pointed out that the influence did not move in one direction only. Although Jan van Eyck's journey to Spain does not seem to have left any traces in his work, except for some exotic motifs, his purported visit to Italy seems to have been the origin of influences traceable to Gentile da Fabriano and Masaccio. Italian influence is much stronger, however, in certain works by Rogier van der Weyden, who went on a pilgrimage to Rome in the Jubilee year of 1450. His 'Medici Madonna' (fig. 95) shows that he had seen Fra Angelico's 'San Marco altarpiece' in Florence, and particularly the *Sacra Conversazione* by Domenico Veneziano (fig. 93).

In addition, his *Entombment* was directly inspired by Fra Angelico's painting of the same subject (figs 96, 97). Yet, for the time being, the Italian influence was limited to the borrowing of certain motifs and compositional schemes.

The religious works of Early Netherlandish masters often contain musician angels. Music, as well as tapestry and painting, was one of the great glories of the Burgundian Netherlands, to which, for the sake of convenience, we might add the neighbouring Bishopric of Cambrai, where Jean, 'Bâtard de Bourgogne' (the illegitimate son of Duke John the Fearless), was bishop between 1439 and 1480. Nevertheless, the Dukes of Burgundy were never able to retain musicians of genius or talent in their territories, unlike their painters and tapestry makers. The Burgundian musicians could be found all over southern Europe, and were particularly prized in Italy.

The great musicians active at the court of Burgundy were Gilles Binchois (d. 1460), who came from Hainaut and worked for Philip the Good; Antoine Busnois (d. 1492), from Picardy, who entered the service of Charles the Bold and then Mary of Burgundy; Heinrich Isaac (d. 1517), from Flanders, who worked for Maximilian (after a spell in Florence, whence he returned permanently in 1512); Alexander Agricola (d. 1506), from the Netherlands, who became chaplain and chanter to Philip the Handsome after he had spent time in Milan (1471–74), Florence (1474), Cambrai (1476), France (1491), Florence again (1491–92), Naples (1492), France again (1492–93) and finally the Netherlands (1500); Pierre de la Rue (d. 1518), from Tournai (?), who worked for Philip the Handsome, Joan of Castile, Margaret of Austria and the young Charles v.

The three most famous composers of Flemish polyphony – Dufaÿ, Ockeghem and Des Prés – never worked for the Dukes of Burgundy. Guillaume Dufaÿ (d. 1474) was born in the region of Cambrai and spent his career wandering between France and Italy: he worked for the Malatesta family in Pesaro (1420–24), in Laon (1424–26), in Bologna (1427–28), the papal chapel in Rome (1428–33), at the court of Savoy (1434–35), in Florence, then in the papal chapel in Rome again (1435–37), in Cambrai (1440–50), once more at the court of Savoy (1451–58) and finally in Cambrai again (1459–74). Johannes Ockeghem (d. 1497), who came from Saint-Ghislain in Hainaut, was first in the service of Charles, Duke of Bourbon, from 1446 to 1448, then went to work at the court of France. Josquin des Prés (d. 1521), from Picardy, was a chorister in Milan Cathedral (1459–72), then in the service of the Duke of Milan, Galeazzo Maria Sforza (1474), before moving to the service of Cardinal Ascagno Sforza in Milan and Rome (1479–86), then to the Popes Innocent VIII and Alexander VI (1486–94); he went on to serve the King of France Louis XII (1501–3), before returning to Duke Ercole d'Este in Ferrara in Italy in 1503; from 1504 he resided in Condé-sur-l'Escaut.

The genres of music made popular by these composers were the *chanson*, the motet (particularly in honour of the Virgin) and the *cantus firmus* Mass, the most successful of which was entitled the Mass of *L'Homme armé*. They introduced the *Requiem* (the first of these was composed by Guillaume Dufaÿ, but is now lost, the first surviving *Requiem* being the one composed for the funeral of Charles VII by Johannes Ockeghem), the *Magnificat*, the *De profundis* and the *Miserere*. The theorist of this music was Johannes Tinctoris (d. 1511), who came from Poperinge or Nivelles and taught at the court of Ferrante of Naples.

It was not only the great composers who sought an audience worthy of their talent and a salary better than the one they could earn in the Netherlands, but also large numbers of choristers, men and boys, who would even be recruited from abroad by agents. The same happened with instrument makers, organ makers in particular. Alfonso of Aragon had a number of such craftsmen in his employ, including Constantino de Tanti, from Modena, in 1451, and 'Rodrigue' of Burgundy, in 1453. Constantino de Tanti

was sent to him, with an organ he had invented, by Lionello d'Este. Alfonso was so excited that two years later he sent Constantino de Tanti to make a similar organ for Philip the Good. Later, in 1456, he bought from Gérard de Hollande an organ with 84 pipes.

The most moving encounter between northern and southern music took place at the wedding of Louis of Savoy and Anne of Cyprus, at Chambéry, in February 1434, at which Philip the Good was present. A celebrated miniature (fig. 194), the only medieval representation of contemporary musicians, commemorates part of it: the meeting between Gilles Binchois and Guillaume Dufaÿ. The miniature does not, however, show the scene which, reportedly, left the two composers dumbfounded and confused: the playing of a glorious melody on the lute and viol by the two blind Castilian-born musicians of Duchess Isabella, Juan de Cordoal and Juan Fernández, who had come with her from Portugal.

Relations between the court of Burgundy and the South were rich and intense. This cultural exchange gave intellectual depth to the debates that took place in courtly circles, on nobility and on the honour of women, for example. The Burgundians emphasized appearances: their preference for splendour and magnificence made their court one of the most brilliant in Europe at the end of the Middle Ages. To support such luxury they took advantage of the wealth of the inhabitants of the Southern Netherlands, established by a long tradition of both hard work and rebellion. It was among this population of enterprising craftsmen that the court found the tapestry weavers, painters and musicians who brought it glory all over Europe.

The Habsburgs and the Cultural Heritage of Burgundy

Dagmar Eichberger

The dynastic links between the House of Habsburg and the Duchy of Burgundy date back to 19 August 1477, when Maximilian (1459–1519), son of Emperor Frederick III, married Mary of Burgundy (1457–82), daughter of Charles the Bold (1433–77).[1] This essay uses a number of selected examples to investigate the significance of the Burgundian cultural legacy for individual members of the House of Habsburg.

Maximilian's father, Frederick III (1415–93), had already called upon the Leiden-born sculptor Nicolaus Gerhaert, who had settled in Strasbourg. Gerhaert came to Vienna in 1467 at Frederick's express wish, to produce a marble tomb for the Emperor.[2] Maximilian I made use of Netherlandish art and culture in a different way to his daughter, Margaret of Austria (1480–1530) and to his grandchildren, especially Charles V (1500–58) and Mary of Hungary. For some members of the family, the Burgundian heritage played a minor role within their own cultural policy. The patronage of Philip the Handsome (1478–1506), who died young, has yet to be examined in any detail. His second son, the future Emperor Ferdinand I (1503–64), was raised in Spain and only spent a brief period in the Burgundian Netherlands, beginning in 1518, before marrying Anne of Hungary in 1521. Ferdinand assumed the administration of the Habsburg ancestral territories and was elected King of the Romans in 1531. Ferdinand does not, therefore, appear to have set much store by his Burgundian heritage. Margaret of Austria, by contrast, played a key role during her period as Governor-General and Regent of the Netherlands, which ended in 1530. Consequently, her contribution to the preservation, dissemination and development of Burgundian culture occupies a prominent place in this essay.

Emperor Maximilian and Burgundy

Maximilian, an ambitious son of the 'Casa de Austria', placed a great deal of importance on his marriage to the sole heiress to the Burgundian territories. It was a judicious move that enabled the future Emperor to add a politically and economically powerful region to his own birthright. Burgundy was, moreover, one of Europe's leading cultural centres. The marital alliance with the House of Burgundy enabled the rising Habsburg empire and the House of Austria to enhance their international esteem.

Maximilian made constant reference to his match with Mary of Burgundy in his artistic projects. The marriage featured centrally, for instance, in the *Triumphal Arch* – a giant woodcut produced in Albrecht Dürer's workshop. The accompanying text by Maximilian's court historian, Johannes Stabius, refers explicitly to the peaceful territorial gain on behalf of future generations: 'Let it be clearly understood / He took a princess in wedlock / The daughter and heir of Burgundy / And used this as a means to / Make his children heirs / To a greater realm through peace and arms alike.'[3] Maximilian immediately appropriated the symbols and emblems of his newly acquired territories, in order to lend additional visual expression to his claim to power. The chain of the Order of the Golden Fleece, the cross of Saint Andrew and the Burgundian steel-and-flint motif were given a central position on the aforementioned triumphal arch. For the Holy Roman Emperor they became key elements of how he conceived himself and his role.[4]

The merging of the Houses of Austria and Burgundy was dealt with in even greater detail in the *Great Triumphal Chariot* of Emperor Maximilian, another oversized (57-metre long), multi-block woodcut depicting an imaginary procession.[5] The small carriage offers a courtly and elegant representation of Maximilian's marriage to the Burgundian heiress. It is led by flag-bearers and musicians representing Austria and Burgundy: 42 horsemen carrying banners which symbolize the various Austrian territories are followed by 30 horsemen with banners referring to the Burgundian territories.[6] Maximilian personally ordered that the Burgundian horsemen ought not to be dressed in armour, but in fine clothes and costly chains, so as to represent the splendour and wealth of the legendary Burgundian court. It is evident from the introductory text that Maximilian was anxious to present himself publicly as an equal partner to Mary.[7] The text on the woodcut reads: 'The noble House of Austria / how it compares to Burgundy / Those who want to learn more about this matter / the following

fig. 204
Jan van Eyck
The Virgin and Child at the Fountain
Koninklijk Museum voor Schone Kunsten, Antwerp (see cat. 26)

coats of arms will tell / which Emperor Maximilian has already merged by marriage.' Maximilian turned to the theme of his Burgundian marriage on a third occasion, too, in his own allegorical and autobiographical romance, *Theuerdank*.[8]

Although he was fully aware of the political importance of his dynastic alliance, he only exploited its artistic potential to a limited degree. Following Mary's premature death in 1482, he fought to have himself appointed regent for his son Philip, who was still a minor, and to defend his family's political claims. Maximilian rarely spent extended periods of time in one place within the Burgundian Netherlands and was only reluctantly accepted as Governor by the Estates General. In reality, therefore, the Emperor remained an outsider in this part of his realm.[9]

When he began to develop his artistic projects in the years after 1500, he entrusted the execution of his ideas almost exclusively to artists from his German-speaking territories. Painters like Jörg Kölderer, Albrecht Dürer, Albrecht Altdorfer, Lucas Cranach, Hans Baldung and Hans Burgkmair were given the task of translating his artistic vision into reality. The proverbial exception to the rule was a Netherlandish painter referred to as 'Jorigen Delfs', who was active in Vienna in 1500 and whom we know only from the court accounts.[10] The artist from Delft may have helped design the stained-glass windows for Saint George's Church in Wiener Neustadt.[11]

Bernhard Strigel from Memmingen was Maximilian's favourite portrait painter for many years, during which time Strigel and his assistants produced official likenesses of the Habsburg prince, who was elected King of the Romans in 1486 and Emperor in 1508.[12] The small panel by the Netherlandish artist Joos van Cleve (Kunsthistorisches Museum, Vienna) is an exception within the extensive group of imperial portraits. Maximilian had Van Cleve paint his portrait around 1508–9, during a visit to the Netherlands.[13] For the Emperor's likeness, the sought-after portraitist, who was probably working in Bruges at the time,[14] adhered to the conventions of Burgundian portraiture. By foreshortening his left arm and by resting the fingers of his right hand on the lower edge of the frame, the borderline between the pictorial space and the real world is blurred. Maximilian is shown wearing a loosely cut brocade coat with a fur collar. In other words, he is not portrayed as a warrior, but as an elegantly dressed statesman. Van Cleve's portrait makes no reference to Maximilian's newly acquired status as Holy Roman Emperor, but solely to his honorary Burgundian title – his membership of the Order of the Golden Fleece. The painting may have been done expressly for a Netherlandish audience, as Margaret of Austria owned two versions of Van Cleve's portrait. The Viennese version, which includes two carnations, was kept in Margaret's *studiolo* in Mechelen (Malines),[15] while the portrait of Maximilian holding a scroll was hung in her official portrait gallery.[16] The latter type was also used shortly afterwards as the model for Maximilian's portrait in the Flemish manuscript with the 'Statutes of the Order of the Golden Fleece', in which each head of the Order is portrayed in a full-page miniature with floral border (fig. 205).[17]

Netherlandish music manuscripts as a cultural export product

The only area in which Maximilian turned frequently and willingly to the achievements of Flemish masters was that of illuminated manuscripts. He owned, for instance, a high-quality Latin and Dutch prayerbook, which was produced in Ghent or Bruges in 1486–87 (Österreichische Nationalbibliothek, Vienna, Cod. Vindob. 1907). Folio 61v features a full-length portrait of Maximilian as King of the Romans kneeling before Saint Sebastian in armour. The anonymous painter responsible for the codex is referred to by art historians as the 'Master of the First Prayerbook of Maximilian' and was the most productive pupil of the Master of Mary of Burgundy.[18] That places him in the circle of book illuminators that had already been active for some years on behalf of the Burgundians.

The small Book of Hours of Mary of Burgundy and Maximilian (Staatliche Museen, Berlin, Kupferstichkabinett, Ms. 78B12) is also of special interest in this context. Following Mary's death, Maximilian gave the richly illuminated manuscript, made in Ghent or Bruges in around 1480 for the newly wed couple, to their daughter, Margaret of Austria.[19]

Flemish manuscripts containing religious music

fig. 205
Simon Bening and workshop
Maximilian I as Grand Master of the Order of the Golden Fleece
Miniature from the 'Statutes of the Order of the Golden Fleece'.
Österreichische Nationalbibliothek, Vienna, Cod. Vindob. 2606, fol. 76v

were favoured diplomatic gifts for high-ranking individuals such as Pope Leo X, Pope Julius II, King Henry VIII and Elector Frederick the Wise.[20] Both the polyphonic music they contained and the sumptuous, historiated initials painted by Flemish illuminators were viewed throughout Europe as masterpieces of the art of the Burgundian Netherlands.[21] Maximilian promoted contemporary music and had his own royal chapel. The Emperor owned a number of Flemish music manuscripts from Mary of Burgundy's homeland and occasionally presented valuable codices to close relatives.[22] In 1511, for instance, he ordered an illuminated missal – which was not completed until around 1515–16 – for either his daughter Margaret or his grandson Charles.[23] Virtually all the members of the immediate imperial family owned manuscripts of this kind – Philip the Handsome and Joan of Castile, (fig. 206), Margaret of Austria, Charles V, Ferdinand I and Anne of Bohemia, Catharine of Austria and João III of Portugal.[24] The Nuremberg-born composer and calligrapher Petrus Alamire (Peter Imhoff) and his workshop played a key role in the production of these costly music manuscripts. Alamire entered the service of the young Archduke Charles in 1508 and joined the latter's chapel in Mechelen. The manuscripts were illuminated by anonymous artists of the Ghent-Bruges school.[25]

The example of Flemish music manuscripts provides an especially clear illustration of the Habsburg network through which the dissemination of Netherlandish cultural products was promoted. The widespread network of dynastic relationships thus functioned as an efficient system of distribution for Netherlandish manuscripts, tapestries and paintings. This phenomenon did not arise with the Habsburgs, however, but represented the continuation of an international cultural exchange that began no later than the marriage of Philip the Good and Isabella of Portugal.

Margaret of Austria and the Burgundian legacy

In many respects, Margaret of Austria played a more decisive role in the preservation and nurturing of the Burgundian legacy than her father did. There were differences of emphasis, in that she was not concerned solely with protecting her family's dynastic interests. Margaret was well aware that Burgundian artefacts were collected throughout Europe because of their high artistic value and she developed a certain feel for the achievements of such artists as Jan van Eyck, Michel Sittow and Jan Gossaert.

The early death of Philip the Handsome on 25 September 1506 left her as the sole adult descendant of the House of Burgundy. Charles – the eldest son of Philip and Joan – was only six years old. To the people of the Low Countries, Margaret, as the daughter of Mary of Burgundy, was a *princesse naturelle*. Unlike Maximilian, she did not face any resistance to her appointment as Regent of the Burgundian Netherlands.[26] Against this background, Margaret was able to create a stately residence for herself in Mechelen, from which she governed the territory for which she was responsible.[27] However, her court – the 'Hof van Savoyen' as it was known – functioned as more than simply the administrative centre for the Burgundian Netherlands between 1506 and 1530. Under Margaret's influence, it became a focal point of cultural and intellectual life, at which a variety of European influences converged. This development was also promoted in the early years of her regency by the fact that the youthful Archduke Charles and three of his sisters lived in close proximity to Margaret. Her status as foster mother to the young Habsburgs gave Margaret and her court an important role in passing on Burgundian family traditions.

Margaret's large art collection and extensive library clearly illustrate the value that the Regent placed on Netherlandish art and culture, and their crucial importance to her identity and self-perception as a Burgundian princess.[28] Margaret of Austria inherited a substantial proportion of the Burgundian patrimony and kept numerous manuscripts and art objects at her residence in Mechelen. In the course of her regency, she acquired additional works of Early Netherlandish art and literature, bestowed commissions on leading artists from the Low Countries and thus did much to promote contemporary culture in her region. Margaret of Austria did not, however, see herself solely as the inheritor of the Burgundian tradition, she also acted as a mediator between the different cultural circles belonging to the expanding Habsburg empire. She was ideally suited to this role, as the same traditions had come together harmoniously in her own life.[29]

The circumstances of her birth made her a natural link between the Houses of Austria and Burgundy. Her first marriage to Juan of Castile (1478–97) meant that she, like her late brother, had close links to the Spanish dynasty. The Spanish kingdom was of growing importance to the Habsburgs and ultimately passed into their hands, in the shape of Margaret's nephew Charles, on the death of King Ferdinand of Aragon (1452–1516). It is not surprising, therefore, that her collection included many valuable objects that had come from Spain – either items of Spanish origin or works of art produced by Flemish and German artists at the Spanish court. Her marriage to Philibert II of Savoy (1475/80–1504) reintroduced Margaret to French courtly culture and brought her into closer contact with the artistic achievements of northern Italy. Italian art may only have featured to a relatively limited extent in Margaret's collection, but it nevertheless played a very important role. The appointment of the Venetian artist Jacopo de' Barbari (c. 1460/70–1516) as the Regent's first court painter illustrates her interest in Italian culture. Family connections played a part once again, as de' Barbari had briefly been employed by her father. Moreover, Maximilian's second marriage to Bianca Maria Sforza (d. 1510) had linked him to the Duchy of Milan, which provided Margaret with further northern Italian connections.

There was no conflict between Margaret's desire to preserve Burgundian traditions and this pursuit of internationalism. Her position as regent and guardian of the imperial children meant that the Burgundian legacy constituted the most important element within the broad spectrum of European cultural possessions which the Governor-General of the Netherlands presented to visitors to her Mechelen court. In the next section, we will investigate which Burgundian works of art Margaret possessed and how she displayed these treasures at her residence.

Three artistic fields are important when discussing this issue – panel painting, book illumination and textile art (although the Regent owned a great deal of embroidery and tapestries, few of these have survived and so this type of work will not be discussed here).[30]

Many of the sculptures which Margaret owned were executed by Conrat Meit, her Worms-born court sculptor. As far as panel painting is concerned, two groups of objects are of special interest – portraits of the Burgundian family and paintings by celebrated Netherlandish masters.

Dynastic family portraits

It is evident from the inventories of her household prepared in 1516 and 1523/24 that Margaret owned many fifteenth-century portraits, a substantial proportion of which were family inheritances. The Regent displayed these paintings at two locations within her private apartments, where they testified to her Burgundian origins. She instituted a dynastic portrait gallery in one of her two large living-rooms – the *première chambre à chemynée*. This 'first room with a fireplace' was notable for both its size and its systematic organization. The pictorial programme, which focused on the political stature of Emperor Charles V and his family, gave an important place to the Dukes of Burgundy, as well as to the Emperor's Habsburg and Spanish relatives and forebears.[31] The presence of John the Fearless, Philip the Good, Isabella of Portugal and Charles the Bold legitimized Charles' claim to the Burgundian Netherlands. The same thematic group also included a portrait of Wenceslas of Luxembourg, who inherited the Duchy of Brabant through his marriage to Joan of Brabant. When the couple died childless, Brabant passed to Anthony of Burgundy, John the Fearless' brother.[32] Some of the paintings were the work of Rogier van der Weyden who, together with his workshop, produced many official portraits for the Burgundian ducal family. The portrait of Duke Charles the Bold is attributed to the Brussels municipal painter ('*par la main de Rogier*') in the Mechelen inventory of 1516.[33]

Family portraits and 'memoria'

In addition to the paintings in the dynastic portrait gallery, Margaret owned a number of more intimate portraits and devotional pictures featuring her Burgundian relatives. She kept these works in the

fig. 207
Pieter van Coninxloo
Philip the Handsome and
Margaret of Austria
National Gallery, London

seconde chambre à chemynée and the adjoining *petit cabinet*, which functioned as the Regent's state bedchamber and *studiolo*.

The group of Burgundian devotional works included a diptych with Philip the Good praying before the Virgin Mary, a diptych with Charles the Bold in a similar pose, an ivory triptych with Philip the Good and Charles the Bold before the Passion of Christ and a small diptych with Charles v and his aunt Margaret before a Madonna icon. The painting of Philip with the Virgin was described in the following terms in 1516: '*ung autre tableau de Nostre-Dame et du duc Philippe qui est venu de Maillardet, couvert de satin brouché gris et ayant fermaulx d'argent doré et bordé de velours vert, fait de la main de Johannes*' ('another painting of Our Lady with Duke Philip, which has come from Maillardet, covered in grey satin and with silver gilt clasps, bordered with green velvet, made by Johannes'). The diptych with Charles v, meanwhile, was summed up in 1523/24 as '*Item, ung aultre petit tableau de N[otre] Dame en chief ou est la representation de l'empereur moderne et de Madame à genoux, adorant ladite ymaige, dessus ung blason aux armes d'Espaigne et de Bourgogne et quatre blasons es quatre coins*' ('Item, another small painting of the head of Our Lady with the Emperor and Madame kneeling in adoration, with the arms of Spain and Burgundy on top and four escutcheons in the corners').[34]

In her bedchamber, Margaret kept a double portrait of herself and her brother Philip the Handsome, which was produced for the marriage negotiations with the Spanish ruling house around 1494 (fig. 207).[35] Her *studiolo* also contained a painted diptych with Charles the Bold and his mother, Isabella of Portugal, and a small but precious panel in gold enamel showing Duke Jean de Berry who, as Philip the Bold's brother, could be placed among the wider forebears of the House of Burgundy.[36] Especially noteworthy is the equestrian portrait of her mother, Mary of Burgundy (1457–82), which Margaret kept in a carved oak casket ('*Une chasse de bois de chasne … et dedens la representacion de madame Marie de Bourgogne, que dieu pardoint, mere de Madame, estant sus ung cheval …*').[37] Margaret kept this one image of her mother, who died prematurely, in the personal surroundings of her bedchamber rather than in the official portrait gallery.

In her bedchamber and *studiolo*, the Regent kept a number of very precious and often small-scale images that were intended for close viewing. Family-related devotional works of this kind were kept in the same intimate space as most of Margaret's other religious art. Her *seconde chambre à chemynée* fulfilled a series of different functions. Among other things, Margaret used her state bedchamber, in which a private altar and *prie-dieu* were installed, as her personal place of worship.[38] It is likely, therefore, that the diptychs and triptychs mentioned above served a religious purpose. Margaret regularly endowed masses to be said for her dead relatives, some of them at the neighbouring Church of Saint Peter, and it is not surprising that she would have wanted to surround herself with the same people in her private prayers.

The examples presented here make it clear that family portraits fulfilled two principal roles within Margaret's residence. The ones in the portrait gallery in the *première chambre* functioned as a kind of family tree. Like the chronicles and genealogies of the House of Burgundy[39] that Margaret kept in her library, the portraits were intended to express the political legacy of the Dukes of Burgundy. Within her bedchamber, however, to which only a handful of privileged individuals had access, the family portraits served a commemorative purpose that went beyond purely dynastic considerations.

Art and its value

In the course of her regency, Margaret earned a reputation as a discerning patron of the arts and an enthusiastic collector. Through her grand collection of sculpture, paintings, tapestries and *objets d'art*, Margaret bestowed on her Mechelen residence a status worthy of a Burgundian princess. Like the Dukes of Burgundy before her, Margaret owned an extensive and well-stocked library.[40] Artists, diplomats and scholars all visited the 'Hof van Savoyen', and, knowing of her pronounced interest in art objects, they regularly presented her with paintings and artfully designed and decorated furniture. By displaying her forebears' art collection at her residence, she was at once able to refer to her Burgundian roots and to place her own activities as a connoisseur within the tradition of courtly patronage. Margaret's collection included several key works of Early Netherlandish painting, which she acquired by inheritance, purchase or in the form of gifts. They are very important for what they tell us about the Regent's passion for the art of her region. It would be wrong, however, to interpret her love of collecting simply as an exaggerated focus on the significance of Burgundian art or the glorification of her ancestral history. Margaret's interest in local culture took in both historical and contemporary developments. It was recently discovered, for instance, that she was kept closely informed of the excavation of a Roman tomb in her territory by Jean Lemaire de Belges.[41]

Margaret's collection of Netherlandish paintings stood out for its high quality and its diversity. Although the artist's name was not always given in the inventories, as a result of which many of the painters responsible for works listed there remain anonymous, we know, for instance, that she owned several paintings by Jan van Eyck and Rogier van der Weyden, both of whom had worked for Philip the Good. Van Eyck, who was celebrated and admired throughout Europe by 1500, had been the favourite court painter of Margaret's great-grandfather.[42] She owned his double portrait of *Giovanni Arnolfini and His Wife* (fig. 127),[43] the portrait of a young Portuguese woman and the *Virgin and Child at the Fountain* (fig. 204).[44] Both the Arnolfini portrait and the *Tüchlein* (canvas painting) of the '*belle portugalaise*', were presented to the Regent of the Netherlands by the Spanish-born court official Diego de Guevara, who was employed by the House of Habsburg. In addition to the portraits mentioned earlier, Margaret owned a 'Holy Trinity' by Rogier van der Weyden and a diptych containing a 'Crucifixion and Mass of Saint Gregory'.[45] It has been suggested that Margaret inherited these works, as Philip the Good was known for his special devotion to the Trinity.[46]

Further fifteenth-century works in her collection included a 'Virgin and Child' by Dieric Bouts;[47] a 'Saint Anthony' by Hieronymus Bosch;[48] a 'triptych with the *Pietà* and Saints' by Petrus Christus;[49] a triptych with a 'Madonna and Saints' by Hans Memling;[50] another *Pietà* triptych, this time with angels, also attributed to Hans Memling;[51] a miniature

fig. 208
Jan van Eyck and workshop
The Virgin and Child at the Fountain
Koninklijk Kabinet van Schilderijen
'Mauritshuis', The Hague. On loan
from Rob Noortman, Maastricht
(see cat. 27)

fig. 209
Michel Sittow
King Christian II of Denmark
Statens Museum for Kunst,
Copenhagen (see cat. 57)

fig. 210
Jan Mostaert
Ecce Homo
Kunsthalle Hamburg

of the Virgin by a painter called 'Sandres' – possibly Sanders (Alexander) Bening[52] – and a 'Lucretia' by the Master of the Holy Blood from Bruges.[53]

In addition to these Early Netherlandish paintings, Margaret owned many works produced in the early sixteenth century. Her Netherlandish court painters, Bernard van Orley, Gerard Horenbout and Jan Vermeyen, provided her with numerous likenesses to complete her collection of portraits. In 1522, Margaret purchased a portrait of the Habsburg ally Christian II of Denmark, done by Gerard Horenbout.[54] Bernard van Orley produced not only paintings and tapestry designs for her personal collection, but works for monastic foundations and diplomatic gifts, too.

In addition to the work of her court painters – only a brief glimpse of which has been provided here – the Regent of the Netherlands also possessed a great many works by contemporary Netherlandish artists.

The following paintings can be attributed to specific masters – a portrait and two devotional works by Jan Mostaert (fig. 210),[55] a battle scene by Joachim Patinir,[56] the aforementioned portrait by Joos van Cleve, a *Portrait of the Artist and His Wife* by the Master of Frankfurt, who was active in Antwerp,[57] and another double portrait and a mythological scene by Jan Gossaert.

Gossaert's paintings were among the most progressive in Margaret's collection, in terms of both iconography and style. They were given to her some time after 1524. The Regent's library housed a large panel painting with a highly unconventional representation of Christian II's court dwarves, a gift from the Danish King. The two courtiers were shown in the manner of Adam and Eve, naked, in the open air and the woman holding an apple.[58] Margaret's garden cabinet contained a small painting by Gossaert, which was displayed along with coral, sea-shells, statuettes and other curiosities.[59] The theme of the painting was *Hermaphroditus and Salmacis* (fig. 211), who, following a furious struggle, metamorphose into a hermaphrodite.[60]

Whereas the Burgundian paintings and manuscripts in the portrait gallery and library primarily served dynastic purposes, the inherent artistic value of Margaret's collection is more apparent from the work displayed in her private quarters. The highest concentration of celebrated paintings was to be found in the *seconde chambre* and the *petit cabinet*. This view is supported by the discriminating quality judgments made in the inventories of her collection.[61] Some 38 paintings and a woven portrait of the Regent hanging on the walls of Margaret's bedchamber are listed under the heading '*riches tableaux de painctures et aultres*'. She kept a further 47 *objets d'art* in a number of wooden cupboards. The following Netherlandish works were rated especially highly: Van Eyck's Arnolfini double portrait ('*fort exquis*') and his *Virgin and Child by the Fountain* ('*fort antique*'), Sittow's *Virgin Reading* ('*fort bien fete*'), the portrait of an old man ('*exquis*'), the portrait of a Spaniard ('*bon tableau*'), the diptych with Charles the Bold ('*riche et fort exquis*'), the tapestry portrait of the Regent ('*riche*') and the paintings by Juan de Flandes ('*bonne, painctures esquises*').

Flemish artists in Spanish and Habsburg service

We will round off this essay by taking a closer look at a group of Netherlandish paintings that were produced in Spain and later came into the possession of Margaret of Austria. The Regent owned several works by the painter Michel Sittow, whom she rated very highly. Having completed his training in Bruges, Sittow was employed by Isabella of Castile for over ten years and completed a number of commissions in England and the Netherlands after 1500. He made the acquaintance of the young Margaret in 1497 at the Spanish court, where he painted a portrait of the newly married couple as Saint Margaret and Saint John.[62] In addition to that diptych, Margaret also owned a small devotional painting by Sittow showing the *Virgin and the Sleeping Child*, which she referred to fondly as '*ma mignonne*' ('my favourite').[63] She acquired two further paintings following the death of her mother-in-law, Isabella of Castile – an *Ascension of Christ* and an *Assumption of the Virgin*.[64] Margaret had these two exquisite paintings combined to form a precious diptych with silver clasps (figs 212–213),

fig. 211
Jan Gossaert
Hermaphroditus and Salmacis
Museum Boijmans Van Beuningen,
Rotterdam

fig. 212
Michel Sittow
Ascension of Christ
Private collection, United Kingdom

fig. 213
Michel Sittow
Assumption of the Virgin
National Gallery of Art,
Washington, DC. Ailsa Mellon
Bruce Fund

which she kept in her bedchamber, along with the other works by Sittow.

The Regent rated the work of the Netherlandish master Juan de Flandes equally highly. Like Sittow, he had been employed at the court of Isabella.[65] Following Isabella's death, Margaret inherited 32 individual panels of an unfinished polyptych (1496–1504), which Juan de Flandes had produced for the King of Spain, together with Sittow and another painter (figs 175, 215–218). She kept the unframed panels in a wooden case and showed them to visitors with an interest in art. In 1527, Margaret had twenty of the paintings combined to form a large diptych with a costly silver frame. She displayed this masterpiece of Netherlandish art in the *riche cabinet* – a small but lavishly appointed reception room on the first floor of her residence.[66]

It was in this period that Spain and the Low Countries were joined together through the marriage of Philip and Joan and the succession of their son Charles. Over the years, Charles V increasingly shifted his seat of government to Spain, leaving relatives to govern the Netherlands and Austria. Margaret, too, contributed to the political unification of Spain and

the Netherlands, as reflected in the furnishing of her residence. The diptych by Juan de Flandes, for instance, contained numerous references to the Spanish royal family, such as portraits-in-disguise, coats of arms and mottoes, as well as a discreet reference to Margaret's marriage to Juan. The Regent's audience chamber, meanwhile, contained a valuable table, decorated with coats of arms and silver ornaments, which also came from Spain. Margaret's Spanish furniture, heraldic tapestries and paintings enabled her to stress the interweaving of the Burgundian and Iberian elements of the Habsburg empire.

In their capacity as 'cultural ambassadors', artists like Sittow and de Flandes made a vital contribution to the integration of that huge empire. Having received their training in the Netherlands, they lived for a time at the Spanish court, just as the dynastic links between the two kingdoms were being forged in earnest. The Kings of Spain had long been attracted to Burgundian art, causing them to import a great many Netherlandish paintings to Spain. In the final decade of the fifteenth century, Netherlandish artists assumed a leading role at Isabella and Ferdinand's court and exerted a direct influence over the cultural life of the Spanish high nobility.[67] Members of the Spanish court had Juan de Flandes and Michel Sittow paint their portraits in the tradition of Dukes Philip the Good and Charles the Bold.

Isabella's polyptych on which both Sittow and de Flandes worked is a particularly interesting example, as it perfectly illustrates the mobility of both people and works of art. The Catholic Queen commissioned the work in Spain and Margaret, as a Spanish princess, witnessed its creation. Years later, Margaret acquired a series of paintings from her late mother-in-law's estate and had them brought to her residence. She then had two functional diptychs with silver frames made from the group of panels. After the Regent's own death, Charles V decided to send the larger of the two back to Spain,[68] where parts of it can still be seen today in the royal collection at the Palacio Real in Madrid (figs 215–218).

It is evident from these few examples that the leading cultural role that Burgundy played during the fifteenth century in a large part of Europe was perpetuated for several decades thereafter under the aegis of the Habsburgs. From Mechelen, Margaret of Austria cultivated the younger generation's awareness of the cultural achievements of the Burgundian realm. After her death, Mary of Hungary and Charles V continued the tradition in their own way, honouring the cultural legacy of their forefathers in both the Netherlands and Spain.

1 Erbe 1993, pp. 74ff.
2 Hertlein 1977, pp. 294–305.
3 Quoted after the original.
4 Wiesflecker 1971–86, I, pp. 228–47, 389–95.
5 Appuhn 1979, p. 183, ill. 57–90.
6 Ibid., p. 183.
7 Ibid., p. 182.
8 Innsbruck 1992, nos 124–25.
9 Wiesflecker 1971–86, I, pp. 113–81, 200–247.
10 Zimerman and Kreyczi 1885, Reg. 2318, p. X; 2331, p. XI and 2345, p. XII. I am grateful to Anja Eisenbeiß, Heidelberg, for bringing this source to my attention.
11 Jahrbuch des allerhöchsten Kaiserhauses 31 (1913/14), p. 253; Vienna 2000, no. 32, p. 187.
12 Otto 1964; Anja Eisenbeiß, Universität Heidelberg, is preparing a study on Strigel's portraits: 'Der Kunstbetrieb am Hofe Kaiser Maximilians I.'
13 Eichberger and Beaven 1995, pp. 230–34; Innsbruck 1992, nos 156, pp. 343–44; Hand 1978, pp. 58–59.
14 Hand 1996.
15 Michelant 1871, p. 92.
16 Ibid., p. 68.
17 Österreichische Nationalbibliothek, Vienna (ÖNB), Ms. 2606, fol. 76v; Thoss 1987, p. 95; Eichberger and Beaven 1995, p. 233.
18 ÖNB, Ms. 1907, see Thoss 1987, no. 67, pp. 104–6; Brinkman 1996. Cf. Innsbruck (1992), no. 1000, pp. 283–85.
19 For the Berlin Book of Hours, see Steenbock 1998, pp. 159–60.
20 Leo X: Biblioteca Apostolica Vaticana, Vatican City (BAV), C. 34, 36 and 160; Julius II: BAV, C. 23; Henry VIII: British Library, London, Royal 8 G VII; Frederick the Wise: Thüringer Universitäts- und Landesbibliothek, Jena, Ms. 2, 3, 4, 5, 7, 8, 9, 12, 20, 21, 22. See Kapp 1987, pp. 176–91.

21 Schreurs 2000.
22 ÖNB, Musiksammlung, S. M. 15495 and 15497; see Kapp 1987, pp. 185–86; Schreurs 2000, pp. 55ff.
23 Bonn and Vienna 2000, no. 31, p. 128; Schreurs 2000, pp. 68–71.
24 Philip: Bibliothèque Royale de Belgique, Brussels (BRB), Ms. 9126; BAV, Chigiana CVIII 234; ÖNB, Ms. 1783; Margaret: Stadsarchief, Mechelen; BRB, Mss. 228, 6428, 9085 and 11239; Charles: Biblioteca del Monestir, Montserrat, Mss. 766 and 773; ÖNB, Ms. 15496; Ferdinand: BAV, Pal. lat. 1976–79; Catherine: BRB, Ms. 15075. See Kapp 1987, pp. 176–91; Schreurs 2000.
25 Kapp 1987, pp. 128–45.
26 Blockmans and Prevenier 1998, pp. 206–34.
27 Eichberger 2000a.
28 Eichberger 2000b; Debae 1995.
29 Eichberger 2001, pp. 4–24.
30 Eichberger 1992, pp. 23–44.
31 Eichberger and Beaven 1995, p. 230.
32 Eisler 1989, no. 1, pp. 35–39.
33 Smith 1979, pp. 279–331.
34 Archives du Nord, Lille, B. 3507; Bibliothèque Nationale, Paris, Cinq Cents de Colbert 128, fol. 70v [1523/4]. Eichberger 1998, p. 301.
35 Campbell 1998, pp. 110–15.
36 Michelant 1871, pp. 93, 97.
37 Österreichisches Staatsarchiv, Vienna, no. 1176, fol. 19v [after 1524].
38 Archives Générales du Royaume, Brussels, AR 41297, fol. 212v [1518].
39 Michelant 1871, pp. 59–60.
40 Debae 1995, Eichberger 2002a.
41 Fontaine 2001 (forthcoming).
42 Smith 1979, pp. 215–39.
43 Campbell 1998, pp. 174–210.

44 See Duverger 1928, pp. 210–20.
45 Eichberger 1998, p. 306 and n. 67; Finot 1895, p. 210; Michelant 1871, p. 93.
46 Smith 1979, pp. 247–49.
47 Finot 1895, p. 210.
48 Ibid.; Michelant 1871, p. 87.
49 Lemaire, Henry and Rouzet 1991, no. 51, pp. 159–60.
50 Finot 1895, pp. 209–10; Michelant 1871, p. 87.
51 Finot 1895, pp. 209–10; Michelant 1871, p. 85; Lorentz and Reynaud 1994, pp. 10–17.
52 Finot 1895, p. 211; Michelant 1871, p. 95. For Alexander Bening, see Winkler 1942.
53 Michelant 1871, p. 83.
54 Eichberger and Beaven 1995, p. 232; Duverger 1930, pp. 85–86.
55 Duverger 1971, pp. 113–17; Eichberger and Beaven 1995, pp. 227; Eichberger 1998, p. 298 and n. 28.
56 Ghent 2000, nos 133–34.
57 Finot 1895, p. 210.
58 Österreichisches Staatsarchiv, Vienna, HLF 1176, fol. 97 [after 1524]; Michelant 1871, p. 58.
59 Eichberger 2002a.
60 Lammertse 1994, pp. 174–79; Eichberger 1996, pp. 259–79.
61 Eichberger 2002b, ch. 5.
62 Eichberger 1998, pp. 301–2.
63 See Finot 1895, p. 210; Michelant 1871, p. 87.
64 Hispania-Austria 1992, no. 53, pp. 233–35; Eichberger 1998, pp. 303–5.
65 Ishikawa 1989; Weniger 1996.
66 Eichberger 2002b, ch. 2.
67 Innsbruck 1992, no. 44, pp. 227–28; no. 191, pp. 376–77; nos 192 and 193, p. 379; no. 197, p. 383.
68 Ishikawa 1989, pp. 24–50.

fig. 214
Jean Hey (Master of Moulins?)
Margaret of Austria
The Metropolitan Museum of Art, New York. Robert Lehman Collection (see cat. 73)

figs 215–218
Juan de Flandes
Four panels from the *Altarpiece
of Isabella the Catholic*
*Raising of Lazarus; Feeding of the Five
Thousand; Christ and the Canaanite
Woman; Arrest of Christ*
Patrimonio Nacional, Palacio Real,
Madrid (see cat. 117)

'Lacking only breath'.
Italian Responses to Netherlandish Portraiture

Paula Nuttall

Among the many aspects of Netherlandish painting which aroused the admiration of fifteenth-century Italian commentators, portraiture was particularly acclaimed, primarily on account of its verisimilitude.[1] Fidelity to appearances was a prime artistic concern of the day, and especially desirable in the context of portraiture. Yet although in Italy the example of classical antiquity endorsed portraiture as an art form, until the last quarter of the century Italian painted portraiture lagged behind that of the North in terms of sophistication and realism, as the Italians readily acknowledged. Writing in Naples around 1456, Bartolomeo Fazio extolled the donor portraits in Jan van Eyck's 'Lomellini triptych' for their lifelikeness.[2] Similar views were expressed by Filarete and Francesco Florio, describing Fouquet's portrait of Pope Eugenius IV (d. 1447), perhaps the earliest Netherlandish-style portrait to be painted in Italy, and Vespasiano da Bisticci, who considered that Justus of Ghent's portrait of Federico da Montefeltro, Duke of Urbino, 'lacked only breath'.[3]

Eugenius IV himself owned works by Van Eyck,[4] and his choice of Fouquet to paint his portrait may reflect awareness of the relative sophistication of northern portraiture. Many of the works which Justus of Ghent produced for the court of Urbino in the 1470s were portraits, and it has been suggested that the Duchess of Milan sent her court painter Zanetto Bugatto to study with Rogier van der Weyden in 1460 in order to improve his skill in portraiture.[5]

Italian visitors to the Low Countries availed themselves of the opportunity to have their portraits painted there. One of the earliest to do so was Cardinal Niccolò Albergati, involved in diplomatic missions to the Burgundian court in the 1430s, who is generally identified as the sitter in Van Eyck's portrait of a Cardinal in Vienna (fig. 7).[6] An inventory of the Sforza library at Pesaro in 1500 lists three paintings by Rogier van der Weyden, which were presumably acquired by Alessandro Sforza, Lord of Pesaro, on his visit to the Netherlands in the 1450s: a portrait of Alessandro himself, another of the Duke of Burgundy, and a triptych of the *Crucifixion*, now in Brussels, which includes the portraits of Alessandro and two other members of his family (fig. 139).[7]

Portraits were also commissioned by the many Italian merchants resident in the Netherlands (and even as far afield as London, where a follower of Van Eyck painted the portrait of the Venetian consul Marco Barbarigo, now in the National Gallery).[8] They were probably the type of Netherlandish painting most popular with this group of patrons, whether independent portraits, or half-length devotional portrait diptychs and triptychs. The latter apparently enjoyed a particular vogue amongst members of the Florentine expatriate community in Bruges, exemplified by Memling's portraits of Tommaso Portinari and his wife Maria Bandini Baroncelli in the Metropolitan Museum, New York, which originally comprised a triptych with a central Virgin and Child, now lost.[9]

In addition to these standard, small-scale formats, Italian merchants had themselves painted in other portrait forms, of which the most remarkable is Van Eyck's full-length double portrait of the Lucchese merchant *Giovanni Arnolfini and His Wife* (fig. 127).[10] The Bolognese merchant Giacomo Loiani was painted together with his two successive wives in a devotional panel in the Courtauld Gallery, London, by the Master of the Baroncelli Portraits.[11] The portraits of Tommaso and Maria Portinari were included by Memling in another devotional image, the *Passion of Christ* in Turin.[12] Donor portraits were also painted on the wings of small-scale domestic triptychs such as Van Eyck's in Dresden (fig. 115), made for an unknown Genoese patron; Van Eyck's lost 'Lomellini triptych', another Genoese commission, must also have been of this type.[13] The Netherlandish formula of winged triptychs with donor portraits was also adopted in commissions for large altarpieces destined for Italian churches, such as Hugo van der Goes' 'Portinari triptych' (fig. 107), or Memling's *Last Judgment* (fig. 76), painted for Portinari's predecessor Angelo Tani.[14]

Such works, whether private images or public altarpieces, constituted distinctive souvenirs of the patron's career abroad. Interest in Netherlandish portraits was, however, also shown by those who had never set foot across the Alps. In Florence, one of the most precious paintings listed in Lorenzo de' Medici's inventory of 1492 was a portrait by Petrus Christus of a 'French lady'.[15] Her anonymity suggests that the portrait was acquired for its own sake, as an object

fig. 219
Jan van Eyck
Man in a Blue Chaperon
Muzeul National de Artă al
Romăniei, Bucharest (see cat. 18)

199

fig. 221
Hans Memling
Diptych of Maarten van Nieuwenhove
Memlingmuseum, Sint-
Janshospitaal, Bruges

HOC · OPVS · FIERI · FECIT · MARTINVS · Đ · NEWENHOVEN · ANNO · DM̃ · 1487 ·

fig. 220
Hans Memling
*Portrait of a Male Donor
(Francisco de Rojas?)*
Estate Fred Ziv, Cincinnati
(see cat. 47)

AN · VERO · ETATIS · SVE · : 23 · :

of beauty and interest. Housed in the *studiolo* of the Medici palace, it ranked as a collector's piece, like the other rare and precious objects kept there, which included Van Eyck's *Saint Jerome in His Study* (fig. 113).

Italian painters as well as patrons shared this enthusiasm for Netherlandish portraits. In Naples, Summonte relates how Colantonio reproduced a portrait of the Duke of Burgundy so faithfully that it was impossible to distinguish it from the original, thereby displaying his familiarity with a fashionable art form, as well as his virtuosity.[16] Increasingly, too, as examples of Early Netherlandish portraiture became known in Italy, painters began to adopt its formulas and techniques.

Van Eyck and his contemporaries had, by 1430, abandoned the profile view, fashionable throughout Europe in the fourteenth century (fig. 222), in favour of the three-quarters view, which reveals more of the face and shows the three-dimensional structure of the head and body; frequently, too, the hands were included (figs 221, 223). The realistic lighting, tonal modulations and rendering of textures permitted by the oil medium further contributed to producing an impression of verisimilitude, which was beyond the reach of Italians working in tempera and still faithful to the more hieratic, two-dimensional profile view. The effect of such portraits on Italian audiences is conveyed by the Pesaro inventory of 1500, which describes Van der Weyden's portraits of Alessandro Sforza and the Duke of Burgundy as '*in due occhi*' – 'two-eyed' – something which was evidently still regarded as noteworthy.[17]

The impression of reality might be further enhanced by the use of naturalistic settings – the corner of a room or a landscape background – and the introduction of devices such as fictive frames, window embrasures or parapets, as in Van Eyck's '*Leal Souvenir*' (fig. 223) or Memling's New York portraits of *Tommaso and Maria Portinari*, introducing deliberate spatial ambiguities which blurred the boundaries between the real and painted worlds.

Netherlandish portraits must have begun to reach Italy by the late 1430s, and occasional responses are seen in portraits of the mid-century, notably by Filippo Lippi, Castagno and Mantegna.[18] It was only in the last quarter of the century, however, that they made a significant impact on Italian portraiture, doubtless because more examples were now available.[19] From about 1470 the three-quarters view rapidly replaced the profile, which was retained apparently only when particular circumstances dictated its use. Additionally, Netherlandish-style portrait backgrounds were adopted, as were parapets and fictive frames, naturalistic lighting and textural effects – often facilitated by the use of a Netherlandish oil medium.

No Italian portraitist of this generation was impervious to this trend, although the type of Netherlandish model varied according to individual (or possibly regional) preference. Antonello da Messina favoured the dark backgrounds and strong directional lighting of Eyckian portraiture, as did many Venetian painters (figs 224, 225, 233, 234). The parapet, possibly of Eyckian derivation, was also favoured in the Veneto.[20] Giovanni Bellini often placed sitters against an expanse of blue sky (fig. 110), introducing a type of naturalistic setting which was perhaps a quicker and more economical alternative to a detailed landscape background. Florentine painters frequently favoured interior settings, and adopted the Netherlandish formula of depicting the sitter as if at a window, itself a continuation of the frame, as in Perugino's *Self-Portrait* (fig. 237), modelled on Memling's *Portrait of a Young Man* in the Lehman Collection, New York (fig. 239).[21] It was, however, the landscape background which enjoyed the greatest success, producing countless variants, including Leonardo's *Ginevra de' Benci* (fig. 230), Botticelli's *Youth with a Medal of Cosimo de' Medici* (Uffizi, Florence), and Cossa's *Man with a Ring* (Museo Thyssen-Bornemisza, Madrid). This is hardly surprising, given that the type was a speciality of Memling, who was particularly popular with Italian patrons in Bruges (fig. 227), and given Italian admiration of Netherlandish landscape painting in general.

Such was the impact of Netherlandish portraiture that in the last quarter of the century the independent portrait in Italy was completely transformed. By 1500 the lessons learned from Netherlandish portraiture had been thoroughly assimilated into the indigenous vocabulary, and are no longer so readily recognized, yet Leonardo's *Mona Lisa*, Raphael's Doni portraits (Uffizi, Florence) or Titian's *Man with a Blue Sleeve* (National Gallery, London) are inconceivable without the precedent of Netherlandish models. Although they employ the larger format, and *contrapposto* poses favoured by Italian portraitists in the new century, and are consequently more ample, more graceful and more animated, they are none the less the direct descendants of the portraits of Van Eyck and his contemporaries.

fig. 222
Pisanello
Lionello d'Este
Pinacoteca dell'Accademia Carrara,
Bergamo

fig. 223
Jan van Eyck
Portrait of a Man ('Leal Souvenir')
National Gallery, London

1 A more extensive discussion of Italian responses to Netherlandish portraiture will be found in my forthcoming book, *From Flanders to Florence: The Impact of Netherlandish Painting, 1430–1500* (Yale University Press, spring 2003).
2 Baxandall 1964, pp. 102–3.
3 Finoli and Grassi 1972, I, p. 265; Salmon 1855, p. 105.
4 Miglio 1975, p. 141 n. 31.
5 Campbell 1990, p. 149.
6 *Ibid.*, p. 170.
7 Mulazzani 1971, pp. 252–53.
8 Campbell 1998, pp. 224–27.
9 For the recently discovered inventory listing this work, see Waldman 2001, pp. 28–33; for a general discussion of Netherlandish portraits of Florentines, see Rohlmann 1994, pp. 85–90.
10 Campbell 1998, pp. 174–211.
11 Rohlmann 1997, pp. 95–99.
12 De Vos 1994, pp. 100–101; Rohlmann 1994, pp. 63–65.
13 Weiss 1956, pp. 1–15.
14 Rohlmann 1993, pp. 41–65.
15 Spallanzani and Gaeta Bertelà 1992, p. 52.
16 Nicolini 1925, p. 162.
17 Mulazzani 1971.
18 See Pope-Hennessy and Christiansen 1980, pp. 57–59; Campbell 1990, pp. 115, 232.
19 Campbell 1990, pp. 227–46.
20 Goffen 1999, pp. 122–30.
21 Campbell 1983, pp. 675–76.

fig. 224
Antonello da Messina
Portrait of a Man
Galleria Borghese, Rome

fig. 225
Antonello da Messina
Portrait of a Man
Museo Civico d'Arte Antica,
Palazzo Madama, Turin (see cat. 88)

fig. 226
Piero di Cosimo
Giuliano da Sangallo
and Francesco Giamberti
Rijksmuseum, Amsterdam
(see cat. 97)

fig. 228
Pietro Perugino
Francesco delle Opere
Galleria degli Uffizi, Florence
(see cat. 104)

fig. 227
Hans Memling
Man with a Roman Coin
(Bernardo Bembo?)
Koninklijk Museum voor Schone
Kunsten, Antwerp (see cat. 48)

fig. 229
Jan van Eyck
Margaret van Eyck
Stedelijke Musea,
Groeningemuseum, Bruges
(see cat. 25)

fig. 230
Leonardo da Vinci
Ginevra de' Benci
National Gallery of Art,
Washington, DC. Ailsa Mellon
Bruce Fund

fig. 231
Domenico Ghirlandaio
Portrait of a Young Woman
The Sterling and Francine Clark Art
Institute, Williamstown, Mass.

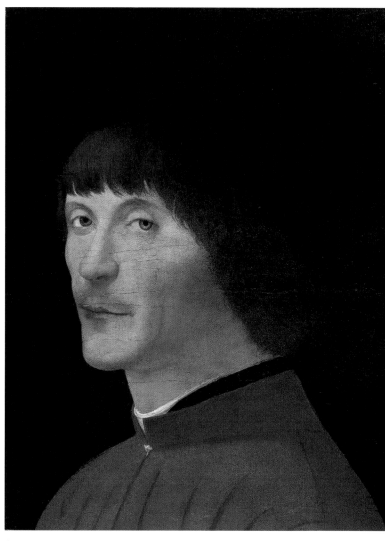

fig. 232
Petrus Christus
Portrait of a Man
Los Angeles County Museum
of Art. Mr and Mrs Allan Balch
Collection (see cat. 14)

fig. 233
Antonello da Messina
Portrait of a Man
Musei Civici, Pinacoteca
Malaspina, Pavia (see cat. 87)

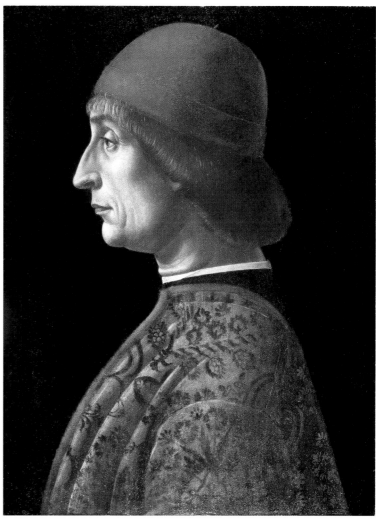

fig. 234
Antonello da Messina
Portrait of a Man
Museo Thyssen-Bornemisza,
Madrid

fig. 235
Vincenzo Foppa
Francesco Brivio
Museo Poldi-Pezzoli, Milan

fig. 236
Michel Sittow
Portrait of a Man
Koninklijk Kabinet van Schilderijen
'Mauritshuis', The Hague
(see cat. 56)

fig. 237
Pietro Perugino
Self-Portrait (?)
Galleria degli Uffizi, Florence

fig. 238
Hugo van der Goes
Portrait of a Man (fragment)
The Metropolitan Museum of Art,
New York. H. O. Havemeyer
Collection, Bequest of Mrs H. O.
Havemeyer, 1929

fig. 239
Hans Memling
Portrait of a Young Man
The Metropolitan Museum of Art,
New York. Robert Lehman
Collection (see cat. 49)

A New Look on the World.
The Invention of Landscape

Manfred Sellink

fig. 241
Master of Hoogstraten
Stigmatization of Saint Francis
Museo Nacional del Prado, Madrid
(see cat. 45)

The Neapolitan court scholar and chronicler Bartolomeo Fazio included four painters in his treatise *De viris illustribus* ('On Famous Men'), which he completed shortly before his death in 1457. This was unusual enough in itself, but even more so was the fact that of the four artists he chose – Gentile da Fabriano, Pisanello, Jan van Eyck and Rogier van der Weyden – two hailed from the Low Countries, providing clear evidence that the fame of the 'Flemish Primitives' had spread deep into Italy by as early as the mid-fifteenth century. Within the artistic quartet, Van Eyck was rated most highly – he 'is deemed the most important painter of our age' – and Fazio wrote admiringly of his brilliant painting technique and the breathtaking verisimilitude of his work. He also referred explicitly in his paean of praise to the handling of the landscape. The Italian – who only discussed works that he had studied in person, or of which he had a detailed description – noted, for instance, regarding the background of a panel with bathing women that was owned by Ottaviano della Carda: '[there are also] horses, minute figures of men, mountains, groves, hamlets and castles carried out with such skill you would believe one was fifty miles distant from another'.[1]

It is apparent from this that what Fazio especially admired was Jan van Eyck's ability to set all of this out so precisely and in such detail as the background to a larger composition. Although the painting of bathing women 'of unprecedented beauty' has sadly been lost, the landscapes in works like the 'Rolin Madonna' (fig. 13) and the centre panel of the Ghent altarpiece (figs 4–5) leave us in no doubt of what it was that Bartolomeo Fazio found so fascinating. Similar observations underpinned his praise of 'a circular map of the world, which he [Van Eyck] painted for Philip [the Good of Burgundy], ... which is held to be the most perfect work to be produced in our age. In it we make out not only the individual places and the position of the regions, it is even possible to measure the distance between them.'[2] Like Ambrogio Lorenzetti's 1345 *Mappamundi* in the Council Chamber at Siena's Palazzo Pubblico and a variety of other world maps from the fourteenth and fifteenth centuries, virtually all of which have since been lost, the painting ascribed to Van Eyck by Fazio (but see

Elena Parma's essay, p. 96) is likely to have been more than just a painted map and will have contained many decorative (landscape?) details. The public's steadily growing interest in geography and cosmography will have been another important stimulus to the rapid growth of the landscape as an autonomous genre in the sixteenth-century Netherlands.[3]

Things had yet to reach such a point, however, in the early fifteenth century. There were, of course, Netherlandish painters prior to Jan van Eyck who were capable of placing a composition in an attractive landscape – a skill displayed in particular by a number of illuminators and by Melchior Broederlam and the Master of Flémalle. Yet it is equally plain that Jan van Eyck and his immediate circle made substantial advances in the development of the landscape. The ability to tie all the landscape elements into a visually convincing unit is certainly their most important achievement. This is particularly apparent in the background landscapes of works like the *Stigmatization of Saint Francis* (figs 242, 243). The saint and his companion, who has nodded off, are placed convincingly in a barren, rocky setting. The desolate

fig. 240
Andrea del Verrocchio
Baptism of Christ
Galleria degli Uffizi, Florence

213

nature in the foreground gradually gives way to a more fruitful and attractive, hilly landscape, bounded by a river valley and a view of a distant city. Van Eyck's use of atmospheric perspective, a technique in which a foreground made up of brown tones gradually shifts to greens and finally to greyish blues in the background, would dominate landscape art for centuries to come. The perspective effect of his paintings, whether the main subject is situated inside or outside, is so strong that Fazio was convinced he must have been a very learned artist, especially when it came to geometry, on which the application of perspective is based. The Italian humanist was struck by the suggestive spatial construction and the virtuosity by which even the smallest landscape details remain legible – the same elements that continue to make Van Eyck's landscapes so attractive today.[4]

The 'discovery' of landscape as an attractive and defining pictorial motif can be dated in Flanders to the second quarter of the fifteenth century. In addition to Jan van Eyck, this is apparent in the work of his contemporary Rogier van der Weyden, not least in his *Saint Luke Drawing the Virgin*, numerous copies and variants of which have survived (fig. 250). The way in which the landscape is incorporated in this composition is strongly reminiscent of Van Eyck's aforementioned 'Rolin Madonna', for instance in the two small figures below the central arch, which draw the viewer's eye into the landscape. A more original work is Van der Weyden's *Entombment* in the Uffizi, Florence (fig. 97), in which a looming Golgotha dominates the background, with charmingly rendered vistas of the city of Jerusalem on either side. A similar landscape in a Rogier triptych prompted the Italian humanist Ciriaco d'Ancona to write that it was produced 'not by the artifice of human hands but by all-bearing nature herself'.[5]

As discussed at length elsewhere in this publication, works by Jan van Eyck, Rogier van der Weyden and their direct circles can be identified in Italy from the mid-1430s onwards, either in autograph form, or as workshop variants or copies. The landscape is indisputably one of the themes that most intrigued and inspired Italian artists. Van Eyck's landscape with Saint Francis – possibly the Turin version – must have been present in Italy from a fairly

early date as it plainly influenced artists such as Botticelli, Andrea del Verrocchio (fig. 240), Filippino Lippi and Domenico Ghirlandaio.[6] It is arguable whether or not Ghirlandaio's *Meeting of Christ and John the Baptist* in Berlin (fig. 247) literally quotes particular details from Van Eyck, but what cannot be disputed is the degree to which the conception and execution of the landscape are indebted to the Flemish master. There are also many documented borrowings by Italian artists from Van der Weyden's *Entombment*, varying from the straightforward copying of the entire landscape in the background to the reproduction of specific details.[7]

The development of the landscape as the decisive pictorial motif is plain in the work of subsequent generations of Early Netherlandish artists. One only has to leaf through a survey of Early Netherlandish art to see that landscape assumes an increasingly prominent place in the work of successive masters

fig. 242
Jan van Eyck
Stigmatization of Saint Francis
Galleria Sabauda, Turin (see cat. 28)

fig. 243
Jan van Eyck and/or workshop
Stigmatization of Saint Francis
Philadelphia Museum of Art.
The John G. Johnson Collection
(see cat. 29)

such as Petrus Christus, Dieric Bouts, Hugo van der Goes, Hans Memling, Geertgen tot Sint Jans, Hieronymus Bosch and Gerard David. The centre panel of the latter's *Baptism of Christ* (fig. 244) provides a perfect illustration. It is hardly surprising, then, that by the first half of the sixteenth century at the latest, landscape had become a distinct genre within Netherlandish painting. The frequently recounted story of landscape art in the Low Countries begins in earnest with the generation of Joachim Patinir and Herri met de Bles, following this impressive fifteenth-century prologue.

As noted already, it did not escape the Italians that landscape was one of the Flemings' most striking contributions to the renewal of art in the fifteenth century. Indeed, after Bartolomeo Fazio and Ciriaco d'Ancona, it became one of the *topoi* in Italian authors' characterization of the art of the *Fiamminghi*. We find the following passage, for instance, in the *Tractato di pictura* that the Florentine Francesco Lancillotti wrote in 1509: 'A certain attitude and discernment are required in order to paint landscapes from close by and far away. To my mind, these come more naturally to Flemings than to Italians.'[8] Lancillotti's view is surprisingly reminiscent of what Fazio wrote fifty years earlier regarding Jan van Eyck's ability to paint every detail so realistically and precisely, whether it was located in the foreground or deep in the background. As the sixteenth century progressed,

painters from the *Paesi bassi* would become even more closely associated with a penchant for landscapes.

For all the praise, however, and the undoubted appreciation of collectors all over Italy, there was still some occasional criticism. The most important factor in this respect is the fact that landscape occupied a relatively lowly position within the theory of art being developed in Italy in the sixteenth century. No less a figure than Michelangelo commented in this regard – if, that is, we are to believe his interlocutor Francisco de Holanda, who quotes the celebrated artist in his *Dialogos em Roma* (1548): '[The Flemish] paint *trapos* [canvases], [with] houses, vegetation in fields, shadows of trees, bridges and rivers, and they call them landscapes, which they dot with little figures. Yet in reality, all of that, even though some find it pretty, is done without reason or artistic sense, without harmony or sense of proportion, without the ability to select, without boldness and, finally, without content or eloquence.' In the same breath, he added that what his Flemish colleagues produced was fit only for women – especially very young and very old ones – for monks and nuns, and for one or two other groups, for which art was not, by definition, intended.[9] In that respect at least, history has proved Michelangelo wrong – admiration for the 'Flemish Primitives' steadily grew in intensity, especially since the epoch-making 1902 exhibition in Bruges, to become all but universal. ✑

1 Baxandall 1964, pp. 102–3.
2 *Ibid.*; see also Steppe 1983; Paviot 1991; Büttner 2000, pp. 72–74.
3 Gibson 1989; Den Bosch 2001.
4 Hockney 2002.
5 As quoted by Crowe and Cavalcaselle 1875, p. 411; see also Torresan 1981; Miedema 1973, pp. 408–11.
6 Rohlmann 1993; Rohlmann 1994, pp. 105–10; Luber 1998; Nuttall 2000.
7 Rohlmann 1993, pp. 243–44.
8 As quoted by Barocchi 1971, p. 745.
9 Venice 1999, p. 424 n. 9.

fig. 244
Gerard David
Baptism of Christ
Stedelijke Musea,
Groeningemuseum, Bruges
(see cat. 17)

fig. 245
Juan de Flandes
*Scenes from the Life of Saint John
the Baptist* ('Miraflores altarpiece',
reconstruction) (see cat. 116)

Birth and Naming of Saint John
The Cleveland Museum of Art

Saint John Preaching to the Multitude
Present whereabouts unknown

Baptism of Christ
Private collection, Madrid

Beheading of Saint John
Musée d'Art et d'Histoire, Geneva

Banquet of Herod
Museum Mayer van den Bergh,
Antwerp

fig. 247
Domenico Ghirlandaio
Meeting of Christ and John the Baptist
Staatliche Museen zu Berlin.
Gemäldegalerie

fig. 246
Rogier van der Weyden
Visitation
Museum der Bildenden Künste,
Leipzig

Van Eyck and the Invention of Oil Painting. Artistic Merits in Their Literary Mirror

Till-Holger Borchert and *Paul Huvenne*

The legend recounted by Vasari to the effect that Jan van Eyck was the inventor of oil painting is one of the eloquent Florentine's most original and doggedly persistent artists' anecdotes. It crops up in the life of Antonello da Messina, the joint lives of Domenico Veneziano and Andrea del Castagno and, in the second edition of the *Lives* of 1568, in the chapter 'De diversi artifici fiamminghi' ('Divers Flemings'). Van Eyck, so the story goes, carried out a number of experiments in the hope of producing an oil-based varnish. He then discovered that pigments, too, could be bound in oil, enabling them to retain a special luminosity. The jealously guarded 'invention' of *colorire a olio* established the Fleming's reputation. He subsequently entrusted the 'secret' to Rogier van der Weyden and Hans Memling, and to Antonello da Messina, who travelled North specifically for that purpose. According to Vasari, Antonello then brought '*il nuovo segreto … di Fiandra*' – the secret of oil painting – back to Italy.[1]

It was not until 1774, when Lessing discovered a copy of Theophilus Presbyter's twelfth-century *Schedula diversarum artium* in the library at Wolffenbüttel, that conclusive proof emerged that Vasari and the art historians who came after him were profoundly mistaken. Lessing realized that Theophilus already knew that pigments could be bound using pressed oil and that this fact could not, therefore, have been discovered by Van Eyck. He felt, however, that Vasari – who was, after all, a painter himself – would not have attributed such an *inventio* to Van Eyck unless there was a grain of truth in the story. He suspected, therefore, that although the Flemish artist did not invent oil painting as such, he may nevertheless have introduced some crucial refinement to the process – 'For it is rare that special fame is entirely groundless'.[2] Generations of art historians, from Raspe to Doerner, have since laboured in vain to solve the problem of Jan van Eyck's painting technique empirically.[3]

The rhetorical character and carefully conceived structure of Vasari's *Lives* and the *ad hoc* combination of literary models and *topoi* in the biographies also permit another approach.[4] The portrayal of the artist as an inventor is, of course, a *topos* already familiar from classical art theory, and one of which Vasari

himself presents several variations. But what precisely are the historical roots of the 'invention of oil painting', to what aspect of Van Eyck's work does the metaphor refer, and how is it related to visual experience? These issues can only be addressed by examining the written tradition regarding Jan van Eyck and his work in humanist correspondence and Italian art literature prior to Vasari.

The earliest surviving testimony regarding the literary reception of Early Netherlandish painting in Italy dates from 1449. In that year, the writer and humanist Ciriaco d'Ancona visited Ferrara, where Lionello d'Este proudly showed him a triptych by Rogier van der Weyden with a Deposition at its centre.[5] The Brussels-based Rogier was, so the learned Ciriaco tells us, the greatest painter of the time, '*post praeclarum illum brugiensem, picturae decus, Johannes*' ('after the famous Bruges painter Johannes, the glory of painting'). Van Eyck's paintings seemed to him to be more divine than human ('*potius divina dicam quam humana arte depictam*'), as the faces appeared to breathe or to be lifeless as appropriate. Every detail of the image, whether it be armour, architecture or flora, seemed not to have been created by human hand ('*non artificis manu hominis*') but by nature herself ('*quin et ab ipsa omniparente natura inibi genita*').[6]

Interestingly, since Van Eyck's fame had spread by the middle of the Quattrocento to the courts of northern Italy if not further south, Ciriaco was able to place him among the foremost painters, without ever having seen the artist's work with his own eyes. No less striking are the criteria by which Rogier's paintings are assessed – the brilliant painting technique is not mentioned, as Ciriaco, drawing on what were ultimately classical notions, considered the imitation of nature to be the highest standard within painting. The figures, he declared, seemed alive (or, indeed, dead) and every detail was true to life.

Remaining in the courtly milieu – this time in Naples – an extensive appreciation of Jan van Eyck and Rogier van der Weyden and several of their works can be found in Bartolomeo Fazio's *De viris illustribus* of 1456. Fazio, who was a native of Liguria, was historian to Alfonso v of Aragon, at whose court he had seen paintings by Jan van Eyck. He appears to have been well informed about the Netherlandish

fig. 248
Antonello da Messina
Virgin of the Annunciation
Galleria Regionale di Sicilia,
Palazzo Abatellis, Palermo

master, although it is not clear from where he derived this knowledge.[7] He too considered Van Eyck to be the pre-eminent painter of his time, though unlike Ciriaco, he focused on the artist's expert knowledge of geometry and other 'aids' to painting (*'literatum nonnihil doctus Geometriae, praesertim et earum artium quae ad picturae ornamentum accederent'*). With the assistance of classical texts – Pliny's *Naturalis Historia* is explicitly cited – Van Eyck supposedly discovered a great deal about the properties of colour (*'putaturque ob eam rem multa de colorem propritatibus invenisse quae ab antiquis tradita ex Plinii et aliorum auctorem lectione didicerat'*): only by resorting to the Classical Age had the Fleming been able to make certain technical discoveries regarding the art of painting.[8] This element is not, however, relevant to Fazio's appreciation of Van Eyck's paintings. In the case of the 'Lomellini triptych', which belonged to Alfonso's collection at the time, what the historian most admired was the brilliance with which Van Eyck appeared to transcend nature. Van Eyck's portrait of the donor, Battista Lomellini, only differed from the real thing, it was said, in that the likeness was mute. Turning to the painting of *Saint Jerome in His Study*, Fazio praised the realism with which Van Eyck rendered the individual books. He was also fascinated by the painter's brilliant illusionism when discussing the execution of a mirror in a lost bathing scene, which belonged at the time to the collection of Ottaviano della Carda.[9] Fazio, like Ciriaco, makes no reference to the technical features of Van Eyck's works, which evidently played a subordinate part in the reception of painting in the middle of the Quattrocento.

It is not until Filarete's *Trattato d'architettura* (c. 1464) that oil painting is explicitly linked to paintings by the *oltramontani*. The treatise on architecture, written at the Sforza court in Milan, mentions northern paintings in the section on the interior decoration of princely residences: '*Nella Magna si lavora bene in questa forma, massime da quello maestro Giovanni di Bruggia e maestro Ruggieri, i quali hanno adoperato ottimamente questi colori a olio*' ('In Germany they do good work of this kind, especially Master *Giovanni di Bruggia* and Master *Ruggieri*, who excelled in this oil painting technique').[10] Where did Filarete obtain this information? Perhaps it was Jean Fouquet who passed it on to the Italian in

Rome, although it is more likely, especially given the detailed knowledge he subsequently displays of binding agents and the range of possible manipulations, that Filarete learned about the technique from the Milanese court painter Zanetto Bugatto, who returned to the Sforza court in 1463, having studied under Rogier van der Weyden himself.[11] In fact, Filarete only touches on Netherlandish painting briefly when discussing Jean Fouquet's portrait of Pope Eugenius IV. Once again, it is the mimetic quality of northern painting that is praised, with Filarete describing the French painter as a '*buen maestro maxime a retrarre del naturale*'.[12]

There can be no doubt that Filarete was familiar with Leon Battista Alberti's *De re aedificatora* (1452) and that he drew on it for his *Trattato*. Tellingly, the scholar and architect Alberti, who was employed at the Mantuan court, referred to the invention of linseed oil (*'novum inventum oleo linaceo'*), without mentioning the Flemings.[13] Giovanni Santi, by contrast, writes in his rhymed chronicle of the Dukes of Urbino, which was produced around 1485, about '*il gran Ioannes, el discepol Ruggero*' ('the great Johannes [and] his pupil Rogier'). Raphael's father was familiar with Netherlandish painting through the work of Joos van Wassenhove (Justus of Ghent), although it is not clear whether the words '*arte e summo magistero di coloriere durno si excellenti / che han superato spesse volte il vero*' ('their art and superior mastery of colour were so outstanding / that they often surpassed nature') refer to the technical aspects of that painting or are merely a general expression of stylistic appreciation.[14]

On the other hand, Vespasiano da Bisticci's *Vite di uomini illustri del secolo XV* (1485) contains an explicit reference to the fact that Federico da Montefeltro sought to attract Flemish artists to his court in Urbino precisely because they were familiar with the technique of oil painting.[15] It was evidently realized that the celebrated mimetic qualities of Flemish painting, which had become so desirable, were closely related to certain specific painterly techniques. This know-how was either imported to Italy, as Federico sought to do, or else court artists like Giovanni di Giusto from Naples and Zanetto Bugatto from Milan were sent to the Burgundian Netherlands to be instructed in it. It was certainly a rare commodity in

fig. 251
Master of the Holy Blood
Saint Luke Painting the Virgin
Fogg Art Museum, Harvard
University Art Museums,
Cambridge, Mass. The John Witt
Randall Fund (see cat. 44)

fig. 252
Lancelot Blondeel
Saint Luke Painting the Virgin
Stedelijke Musea,
Groeningemuseum, Bruges
(see cat. 5)

Italy, which may help explain why the technique underpinning such costly paintings is mentioned with increasing frequency in a variety of documents. The inventory of Piero de' Medici, for instance, still described the Detroit *Saint Jerome* (fig. 113) as '*Una tavoletta di uno San Girolamo*', whereas the 1492 list defines it as a work by Jan van Eyck painted in oil ('*Una tavoletta di Fiandra suvi uno San Girolamo a studio… opera di maestro Giovanni di Bruggia, cholorita a olio…*').[16] The Venetian Marcantonio Michiel was equally conscientious when describing the Flemish paintings he had examined. In his *Notizie del disegno* – the notes he wrote between 1521 and 1543 in preparation for a history of Italian art that was never published – he wrote that he had seen in the house of Zuan Ram '*el ritratto de Rugerio da Burselles pittor antico celebre, in un quadretto de tavola a oglio*' ('the portrait by the famous master Rogier of Brussels, painted in oil on panel').[17]

Like Vasari, the publication of whose *Lives* appears to have rendered Michiel's project obsolete, the Venetian corresponded with scholars, who informed him about artists, their work and the development of art in their native regions. This is the context in which the Neapolitan Pietro Summonte wrote to Michiel in 1524 with information about art in Naples. Summonte's remarks are the most important source since Fazio on the presence of Netherlandish paintings at the Neapolitan court and provide additional information regarding the reception of Van Eyck's work by painters in Naples.[18] Unlike Vasari, who presents Van Eyck as the inventor of oil painting and declares him in this respect to be the teacher of Antonello da Messina, Summonte stresses that the latter was actually the pupil of '*Colantonio nostro neapolitano*' ('our Neapolitan master Colantonio'), whom he further describes as follows: '*La professione del Colantonio tutta era, sì come portava quel tempo, in lavoro di Fiandra e lo colorire di quel paese. Al che era tanto dedito che avea deliberato andarci. Ma il re Raniero le ritenne qua, con mostrarli ipso la pratica e la tempera di tal colorire*' ('As was customary at that time, Colantonio looked to the work of Flemish painters and to the use of colour emanating from that country. So devoted was he to them that he actually decided to move to Flanders, but King Raniero [*sic*] kept him here by showing him himself how to mix and use these colours').[19] In other words, a specifically Flemish art of *colouring* was established in Quattrocento Naples, prompting a desire on the part of local painters at that time to travel to the Netherlands to perfect their training. Colantonio, so Summonte tells us at any rate, was taught this Netherlandish colouring technique by René of Anjou, King of Naples, between 1438 and 1442 – that is to say, he learned it from Angevin court artists from the North, such as Barthélemy d'Eyck's stepfather, Pierre du Billant. Summonte's account is somewhat undermined by recent discoveries regarding Antonello da Messina's painting technique, which show that, despite his use of oil as a binding agent, his working methods otherwise had little in common with the transparent glazes used by Van Eyck.[20] But none the less Antonello's works demonstrate a true *emulation* of Netherlandish painting, which represents a remarkable parallel with Colantonio and artists active around René of Anjou, such as Barthélemy d'Eyck, the Master of the Aix Annunciation.

Vasari did, indeed, misinterpret the nature of the relationship with Flemish painting, which, in Antonello's case, rested solely on the visual effect of the colouring, while for Marcantonio Michiel, too, Antonello's *Saint Jerome* could have been painted by Van Eyck.[21] However, in ascribing the discovery of oil painting to the Fleming, Vasari ultimately appealed to an idea that was becoming increasingly widespread in Italy towards the end of the Quattrocento. According to this reading, the unique colourfulness of Early Netherlandish painting, identified with the name of Van Eyck, required that pigments and binding agents, which were not unfamiliar to Italian painters per se, were combined in a way that was hitherto unknown in Italy.[22] And, as it happened, it was not the ingredients but the recipe that played a crucial part in conveying the verisimilitude of Netherlandish art that was long coveted in Italy.

1 Vasari (Milanesi ed.), I, pp. 184–87; II, pp. 565–66.
2 Lessing 1974, VI, pp. 509–51.
3 Brinkman 1993, pp. 134–205; Roy 2000, pp. 97–100; White 2000, pp. 101–5.
4 Kris and Kurz 1980; Barolsky 1991; Barolsky 1992.
5 Dhanens 1995, p. 104; De Vos 1999, B31.
6 Dhanens 1995, p. 104.
7 Baxandall 1964, pp. 90–107; Baxandall 1971, pp. 98–111; for Fazio, see also Kristeller 1965;

Bentley 1987, pp. 100–108.
8 Preimesberger 1991; Preimesberger 1992; Belting and Kruse 1994, pp. 65–66.
9 Baxandall 1964, p. 103.
10 Filarete (Von Oettingen ed.), p. 641; Dhanens 1995, p. 112; see also Koster's essay in this book, pp. 89–90.
11 De Vos 1999, pp. 63–64.
12 Brinkman 1993, p. 28.
13 *Ibid.*
14 Dhanens 1995, p. 124; Rohlmann 1994, p. 120.

15 D'Ancona and Aeschlimann 1951, p. 209.
16 Müntz 1888, pp. 26, 78; Garzelli 1984, pp. 347–53; Rohlmann 1994, pp. 96–97.
17 Frimmel 1888, p. 104.
18 Nicolini 1925; Bologna 1977; Jolly 1976, pp. 80–100.
19 Nicolini 1925, p. 160.
20 Dunkerton 1999.
21 Venice 1999, no. 16.
22 Campbell, Foister and Roy 1997, pp. 6–55.

Catalogue

Note on the catalogue

The catalogue entries are subdivided into
the following geographical sections:
Netherlands, cats 1–62
France, cats 63–83
Italy, cats 84–105
Spain, cats 106–123
Portugal, cats 124–131.
Within these sections, the artists are arranged
in alphabetical order.

Provenance: As a rule, only the earliest known
location of the work is given.
References: Only the most authoritative and/or recent
publications (usually containing a comprehensive
bibliography) are included.

1   **Anonymous (Bruges?)**
Crucifixion with Saints Catherine and Barbara
('Calvary of the Tanners'), *c.* 1400
Panel, 70.5 × 141 cm (see fig. 2)
Stedelijke Musea, Groeningemuseum, Bruges.
(Depot Sint-Salvator, 92.28)

This altarpiece in the form of a chest, the original
cover of which has survived, is one of the earliest
paintings in Bruges to have come down to us. Said to
have been painted around 1400 for the Bruges Tanners'
Guild, it is probably the work of a master from the
same city. Although the Bruges *Crucifixion* falls short
of the quality attained by Franco-Flemish court
painting around 1400, it is an outstanding example of
contemporary art production in the cities of Flanders,
from which artists such as Broederlam were to emerge
prior to entering court service.

2   **Anonymous (Netherlands)**
Crucifixion with Saints (triptych), *c.* 1420
Panel, 35.5 × 28 cm (centre); 35.5 × 16 cm (wings)
(see fig. 68)
Gallinat-Bank AG, Essen

This small triptych with the *Crucifixion* in the centre
panel and two saints in either wing was probably
intended for use in private devotion. It appears
to be the work of a master active in the Northern
Netherlands in the early part of the fifteenth century.
Although the figures are rather provincial compared to
the early 'Calvary of the Tanners' from Bruges (cat. 1),
the composition – especially that of the wings –
displays the painter's desire to present the figures
in a spatially consistent manner, influenced by the
Flemish *ars nova*.

Provenance: Sint-Salvatorkerk, Bruges.
Reference: De Vos 1989.

Provenance: Thomae collection, Essen.

3   **Anonymous (Bruges)**
Scenes from the Passion of Christ, c. 1500–10
Panel, 196 × 206 cm (see fig. 193)
Museu Nacional do Azulejo, Lisbon.
On loan from Museu Nacional de Arte Antiga

This work of an anonymous Bruges workshop around 1500 belongs to a tradition – essentially created by Memling – of simultaneous narratives, in which the main events, above all those from Christ's Childhood and Passion and from the life of the Virgin, are presented in a single pictorial sequence. Whereas Memling's *Panorama of the Passion* (Galleria Sabauda, Turin) probably found its way to Italy as early as the 1470s, his second simultaneous narrative – the altarpiece with the *Seven Sorrows of the Virgin* (Alte Pinakothek, Munich), which was commissioned by Pieter Bultynck – decorated the Tanners' Chapel in the choir of Our Lady's in Bruges, where it undoubtedly functioned as a model for other local painters.

The link between the anonymous Lisbon panel and Memling's Turin painting has long been acknowledged, although it is questionable whether the latter was the actual model for the unidentified workshop. Memling's Passion triptych of 1491 (Sankt-Annen-Museum, Lübeck), which also contains a simultaneous narrative, is closer in date to the Lisbon work and may have functioned as its immediate model. The Passion miniatures produced by the Ghent-Bruges school are another possible source for the painting, although the question of whether illuminators might therefore have had a hand in it must remain unanswered.

In a chronicle of the Clarissan Convent of Madre de Deus in Xabregas, near Lisbon, the monk Jeronomo de Belém wrote in 1755 that Emperor Maximilian I had presented the *Scenes from the Passion* to his cousin, Eleanor of Portugal. Although this piece of information, which probably derives from an oral tradition, is not mentioned in the anonymously authored chronicle of the same convent in 1639, it is not improbable, as the Emperor will undoubtedly have been familiar with the Regent's interest in Flemish painting. Eleanor of Portugal, who is shown at prayer in the lower left of the painting, accompanied by what appears to be a female servant, was a patron and member of the Clarissan Convent at Xabregas, for which Massys also painted his altarpiece with the *Seven Sorrows of the Virgin* (see cat. 41).

4   **Anonymous (Flanders?)**
Christ Carrying the Cross, c. 1510–20
Panel, 47 × 49.5 cm
Fine Arts Museums of San Francisco (inv. 47.8)

The trefoil shape of *Christ Carrying the Cross* suggests that the panel once formed part of a larger altarpiece configuration. It is less likely to have belonged to a Passion cycle than to a work devoted to the Seven Sorrows of the Virgin. In images of this type, the grieving Virgin Mary, her anguish symbolized by a sword piercing her heart, is linked to the *Septem Dolores Mariae* – events from the Childhood and Passion of Christ, including the Carrying of the Cross. The associated iconography became increasingly widespread in the Low Countries towards the end of the fifteenth century, reflecting the growing popularity of religious brotherhoods, which emphasized the veneration of the Virgin and her *compassio*. The images of the Seven Sorrows of the Virgin painted by Barend van Orley and Quentin Massys (see cat. 41) were destined to exert a crucial influence within Netherlandish art.

The panel shown here also depends, indirectly at least, on those models, although that does not necessarily imply its Netherlandish origin. The unusual colouring in particular makes it more likely that the painting was produced in southern Europe. Although its precise origin cannot be determined at this stage, the previously proposed attribution to Juan de Flandes does not appear plausible.

5   **Lancelot Blondeel** (c. 1498–1561)
Saint Luke Painting the Virgin, c. 1545
Canvas (rounded at the top), 144.5 × 103 cm
(see fig. 252)
Stedelijke Musea, Groeningemuseum, Bruges
(inv. 0.GRO0018.1)

This composition draws on a hundred-year-old tradition of images depicting Saint Luke as the patron saint of painters. Blondeel essentially combines two types here. The influence of Rogier van der Weyden's *Saint Luke* (see cat. 61) is plain – the Madonna sits on the left below a canopy, while the painter kneels to the right, while Luke's workshop/study can be seen in the background through a doorway.

The canvas does, however, differ from Rogier's panel in several essential respects. While Rogier's Luke is shown *drawing* the Virgin's portrait on a sheet of paper or parchment, Blondeel's saint kneels rather awkwardly behind his easel and is clearly *painting* the Madonna's portrait, working with paintbrush, palette and mahlstick. Moreover, and contrary to the Van der Weyden tradition, the Madonna is sitting on the throne, rather than on the footstool in front of it. The easel and enthroned Virgin are, in fact, distinguishing features of the compositions done after Robert Campin's lost original by artists such as Derick Bagaert and Colyn de Coter.

Blondeel's composition is more enclosed than either Van der Weyden's or Campin's. He makes no attempt, for instance, to open it up to include a landscape. Instead, he places the scene in one of the golden *trompe-l'œil* architectural settings that are his trademark, and which appear to reflect contemporary Italian debates about the grotesque. This illusionistic enlargement lends greater depth to the overall work, as a result of which the central scene is seemingly pushed into the background.

The canvas originally adorned the altar of the Bruges painters' corporation, together with the *Virgin and Child Enthroned with Saints Luke and Eligius* (Cathedral, Bruges). It is widely believed that the two works were used as the guild's banner (possibly joined together) during Saint Luke's Day celebrations on 18 October.

Provenance: Madre de Deus Monastery, Xabregas (Lisbon).
Reference: Lievens de Waegh 1991, pp. 46–105.

Provenance: Before 1947, George T. Cameron collection.

Provenance: Until 1799 (?), chapel of the painters' guild, Bruges.
References: De Vos 1979; Huvenne 1984; Tahon 1998; Bruges 1998.

6   **Dieric Bouts** (*c.*1410/20–1475)
The Virgin and Child with Angels on a Porch,
*c.*1465–70
Panel, 53.8 × 39 cm (see fig. 171)
Capilla Real, Granada

As is the case with Bouts' other paintings in the Capilla
Real, it is not clear when and how this *Virgin and Child*
arrived in the Iberian peninsula and whether it was
installed in the Catholic Kings' burial chapel in
Granada Cathedral at the same time as the other items
from the royal collection. The relationship between
Bouts and his workshop and the Kingdom of Castile,
which may have been quite close, given the examples
of his work that survive in the region, remains obscure
at this stage. Martens (1998) recently highlighted the
reception of Bouts' Madonnas in Castilian painting,
focusing in particular on the '*Retablo de los Luna*' (*c.*1488)
in Toledo Cathedral. The central image of the Madonna
in the upper register of that altarpiece recalls Van der
Weyden's 'Durán Madonna' (Prado, Madrid), while
the barrel-vaulted porch seems to draw directly on
Bouts' painting. The reference to one of Castile's
most important noble families, the Lunas, provides
significant evidence that the Netherlandish model must
have entered Castilian court circles at an early date.

    Bouts' composition shows the Virgin and Child
enthroned in a raised, porch-like setting with a barrel
vault. Two singing angels kneel on the steps on either
side of them. The picture is closely related to Petrus
Christus' *Virgin and Child Enthroned on a Porch* in the
Prado, Madrid, which shares the same composition
and also has a Spanish provenance. Assuming that the
two paintings are not based on a common model, Bouts
might have borrowed the composition of Christus'
painting, which was produced in Bruges in the mid-
1450s. His own version represents a clear advance,
however, as its perspective construction is more
precise, with the orthogonals all converging in a single
point. Bouts was the first Netherlandish artist to be
demonstrably familiar with the geometric construction
of space – a knowledge that he first applied in his *Last
Supper* altarpiece in Leuven (1466–67).

7   **Dieric Bouts** (*c.*1410/20–1475)
and Hugo van der Goes (*c.*1440–1482)
Martyrdom of Saint Hippolytus (triptych),
after 1470
Panel, 92 × 89.2 cm (centre); 92 × 41 cm (wings)
(see fig. 73)
Stedelijke Musea, Groeningemuseum, Bruges.
(Depot Sint-Salvator, 92.30)

Hippolyte de Berthoz, councillor to Philip the
Handsome, must have commissioned Dieric Bouts to
paint this martyrdom of his patron saint, Hippolytus,
shortly after 1470. The centre panel shows the
unfortunate Roman officer being pulled apart by four
horses, in what is a late-medieval conflation of several
different stories. Bouts uses a striking, circular
composition, with an ambitious but not entirely
successful emphasis on depth effects, reminiscent
of works by the artist's Italian contemporaries.

    The hilly landscape in the centre continues in more
detail and with greater refinement in the wings. The
scene on the right is difficult to interpret. It might be
intended to show the Emperor Decius, standing with
a staff, addressing his 'disloyal' officer shortly before he
is sentenced to death. The left wing shows the donor
with his wife, Elisabeth de Keverwyck. The panel is
unusual for two reasons. To begin with, donors are
rarely shown as a couple in a single panel of an
altarpiece. More important, however, is the fact that
the donors were not painted by Bouts, but by Hugo
van der Goes. The style, technique and tonal subtleties
differ sharply from the figures in the other panels. The
attribution to Hugo is not seriously challenged. It is
generally believed that he completed Bouts' triptych
after the latter's death in 1475. The closed wings,
which, in the traditional manner, show the donors'
patron saints, are certainly the work of Van der Goes.

    Another unusual feature, finally, is the fact that,
shortly afterwards, the same couple commissioned a
second triptych devoted to the martyrdom of Saint
Hippolytus from an as yet unidentified master
belonging to Hugo's immediate circle. That painting,
now in the Museum of Fine Arts, Boston, clearly and
successfully attempts to outdo Bouts' earlier central
panel in the complexity of its composition and its
perspective effects.

8   **Robert Campin (Master of Flémalle)**
(*c.*1375–1444) **and Rogier van der Weyden** (?)
(*c.*1399–1464)
*The Virgin and Child in a Glory with Donor
and Saints Peter and Augustine, c.*1435–40?
Panel, 48 × 31.6 cm (see fig. 44)
Musée Granet, Aix-en-Provence (inv. 300)

This small panel shows Saint Peter, dressed in papal
robes, and the Church Father Saint Augustine. The
latter, who is presented as a bishop, reads a book while
holding a heart in his left hand, a symbol of religious
fervour. The Augustinian monk kneeling before Saint
Peter gazes up with a gesture of astonishment at the
Virgin and Child who appear in a glory, ringed by
clouds. An aureole blazes behind the enthroned
Madonna's head, while her feet rest on a crescent
moon, symbolizing the Immaculate Conception.
A distant landscape with a low horizon and a city at
its centre can be made out beyond the grassy bank.
The as yet unidentified coat of arms that appears on
the lower member of the frame might be original.

    According to a note attached to the reverse of the
panel in the seventeenth or eighteenth century, the
monk was Pierre Ameil, a member of the Papal Curia
and the Augustinian community at Limoux, Bishop
of Senigallia and Patriarch of Grado, who died in 1401.
As Châtelet suspected, the painting, which was not
produced until the late 1430s, probably served a
commemorative function. It might have been
commissioned by Ameil's nephew, Pierre Assalbit,
Bishop of Alet and member of the Council of Basle,
for the Augustinian Monastery at Limoux.

    The painting is probably a late product of the
Campin workshop in Tournai and is closely related
in stylistic terms to the wings of the 'Werl altarpiece'
(dated 1438 and now in the Prado, Madrid) and the
Holy Trinity diptych in Saint Petersburg. Kemperdick
noted similarities with the two small Vienna panels
with the *Virgin and Child* and *Saint Catherine*, in which
Rogier van der Weyden responded to Van Eyck's
Virgin and Child at the Fountain (1439; cat. 26).
This suggests that Rogier did indeed have a hand
in the execution of the Aix Madonna.

    The late dating undermines the hypothesis
advanced by Troescher and Sterling that the painting
was done around 1430, at the time of Campin's
disputed pilgrimage to Saint-Gilles-du-Gard in
southern France.

Provenance: Collection of Isabella the Catholic (?).
References: Schöne 1938; Van Schoute 1963, pp. 29–35; Bermejo 1982;
Leuven 1998; Martens 1998.

Provenance: From 1694, recorded in Sint-Salvatorkerk, Bruges.
References: Schöne 1938; Winkler 1964; Sander 1992; Dhanens 1998;
Leuven 1998.

Provenance: Before 1863, Jean Baptiste Marie de Bourguignon
de Farbregoules, Aix-en-Provence.
References: Troescher 1966; Troescher 1967; Sterling 1969; Davies 1972;
Châtelet 1996; Kemperdick 1997; Madrid and Valencia 2001.

9 **Petrus Christus and/or**
  workshop of Jan van Eyck
  *John the Baptist – 'Ecce Agnus Dei', c.*1445
  Panel, 40 × 12.5 cm (see fig. 9)
  The Cleveland Museum of Art. Leonard
  C. Hanna Jr. Bequest (inv. 79.80)

Ever since this image of John the Baptist first surfaced in 1979, it has been a key work in the study of Van Eyck's workshop after the artist's death in 1441. It is particularly important to the issue of the contacts that existed between the workshop and Petrus Christus.

 Christus, who registered as a citizen of Bruges in 1444, was a native of Baarle in the Duchy of Brabant. Before settling in Flanders, he appears to have worked as a manuscript illuminator in Holland. Members of the Van Eyck workshop were not only active as panel painters in the 1440s, they also continued their late master's work in the miniatures decorating the Turin-Milan Hours. This may have resulted in contacts in the mid-1440s with Petrus Christus, providing him with access to model drawings from the Van Eyck workshop.

 The miniature-like *John the Baptist* panel, which once functioned as part of a triptych or polyptych, appears to derive from such a model. The precise rendering of the figures and the detailed landscape are reminiscent of Van Eyck and the composition of the painting might even reflect Van Eyck's lost 'Lomellini triptych' (Strehlke 1997), which was extolled by Bartolomeo Fazio among others and did so much to shape the literary reception of his work in Italy.

 As Ainsworth has noted, the underdrawing of this little panel displays the stylistic characteristics of Petrus Christus, more specifically those of his late works. However, the subsequent execution of the painting, which is entirely in the Eyckian idiom, differs from the works that have been securely attributed to Christus. For that reason, his contribution to the panel, which was based on workshop designs, must have been limited to a very early stage, with the completion of the work being entrusted to an experienced member of the Van Eyck workshop. The Friedsam *Annunciation* (fig. 16; Ainsworth and Martens 1994, no. 10) – a fragment of a larger work, which most closely matches the style of the Baptist panel – might represent the continuation of the successful collaboration between the two masters. Christus used the composition and landscape elements of the Cleveland *John the Baptist* in a donor portrait (cat. 11) and in the Baptist wing – destroyed by fire in 1945 – of the triptych with the *Death of the Virgin* (cat. 13).

10 **Petrus Christus** (*c.*1410–1475/76)
  *Christ as the Man of Sorrows, c.*1450
  Panel, 11.2 × 8.5 cm (see fig. 66)
  Birmingham Museums and Art Gallery
  (inv. P.306.35)

This tiny painting shows Christ as the 'Man of Sorrows', displaying his wounds. He is flanked by two small angels who pull back a green curtain. They hold a lily and a sword – the traditional attributes of Christ as he presides over the Last Judgment. The combination of the latter iconography with that of the *Imago pietatis* was well established in devotional art long before the advent of Early Netherlandish painting, in the work of Master Francke (Kunsthalle, Hamburg), for instance, in illuminated manuscripts and, later, in woodcuts produced for a mass audience. The stage-like setting evoked by the curtains is an original reworking of the traditional iconography, in which the angels hold up Christ's robe.

 Owing to the virtual absence of glazes, the painting is also reminiscent of miniatures in terms of technique. It was probably intended as a portable image for use in private meditation on Christ's Passion and the promise of Salvation, as propagated by Netherlandish humanists around Jan van Ruusbroec and the Brethren of the Common Life. The painting, which has been considered a key work of Petrus Christus ever since Rowlands attributed it to that artist in 1962, is in excellent condition. It must have been treated with great care, as befits an object perceived to be of exceptional value, and was probably kept in its own protective container.

 The iconography of the diminutive painting points to Bruges, and may well have been linked to the prominent cult centring on the precious relic of the Holy Blood, which was carried through the city streets in an annual procession instituted in 1281. Hans Memling, too, painted a recently reconstructed triptych devoted to the relic (centre panel: National Gallery of Victoria, Melbourne). Once again, this features two angels holding the attributes of Christ as divine judge, flanking a Man of Sorrows surrounded by the instruments of his Passion.

11 **Petrus Christus** (*c.*1410–1475/76)
  *Saint Anthony and a Donor, c.*1450
  Panel, 59 × 32.7 cm (see fig. 8)
  Statens Museum for Kunst, Copenhagen
  (inv. 113)

The image of Saint Anthony accompanying a kneeling male donor is attributed to Petrus Christus. It once formed the left wing of a triptych, whose centre panel and right wing seem to have been lost by the eighteenth century. The remains of a grisaille Angel of the Annunciation can still be made out on the reverse of this panel. A *Virgin and Child* by Van Dyck had been attached on the right-hand side by the time the painting was purchased – as a Van Eyck – in Holland in 1763 for the collection of King Frederick v of Denmark. The extension, which remained in place until the 1920s, necessitated significant overpainting, as a result of which the donor's coat of arms was concealed and not revealed again until the panel's recent restoration. The arms have yet to be identified.

 The relationship between the figures and the landscape gives the composition a strikingly archaic feel, which prompted Friedländer to place the painting in Christus' early period. The figure of Saint Anthony – identifiable from the Egyptian cross with its small silver bell and his Antonine habit – appears especially huge in comparison with the rocky formation behind him. There are unmistakable links with the Hermits wing of the Ghent altarpiece (fig. 4), while the mossy surface of some of the rocks is also reminiscent of Eyckian paintings (cats 28–29).

 On the other hand, the portrait of the praying man is closely related both stylistically and in terms of the clothing, to the two donor wings in Washington (cat. 12), which date from the 1450s. There are similarities, moreover, with the image of John the Baptist, which once formed part of Christus' *Death of the Virgin* (cat. 13) and was destroyed by fire in Berlin. It is plausible, therefore, that Christus also painted this work in the 1450s.

 The parallels with the small, Eyckian *Saint John* panel, by contrast, which was finished after Van Eyck's death, possibly with Christus' assistance (cat. 9), are largely restricted to individual motifs. Rather than being chance similarities, the plateau-like rocks with their scattered trees and the city gate in the background could refer to a common model.

Provenance: Heirs John Frere (1740–1807), Roydon Hall, Norfolk.
References: Lurie 1981; Ainsworth and Martens 1994; Ainsworth 1995; Strehlke 1997; Madrid and Valencia 2001.

Provenance: Collection of Empress Maria Theresa, Vienna (?).
References: Rowlands 1962; Sterling 1971; Schabacker 1974; Panhans Bühler 1978; Upton 1990; Ainsworth and Martens 1994.

Provenance: 1763, purchased in Holland for the Danish Royal Collection.
References: Bruyn 1957; Schabacker 1974, pp. 108–9; Lurie 1981; Dhanens 1984; Ainsworth and Martens 1994.

12   Petrus Christus (*c.* 1410–1475/76)
Portrait of a Male Donor; Portrait of a Female Donor
(wings of a triptych)
Panel, 42 × 21.2 cm (man); 41.8 × 21.6 cm
(woman) (see fig. 125)
National Gallery of Art, Washington, DC.
Samuel H. Kress Collection (inv. 1961.9.10–11)

Members of the Italian *natione* in Bruges – merchants
and their staff from Florence, Genoa, Lucca, Pisa and
Venice – were among the most important patrons
of Flemish panel painters, from whom they
commissioned portraits, altarpieces and other works.
Petrus Christus, who was active in Bruges from 1442,
appears to have profited from this clientele more than
any artist since Van Eyck. Many of his paintings ended
up in Italy or Spain, apparently before the fifteenth
century was out.

　　These two altarpiece wings with donors' portraits,
both of which have been cut down on all sides, were
discovered in Italy and probably come from Genoa.
This view is supported by the donors' respective coats
of arms, which refer to families in the Ligurian trading
metropolis. The female donor's arms are those of the
Vivaldi family, who were related to the Genoese
nobility. Those of the man, meanwhile, appear
to belong to the prominent and widely branched
Genoese merchant family, the Lomellini. A member
of the same dynasty – the businessman and diplomat
Giovanni Battista Lomellini – had previously
commissioned a triptych from Van Eyck. That work
entered the Neapolitan collection of King Alfonso V
of Aragon in 1444 and was universally praised in
Quattrocento art literature, not least because of the
donors' portraits. The couple who commissioned their
own triptych in the 1450s from Bruges' then leading
painter, Petrus Christus, might well have had Van
Eyck's model in mind.

　　Because of the complex and rather incoherent
spatial construction of the interiors in the two wings,
scholars have focused primarily on the iconography
and spatial structure of the original centre panel.
Several authors have suggested that the donor
portraits were originally the wings of the *Virgin
and Child Enthroned Between Saints Francis and Jerome*
(fig. 94), the frame of which is inscribed with the
artist's name and dated 1457. This proposed
reconstruction has, however, been disputed, despite
the fact that all three panels come from the same tree
and the combination of saints, which is unusual for
the Low Countries, points towards Italy.

13   Petrus Christus (*c.* 1410–1475/76)
Death of the Virgin, c. 1460–65
Panel (transferred), 171.1 × 138.4 cm (see fig. 45)
Timken Art Gallery, San Diego. Putnam
Foundation

Christus' *Death of the Virgin* was originally the centre
panel of a triptych that had already found its way to
Sicily by the end of the fifteenth century. It was
probably an Italian commission. The wings, which
featured a grisaille *Crucifixion* on the outside and
John the Baptist and *Saint Catherine of Alexandria* on
the inside, were destroyed by fire in Berlin in 1945.
The painting is unusually large for Christus and, as
Ainsworth (1994) has pointed out, it leans towards
Sicilian works – features that may reflect the wishes
of the unidentified patron. Both the panel's provenance
and echoes of its composition found in local Sicilian
painting and sculpture in the early sixteenth century
argue against the hypothesis (reiterated most recently
by Châtelet 1995) that the work might be the Marian
painting installed at Santa Maria del Carmine in
Florence in 1451. That painting – possibly
commissioned by the Barbarigos – was delivered to
Venice by a certain 'Piero de Fiandra'. What is more,
the work cannot have been painted prior to the 1460s,
as the *Death of the Virgin* is based on a perspective
system in which most of the orthogonals – leaving
aside the barrel vault – meet at a vanishing point to
the left of the window. The *Death of the Virgin* thus
represents a more advanced stage than the 1457 *Virgin
and Child Enthroned Between Saints Francis and Jerome*
(fig. 94) in which Christus first applied his knowledge
of a geometrically constructed, central perspective.

　　Since the Death of the Virgin is not a very
common theme in Early Netherlandish panel painting,
Christus apparently drew his inspiration from early
miniatures. Ainsworth's reference (1995) to the
celebrated *Hours of Catherine of Cleves* (Morgan Library,
New York, Ms. M.917) – the work of a Utrecht
illuminator – is especially persuasive in this respect.

　　Although Christus' triptych probably arrived in
Sicily shortly after its completion, its centre panel was
destined to be one of the painter's most influential
creations. Bermejo's *Death of the Virgin* (cat. 110)
unmistakably draws its motifs from the composition,
while Van der Goes' early depiction of the theme
(see cat. 40) does not derive from, say, a lost work
from the Campin workshop, but is plainly based
on Christus' model.

14   Petrus Christus (*c.* 1410–1475/76)
Portrait of a Man, c. 1465
Panel, 47.6 × 32.5 cm (see fig. 232)
Los Angeles County Museum of Art. Mr and
Mrs Allan Balch Collection (inv. m.44.2.3.)

This bust portrait of a man, turned to the right, is set
against a dark, neutral background. The painting
follows the customary Flemish three-quarter portrait
scheme, as developed in the period around 1430 by
Jan van Eyck, Robert Campin and Rogier van der
Weyden. Christus' portrait differs from those models,
however, in its concentrated treatment of the lighting.
This is crucial to the plasticity suggested by the artist,
which lends the sitter's face a monumentality
reminiscent of a sculpted portrait bust. The half of
the face that is turned towards the viewer is lit directly
from the left, leaving the other half in heavy shadow.
The sculptural quality of the modelling is further
heightened by the contrast with the dark background.
Christus carefully prepared this three-dimensional
effect in the underdrawing (Ainsworth and Martens
1994; Fronek 1995). In spite of differences in the choice
of means, this gives the painting its rightful place
within Petrus Christus' portraiture, in which great
importance is placed on volume – a feature that is
equally apparent in the early *Portrait of a Carthusian*
(Metropolitan Museum, New York) and in the late
Portrait of a Lady (Staatliche Museen, Berlin).

　　Since the sitter's costume and the way the light
is handled are reminiscent of Christus' *Death of the
Virgin* (cat. 13), *Nativity* (National Gallery of Art,
Washington) and *Holy Family* (fig. 30), this painting,
too, might have been completed in the 1460s. The
panel probably began life as the left wing of a portrait
diptych, whose right wing – a likeness of the sitter's
wife – has been lost. Photographs exist of a diptych
attributed to Christus containing portraits of Pieter
Adornes and his wife (see Gellman 1995). Although
this offers the closest parallel to the work under
discussion within Early Netherlandish portraiture,
the identification of the man must remain tentative.
Memling's success in Bruges at that time with
portraits set in front of landscapes might help explain
why Christus' *Portrait of a Man* was not emulated in
Flanders. The same cannot be said of northern Italy,
however, where Antonello da Messina painted equally
monumental portraits in the 1470s (cats 87, 88).

Provenance: Before 1937, Count Alessandro Contini-Bonacossi, Florence.
References: Lane 1971; Schabacker 1974; Upton 1975; Eisler 1977; Hand
and Wolff 1986; Ainsworth and Martens 1994.

Provenance: Sciaccia, Sicily (sixteenth century).
References: Schabacker 1974; Upton 1990; Ainsworth and Martens 1994;
Ainsworth 1995.

Provenance: Until 1928, Sir George Lindsay Holford, London
and Westonbirt, Gloucestershire.
References: Schabacker 1974; Ainsworth and Martens 1994; Ainsworth 1995;
Fronek 1995; Gellman 1995; Venice 1999, no. 2.

15   Assistant or follower of Petrus Christus
      (c. 1410–1475/76)
      *Saint Elizabeth of Hungary with a Female Donor
      (Isabella of Portugal?)*
      Panel, 79 × 33 cm (see fig. 197)
      Stedelijke Musea, Groeningemuseum, Bruges
      (inv. 0.1614)

This panel originally formed the left wing of a triptych.
It shows a richly attired donatrix with her patron saint,
Elizabeth of Hungary, in a portico-like interior that
opens to the left and rear on to a landscape vista.
The headgear and the long, costly brocade gown
edged in white fur identify the figure, who kneels
before a prayerbook, as a noblewoman. The headgear
in particular recalls portraits of Isabella of Portugal
(1397–1471), whose patron saint was Elizabeth.
      The identification of the donor as Philip the Good's
third wife is supported by the fact that, until the late
nineteenth century, the panel had an image of Saint
Catherine as its companion piece. A triptych with the
Mater Dolorosa, the wings of which showed Isabella
with Saint Elizabeth and Saint Catherine, with an
Annunciation on the reverse, is listed in the 1526
inventory of Margaret of Austria's collection in
Mechelen. The fact that the Bruges panel still shows
traces of grisaille on the reverse suggests that this
might well be a wing of the Mechelen triptych, which
would confirm the identity of the donor.
      Isabella fell out with Philip the Good in the mid-
1450s and left his court in 1457. Previously, however,
she had exerted her influence on Burgundian foreign
policy, taken part in the negotiations that led to the
Treaty of Arras (1435) and championed the alliance
with the English House of York. In the final years of
her life, Isabella founded a number of charitable and
religious institutions. Her donor portrait emphasizes
her piety and might thus have been painted around
that time.
      The panel's attribution to Petrus Christus, first
proposed by Stange and Marlier (see De Vos 1979),
has not been widely accepted. Although the spatial
conception is closely related to Christus' work,
there are undeniable qualitative discrepancies, even
allowing for the poor state of preservation of the
painting. The author of the Bruges panel is more likely,
therefore, to have been one of Christus' assistants –
possibly one of his sons.

16   Jacques Daret (c. 1403–1468/70)
      Portrait of a Woman, c. 1440
      Panel, 50.5 × 35.5 cm (see fig. 47)
      Dumbarton Oaks Research Library and
      Collections, Washington, DC. House
      Collection (inv. HC.P.1923.01)

An elegant lady is shown against a dark background,
her head turned to the left and a prayerbook in her
hands. Judging by her luxurious clothes, headdress
and jewelry, this is a portrait of a noblewoman, which
was probably combined with an image of the Virgin
Mary or Christ to form a devotional diptych. The
structure and composition of the portrait seem to
indicate that it was produced in the Netherlands
before the mid-fifteenth century, but definitely
not in Bruges.
      First documented in Italy in the nineteenth
century, the painting was attributed to the Master
of Flémalle (Robert Campin) by Friedländer (1899
and 1924). The inscription in the upper left zone has
become partially illegible, but the words 'Sibylla Agripa
Aloisia Sabauda' can still be seen in a sixteenth-century
copy, now in Verona (Collobi Ragghianti 1990).
As is the case with other Early Netherlandish female
portraits with inscriptions identifying the sitter
as a sibyl (e.g. Memling's *Portrait of a Woman*,
Memlingmuseum, Bruges; De Vos 1994, no. 36),
the text is a later addition. Consequently, the name
'Aloisia Sabauda' is only of limited use in identifying
the sitter; at best it tells us that the painting may once
have belonged to a member of the House of Savoy.
If so, the inscription could be a reference to Louise of
Savoy (1476–1503), Duchess of Angoulême and mother
of François I.
      There is certainly no evidence to support the
identification proposed by Hulin de Loo (1932),
who argued that the subject of the portrait is Mary
of Savoy, who married the Duke of Milan, Filippo
Maria Visconti in 1427. The same goes for Troescher's
suggestion (1967) that the portrait was painted during
Robert Campin's pilgrimage to Saint-Gilles-du-Gard
in 1428.
      The painting is rarely ascribed to Campin
nowadays, for most art historians agree that it is the
work of Campin's pupil, Jacques Daret (Campbell
1996; Châtelet 1996), whose oeuvre has been taking
clearer shape in recent years.

17   Gerard David (1460/65–1523)
      Baptism of Christ (triptych), c. 1502–8
      Panel, 127.9 × 96.6 cm (centre); 132 × 43.1 cm
      and 132.2 × 42.2 cm (wings) (see fig. 244)
      Stedelijke Musea, Groeningemuseum, Bruges
      (inv. 0.35)

The monumental triptych with the *Baptism of Christ*
is generally considered to be one of Gerard David's
greatest masterpieces. Saint John baptizes Christ in
the river Jordan, assisted by an angel dressed in a richly
decorated liturgical robe, who holds the Messiah's
simple garments. John appears again in the deep
middleground preaching in the wilderness, while
somewhat nearer, on the right, he is shown
introducing Jesus to his followers after the baptism.
      The donor and his family are depicted in the wings.
On the left we see Jan de Trompes, the influential
Flemish civil servant who commissioned the triptych
in 1502, accompanied by his son and his patron saint,
John the Evangelist. His wife, Elisabeth van der
Meersch, appears on the right with her patron saint
and the couple's four daughters. The closed wings,
which seem to have been painted at a later date,
contain a Virgin and Child and Jan de Trompes' second
wife, with her young daughter and patron saint.
      The most striking features of the triptych are the
painting technique and the landscape. The masterly
precision and the detailed rendering of the different
materials emphasize David's close relationship with the
Van Eyck/Memling tradition. The landscape, which
extends across all three panels, is even more impressive.
The powerful illusion of depth enables the artist to
place the main figures convincingly in the foreground
of this magnificent landscape, without them being
overwhelmed by the scenic elements. The marvellously
detailed painting also includes sumptuously executed
plants, flowers and trees, which contribute
significantly to its overall charm. The luxuriant flora
is not, however, merely intended as decoration – most
of the plants also have a symbolic meaning.
      In 1520, the family donated the *Baptism of Christ*
to a more publicly accessible chapel in the Basilica of
the Holy Blood in Bruges. The influence of David's
masterpiece is clearly detectable in works produced
shortly afterwards by such painters as Joachim Patinir
and Simon Bening.

Provenance: Probably collection of Margaret of Austria, Mechelen (1526).
References: Schabacker 1974; De Vos 1979, pp. 96–98; Janssens
de Bisthoven 1981.

Provenance: 1858, Pozzi collection, Cremona.
References: Troescher 1967; Sterling 1969; Davies 1972; Collobi
Ragghianti 1990; Campbell 1996; Châtelet 1996; Kemperdick 1997.

Provenance: Chapel of Saint Lawrence, Sint-Basiliuskerk, Bruges.
References: De Vos 1979; Janssens de Bisthoven 1981; Van Miegroet 1989;
Ainsworth 1998; Bruges 1998.

18 **Jan van Eyck** (*c.* 1390–1441)
Man in a Blue Chaperon, *c.* 1429
Panel, 19.1 × 13.2 cm (including extensions:
22.5 × 16.6 cm) (see fig. 219)
Muzeul Naţional de Artă al României,
Bucharest (inv. 8100/134)

This is probably the earliest surviving portrait
by Jan van Eyck. Having been extended on all sides
– probably in the seventeenth century – and provided
with a Dürer monogram and the date '1492', it was first
attributed to the Flemish artist by Frimmel in 1894.
Panofsky did not accept the attribution to Van Eyck,
but this has recently been confirmed by the results of
technical examination.

The sitter is a middle-aged man, shown from the
chest up against a neutral, dark background. His upper
body and gaze are turned to the left. His aristocratic
rank is apparent from the fur cloak worn over a black
shirt and the blue chaperon, with dangling *cornette*, on
his head. He holds a ring in his right hand, while his
left hand probably rested on the portrait's lost original
frame. The ring does not refer in this instance to the
sitter's profession, as it does in Van Eyck's portrait of
the goldsmith *Jan de Leeuw* (1436), but reflects the
original function of the panel as a betrothal portrait.
Producing works of that kind was one of Van Eyck's
duties as Burgundian court artist. During the
diplomatic mission to Portugal (1428/29), for instance,
he painted the portrait of Princess Isabella and
probably took a likeness of Philip the Good with him.

19 **Jan van Eyck** (*c.* 1390–1441)
Annunciation, *c.* 1434–36
Canvas (transferred), 92.7 × 36.7 cm
(see fig. 17)
National Gallery of Art, Washington, DC.
Andrew W. Mellon Collection (inv. 1937.1.39)

Jan van Eyck places this *Annunciation* in a church
interior, the architecture of which is based on real
models, though without actually representing a
particular cathedral. The Archangel Gabriel appears
on the left, wearing a crown, his multicoloured wings
protruding from the back of his costly brocade robe.
He holds a sceptre in his left hand and points upwards
with his right, while speaking his greeting '*Ave gratia
plena …*'. The words, which are inscribed in the
painting in golden letters, are addressed to the Virgin
Mary, who kneels before a *prie-dieu* on which lies an
open book. She replies, with a gesture of surprise,
'*Ecce ancilla domini …*'. Van Eyck presents the words
upside-down, so that they can be read from above.
As in the Ghent altarpiece, this is done to suggest that
the answer is intended for God himself. The golden
rays entering from the clerestory and the dove of
the Holy Spirit represent the mystery of Christ's
conception, which marks the beginning of the
New Covenant.

Many of the pictorial motifs serve to symbolize
Mary's virginity and the Passion of Christ. In this way,
Van Eyck places his Annunciation in its broader
theological context. The murals and the stained-glass
window in the clerestory, for which the painter has
deliberately chosen the Romanesque style, relate,
for instance, to the presentation of the Ten
Commandments and hence to the beginning of the
Old Covenant, which is to be replaced following the
Annunciation, by the New Covenant. The tiled floor,
meanwhile, is decorated with astrological symbols
and with Old Testament scenes prefiguring Christ's
sacrificial death.

The painting might have been done for Philip the
Good, by whom Van Eyck was employed as court
painter. In addition to the complex content of the
image, this is also suggested by the fact that the panel
was brought to Paris from Dijon in 1819, while a 1791
description of the Charterhouse of Champmol near
Dijon mentions an upright *Annunciation* in the ducal
chapel. That would make the painting the only
surviving example of the work that Van Eyck produced
for the Duke's court. The composition was taken up
around 1450 by an illuminator with close links to the
Van Eyck workshop in the 'Llangattock Hours' (J. Paul
Getty Museum, Los Angeles, Ms. Ludwig IX 7).

20 **Jan van Eyck** (*c.* 1390–1441)
Annunciation (diptych), *c.* 1435?
Panel, 38.8 × 23.2 cm each (see fig. 26)
Museo Thyssen-Bornemisza, Madrid
(inv. 137a–b; Acc. 1933.11.1–2)

Although the *Annunciation* diptych was only discovered
in the early 1930s, it is indisputably one of Jan van Eyck's
most exquisite works. As Preimesberger (1991) was able
to show, it demonstrates both the artist's perfect
mastery of optics and catoptrics as understood in his
time, and his artistic and intellectual self-assurance.
Working only with the means available to his craft, the
painter applies his brilliant visual illusionism to create
several different levels of pictorial reality with clear art-
theoretical implications and allusions to classical
anecdotes regarding celebrated artists.

The Virgin Mary and the Angel of the
Annunciation are placed in frames painted as red
imitation marble. Their figures are presented as stone
statues, each of which stands on an octagonal plinth in
front of a flat niche with a stone frame. Not only does
the painting emulate the medium of unpolychromed
stone sculpture, it also suggests the closed wings of
an altarpiece, which were frequently adorned in
Netherlandish art – as in Van Eyck's *Virgin and Child*
triptych of 1437 (cat. 23) – with monochrome images of
statues. This *Annunciation*, by contrast, is by no means
monochrome and it appears on the *inside* of a diptych,
as the reverse of each panel is painted with the imitation
porphyry that we know from other works by Van Eyck.
The artist further teases the viewer by allowing the two
plinths to protrude beyond the painted edge of the
niche and by making the statues cast shadows on the
imitation stone frames to the left. In so doing, he
creates a *trompe-l'œil* effect which, together with the
painted reflections in the highly polished black stone
of the rear wall of the niches, heightens the illusion of
three-dimensionality. Meanwhile, the dove of the Holy
Spirit, hovering above the Virgin, defeats sculpture on
its own ground and enables painting to claim the title
of greatest of the arts.

We do not know for whom this intellectually and
aesthetically fascinating diptych was painted. Elsig's
recent hypothesis (Madrid and Valencia 2001) that
the work was commissioned by René of Anjou is
not convincing.

Provenance: Baron von Brukenthal, Hermannstadt (now Sibiu, Romania).
References: Ridderbos 1991; Van Asperen de Boer 1991; Belting and
Kruse 1994; Borchert 2000.

Provenance: Probably Charterhouse of Champmol near Dijon.
References: Purtle 1982; Hand and Wolff 1986; Pächt 1989, p. 167;
Harbison 1990, pp. 175–76; Gifford 1999; Purtle 1999; Gifford 2000;
Purtle 2000.

Provenance: Comte de Menthon, Château-Bernard (Haute-Savoie, France).
References: Friedländer 1934; Bruyn 1957; Snyder 1973; Sterling 1976;
Dhanens 1980; Eisler 1989; Preimesberger 1991; Bosshard 1992; Madrid
and Valencia 2001.

21 **Jan van Eyck** (*c.* 1390–1441)
Virgin and Child ('Lucca Madonna'), *c.* 1435?
Panel, 65.7 × 49.6 cm (see fig. 29)
Städelsches Kunstinstitut und Städtische
Galerie, Frankfurt (inv. 944)

This *Virgin and Child* is frequently referred to as the
'Lucca Madonna', as it once belonged to the Marquis
of Lucca's collection. Art historians are unanimous
in ascribing the painting to Jan van Eyck, but disagree
as to its date. Some authors believe it to have been
executed immediately after the Ghent altarpiece,
while others place it in the mid-1430s or near the
end of the artist's life.

The dating issue has yet to be settled. Every
attempt to date the painting has, however, inevitably
taken account of two closely related Van Eyck
Madonnas that *are* inscribed with the date of their
execution. The 'Van der Paele Madonna' (1436; cat. 22)
and the centre panel of the Dresden triptych (1437;
cat. 23) both show the Virgin and Child enthroned
beneath a canopy in an interior. The spatial conception
is more complex in those works than it is in the 'Lucca
Madonna' and the relationship between the enthroned
Virgin and Child and the surrounding space seems
more progressive. In this instance, the space around
the throne is substantially tighter, as the monumental
figure of the Madonna virtually fills the interior.

It is, however, this very feature that enables
the artist to heighten the immediacy of the divine
presence in the painting. The interior seems
deliberately to transcend the boundaries of the panel
and continues into the viewer's own world. Sander
(1993) rightly pointed out a fundamental difference
between the Frankfurt painting and the two other
Van Eyck Madonnas mentioned here. In the latter
works, the donor is shown in Mary's immediate
presence, while in this painting the artist implicitly
places the donor before the image. Although we are
ignorant as to the original function and destination
of the 'Lucca Madonna', which might have been
commissioned by an Italian patron, it could well have
been intended for private devotion. It is plain at all
events that in opting to present the Virgin as *Madonna
lactans* – suckling the Christ Child – Van Eyck was
drawing on a well-known miraculous Madonna image
from Cambrai.

22 **Jan van Eyck** (*c.* 1390–1441)
*The Virgin and Child with Saints Donatian
and George and Canon Joris van der Paele*
('Van der Paele Madonna'), 1436
Panel, 141 × 176.5 cm (including frame)
(see fig. 92)
Stedelijke Musea, Groeningemuseum, Bruges
(inv. 0.161)

This is the largest known painting by Jan van Eyck
after the Ghent altarpiece. The frame is inscribed with
the artist's name and the date '1436', and also states the
name of the donor and the context in which the work
was commissioned. Joris van der Paele was a canon at
Saint Donatian's in Bruges. The ailing clergyman
commissioned the painting to commemorate his
foundation of two chaplaincies at the church.
We know from surviving documents that the panel
was placed close to Van der Paele's tomb, where the
chaplains were to perform 'perpetual' masses for the
dead man's soul (Viaene 1965). Although the painting
thus had a clear commemorative function, there is
some dispute as to whether it functioned as an
altarpiece or as a straightforward memorial.

Joris van der Paele kneels to the right of the Virgin,
who is enthroned with the Christ Child below a
brocade canopy in a round building reminiscent of
a medieval apse. His patron saint, George, clad in
golden armour and respectfully doffing his helmet,
stands at his side and presents him to the Virgin.
The figure on the left is Saint Donatian, titular saint
of the Bruges church. Van Eyck's painting combines
several levels of reality and meaning to produce a
visual construction that is both extremely complex
and deeply theological. The Madonna symbolizes
the altar, with the Christ Child on her lap as the
Eucharistic Host. Her throne is decorated with figures
of the first human couple and Old Testament
prefigurations of Christ's sacrifice and Resurrection,
while additional prefigurations of the Christian
Redemption can be seen in the capitals.

Saint George's armour reflects the Madonna's
red cloak – an allusion to the Marian metaphor of the
'Flawless Mirror' (*'speculum sine macula'*) mentioned
in the inscription on the frame. The artist painted
his own reflection in the saint's shield in a deliberate
reference to classical anecdotes about great artists
(Preimesberger 1991).

23 **Jan van Eyck** (*c.* 1390–1441)
*The Virgin and Child with Saints Catherine
and Michael and a Donor* (triptych), 1437
(reverse) *Annunciation*
Panel, 33.1 × 27.5 cm (centre); 33.3 × 13.6 cm
(wings) (see fig. 115)
Staatliche Kunstsammlungen, Dresden.
Gemäldegalerie Alte Meister (inv. 799)

This miniature-like, winged altarpiece is Jan van
Eyck's only surviving triptych. The composition and
iconography of the open altarpiece draw on the
monumental 'Van der Paele Madonna' of 1436 (cat. 22),
while the grisaille *Annunciation* on the closed wings
recalls the undated *Annunciation* diptych in the
Museo Thyssen-Bornemisza (cat. 20). Similarities
also exist with Van Eyck's Mellon *Annunciation* (cat. 19).

In the narrowest possible space, the left wing
shows the unidentified donor accompanied by the
Archangel Michael in the ambulatory of an essentially
Romanesque church. The man is dressed in the
Burgundian style and kneels before the Virgin and
Child, who are positioned in the centre panel below
a brocade canopy in the nave of the same church. The
Infant Christ holds a banderole on which is inscribed
a quotation from Matthew's Gospel: *'Discite a me,
quia mitis sum et humilis corde'* ('Learn from me; for I am
gentle and humble in heart'). The figure in the right
wing is that of Saint Catherine, behind whom we
catch a glimpse of landscape through the window
on the right-hand edge of the painting.

The inscription on the frame was only rediscovered
during the triptych's restoration in 1959. In addition
to passages from the Old Testament, which formed
part of Marian liturgy in the fifteenth century,
the inscription names Jan van Eyck as the painter,
states his motto 'ALC IXH XAN' and gives the year
of execution as '1437'. The triptych had hitherto been
widely viewed as one of the master's early works.

Moreover, coats of arms referring to the prominent
Giustiniani family of Genoa were discovered in the
upper corners of the frames of the wings. Although
these were painted over earlier sets of arms, the
triptych is still likely to have been commissioned from
Van Eyck by Bruges-based Genoese merchants and to
have been transported soon afterwards to Liguria.
The Master of the Del Monte Annunciation may have
drawn partially on Van Eyck's composition for his
Virgin and Child altarpiece in Pontremoli (fig. 109).
The size of the triptych, which was probably intended
for private devotion, suggests that it might have
served as a travelling altarpiece.

Provenance: Before 1840, Charles de Bourbon, Duke of Lucca.
References: Snyder 1973; Ames Lewis 1979; Dhanens 1980; Purtle 1982;
Ruda 1984; Pächt 1989; Elkins 1991, pp. 53–62; Sander 1993, pp. 244–63.

Provenance: Sint-Donaaskerk, Bruges.
References: Viaene 1965; Farmer 1969; Snyder 1973; Sterling 1976;
De Vos 1979; Janssens de Bisthoven 1981; Purtle 1982; Pächt 1989;
Preimesberger 1991; Belting and Kruse 1994.

Provenance: Before 1597 (?), Vincenzo i Gonzaga, Mantua.
References: Weiss 1955; Menz 1959; Snyder 1973; Purtle 1982; Pächt 1989;
Faries 1999; Neidhart and Schölzel 2000; Zeman 2001.

24   Jan van Eyck (*c.* 1390–1441)
Niccolò Albergati, 1438
Panel, 34.1 × 27.3 cm (including vertical strips,
1.0 and 1.1 cm, added on both sides) (see fig. 7)
Kunsthistorisches Museum, Vienna.
Gemäldegalerie (inv. 975)

The portrait once belonged to the Antwerp art dealer
Peter Stevens, who sold it in 1648 to Archduke
Leopold Wilhelm. Its provenance is supported by a
cabinet piece by Frans II Francken and David Teniers
the Younger (*c.* 1642; Courtauld Institute Galleries,
London) showing Stevens' art collection. This is
important, as the identification of the sitter goes back
to Stevens, who annotated his copy of Van Mander's
Schilder-boeck with information about painters and
their work that has since proved reliable (Briels 1980).
His note about the portrait reads: '… a fine work by
Jan van Eyck, dated 1438, showing the Cardinal of
Santa Croce, whom the Pope sent to Bruges to make
peace between Duke Philip and the Dauphin about the
death of Philip's father'. The information in question
probably came from the painting's lost original frame.

The evidence strongly suggests, therefore, that this
is Cardinal Niccolò Albergati (1375–1443) who, in
1426, was appointed titular cardinal of the Roman
Church of Santa Croce in Gerusalemme. Albergati
acted as papal legate to the peace negotiations held in
France in 1422 and 1431. In 1435, he took part in the
peace conference that led to the Treaty of Arras,
which ended the conflict between Philip the Good
and Charles VII over the murder of the Duke's father,
John the Fearless (1419).

The Duke of Burgundy appears to have sent Jan van
Eyck from Bruges to Arras to attend the conference
(Paviot 1990), where he probably sketched the portraits
of prominent delegates. The silverpoint drawing on
which the Vienna portrait is based has survived (fig. 12).
Not only did Van Eyck record the elderly Cardinal's
features, he also made colour notes in his native Mosan
dialect (Dierick 1999). The reason why Van Eyck
painted the portrait fully three years after he had made
the portrait study has yet to be explained.

Hunter (1993) and Hall (1998) have expressed doubt
as to whether this really is Albergati, because of
discrepancies in terms of portrait tradition and the
clothing, which does not appear to match the kind of
robes worn by cardinals at that time. These objections
would, however, appear to be outweighed by the
precise information supplied by Peter Stevens.

25   Jan van Eyck (*c.* 1390–1441)
Margaret van Eyck, 1439
Panel, 41.2 × 34.6 cm (see fig. 229)
Stedelijke Musea, Groeningemuseum, Bruges
(inv. 0.162)

Like the small *Virgin and Child at the Fountain* (cat. 26),
the portrait of *Margaret van Eyck*, which is inscribed
with the date 1439 and was probably the companion
piece to a lost self-portrait, is one of the latest surviving
paintings by Jan van Eyck. It was done about a year
after the portrait of *Niccolò Albergati* (cat. 24), but
the two works differ in that the Cardinal's likeness
was an official portrait, while the other was intended
for private use. This is plain from the way Van Eyck's
wife looks the viewer in the eye and the direct manner
in which the 'talking' inscription on the original frame
states her identity: 'My husband Jan painted me in
the year 1439 on 17 June, at the age of 33. ALC IXH XAN'.
The only other instance in which these two elements
are combined is in the 1436 portrait of the Bruges
goldsmith *Jan de Leeuw* (Kunsthistorisches
Museum, Vienna).

Van Eyck appears to have married in 1432/33 –
immediately after his arrival in Bruges and the
completion of the Ghent altarpiece (figs 4–5) – as the
couple's first child was born in 1434. We do not know
his wife's maiden name. Contemporary documents
merely state her first name, while the ducal accounts
refer to her – even after the painter's death – as
Damoiselle Marguerite, suggesting that she might have
come from a noble family. The theory that, with the
Duke's mediation, Jan van Eyck married a daughter
of the minor nobility is certainly supported by the fine
clothes that Margaret wears in the portrait, although
these were increasingly the preserve of the urban élite,
too. Margaret van Eyck remained in Bruges for almost
a decade after her husband's death before she finally
sold the painter's house. She may have continued to
run the Bruges workshop, together with Jan's brother
Lambert, as often occurred with the widows of
members of the painters' corporation.

26   Jan van Eyck (*c.* 1390–1441)
The Virgin and Child at the Fountain, 1439
Panel, 19 × 12.5 cm (see fig. 204)
Koninklijk Museum voor Schone Kunsten,
Antwerp (inv. 411)

Van Eyck's motto 'ALC IXH XAN' appears in classical
Greek-style lettering on the lower member of the
original frame, above the inscription 'JOH[ANN]ES
DE EYCK ME FECIT + [COM]PLEVIT AN[N]O 1439'.
The *Virgin at the Fountain* was painted two years before
the painter's death and is the last religious work to
be inscribed with a date.

The tiny painting shows the Virgin Mary with
the Christ Child in a rose garden. The Madonna is
presented against a cloth of honour, held up by two
angels. The latter have wings with shimmering
rainbow colours, like the Archangel in the Mellon
Annunciation (cat. 19) and the New York diptych
(fig. 15). A brass fountain surmounted with a lion
appears on the left. In spite of the limited space,
Van Eyck manages to imbue this devotional image
– which draws, appropriately enough, on the
Byzantine miraculous type of the *Maria Eleousa* –
with a multiplicity of symbols referring directly
to the Mother of God and her virginity.

The garden, for instance, which is closed off to the
rear with a bed of roses, alludes to the *hortus conclusus* –
the paradisiacal garden mentioned in such texts as
the Song of Songs. The flora and the fountain motif
– a common feature of late-medieval gardens – also
refer to the Virgin Mary, who is described in the Song
of Songs as the *fons hortorum* ('fountain of gardens').
The fountain motif can, however, also be interpreted
as an allusion to Christ as the source from which
springs the Water of Life.

This complex symbolism and the miniature-like
format of Van Eyck's painting suggest that the
unidentified patron purchased it for use in private
devotion. Nevertheless, the composition must have
been more widely accessible to some extent, as it was
still being imitated in sixteenth-century Bruges and a
copy of the painting belonged to Margaret of Austria's
art collection.

A replica was painted in Van Eyck's own workshop
around the same time (cat. 27), and the composition is
also echoed in the 'Charterhouse Madonna' (fig. 22),
produced by the workshop after the master's death.

Provenance: Until 1648, Peter Stevens, Antwerp; Archduke
Leopold Wilhelm; Stallburg collections, Vienna.
References: Snyder 1973; Dhanens 1980; Demus, Klauner and Schütz 1981;
Anzelewsky 1985; Pächt 1989, pp. 112–13; Campbell 1990; Dülberg 1990,
pp. 218–19; Harbison 1990, pp. 164–67; Hunter 1993; Rohlmann 1994;
Hall 1998, pp. 11–37; Dierick 1999, pp. 79–82.

Provenance: Chapel of the painters' guild, Bruges.
References: Snyder 1973; De Vos 1979; Dhanens 1980;
Janssens de Bisthoven 1981; Pächt 1989; Harbison 1990.

Provenance: Before 1830, collection of the parish priest of Dikkelvenne
(East Flanders).
References: Snyder 1973; Dhanens 1980; Purtle 1982; Silver 1983;
Vandenbroeck 1984; Pächt 1989; Harbison 1990; Belting and Kruse 1994;
Verougstraete and Van Schoute 2000; Jones 2000.

27 **Jan van Eyck and workshop** (*c.* 1390–1441)
The Virgin and Child at the Fountain, *c.* 1440
Panel, 21.3 × 17.2 cm (see fig. 208)
Koninklijk Kabinet van Schilderijen
'Mauritshuis', The Hague. On loan from
Noortman BV, Maastricht

28 **Jan van Eyck** (*c.* 1390–1441)
Stigmatization of Saint Francis, *c.* 1435–40
Panel, 29.3 × 33.4 cm
Galleria Sabauda, Turin (cat. no. 147)

29 **Jan van Eyck and/or workshop** (*c.* 1390–1441)
Stigmatization of Saint Francis, *c.* 1440
Parchment mounted on wood, 12.4 × 14.6 cm
(see fig. 243)
Philadelphia Museum of Art. The John
G. Johnson Collection (cat. no. 314)

This excellently preserved little painting – though its original frame has not survived – is a detailed copy of Jan van Eyck's late *Virgin and Child at the Fountain* (1439; cat. 26). It was initially identified as an anonymous replica of the Bruges master's influential composition. In addition to the exceptional quality, recent detailed technical examination of the paint layers and dendrochronological analysis of the wooden support indicate, however, that it is more likely to be a workshop copy produced at more or less the same time as the original, currently in Antwerp.

This view is supported by the nature of the many Early Netherlandish 'copies' of Van Eyck's *Virgin at the Fountain*, which were chiefly produced after 1500 in the circle of Gerard David and Adriaen Isenbrant, and which either reinterpret or extend the iconography of the original or else follow Van Eyck's composition, but not his style. The fact that this is an exact replica and that it dates, moreover, from the fifteenth century, suggests a closer relationship with Van Eyck's Bruges workshop.

The dubious, though long unchallenged notion that Van Eyck never repeated his pictorial inventions ought to be thoroughly overhauled in the light of the two *Virgins at the Fountain,* the images of the *Stigmatization of Saint Francis* in Turin and Philadelphia (cats 28, 29) and the Eyckian *Crucifixion* that has come down to us in both the Turin-Milan Hours (fig. 18) and a panel now in Venice (cat. 34). In doing so, proper account ought to be taken of the organization and working methods of Jan van Eyck's workshop.

The fact that assistants at that workshop reused their master's compositions after his death is apparent from the 'Madonna of Jan Vos' (fig. 22), completed in 1443, which derives from the 1439 *Virgin at the Fountain.* Model drawings of Eyckian compositions were probably available to at least the master's former assistants and colleagues in Bruges, where they appear to have remained in use until the 1450s.

After the Ghent altarpiece (figs 4–5) and the 'Rolin Madonna' (fig. 13), this painting is the most important example of Van Eyck's contribution to the development of landscape painting. It shows Saint Francis receiving the stigmata in a panoramic landscape with a city by a river in the distance, to the left of which is a hilly landscape that stretches into the foreground. The founder of the Franciscan Order kneels before a winged crucifix, the wounds in his hands and feet clearly visible, while the wound in his side is hidden by his robes. His fellow friar, Leo, is huddled in sleep on the right, next to a rocky outcrop from which flows a spring.

Van Eyck's composition is probably the earliest rendering of this subject in Netherlandish art and is entirely independent of the Italian pictorial tradition deriving from Giotto, which was popular in southern Europe. The painting, of which a smaller replica is known (cat. 29), has been linked to two *Saint Francis* paintings by Van Eyck, which the prominent Bruges merchant Anselmus Adornes willed to his two daughters, who lived as nuns in the Bruges area, on the eve of his 1470 pilgrimage to the Holy Land.

Echoes of the composition can be detected in Bruges painting centring on the Van Eyck workshop and its immediate circle from the 1440s onwards (cat. 29), and copies were still being produced around 1500 (cats 45, 121). Direct borrowing of motifs – evidence of first-hand knowledge of the Eyckian composition and of the immense impact of Flemish painting on Italian artists – is apparent in Florence in the 1470s in the landscape backgrounds of paintings by Verrocchio, Botticelli and Filippino Lippi, and in the work of the Venetian Giovanni Bellini. It is possible, therefore, that Adornes took one of his Saint Francis panels with him on his journey to Jerusalem.

A *Stigmatization of Saint Francis* by the Master of Porciúncula (cat. 121), which recently came to light in the Valencia area, also draws on Van Eyck's composition. This may derive from a third Van Eyck *Saint Francis,* which belonged to the Valencian painter Juan Reixach and was mentioned in his will in 1448.

The Philadelphia *Saint Francis* is a very faithful, reduced replica, painted on parchment, of the panel in Turin (cat. 28). Minor differences can be made out in the brushwork of the surface of the rock formation and other details, but the overall impression is identical. Only the Turin panel has an underdrawing similar to other Van Eyck paintings, which, moreover, features adjustments and corrections that have been carried through to the paint layer. It would seem likely, therefore, that the Philadelphia painting served as the model for the one in Turin. Yet dendrochronological analysis of the wooden support has demonstrated that the Philadelphia panel came from the same tree trunk as those used for Van Eyck's portraits of *Baudouin de Lannoy* and *Giovanni Arnolfini* (both Staatliche Museen, Berlin). This confirms the conclusion already suggested by the painterly quality of the smaller version, namely that the latter also originated in Van Eyck's workshop.

The precise relationship, circumstances of production and firm attribution of the two paintings, which have been associated with Jan van Eyck and his workshop since the early twentieth century, remain open to question, despite scientific examination and the knowledge gained during restoration. The dating of the two works and their relationship to working practices, organization and division of labour within Van Eyck's workshop all require further study, as do their links with the Eyckian miniatures in the Turin-Milan Hours.

The recently postulated dating of the two panels to the beginning of the 1430s (see Valencia 2001) is seemingly contradicted by the observation that the Saint Francis figure appears to derive from the donor portrait in the 'Rolin Madonna' (fig. 13), to which a pair of anatomically awkward feet were added (Reynolds 2000). Motifs from the *Saint Francis* panels were, moreover, incorporated in several miniatures in the Turin-Milan Hours and in other works produced by the workshop or in its immediate circle after Van Eyck's death (cat. 9). Consequently, both paintings might also have been produced around 1440.

Provenance: Private collection, England.
References: Silver 1983; Vandenbroeck 1985.

Provenance: Before 1866, private collection, Casale Monferrato.
References: Dhanens 1980; Rohlmann 1993; Van Buren 1996; Philadelphia 1997; Turin 1997; Luber 1998; Venice 1999; Geirnaert 2000; Jones 2000; Nuttall 2000; Reynolds 2000; Madrid and Valencia 2001.

Provenance: Purchased *c.* 1824–28 in Lisbon by William à Court (Lord Heytesbury).
References: Dhanens 1980; Rohlmann 1994; Van Buren 1996; Philadelphia 1997; Luber 1998; Geirnaert 2000; Jones 2000; Nuttall 2000; Reynolds 2000; Valencia 2001.

30   Jan van Eyck and assistant (*c.* 1390–1441)
Saint Jerome in His Study, c. 1440–42
Paper mounted on panel, 19.9 × 12.5 cm
(see fig. 113)
Detroit Institute of Arts (inv. 25.4)

The fact that this work was executed on a paper
support, together with a number of supposed
peculiarities in terms of painting technique, led
to the questioning of its authenticity in the 1960s
(see Marijnissen 1978). However, recent technical
examination (Heller and Studolski 1995 and 1998)
has shown such doubts to be unfounded.

The miniature-like, Eyckian image shows the
Father of the Church dressed as a cardinal in his study.
Jerome, the lion at his feet, sits reading at a table
covered with writing equipment, an hourglass and
a letter. The wall of the study is lined with shelves,
protected by a blue curtain and stacked with books,
documents, an astrolabe and other objects. The letter
on the table is addressed to the titular cardinal of Santa
Croce in Gerusalemme in Rome, prompting the
identification of this Jerome as a historicizing portrait
of Cardinal Niccolò Albergati (cat. 24). Furthermore,
the astrolabe refers to the date of the Treaty of Arras
(1435), in which Albergati (1375–1443) was involved
as papal legate.

This link to the Cardinal – the painting's most
likely original owner – suggests that the work is the
picture of Saint Jerome by Van Eyck that appears in
the inventory of the Medici collection in 1492. The
painting might well have reached Florence prior to
1480, as its composition is echoed in the Ognissanti
frescoes by Ghirlandaio and Botticelli (fig. 112).

The attribution of the Detroit painting is rendered
problematic by partial overpainting and the date
(1442?) inscribed on the wall behind the saint. An
initial attribution to Petrus Christus is, however,
untenable (Ainsworth 1994). As is the case with the
'Charterhouse Madonna' (fig. 22), the painting is more
likely to have been a Van Eyck composition completed
by a workshop assistant after the master's death.
Van Eyck's workshop – the same painter perhaps –
reused the composition in a miniature depicting Saint
Thomas Aquinas (Turin-Milan Hours, destroyed
by fire in 1904), which circulated among Flemish
illuminators. It is unclear to what extent the
composition corresponded with the Saint Jerome
wing of Van Eyck's lost 'Lomellini triptych'.

31   Assistant of Jan van Eyck (*c.* 1390–1441)
Virgin and Child ('Ince Hall Madonna'), *c.* 1435
Panel, 26.3 × 19.4 cm (see fig. 27)
National Gallery of Victoria, Melbourne
(inv. 1275/3)

The Virgin with the Infant Christ on her lap sits on
the floor below a canopy in an interior lit by a window
on the left. The canopy serves to link this example of
the 'Virgin of Humility' with another pictorial type
– that of the Virgin and Child Enthroned (cat. 23).
The pomegranates on the windowsill symbolize the
Passion of Christ, while the glass carafe on the bench
alludes to Mary's virginity. A metal jug stands on the
sideboard to the right, together with a three-armed
brass candleholder with snuffed candles. A wash-basin
can be seen on the floor nearby. These seemingly
everyday items also have a Marian or Eucharistic
significance – similar objects appear not only in
Van Eyck's paintings, but also in those of the
Campin workshop.

A painted inscription to the left of the canopy
indicates that the painting was completed in 1433 by
'IOH[ANN]EM DE EYC BRUGIS', while Van Eyck's motto
appears on the right. The inscription, in spite of being
part of the original paint structure, is problematic
because of the toponymical addition '*Brugis*' – 'from
Bruges', which might indicate that it was painted for a
temporary resident in the city, say a foreign merchant.
Starting from the inscription's clearly retrospective
character, Davies and Hoff (1971) questioned the
hitherto all but unchallenged attribution to Van Eyck.
They identified the painting as a late pastiche,
comprising various pictorial elements from
Van Eyck's oeuvre.

In the light of recently discovered *pentimenti*
(Madrid and Valencia 2001), it would seem logical to
reconsider the painting in the context of Van Eyck's
work and that of his workshop. Although the artist
falls well short of Jan van Eyck as far as the spatial
construction and flesh areas are concerned, he is more
successful in 'the brilliant registration of the lighting'
(Pächt 1989), which is reminiscent of Piero della
Francesca. The painting might be a workshop replica
of a lost Van Eyck, the composition of which was
paraphrased somewhat later in the 'Covarrubias
Madonna' (cat. 42). A third version, painted in
Flanders around 1500, belonged to a collection in
Messina (Collobi Ragghianti 1990, no. 3). It is possible
that the inscription refers to the year in which the lost
prototype was painted.

32   Assistant of Jan van Eyck (*c.* 1390–1441)
The Fountain of Life (*Triumph of the Church
over the Synagogue*), *c.* 1445–50
Panel, 181 × 119 cm (see fig. 24)
Museo Nacional del Prado, Madrid (inv. 1151)

The composition is arranged into three horizontal
registers, set in and before a powerful and fantastic
architectural structure flanked by a pair of towers.
God the Father sits on his throne below a monumental
Gothic baldachin, a stone statue of the Lamb of the
Apocalypse at his feet. The Virgin Mary and Christ
sit on either side of him. The sides of the throne are
decorated with the symbols of the Evangelists, while
statues representing Old Testament prophets adorn
the baldachin. As described in the Book of Revelation,
the Fountain of Life – in which float wafers of the
Host – flows from the Lamb. The water passes
through a paradisiacal meadow with musician angels
who accompany the singers in the towers. The River
of Life leads to a fountain, to the right of which stand
the despairing adherents of the Jewish faith, and on
the left the representatives and estates of a triumphal
Christendom.

The painting, which is explicitly described as
Flemish in the deed of endowment, was commissioned
by King Henry IV of Castile (r. 1454–74) for the recently
established Hieronymite Monastery of Nuestra Señora
del Parral (Segovia). That makes the painting one of the
first Early Netherlandish works to be identified in
Castile, together with the Marian altarpiece that
Rogier van der Weyden painted in 1445 for John II
on behalf of the Charterhouse of Miraflores (fig. 131).

Art historians are divided in both their assessment
of the painting and their interpretation of the artist's
relationship to Jan van Eyck. Iconographical and
supposedly stylistic similarities to the Ghent altarpiece
initially led to either the painting's identification
as an early work by Hubert or Jan van Eyck, or its
attribution to Petrus Christus because of the
discrepancies in quality. Nowadays, the dispute tends
to focus on whether the painting is a copy of an earlier,
lost work by Van Eyck or, as we suspect, an
autonomous pictorial invention by an assistant or
follower familiar with the repertory of motifs kept
within the Van Eyck workshop.

The Madrid *Fountain of Life* was copied several
times in Spain around 1500. The most important copy
of the Eyckian panel was displayed in the Cathedral in
Palencia until the eighteenth century (fig. 23).

Provenance: Probably Medici collection, Florence (1492).
References: Panofsky 1954; Sterling 1976; Jolly 1976; Marijnissen 1978;
Dhanens 1980; Ainsworth and Martens 1994; Rohlmann 1994; Heller and
Studolski 1995, pp. 131–42; König 1996; Nuttall 1996; Smeyers 1997;
Hall 1998; Heller and Studolski 1998, pp. 38–55; Venice 1999, no. 15.

Provenance: Henry Blundell, Ince Hall.
References: Baldass 1952; Hoff and Davies 1971, pp. 29–50; Dhanens 1980;
Pächt 1989; Cologne 1993; Madrid and Valencia 2001.

Provenance: Monasterio de Nuestra Señora del Parral, Segovia.
References: Bruyn 1957; Pächt 1959; Pemán y Pemartín 1967; Sterling 1976;
Bermejo 1980; Dhanens 1980; Pächt 1989; Herzner 1995; Jones 2000.

33   **Assistant of Jan van Eyck (Master of the Grimacing Saint John)** (*c.*1390–1441)
John the Baptist; Virgin and Child (diptych), *c.*1440–45
Panel, 38.3 × 23.5 cm each (see fig. 25)
Musée du Louvre, Paris (inv. RF 38–22)

The figures of the Baptist and the Virgin and Child are shown as imitation stone sculptures, illuminated from the left, standing on octagonal plinths before rectangular niches. These are bounded by an arch with traceried lunettes and by two pillars incorporated in the *trompe-l'œil* stone frame. The two panels probably once formed the inside of a diptych, as there are traces of imitation porphyry or marble on the rear. The frame, imitating the effect of book binding, is a later addition of the seventeenth or eighteenth century (Verougstraete and Van Schoute 2000, however, consider it to be original).

The image is indisputably related to the Van Eyck workshop and plainly shows a direct link with the pictorial inventions of the Bruges master. The figure of John the Baptist is, however, more reminiscent of the monumental grisailles of the Ghent altarpiece (fig. 5), while a direct comparison of the diptych with Van Eyck grisailles of the same format, such as the Thyssen *Annunciation* (cat. 20) and the outside of the Dresden triptych (cat. 23), reveals significant differences in quality. Although it is widely agreed that the diptych is not an autograph Jan van Eyck, the question remains as to whether it is a copy after a lost early work or an – at least partially – independent invention of a workshop assistant.

Bruyn (1957) argued that the diptych was the key work of an assistant of Van Eyck active in the mid-1430s, to whom he gave the name the 'Master of the Grimacing Saint John', because of the expression on the Baptist's face. He attributed to that master a series of Eyckian drawings that resemble the painting in terms of the facial features and heavy physicality of the figures. Reynaud (Paris 1990), by contrast, detected a closer relationship with the *Saint John* panel produced by the Van Eyck workshop (cat. 9), though this was in turn challenged by Ainsworth (Ainsworth and Martens 1994).

Perhaps we are dealing here with a member of the Van Eyck workshop who deliberately focused after 1441 on the master's early designs, and who might also have been responsible for the Berlin *Crucifixion* (fig. 19).

34   **Assistant of Jan van Eyck** (*c.*1390–1441)
*Crucifixion, c.*1440–50
Panel, 46 × 31 cm (see fig. 21)
Galleria Giorgio Franchetti alla Ca' d'Oro, Venice (inv. CGF/d128)

The Virgin Mary and John the Evangelist stand grieving on either side of the dead Christ on the cross. Behind them is an imposing view of Jerusalem, with its extensive city walls, Temple and houses, which occupies the middleground of the composition. Some distance away on the left, we see a group of mourning women, while on the right, a number of people on horseback begin to make their way back from Golgotha.

The rich colours, wealth of detail and quality of execution suggest that this is the work of a Flemish painter, who could have spent some time in Jan van Eyck's workshop, where he would have been able to use the master's workshop drawings. The composition plainly draws on a lost original *Crucifixion* by the Bruges painter, to which another workshop assistant turned after Van Eyck's death for the equivalent scene in the Turin-Milan Hours (fig. 18). The panel painting and the miniature were probably based on a common model, therefore, rather than being dependent on one another. The differences between them in terms of viewpoint and the way the image is framed are likely to reflect their varying sizes and functions.

To judge by individual motifs, Van Eyck's lost original must have been most closely related to the left wing of the New York diptych (fig. 15). Although this appears to be a later work that Van Eyck finished with the help of workshop assistants, it may well have drawn on one of the master's earlier compositions (fig. 19).

It is not impossible that Jan van Eyck's lost *Crucifixion* was located in Venice in the mid-fifteenth century. Echoes of its composition and specific motifs can be identified in the Crucifixion scenes produced in the circle of Squarcione, while Van Eyck's mounted figures appear to have inspired Andrea Mantegna during the execution of his *Crucifixion* for the predella of the San Zeno altarpiece (fig. 102). It is more likely, however, to have been this copy by a workshop assistant that found its way to Italy at an early date, where it was copied by another anonymous artist (cat. 85). Strehlke (2001) recently suggested that Barthélemy d'Eyck might have been responsible for the Venetian *Crucifixion*.

35   **Copy after Jan van Eyck** (*c.*1390–1441)
Portrait of a Member of the Order of Saint Anthony ('Man with Carnation'), after *c.*1475
Panel, 41.5 × 31.5 cm (see fig. 196)
Staatliche Museen zu Berlin, Preussisches Kulturbesitz. Gemäldegalerie (inv. 525A)

The sitter is shown from the chest up against a dark background. He is turned to the left and looks out of the painting with its *trompe-l'œil* frame. The man wears a high fur hat and a grey jacket, and holds three carnations in his right hand. His left hand is shown in front of his chest, where we see a little bell with a T-shaped cross on a silver chain. These are the insignia of the Order of Saint Anthony – a chivalric order founded in 1382 by Albert of Bavaria, Count of Holland, Zeeland and Hainaut, and revived as a religious fraternity by John of Bavaria (1419–25). By the 1420s, when Jan van Eyck was employed as John's court painter in The Hague, membership of the order was no longer the preserve of the aristocracy but was also open to the high bourgeoisie. The importance of the Antonine Order declined sharply following the end of Wittelsbach rule in Holland.

This portrait was celebrated for its realism and was long thought to be an early work of Jan van Eyck. However, closer study of its technical execution and dendrochronological dating have shown that it cannot actually have been produced before the end of the fifteenth century. The inclusion of the Antonine insignia suggests that it is a copy – possibly enlarged – of a lost Van Eyck portrait from his Hague period (*c.*1422–25). The overall realism of the painting – especially the illusionism of the painted frame, on which the sitter seems to cast a shadow with his right hand – and the way the man looks out of the image are characteristic features of Van Eyck portraits after 1432, but would, if the above assumption is correct, also appear to have been established elements of the painter's repertoire in the 1420s.

The subject of the portrait has not been identified. He must, however, have been an important individual, as his portrait (also based on the original) can be seen in at least two Cologne *Adorations* (Faggin 1968/70). A portrait of John of Bavaria dressed in a cardinal's robes, which probably also derived from Van Eyck's painting, was recorded in Spain in the early part of the twentieth century (Bermejo 1980).

Provenance: Before 1896, Carlo Micheli, Paris.
References: Bruyn 1957; Lurie 1981; Bosshard 1992; Ainsworth and Martens 1994; Comblen-Sonkes and Lorentz 1995, pp. 1–10; Verougstraete and Van Schoute 2000.

Provenance: Dondo dell'Orologio collection, Padua (?).
References: Bruyn 1957; Châtelet 1980; Belting and Eichberger 1983; Limentani Virdis 1997; Turin 1997; Luber 1998; Venice 1999; Madrid and Valencia 2001; Strehlke 2001.

Provenance: Before 1867, Philipp Engels, Cologne.
References: Baldass 1952; Bauch 1961; Friedländer I (1967); Faggin 1968/70; Dhanens 1980; Bermejo 1980; Pächt 1989.

36   Copy after Jan van Eyck (*c.* 1390–1441)
Woman at Her Toilet, fifteenth century
Panel, 27.5 × 16.5 cm (see fig. 126)
Fogg Art Museum, Harvard University Art
Museums, Cambridge, Mass. Francis H. Burr,
Louise Haskell Daly, Alphaeus Hyatt and
William M. Prichard Funds

Willem van Haecht's 1615 painting of the *Kunstkammer*
of Cornelis van der Geest, Burgomaster of Antwerp
(Rubenshuis, Antwerp), includes a picture (to the
right above a classical *Venus Pudica*) of a naked woman
in an interior, who is helped by her maid as she washes.
Van der Geest's paintings were acquired after his death
by the Antwerp art dealer Peter Stevens, the 1668
catalogue of whose collection includes a panel by Jan
van Eyck in which the painter's wife Margaret is said
to have been portrayed both dressed and undressed.
All the evidence suggests that the description refers
to the painting in Van der Geest's collection.

   The panel reproduced here is a fifteenth-century
copy of the lost Van Eyck. In spite of its poor
condition, the similarities with Van Eyck's celebrated
Arnolfini double portrait in the National Gallery,
London (fig. 127), are overwhelming. In addition
to the box-like conception of the interior and the
positioning of the figures, motifs like the mirror,
sideboard, bed, shoes and even the dog appear in
almost identical locations in the two paintings. Held
suspected that the Van Eyck original showed the ritual
wedding toilet of Arnolfini's wife, Giovanna Cenami,
and that it was the painting's original companion
piece. This view was shared by Ridderbos, although
he interpreted the painting as an allegorical
representation of *Fides*, while Seidel preferred to see
it as an allegory of desire.

   The idea that Van Eyck might have painted his
own wife both naked and dressed ought not, however,
to be dismissed out of hand, especially as the
composition includes elements that might be
interpreted as alluding to his profession. Van Haecht
had already made the link between the classical statue
of the nude Venus and the Eyckian toilet scene in his
image of Van der Geest's *Kunstkammer*, and it is well
established that Van Eyck painted non-religious nudes.
Fazio, for instance, wrote in 1456 of the *Bathing Women*
owned by Ottaviano della Carda.

37   Copy after Jan van Eyck (*c.* 1390–1441)
Portrait of Christ, after 1635
Panel, 33.4 × 26.8 cm (see fig. 100)
Stedelijke Musea, Groeningemuseum, Bruges
(inv. 0.206)

This idealized image of the *vera effigies* of Christ
derives, as the inscription on the *trompe-l'œil* frame
tells us, from Jan van Eyck. The Bruges painter, whose
motto appears on the frame to the right, is described
as the *inventor* of this composition, echoes of which are
found in Flemish illuminated manuscripts until well
into the sixteenth century. The painting itself is said
to date from 30 January 1440. Jesus is presented in a
strictly frontal manner against a dark background.
He has a cross-shaped golden halo. The initials
I(nitium) and F(initum) are attached to it, referring to
God's words 'I am the first and the last', as expressed
by the Greek letters alpha and omega. Christ is
described on the upper part of the painted frame as
the Way (*via*), the Truth (*veritas*) and the Life (*vita*).

   Van Eyck's lost original composition came down
to us in several early copies, examples of which can be
seen in Bruges, Berlin, Munich and an English private
collection. Whereas Christ's collar in Bruges is
trimmed with precious stones, these are replaced in
Munich and Berlin with inscriptions referring to the
King of Kings (*Rex Regum*). The Berlin version, like
the Bruges panel, has an inscribed frame, though in
this instance the prototype is dated to 1438. All the
evidence suggests that, within the space of a few years,
Jan van Eyck and his workshop painted at least two
virtually identical versions of the Holy Face, just as
they did with the *Virgin at the Fountain* (cat. 26) and
Saint Francis Receiving the Stigmata (cat. 28).

   The Bruges copy prompts the question of whether
the *trompe-l'œil* frame was added by the follower, or
whether this noteworthy detail actually reflects the
lost original. Van Eyck is sure to have been familiar
with the legend that the *vera effigies* was not the work
of a human hand but of divine origin. It is entirely
possible that, by painting a frame of this kind, he
wanted to counter this popular belief with the skills
available to him as a painter.

38   Hugo van der Goes (*c.* 1440–1482)
Saint Luke Drawing the Virgin
(left panel of a diptych), *c.* 1475–80
Panel, 104.5 × 62.8 cm (see fig. 249)
Museu Nacional de Arte Antiga, Lisbon
(inv. 1459)

It was discovered during restoration in 1974 that this
originally rounded panel has been cut off to the left
and right of the top and once formed part of a diptych.
The complete composition is known from an
engraving by Antoon Wierix, although the latter
probably worked from a copy of the diptych painted
by Quentin Massys rather than from the original.

   Saint Luke is shown in his workshop, kneeling on
two cushions. Behind him, to the left, is a window,
next to which stands an easel with a panel ready for
painting, and a stool for the painter to sit on. An ox
– the emblem of Luke the Evangelist – gazes across the
stool. A number of traditional artist's implements are
positioned behind the saint, including a leather pouch
containing pigment and a seashell in which to mix
paint, while the book refers to the saint's activity as the
Gospel writer. In his hands, Luke holds another book,
on which rests a sheet of paper, and a silverpoint
stylus. He is intently studying the vision of the
enthroned Virgin and Child. Unlike Rogier's version
of the theme (see cat. 61), the drawing is not visible, but
the contemporary viewer would have seen the results
of the artist's labours in the now-lost right-hand panel.
Hugo van der Goes, who appears to have been
deliberately vying with both Rogier van der Weyden
and Robert Campin, subtly refers in this painting to
his knowledge of Italian Renaissance ideas on subjects
like creation, observation and composition. The still
life in front of Saint Luke, with the quill, penknife and
sharpened stick of charcoal, are literal references to
Cennini's description of the art of drawing in the
Libro dell'Arte.

   Dürer noted in his diary in 1521 that he had seen
a painting by '*Meister Hugo*' in the Nassau chapel in
Brussels. The Nassau Palace's 1568 inventory lists an
altarpiece showing Saint Luke and the Virgin Mary,
which might just have been the diptych of which this
panel is the survivor.

Provenance: Private collection, England.
References: Schabacker 1974–76; Dhanens 1980, pp. 208–11; Ridderbos 1993;
Seidel 1993; Paviot 2000.

Provenance: 1787, Joseph de Busscher, Bruges.
References: De Vos 1979, pp. 228–29; Dhanens 1980, p. 293.

Provenance: Until 1867, Pedro de Madrazo, Madrid.
References: Lievens de Waegh 1991; Sander 1992; Dhanens 1998; White 1997.

39	**Hugo van der Goes** (c. 1440–1482)	

39   **Hugo van der Goes** (c. 1440–1482)
Death of the Virgin, after 1475
Panel, 147.8 × 122.5 cm (see fig. 57)
Stedelijke Musea, Groeningemuseum, Bruges
(inv. 0.204)

The Virgin Mary is shown here in the final moments
of her life, surrounded by her son's disciples. Dressed
in the manner of a fifteenth-century clergyman, the
chief apostle, Saint Peter, lights a candle to place in the
dying person's hands in the traditional way. Christ
appears above the bed accompanied by a group of
angels. The painting is noteworthy for the quiet yet
highly expressive way in which it renders the emotions
that we read in the faces of the deeply moved apostles.
Each of those present is plainly dealing with the
dramatic moment in his own specific way.

The popular theme of the Virgin on her deathbed
does not derive from the Bible, as is often thought, but
from the *Legenda Aurea* (*Golden Legend*)– a frequently
consulted collection of saints' lives compiled by Jacopo
da Voragine in the second half of the thirteenth
century. The theme was adopted by several of the
greatest northern European artists of the fifteenth and
sixteenth centuries, including, in addition to Van der
Goes himself, Dieric Bouts, Martin Schongauer,
Albrecht Dürer and Pieter Bruegel.

Although Hugo's small but entirely unsigned and
undated oeuvre has yet to be properly studied, most
authorities agree that the *Death of the Virgin* must be
one of the artist's later works, produced some time
between 1477 and 1482. He probably drew inspiration
from Schongauer's engraving, which dates from
around 1470–75. Van der Goes' painting influenced
further artists in turn. There are surviving copies and
imitations from the fifteenth and sixteenth centuries.
However, unlike an earlier, lost painting of the same
theme (see cat. 40), this Bruges masterpiece does not
seem to have had any discernible influence on
southern European painting.

40   **Follower of Hugo van der Goes** (c. 1440–1482)
Death of the Virgin, c. 1480–90
Panel, 35 × 36.5 cm (see fig. 43)
Prague Castle Collection

This small panel probably derives from a lost *Death of
the Virgin* by Hugo van der Goes. Two other versions
of the composition survive, the style of which suggests
that they too were painted by followers of Hugo.
If this is correct, the original work must have been
a relatively early one. The composition differs
significantly from the Bruges masterpiece (cat. 39)
and the work is without doubt less ambitious and less
successful both in terms of the internal coherence
between the depicted figures and in the expression
of their individual emotions. It is impossible to say,
however, how much of this is attributable to the
artistic limitations of the anonymous follower.

Whether or not the original was the work of
Van der Goes, its painter clearly drew inspiration
from Petrus Christus' *Death of the Virgin* (cat. 13). It is
tempting to suggest that, as an up-and-coming painter
in Ghent, Hugo van der Goes wished to demonstrate
his skills by taking up the challenge offered by a
famous composition of the celebrated Bruges master.
Judging by the three copies that have survived, the
original painting must have been well received. It was
this composition, at any rate, and not the later Bruges
Death of the Virgin as is usually supposed, on which
Pieter Bruegel drew for his 1564 grisaille interpretation
of the theme (Upton House, Banbury).

The interesting feature of the Prague painting is,
however, precisely its use of colour. Its brightness and
tonality recall French painters in the circle of Simon
Marmion, although it is not possible to venture an
attribution at this stage. The issue is further
complicated by the fact that Hugo van der Goes had a
particularly strong influence on French painting in the
late fifteenth century and may have been the teacher of
Jean Hey (also known as the Master of Moulins, see
cats 72–75). The panel can probably be dated to the
final decade of the fifteenth century.

41   **Quentin Massys** (1465–1530)
Two panels from the altarpiece with the *Seven
Sorrows of the Virgin*, c. 1510
(1) *Rest on the Flight into Egypt*. Panel, 82.6 ×
79 cm. Worcester Art Museum (Acc. 1937.4)
(2) *Saint John and the Three Marys at the Tomb*.
Panel, 82.5 × 79 cm (see figs 34–35)
Museu Nacional de Arte Antiga, Lisbon
(inv. 1829 Pint)

Portuguese painting was indisputably influenced
by Antwerp art in the early sixteenth century
– a period in which the traditionally close ties between
Flanders and Portugal were especially strong. The
Netherlandish painters Francisco Henriques (cat. 129)
and Frey Carlos (cats 125–27), together with the
principal master behind the Évora altarpiece (cat. 130),
were among the most important artists of their time
in Portugal, while Portuguese painters were also
active in Antwerp.

The pupils who trained in Antwerp under Quentin
Massys included a certain 'Eduwart Portugalois', who
entered the master's workshop in 1504 and became an
independent painter in the city in 1508. Works by
followers of Massys have been ascribed to him, though
none securely. The altarpiece with the *Seven Sorrows of
the Virgin*, which is made up of eight individual panels,
is generally viewed as being largely the production of
Massys' studio, even though it was an important royal
commission. It originally belonged to the Clarissan
Convent of Madre de Deus in Xabregas, which Queen
Eleanor of Portugal (1485–1522) founded in 1509, but
was subsequently broken up and is now divided among
museums in Lisbon, Rio de Janeiro and Worcester.
The altarpiece was ordered from Massys through João
Brandao, who was Portuguese factor in Antwerp in
1504–9 and again in 1520–25. The commission was
undoubtedly linked to Eleanor's foundation of the
Lisbon convent and is thus likely to have been placed
around 1509, with completion a short time later.
Portuguese sources first refer to the altarpiece in 1513.

The panels are closest chronologically to Massys'
early *Saint Anne* altarpiece (Musées Royaux, Brussels),
to which they are also linked stylistically. Although the
large size of the two works suggests that assistants will
have had a hand in their completion, the question has
once again arisen in the wake of the recent restoration
of the *Rest on the Flight into Egypt* of how much Massys
himself contributed to the execution of this pair of
important commissions.

Provenance: Ter Duinen Abbey, Koksijde (?).
References: Winkler 1964; Campbell and Thompson 1974; De Vos 1979;
Sander 1992; Dhanens 1998.

Provenance: Emperor Rudolf II, Prague.
References: Winkler 1964; Davies 1972; Châtelet 1996; Campbell 1998.

Provenance: Before 1513, Madre de Deus Monastery, Xabregas (Lisbon).
References: Friedländer VII; Silver 1984; Dacos 1991.

42   Master of Covarrubias (active 1440–1450)
Virgin and Child ('Covarrubias Madonna'),
c. 1445–50
Panel, 46.1 × 35 cm (see fig. 28)
Museo de la Colegiata de San Cosme
y Damián, Covarrubias (Burgos)

The 'Ince Hall Madonna' (cat. 31) was still considered to be an authentic early work by Jan van Eyck when Reinach (1923) published the 'Covarrubias Madonna' as a copy of a lost *Virgin and Child* by the Bruges master. Attention was drawn at the time to differences between the two paintings and it was concluded that the 'Covarrubias Madonna' was definitely not a copy of the Melbourne panel. On the other hand, historians found it hard to imagine that an anonymous copyist would have had the ability to paraphrase such a plainly Eyckian composition.

The Covarrubias picture features a series of compositional details that are too reminiscent of the Melbourne panel – which was probably painted by one of Van Eyck's workshop assistants – to be dismissed as coincidence. It seems possible, therefore, that both paintings actually derive from a lost Van Eyck Madonna or, indeed, the associated workshop drawing. The two putative copies clearly differ in terms of spatial conception. In this respect, the 'Covarrubias Madonna' recalls the 1437 Dresden triptych (fig. 23), while the Melbourne panel is closer in its spatial arrangement to Van Eyck's 'Lucca Madonna' (cat. 21). The two paintings might thus have been the work of assistants employed in Van Eyck's workshop at different periods.

König (1994 and 1998) argued that the Master of Covarrubias was still active in the workshop around 1440–45 – after Van Eyck's death – and attributed to him the miniature *Pietà* in the section of the Turin-Milan Hours that was destroyed by fire in 1904. Brinkmann (2000) has suggested that a number of panel paintings should be ascribed to this Van Eyck assistant, who appears to have been German in origin (the inscription on the wall to the left of the 'Covarrubias Madonna' probably reads '*wer sich des sicher …*'). Prudence is called for, however, in view of the extensive additions to the panel's paintwork, which has only survived in fragmentary form. Natale (2001) has gone so far as to suggest because of this that the painting actually dates from the late nineteenth century.

43   Master of the Portraits of Princes
(active *c.* 1480–1500)
Louis of Gruuthuse, *c.* 1480–90
Panel, 34.2 × 22.8 cm (see fig. 201)
Stedelijke Musea, Groeningemuseum, Bruges
(inv. 0.1557)

The sitter of this portrait can be identified as Louis of Bruges, Lord of Gruuthuse (*c.* 1442–92), from the coat of arms and the motto '*Plus est en vous*', inscribed on the original frame. Gruuthuse was a member of the old nobility and one of the most important aristocratic patrons in Bruges. He also owned a prominent library that included classical and humanist texts (Martens 1992). His grandfather, Jan van der Aa, had a mansion built close to the Church of Our Lady. Louis extended the building and added the famous oratory linking it to the choir of the church.

Louis of Bruges pursued an impressive political career. He was councillor to both Philip the Good and Charles the Bold, served as governor on their behalf in Holland, Zeeland and Friesland, and was made Earl of Winchester by King Richard III of England. In 1461, he became a Knight of the Golden Fleece, the prestigious Burgundian chivalric order used by the Dukes to cement the loyalty of their most prominent subjects and political allies. However, following the death of Mary of Burgundy (1482), Gruuthuse increasingly found himself in opposition to Archduke Maximilian. He became a key figure in the pro-French camp within Flanders, causing him to fall out of favour with the Habsburgs.

The Bruges portrait, which originally formed the right wing of a diptych with a *Virgin and Child*, shows him from the waist up before a neutral, red background. He wears the chain of the Golden Fleece around his neck and holds a marvellous rosary in his clasped hands. He is dressed in a black tunic in the Burgundian courtly style.

The painting is the work of the anonymous Master of the Portraits of Princes, who was active in Brussels in the final decades of the fifteenth century, and who collaborated with a number of minor masters from the circle of Rogier van der Weyden.

44   Master of the Holy Blood (*c.* 1465–1529)
Saint Luke Painting the Virgin, first quarter
sixteenth century
Panel, 43.3 × 32.7 cm (see fig. 251)
Fogg Art Museum, Harvard University Art
Museums, Cambridge, Mass. The John Witt
Randall Fund (Acc. 1910.6)

This depiction of Saint Luke's vision of the Madonna brings together the different pictorial traditions that developed alongside one another in the second half of the fifteenth century (see cats 38, 61). The image of the Virgin suckling the Christ Child was a popular one on the free market. The anonymous master combines it here with a view of a Renaissance master's studio, without making too much of an effort to integrate the two. The painter is shown kneeling awkwardly as he prepares his portrait of the Virgin and Child. The scene is festively adorned with garlands held by putti, recalling the *Judgment of Cambyses* by Gerard David (1498; Groeningemuseum, Bruges), with which the Master of the Holy Blood is relatively closely related. The composition is highly contrived and hence not very successful, but the artist none the less displays his knowledge of pictorial tradition. The inclusion of the easel refers to the lost Campin type of the vision of Saint Luke, while the mirror behind the saint, which appears in both Derick Bagaert and Colyn de Coter's versions, is also given a prominent place here. The *Maria Lactans* motif, on the other hand, is found in Rogier van der Weyden's work – and only there.

The Master of the Holy Blood evidently drew inspiration from traditional representations, without copying them too slavishly. His own contribution lay in the creative way he combined existing motifs.

Provenance: Colegiata de San Cosme y Damián, Covarrubias.
References: Bruyn 1957; Bermejo 1980; König 1994; Van Buren 1996; Madrid and Valencia 2001.

Provenance: Before 1866, A. van den Bogaerde, Bruges.
References: Duverger 1969, pp. 100–103; Martens 1992b; Wilson 1998.

Provenance: Before 1910, private collection, Spain.
References: Friedländer IX (1973); Spronk 1997.

45	**Master of Hoogstraten** (active *c.* 1485–*c.* 1520)

45 **Master of Hoogstraten** (active *c.* 1485–*c.* 1520)
Stigmatization of Saint Francis
Panel, 47 × 36 cm (see fig. 241)
Museo Nacional del Prado, Madrid (inv. 1617)

The Master of Hoogstraten takes his name from a
polyptych in the Koninklijk Museum in Antwerp,
which originally belonged to the Church of Saint
Catherine in Hoogstraten. The anonymous artist
was probably a painter from Holland who settled in
Antwerp some time before 1500. He may have been
active in Bruges prior to this, as he drew repeatedly
on the compositions of Bruges masters.

His image of Saint Francis of Assisi receiving the
stigmata is interesting in this respect, as it derives
directly from a composition of Jan van Eyck, which
probably once belonged to Anselmus Adornes in
Bruges. Two versions of it have survived (cats 28, 29).
The fact that artists like Botticelli, Filippino Lippi and
Giovanni Bellini borrowed landscape motifs from it
suggests that one of the versions must have found its
way to Italy by 1470, probably around the time that
Adornes made his pilgrimage to Jerusalem.
Knowledge of Van Eyck's *Saint Francis* subsequently
spread from Italy to the Western Mediterranean
(see Valencia 2001).

The panel by the Master of Hoogstraten, together
with a number of works from Cologne, is one of the
rare examples that confirm the influence of the
composition in the North and testify to its presence
in the Burgundian Netherlands. The Master of
Hoogstraten based his composition on the Eyckian
model, but otherwise 'modernized' the painting,
correcting, for instance, the awkward position of the
figures' feet in the original. The landscape, by contrast,
is treated more ambivalently – although the painter
retained Van Eyck's strange rock formations, he
replaced the distant landscape of the original with
a more panoramic view of the kind associated with
the Antwerp school. He has inserted a farm in the
middleground and brought forward the tree which,
in Van Eyck's version, appeared in the left background.
Although it was painted around 1495, the panel
illustrates the immense value that continued
to be placed on Jan van Eyck's painting in the
Low Countries.

46 **Master of the Saint Lucy Legend**
(Jean Hervey?) (active 1472–1506)
Saint Nicholas, c. 1486–93
Panel, 101.5 × 81.5 cm (see fig. 178)
Stedelijke Musea, Groeningemuseum, Bruges
(inv. 0.676)

With its sense of monumentality, this image of Saint
Nicholas, enthroned and dressed in bishop's robes,
once formed the centre panel of a triptych. The
original wings, which were fixed, show two scenes
from the saint's life and are now in a private collection
in Madrid (see Bruges 1994, no. 74). The painting's
Spanish provenance suggests that it was
commissioned by one of the many Iberian wool
merchants residing in Bruges and shipped to the
patron's native country. This might also explain the
particular nature of this saint's image, which is unusual
within Bruges painting. The artist appears to have
deliberately based himself on Spanish models, the best
known of which is Bartolomé Bermejo's painting of
Saint Dominic of Silos for the church of the same name
in Daroca (*c.* 1474–77; fig. 152). The type of the
enthroned holy bishop was, however, so well
established in Spanish art towards the end of the
fifteenth century (see also cat. 111) that there is no
reason to suppose a direct influence on Bermejo's part.

It is plain in this instance that the Bruges painter
was working in an idiom that was strange to him,
unlike that of the narrative scenes in the wings. In spite
of stylistic differences with respect to his other work,
it is plausible to attribute the panel to the Master of the
Saint Lucy Legend, not least because of the view of
Bruges in the background – a characteristic feature
of that anonymous master's style (De Vos 1979).
The precision with which a number of identifiable
buildings, including the Belfry, are depicted allows
the painting to be dated to between 1486 and 1493.
This detailed view of the city probably reflects the
patron's desire to record his temporary stay in the
Flemish trading metropolis. Reasons of social
prestige might also have prompted a desire for the
Netherlandish origin of the painting to be emphasized
within it. The function of the *veduta* might thus match
that of the topographical labels that appear in certain
Flemish works for Italian patrons.

47 **Hans Memling** (*c.* 1433–1494)
Portrait of a Male Donor (Francisco de Rojas?)
(left wing of a triptych), *c.* 1480
Panel (transferred), 106 × 50.4 cm (see fig. 220)
Estate Fred Ziv, Cincinnati

This painting, which is all but unanimously viewed
as being by Memling, resurfaced only recently. It used
to be regarded as an early work, but following the
removal of earlier, disfiguring overpainting its dating
will have to be reconsidered. Taking account of
elements like the landscape in the background,
a date around 1480 would also seem plausible.

The donor is shown in an open portico, framed
by a stone archway. He is dressed in a white shirt and
brocade tunic, over which he wears a black velvet robe
with slit sleeves. With a gold chain around his neck
and a short, ceremonial sword at his waist, he kneels
with his hands clasped before a *prie-dieu*, on which
lies an open prayerbook. The austere composition is
more reminiscent of Spanish donor portraits by artists
such as Jorge Inglés and the Sopetrán Master than
of Flemish works.

The man has been identified from the coat of arms
as the influential diplomat Francisco de Rojas. As the
envoy of the Catholic Kings, he was a regular visitor
to the Low Countries from 1492 onwards, working
to prepare the ground for the historic double wedding
between the Houses of Habsburg-Burgundy and
Tastamara in 1496/97. However, the stars in de Rojas'
coat of arms had seven points (see the *Breviary of
Isabella the Catholic*, British Library, London,
Ms. Add. 18851, fol. 437), whereas the ones shown here
have only six – as is also the case in Rietstap's *Armorial
Général*. Although the painting shows some wear in
this area, the discrepancy cannot be blamed on later
modifications. There is, at present, no explanation for
this anomaly. The way the donor portrait is presented
certainly suggests that Memling's sitter was a
prominent individual, who may indeed have come
from the Iberian peninsula.

The donor's portrait was originally the left wing
of a triptych, the lost centre panel of which probably
featured a Resurrection. This interpretation is
supported by the secondary scene that appears in the
left background, in which Joseph of Arimathea stands
before the empty sarcophagus and tomb of Christ.

Provenance: 1746, Spanish Royal Collection, La Granja.
References: Friedländer VII (1971), p. 90; Luber 1998.

Provenance: Comte de l'Epine (Paris?).
References: De Vos 1979; Bruges 1994.

Provenance: Private collection, Spain; before 1936, Knoedler & Co., London.
References: Friedländer 1937; De Vos 1994; Faries 1997.

| 48 | Hans Memling (c. 1435–1494) | 49 | Hans Memling (c. 1435–1494) | 50 | Hans Memling (c. 1435–1494) |

48   **Hans Memling** (*c.* 1435–1494)
Man with a Roman Coin
(Bernardo Bembo?), *c.* 1475
Panel, 31 × 23.2 cm (see fig. 227)
Koninklijk Museum voor Schone Kunsten,
Antwerp (inv. 5)

49   **Hans Memling** (*c.* 1435–1494)
Portrait of a Young Man, *c.* 1475–80
Panel, 40 × 29 cm (vertical strip 0.7 cm wide
added on right) (see fig. 239)
The Metropolitan Museum of Art, New York.
Robert Lehman Collection (inv. 1975.1.112)

50   **Hans Memling** (*c.* 1435–1494)
Triptych of Jan Floreins, 1479
Panel, 56.7 × 67 cm (centre); 56.7 × 33.7 cm
(wings) (see fig. 75)
Stedelijke Musea, Memlingmuseum, Bruges
(inv. o.SJ173.1)

Weale (1871) was the first to identify this male portrait as the work of Hans Memling, following its earlier attribution to Antonello da Messina. As in so many of Memling's portraits, the sitter here was in all likelihood an Italian – the Bruges-based painter was evidently the preferred portraitist of his day for the Italian merchants who lived and worked in the Flemish commercial metropolis. The small panel shows a man dressed in black with a landscape in the background. In his left hand he holds a Roman coin with the head, so the inscription tells us, of Emperor Nero. The sitter is shown from the chest up and turned to the right. He looks out of the painting at the viewer.

A pair of laurel leaves can be made out in the middle of the painting's lower edge. Together with the coin, which probably alludes to the sitter's antiquarian interests, and the palm tree in the right middleground, the leaves are the only clue as to the subject's identity. They could be attributes or pictograms referring to his name, or else they might derive from a visual motto.

The palm and laurel leaf were emblems of the Venetian humanist Bernardo Bembo (d. 1491), who lived in the Burgundian Netherlands between 1471 and 1474 as envoy of the Republic (Fletcher 1989). Not only was Bembo an important collector of antique coins, his collection of paintings, which he gave to Isabella d'Este just before his death, also included a Memling diptych (see De Vos 1994, no. 50), which he left to his famous son, the poet Pietro Bembo. The identification of the man in Memling's portrait as Bernardo Bembo (see Bruges 1998) cannot, however, be confirmed.

The similarity between Memling's painting and Sandro Botticelli's *Man with a Coin* in the Uffizi has been widely noted. Neither work is dated, however, leaving it unclear as to whether or not the Florentine artist borrowed Memling's pictorial invention.

Memling's portrait shows a young man from the chest up in three-quarter view. Turned to the left, he gazes into the distance. His dark claret tunic, worn tied up over a dark shirt, is trimmed with fur and decorated with a brocade pattern. The man's hands rest, one on top of the other, on an imaginary balustrade, which coincides optically with the frame of the painting. This technique dates back to Van Eyck, who used it on figures in niches, and has the effect of blurring the boundary between image and reality.

It is evident from the background that the portrait is set inside some kind of tower. The window on the left, with its decorative porphyry columns, leads the viewer's eye out into the landscape that unfolds into the distance. This is unusual for Memling, whose earliest portraits are set against neutral backgrounds, while his later ones are mostly located before a landscape (cat. 48). It recalls the 1462 male portrait by Dieric Bouts (National Gallery, London), which introduced the view through a window as a motif in northern portraiture.

It was through Memling's portraits, however, that this visual scheme found its way into Florentine painting. Campbell (1983) pointed out that a Madonna image in the Louvre from the circle of Verrocchio (recently attributed to the latter's pupil, Domenico Ghirlandaio), which dates from around 1480, incorporates a detailed borrowing of Memling's background landscape. Campbell showed that Perugino's *Self-Portrait* (fig. 237) also clearly draws on Memling's panel.

It is likely, therefore, that this is a portrait of a member of the Florentine merchant community in Bruges and that it was sent to Italy as soon as it was completed, enabling its assimilation by Florentine painters from around 1480. Italian businessmen and bankers – above all Florentines – were among Memling's most important clients after he settled in Bruges in 1465. There appears to have been considerable demand from that quarter, especially for his portraits.

Despite his German origins and the influence of the Cologne painter Stefan Lochner, which is clearly visible in some of his paintings, Memling was a key figure in fifteenth-century Flemish painting. He settled in Bruges in 1465 and appears to have painted most of his surviving works in that city. Like his contemporaries Bouts and Van der Goes, he followed in the footsteps of his illustrious predecessors Jan van Eyck and Rogier van der Weyden. His work is a synthesis of Eyckian and Rogierian ingredients: while the influence of the former is evident in his handling of light and colour, the skilful rendering of tactile values and a focus on landscape, his compositions, poses and portrait formulas are more closely related to Van der Weyden. Assimilating these elements, Memling created a canon that was to serve as a model for contemporaries such as Gerard David and for the following generation of Bruges artists.

The triptych was commissioned by Brother Jan Floreins and remains at its original location – Saint John's Hospital in Bruges. Memling borrowed a variety of compositions and figures for the 'Floreins triptych' from his supposed master, Rogier van der Weyden. The architecture and the Holy Family group in the centre panel are reminiscent of those in the *Annunciation* of Rogier's 'Columba altarpiece' (Alte Pinakothek, Munich). The left wing, meanwhile, draws on the *Nativity* in the centre panel of Van der Weyden's 'Bladelin triptych' (Berlin). The device of using porticos as a setting had also previously been applied by Van der Weyden and Petrus Christus. Memling drew inspiration for the architectural design of the archways on the outside from contemporary architecture – more specifically the Paradise Porch beneath the tower at the nearby Church of Our Lady.

The artist reused the iconography of the closed wings – featuring *John the Baptist* (possibly based on an Eyckian composition) and *Saint Veronica* – in the 'Bembo diptych' (1480–83; Alte Pinakothek, Munich, and National Gallery of Art, Washington), which had entered the Bembo collection in Venice by 1502.

Provenance: Purchased in Lyons by Baron Vivant Denon.
References: Campbell 1981b; Fletcher 1989; De Vos 1994, no. 42; Bruges 1994; Bruges 1998.

Provenance: Before 1854, 9th Earl of Wemyss, Gosford House, Longniddry (Scotland).
References: Campbell 1983, pp. 675–76; Bauman 1986, pp. 42–43; De Vos 1994, no. 48; New York 1998, no. 28; Wolff 1998, no. 13.

Provenance: Sint-Janshospitaal, Bruges.
References: De Vos 1994; Bruges 1994; Bruges 1998.

51 **Hans Memling** (*c.*1435–1494)
Christ Crowned with Thorns
(companion piece to cat. 52), *c.*1480
Panel, 53.4 × 39.1 cm (including vertical strips
approx. 3.5 cm added on both sides) (see fig. 63)
Galleria di Palazzo Bianco, Genoa

Since its discovery in 1947, this panel has generally
been viewed as a late work by Memling – a reading
confirmed by analysis of the painting technique and
underdrawing. The image of Christ formed the left
wing of a diptych and the reverse was probably
painted in imitation porphyry. The original right
wing, the back of which has been cradled, shows
the grieving Virgin Mary (cat. 52).

Jesus is shown half-length, wearing a dark robe
against a neutral, dark background. The wounds in
his hands and the crown of thorns, which causes the
blood to flow down his forehead, allude to his Passion,
but the tears on his cheeks – the simultaneously
transparent and reflective character of which Memling
captures brilliantly – evoke Mary's grief at her son's
suffering. In the context of the diptych, which was
painted for private devotion, not only is Christ
presented as the focus of that grief and as the subject
of the viewer's sympathy, he also provides an example
of *compassio*.

Memling displays immense subtlety in this diptych
in the way he successfully integrates the viewer/
worshipper in the image. Contrary to the Flemish
pictorial tradition, in which Christ's head is shown
more frontally and the wounds of the Passion are
displayed much more graphically, the painter
deliberately avoids direct eye contact between Christ,
the Virgin and the viewer. Instead, the latter is directly
'addressed' by the way Jesus points with his left hand
and encouraged to display empathy during his or her
devotions. Through the gesture of his right hand the
Saviour offers his blessing as reward for the *compassio*
demanded by the painting and embodied by the Virgin.

Memling's interpretation of a devotional theme
common in the Netherlands was emulated by some
of his Italian contemporaries (see cat. 99), most likely
because of its 'human' character.

52 **Hans Memling** (*c.*1435–1494)
The Virgin Mary
(companion piece to cat. 51), *c.*1480
Panel, 53.2 × 37.2 cm (including vertical strips
approx. 2.5 cm wide added on both sides)
(see fig. 64)
Private collection, United Kingdom

This image of the Virgin Mary praying, which was
only recently reattributed to Memling, was originally
the right wing of a diptych for use in private devotion
(see cat. 51). Memling completed the painting in the
late 1480s, drawing on a pictorial scheme that can
probably be traced back to the workshop of the
Leuven (Louvain) town artist Dieric Bouts. It links
Christ as the Man of Sorrows with a half-length image
of the grieving Virgin Mary and appears to have been
widely disseminated in the Netherlands. Like the
Bouts type, of which several versions have survived,
Memling's diptych is a powerful invitation to the
viewer to empathize with Christ's suffering and
sacrifice and with Mary's grief.

The figure of the Virgin appears to refer indirectly
to the Deisis group in Van der Weyden's Beaune
Last Judgment (figs 60–61), which Memling first
paraphrased around 1467 – probably from a workshop
drawing created by his Brussels-based master – in
the Gdansk *Last Judgment*, painted for Angelo Tani
(fig. 76). As far as the execution of the flesh parts and the
white headdress is concerned, the painting resembles
the female members of the donor's family in the
'Madonna of Jacob Floreins' (Louvre, Paris), another
late work. As is the case with its companion piece, the
chalk underdrawing of the Virgin panel contains a
series of modifications – typical of Memling – especially
in relation to the position of the Virgin's hands, which
are folded in prayer. Although several late fifteenth- and
early sixteenth-century copies of the two wings have
survived, the corrections in the underdrawing indicate
that this is the original version of an autonomous
pictorial invention by the Bruges painter.

It is not known whether Memling painted the
diptych as a commission and, if so, for whom. It
appears, though, that the work was sent to Florence
shortly after its completion. The copies of the left wing
attributed to Domenico Ghirlandaio (cat. 99) as well as
later variations demonstrate the success of Memling's
composition, especially in Italy.

53 **Hans Memling** (*c.*1435–1494)
Triptych of Saint Christopher
('Moreel triptych'), 1484
Panel, 141 × 174 cm (centre); 141 × 86.5 cm
(wings) (see fig. 74)
Stedelijke Musea, Groeningemuseum, Bruges
(inv. 0.91.1)

This triptych was commissioned by the merchant and
banker Willem Moreel, a prominent Bruges citizen.
Moreel, who was given permission in 1484 to install
the altarpiece and a tombstone in the Church of Saint
James, is accompanied in the left wing by his sons and
his patron saint, William of Malavalla; his wife,
Barbara van Vlaenderberch, is shown in the opposite
wing with her daughters and Saint Barbara.
The concept of the composition, incorporating the
portraits of the donors' children, was subsequently
imitated in Bruges.

Most striking, however, are the three monumental
saints' figures, with Saint Christopher in the middle,
that dominate the centre panel. Instead of the small,
narrative groups that were so often used to illustrate
saints' *vitae*, the three large male saints are placed in a
landscape that extends into both wings and includes
a number of typical Memling features. The device
of placing monumental saints' figures alongside one
another recalls Italian altarpieces like the one
Domenico Veneziano painted for the Church of
Santa Lucia dei Magnoli (fig. 93). The triptych is also
reminiscent of paintings by Piero della Francesca, such
as the *Saint Augustine* altarpiece, painted in 1460–69
(Galleria Nazionale dell'Umbria, Perugia), and the
monumental figures in the *Misericordia* polyptych,
which dates from 1445–60 (Museo Civico,
Sansepolcro). This prompts the question of whether
Memling was familiar with those works, and if so,
how? He certainly had widespread contacts with
Bruges' Italian community.

Provenance: Marchesi Tempi collection, Florence.
References: Galassi 1989; De Vos 1994; Buijsen 1996, pp. 57–69; Galassi 1997.

Provenance: 1953, private collection, Florence.
References: De Vos 1994, p. 226; Buijsen 1996, pp. 57–69.

Provenance: Sint-Juliaanshospitaal, Bruges.
References: De Vos 1994; Bruges 1994.

54   **Jan Provoost** (*c.* 1465–1529)
Crucifixion, *c.* 1501–5
Panel, 117 × 172.5 cm (see fig. 56)
Stedelijke Musea, Groeningemuseum, Bruges
(inv. O.GRO1661.I)

Jan Provoost sets the Crucifixion against a background
that clearly betrays first-hand knowledge of the Holy
Land. It is almost certain that Provoost, who belonged
to a confraternity of Jerusalem pilgrims, visited the
region in person. At any rate, his image of Jerusalem,
with the Temple Mount in the upper right corner,
is relatively accurate. The city on the left might be
Constantinople – one of the stopping points on the
pilgrim's journey.

In the centre of the image, we see the legend of
Longinus – the blind Roman centurion who uses
his lance to check whether Jesus is dead. This theme
from the *Golden Legend* was frequently inserted into
Crucifixion scenes from the fourteenth century
onwards. Unusually, however, Provoost combined
different traditional motifs of the Crucifixion, for he
also included the group with Saint John and the Virgin
Mary, swooning with grief, the men squabbling over
their dice game and the angels holding up Christ's
loincloth (cats 1, 2).

The bright colours and turbulence of the
secondary groups contrast sharply with the silent
presence of the dead Christ. Analysis of the
underdrawing reveals that the composition was
formulated in such a way as to heighten this contrast.
The line of spectators and soldiers, who are beginning
to drift back to the city, is unusual for a Crucifixion
scene. Provoost used these figures to add dramatic
expression to the background, through a kind of
reversal of the Carrying of the Cross theme.

55   **Jan Provoost** (?) (*c.* 1465–1529)
*The Virgin of Mercy with Members of the Portuguese
Royal Family*, *c.* 1515
Panel, 154.5 × 142.5 cm (see fig. 190)
Museu Nacional de Arte Antiga, Lisbon
(inv. 697 Pint)

This is the central panel of a triptych ascribed to Jan
Provoost. It shows the Virgin Mary and the Christ
Child enthroned beneath a baldachin, with two angels
lifting Mary's cloak. Her throne stands on an altar.
King Manuel I of Portugal (1469–1521) kneels before
the altar with his daughters. Pope Leo X kneels to the
left, accompanied by a group of clergymen and what
appear to be merchants. The artist skilfully links the
traditional iconography of the 'Virgin of Mercy' or
'Misericordia', sheltering supplicants under her cloak,
with the theological conception of the Eucharist, in
which Mary functions as altar and Christ as the Host.

The open wings of the triptych show Saints
Sebastian and Christopher before a landscape, while
the reverses display grisaille images of the Apostles
Peter and Paul. The altarpiece came from the Church
of Santa Casa da Misericordia in Funchal, on the
Portuguese island of Madeira, which also sustained
a Flemish merchant community. It was probably
commissioned to mark the granting of diocesan status
to Funchal by Pope Leo X in 1514. The worldly and
spiritual rulers of the sugar-producing island, which
lies off the coast of Morocco and was thus under
constant threat, used the altarpiece to invoke the
protection of the Mother of God and the Christ Child.

The triptych's attribution to Provoost requires
scrutiny. There are stylistic discrepancies between
the wings and the centre panel, suggesting the
involvement of workshop assistants. What is more,
Weniger (1999) reported that the underdrawing of the
Lisbon painting includes colour indications that are
not in French as we find in the Bruges *Last Judgment*,
which has been securely attributed to Provoost, but
in Flemish. On the other hand, there are more than
superficial links to key works of Provoost, who was
active in both Bruges and Antwerp (Spronk 1998).
Weniger is right to state, therefore, that Provoost's
workshop activity also had an influence on Portuguese
painting in the early sixteenth century.

56   **Michel Sittow** (1468/69–1525)
Portrait of a Man, *c.* 1500–10
Panel, 35.9 × 25.9 cm (see fig. 236)
Koninklijk Kabinet van Schilderijen
'Mauritshuis', The Hague (inv. 832)

This small male portrait, which Friedländer attributed
to Jan Gossaert, is now viewed as a characteristic
example of Michel Sittow's portraiture. The Estonian
painter trained in Bruges, where he is first
documented in 1486. He subsequently moved to Spain
– possibly through the intermediary of the Habsburgs
or the Burgundian court – where Isabella the Catholic
appointed him court painter in 1492.

Sittow painted a number of portraits for the Spanish
Crown. He collaborated, for a while at least, with the
Netherlandish painter known as Juan Flamenco or Juan
de Flandes, who also probably trained in Bruges, from
where he later moved to the Spanish court (see cats 116,
117). Sittow left Spain in 1502 to return to his native city
of Tallinn, where he registered as a painter in 1507.
From his Estonian base, he worked on various
occasions for the courts of Denmark and, probably,
England, which were either allied to the House of
Habsburg or linked to it by marriage.

This portrait, which belonged to an aristocratic
family in the Baltic region, might have been painted
during Sittow's time in Estonia, where the
Netherlandish three-quarter, head-and-shoulders
portrait type was also established. The painting,
which focuses on the rendering of the sitter's facial
features, recalls the portraits of Spanish princesses
that Sittow and Juan de Flandes produced at the court
of the Catholic Kings, while the details are still
reminiscent of Bruges painting (Bruges 1994).
The portrait might thus date from the first decade
of the sixteenth century.

Provenance: Before 1786, Frans Cortals, Bruges (Koolkerke).
References: De Vos 1979; Spronk 1998.

Provenance: Santa Casa da Misericordia, Funchal (Madeira).
References: Porfírio 1991; Curvelo 1999; Weniger 1999b.

Provenance: Von Liphart collection, Dorpat (Estonia).
References: Trizna 1976, no. 25; Bruges 1994, no. 93; Weniger 1997.

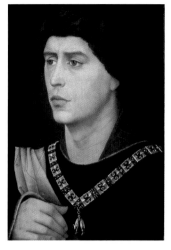

57   Michel Sittow (1468/69–1525)
King Christian II of Denmark, 1515
Panel, 32 × 21 cm (see fig. 209)
Statens Museum for Kunst, Copenhagen
(cat. 1951, no. 663)

In 1514, King Christian II of Denmark (1481–1559)
married Elizabeth of Austria (1501–1526) – second
sister of Archduke Charles – by proxy in Brussels.
Earlier that same year, Sittow had painted the King's
portrait in Copenhagen so that his likeness could be
presented to Elizabeth. Sadly, the 1514 portrait has not
survived, but the panel reproduced here is the only
known copy and is considered to be autograph.
Although the date '1515' was probably added later,
all the evidence suggests that it is correct. An X-ray of
the panel has revealed a portrait of Charles V beneath
that of the Danish King. Not only does this closely
resemble the portraits of Charles painted in the period
in question by Van Orley, among others, but the date
also corresponds exactly with Sittow's visit to the Low
Countries in 1514–15 *en route* for Spain (Trizna 1976).
Margaret of Austria is recorded as having paid him for
a commission in 1515, which might have been for this
very painting.

Both painted and printed portraits of Christian II
have survived. In the engravings and woodcuts of
artists such as Jacob Binck and Lucas Cranach, the
King's idealized portrait is invariably given a
Renaissance architectural setting and provided with
coats of arms, including those of the Scandinavian
nations. Works of this nature have to be interpreted in
the context of a propaganda campaign, through which
the deposed King was obliged to seek support in the
years between 1523 and 1530 for his Scandinavian
territorial ambitions. Painted portraits of Christian II
do not feature the same architectural and heraldic
elements, as they were intended for a smaller circle
of viewers. The 1514 prototype probably served as
the model for the portrait of the King in larger
compositions, including the *Last Judgment*
(Nationalmuseum, Copenhagen) attributed
to Jan Mostaert.

58   Rogier van der Weyden (*c*. 1399–1464)
Anthony, 'Grand Bâtard de Bourgogne',
c. 1460–70
Panel, 33.5 × 23.5 cm (see fig. 202)
Private collection

This head-and-shoulders portrait shows Anthony,
the illegitimate son of Duke Philip the Good and
Jeanne de Presle, bareheaded against a dark, neutral
background. The 'Grand Bastard of Burgundy' was
born in around 1430 and was probably the third
natural son of the Duke. Since Philip's first two
marriages were childless, the Burgundian line was
not in fact secured until Charles the Bold was born
to Philip's third wife, Isabella of Portugal, in 1432.

Philip the Good provided his illegitimate children
with an education befitting their station, and as they
were allowed to play significant roles in Burgundian
politics, their loyalty to the dynasty was assured.
David of Burgundy, a younger natural child of the
Duke, was appointed Bishop of Utrecht, while
Anthony, who also owned an extensive library, made
his career as a soldier and was a leading champion at
tournaments. He was knighted in 1452 and admitted
into the Order of the Golden Fleece four years later.
The 'Grand Bâtard' remained a loyal Burgundian
subject under Charles the Bold, but switched
allegiance to France following Charles' death in 1477.

Anthony is firmly identified as the subject of this
portrait by the emblems featured on the damaged
reverse of the panel: two towers with embrasures,
from which a fiery torch falls, are edged with a golden
band, above which appear the three letters 'N [I] E'. The
second part of Anthony's motto, '[NUL NE SI FROTE]
AINSI LE VEUL' appears below. The inclusion of the
chain of the Order of the Golden Fleece indicates that
the portrait cannot have been painted prior to 1456.
The sitter's physiognomy perfectly matches that in a
second painting by Van der Weyden, which shows the
'Grand Bâtard' with a cap and arrow (Musées Royaux,
Brussels). Both paintings probably derive from the
same portrait study by the Brussels town artist and
will have been painted around the same time.

59   Workshop of Rogier van der Weyden
(*c*. 1399–1464)
Triptych of the Crucifixion
('Sforza triptych'), before 1459?
Panel, 60.5 × 51.6 cm (centre);
60.5 × 25.8 cm (wings) (see fig. 139)
Musées Royaux des Beaux-Arts de Belgique,
Brussels (inv. 2407)

The centre panel and wings of this altarpiece are
divided into two equal horizontal registers. Christ
is shown on the cross in the middle of the painting,
flanked by his grieving mother and Saint John.
They are set against a hilly landscape that rises into the
wings on either side. Images of the donor family are
placed in the foreground below the Crucifixion group.
The man, dressed in armour, appears on the right with
the family's crested coat of arms, while his wife and
son are shown on the left. The left wing has a Nativity
in the upper register and two saints – only one of
whom, Saint Francis, is identifiable – below. The right
wing shows Saint John the Baptist at the top and
Saints Catherine and Barbara beneath. The closed
altarpiece has two *trompe-l'oeil* stone tableaux placed
on marble consoles in niches. The one on the right
depicts Saint Jerome and the lion, while the one on
the left has Saint George slaying the dragon.

The donor's arms in this triptych, attributed to
the workshop of Rogier van der Weyden, have been
identified as those of the Sforza family. The donors
are not, however, Duke Francesco Sforza of Milan,
his wife and their son Gian Galeazzo, as was once
supposed. As Mesnil (1909) realized, they are more
likely to be members of a different branch of the
Sforzas, namely Alessandro, who became ruler of
Pesaro in 1445, with his wife Costanza da Varano,
who died in 1447, and their son Costanzo. The Pesaro
Sforzas are known to have owned three Early
Netherlandish paintings in 1500, including a *'tavoletta
del christo in croce con li paesi di man de Rugieri'* ('a painting
with the Crucifixion in a landscape by *Rugieri*'), which
probably refers to the 'Sforza triptych'. Alessandro
Sforza may have commissioned the work from
Van der Weyden during a visit to the Burgundian
Netherlands in 1458.

This identification undermines the hypothesis that
the triptych was painted by the Milan court painter
Zanetto Bugatto, who spent the period 1460–63 in
Van der Weyden's Brussels workshop. The attribution
to Bugatto of a northern Italian *Saint Jerome* panel
(cat. 103), the composition of which is a detailed copy
of the reverse of the left wing of the 'Sforza triptych',
is also unconvincing.

Provenance: Probably collection of Margaret of Austria, Mechelen (1515).
References: Trizna 1976; Campbell 1990; Villadsen 1998; De Vrij 1999;
Hendrikman 2001.

Provenance: Before 1895, Robert Jackson, England.
References: Brussels 1979 (Campbell); Dülberg 1990;
Stroo and Syfer-d'Olne 1996; De Vos 1999.

Provenance: *c*. 1500, Giovanni Sforza, Pesaro.
References: Cavalieri 1990, pp. 42–49; Campbell 1990, p. 578;
Stroo and Syfer-d'Olne 1996, no. 9; De Vos 1999.

60   Workshop of Rogier van der Weyden
(*c.*1399–1464)
*Nativity, c.*1460–70
Panel, 43.5 × 35 cm (see fig. 71)
Gallinat-Bank AG, Essen

This virtually unknown *Nativity* is a reduced copy of
the centre panel of Rogier van der Weyden's 'Bladelin
altarpiece' (Staatliche Museen, Berlin), from which
it differs in the background landscape and minor
details. Pieter Bladelin, the Burgundian treasurer,
commissioned the original triptych – whose wings
show the *Vision of Emperor Augustus* and the *Christ Child
Appearing to the Magi* – from Rogier around 1445. It is
one of the Brussels town painter's most influential
compositions (see De Vos 1999, no. 15). Rogier's
conception of the Nativity, in particular, was
emulated on numerous occasions, or else provided the
basis for images by the Master of the Saint Catherine
Legend and Hans Memling among others.

    The Essen panel closely follows Rogier's
composition but is more tightly cropped to the right.
The birth of Christ is shown in a ruined building used
as a stable that is positioned diagonally across the
picture plane. Mary kneels before the Christ Child,
who is laid on the floor on his mother's cloak. Angels
have gathered by his head. Joseph approaches from the
left with a lighted candle, using his right hand to shield
the flame. The Romanesque architecture, which was
long out of date by the fifteenth century, identifies
the building as the synagogue of the Old Covenant,
which was replaced on the birth of the Son of God
by the New Covenant.

    A woman dressed in black is shown at prayer in the
position where Rogier's original work has the donor,
Pieter Bladelin. This perfectly preserved figure, which
was only recently uncovered, provides an impression
of the painterly quality of the panel, suggesting that it
might well have been a replica produced in Rogier's
own workshop. The donor was overpainted in the
early sixteenth century and replaced with the portrait
of a praying Compostela pilgrim, which Friedländer
wrongly interpreted as a shepherd. The overpainting
undoubtedly encouraged the attribution of the panel
to an anonymous copyist.

61   Copy after Rogier van der Weyden
(*c.*1399–1464)
*Saint Luke Drawing the Virgin, c.*1500
Panel, 133 × 107 cm (see fig. 250)
Stedelijke Musea, Groeningemuseum, Bruges
(inv. 74.GRO0035.I)

The composition of Rogier's *Saint Luke*, with its vista
of a vast landscape divided by a river, is reminiscent of
Jan van Eyck's 'Rolin Madonna' (fig. 13). In both works,
the view serves to separate the Virgin and Child
within the composition from Saint Luke and
Chancellor Rolin, respectively.

    Saint Luke's vision of the Madonna became a
popular theme after the dissemination of the *Golden
Legend* in the fourteenth century. From that time on,
Luke was chosen as the patron saint of many painters'
corporations, some of which commissioned works like
this to decorate their guild chapels or altars. Rogier van
der Weyden's panel (*c.*1435; Museum of Fine Arts,
Boston), of which this painting is a faithful copy, was
probably used as the altarpiece for the painters' chapel
in the Cathedral of Saint Gudula in Brussels. The fact
that two other close copies have survived (Alte
Pinakothek, Munich, and Hermitage, St Petersburg)
suggests that the painting was highly appreciated.
The copies might themselves have been used as guild
altarpieces elsewhere in the Low Countries.

    Van der Weyden shows Saint Luke with a sheet of
paper in his hand, rapidly sketching the vision before
it disappears. The result of his work is contained in the
panel itself, with its painted likeness of the Madonna.
The image reflects the notion that a good drawing
(*disegno*) is the foundation of a successful composition
– an idea promulgated in southern Europe in the
writings of Cennini and Alberti. The same art-
theoretical discourse was conveyed in the North
through silverpoint and paintbrush, with the
iconography of Saint Luke affording an important
model by which painters could visually express the
way they perceived their own craft. Rogier's invention
deliberately contrasts with earlier representations of
the same theme, in which Luke is placed behind an
artist's easel, capturing the scene with his paintbrush.
The latter approach appears to draw on a lost
prototype by Robert Campin, whose composition
is believed to have survived in Colyn de Coter's
Saint Luke (Parish church, Vieure).

62   Copy after Rogier van der Weyden
(*c.*1399–1464)
*Duke Philip the Good, c.*1500
Panel, 32.5 × 22.4 cm (see fig. 199)
Stedelijke Musea, Groeningemuseum, Bruges
(inv. 0.203)

Philip the Good of Burgundy (1396–1467) is shown
from the chest up against a neutral, dark-blue
background. The Duke, wearing a black chaperon on
his head, is dressed in a black velvet robe with a fur
collar over a white shirt and holds a scroll in his hands.
The only emblem of power worn by the 40- to 50-year-
old ruler is the chain of the Order of the Golden Fleece.
Philip founded the Burgundian chivalric order in 1430,
adopting as its symbol the emblem of the classical hero
Jason and his fellow Argonauts. It rapidly assumed
European significance, its membership extending
beyond the high Burgundian and Netherlandish
nobility to take in the Kings of Aragon and Naples.
As its Grand Master, the Duke – who never attained
the crown he so coveted – was *primus inter pares*, which
helps explain the central position afforded to the
Golden Fleece within the representational
iconography of the Burgundian dynasty.

    Several surviving versions closely resemble the
portrait shown here. A second pictorial type, which
also exists in a number of variants, shows the Duke
bareheaded and appears to have been developed
somewhat later. None of the surviving works is the
original version – all are variants of the official portraits
that circulated in Philip's territories and which may
have served some kind of proxy function. Like the
Bruges panel, many of them may not have been
painted until Charles the Bold had succeeded his
father or even later, and they were probably intended
as gifts. Margaret of Austria owned likenesses of her
Burgundian ancestors, which she displayed in the
portrait gallery at her palace in Mechelen.

    All the known portraits of the Duke appear
to derive from models by Rogier van der Weyden.
The version shown here essentially corresponds with
the image of the Duke in the dedicatory miniature in
the *Chroniques de Hainaut* (1448; Bibliothèque Royale,
Brussels), which might have been based in turn
on a painted portrait.

    Jan van Eyck also painted portraits of the Duke in
the early part of his career as Burgundian court artist,
one of which found its way into the collection of King
Alfonso v of Aragon. Sadly, no trace has survived of
any such youthful likeness of Philip the Good.

Provenance: Before 1912, Weber collection, Hamburg.
Reference: Friedländer II, no. 38b.

Provenance: 1858, Hauber collection, Munich.
References: De Vos 1979, pp. 216–19; Borchert 1997;
Spronk and McBeth 1997; De Vos 1999.

Provenance: George Salting, London.
References: Bruges 1962; De Vos 1979, pp. 214–16; Brussels 1979;
De Vos 1999.

63   **Anonymous (Savoy?)**
Nativity with Saint Jerome, a Pope (Saint Gregory?)
and a Praying Cardinal, c. 1440–50
Panel, 52.5 × 41.8 cm (see fig. 54)
Kelvingrove Art Gallery and Museum,
Glasgow (inv. 203)

This panel confronts us with a number of problems –
iconographical as well as in terms of attribution and
dating. It is plainly a Nativity, but the artist has also
drawn on the visual scheme of an Adoration of the
Magi, adding two saints and a cardinal, possibly the
donor, who kneels before the Christ Child. Saint
Jerome, dressed in blue robes and a cardinal's hat, is
identifiable from the lion at his side, but it is not clear
whether the other figure is meant to be Saint Gregory
or another pope.

   The Nativity scene appears to refer at least
indirectly to Robert Campin and his circle. The straw-
covered stable recalls the Tournai master's *Nativity*
(fig. 200), which was probably already in Dijon by that
time, while the style of the figures and the drapery also
resembles works from Campin's workshop. Although
the execution seems a little crude compared to
Netherlandish paintings, the anonymous artist seems
to have been at least superficially acquainted with
paintings like the Brussels *Annunciation* (Musées
Royaux), as witnessed by the highlights of the drapery.
The painting technique, by contrast, is far more
indicative of an artist rooted in the Italian tradition.
The schematic rendering of the mountainous
landscape in the background and the distant city view
suggest that the painting might have been produced in
the Duchy of Savoy, which lay between the
Burgundian territories and Italy, and enjoyed dynastic
ties with the House of Burgundy.

   The links with the Campin workshop and parallels
with the style of Conrad Witz suggest that the
painting might have been completed before 1450.
This was the period of the schismatic council, when
Duke Amedeo VIII of Savoy (1383–1451), having been
elected Antipope Felix V (1439–41), passed control
of the duchy and his court to his son, Louis I of
Savoy (1402–65).

64   **Anonymous (Southern France/Provence)**
Dionysius the Areopagite, c. 1510
Panel (transferred), 49 × 35 cm (see fig. 88)
Bonnefantenmuseum, Maastricht. On loan
from Mauritshuis, The Hague

It was during the Carolingian period that Saint Denis,
the legendary Bishop of Paris and French martyr, was
confused with the author of a number of theological
treatises, who had adopted the misleading pseudonym
of Dionysius the Areopagite, Saint Paul's convert,
mentioned in the Bible (Acts, 17:34). The otherwise
unknown author is referred to as the 'Pseudo-
Dionysius'. The anonymous painter of this panel
follows the traditional conflation of the figures
– the *cartellino* attached to the book-case on the right
identifies the saint, who is shown worshipping in his
study, as '*Divus Dionysius Parisior Episcopus Theologus
Areopagita*'. The words on the seat to the left of the
image tell us that Dionysius, presented here as
a theologian rather than a bishop, was originally
praying to: '*Magnum Mysterium et mirabile Sacramentum*'
– the Miracle of the Holy Sacrament.

   This prompts several questions regarding the
original purpose of the painting. Judging by its
composition, it is unlikely to have been the wing of a
diptych or triptych. Moreover, the portrait character
of the panel rather suggests that it is the fragment
of a larger work, in which it was balanced by another
saint's image with a Virgin and Child in the centre.
This cannot be verified, however, as the original
support was removed during the twentieth century
and replaced with modern fibreboard.

   The presentation of the bookshelves, on which
numerous codices can be made out, seems to echo
the *trompe-l'œil* props in Barthélemy d'Eyck's Aix
Annunciation (see fig. 142 and cat. 65) and Colantonio's
Saint Jerome (fig. 148), and enables us to place the
anonymous master in southern France. The 'portrait'
and, above all, the rendering of the white vestment
bear witness, however, to an early knowledge of the
work of Quentin Massys and Jan van Scorel,
suggesting that the panel cannot have been painted
before the early sixteenth century.

65   **Barthélemy d'Eyck (Master of the Aix**
      Annunciation) (active 1440–1470)
Triptych of the Annunciation, c. 1442–45
The Prophet Isaiah; Still Life, c. 1442–45.
Canvas (transferred), 101.5 × 67.5 cm;
30 × 56 cm (*Still Life*). Museum Boijmans
Van Beuningen, Rotterdam (inv. 2463);
Rijksmuseum, Amsterdam (inv. A2399)
Annunciation. Panel, 155 × 176 cm. Sainte-Marie-
Madeleine, Aix-en-Provence
The Prophet Jeremiah. Panel, 152 × 86 cm. Musées
Royaux des Beaux-Arts de Belgique, Brussels
(inv. 4494) (see figs 142, 146–47)

This triptych, originally located at Saint-Sauveur in
Aix-en-Provence, is a key work of both Provençal and
Neapolitan painting and is the focus of the debate
regarding early influences of northern painting in the
South. The centre panel shows an Annunciation set in
a church, which derives ultimately from earlier Sienese
models. The wings are devoted to the Prophets Isaiah
and Jeremiah (fig. 147). They recall grisaille saints'
images, such as those in the Ghent altarpiece, which
also appear on plinths and in niches, but the colouring
and the portrait character of the prophet figures give
them a more lifelike appearance. The still life with
books – possibly a motif borrowed from the Ghent
altarpiece – is brilliantly rendered from below.

   The triptych, which displays the unmistakable
influence of Campin and above all Van Eyck, was to
have a significant impact on Colantonio (fig. 144).
It was painted in 1442–45 for the cloth merchant Pierre
Corpici from Aix, who was court draper at the time to
René of Anjou. The altarpiece originally had a predella
and decorative top. According to Corpici's will, it was
installed on an altar which he had endowed in the choir
of Aix Cathedral, where he was subsequently buried.

   There is no documentary evidence as to the artist's
identity, but he is likely to have been Barthélemy
d'Eyck, who is recorded in Aix together with
Enguerrand Quarton in 1445 and who was employed
at the court of René of Anjou from 1447 to 1470.
D'Eyck provided the miniatures for the Vienna
manuscript (Österreichische Nationalbibliothek,
Ms. 2597) of René's romance *Cœur d'amour épris* (1457),
which, in spite of the difference in technique and scale,
are closely related to the triptych.

   D'Eyck appears to have come from the Prince-
Bishopric of Liège, and was presumably related to Jan
van Eyck, in whose Bruges workshop he might have
worked as an illuminator (König 1996).

Provenance: Before 1851, Archibald McLellan, Glasgow.
References: Ring 1949; Sterling 1972; Madrid and Valencia 2001.

Provenance: Klönne collection, Amsterdam; 1930, Rijksmuseum
Amsterdam (inv. A 3116).
Reference: Laclotte and Thiébaut 1983, no. 103.

Provenance: Saint-Sauveur Cathedral, Aix-en-Provence.
References: Reynaud 1989; Avril and Reynaud 1993; Chapuis 1995, pp. 93–111;
Châtelet 1996; König 1996; Châtelet 1998.

66   Barthélemy d'Eyck (Master of the Aix
     Annunciation) (active 1440–1470)
     Portrait of a Man, 1456
     Parchment mounted on panel, 51 × 41.8 cm
     (see fig. 89)
     Sammlungen des Fürsten von Liechtenstein,
     Schloss Vaduz (inv. 729)

67   Barthélemy d'Eyck (Master of the Aix
     Annunciation) (active 1440–1470)
     Holy Family, c. 1450–60
     Canvas, 207 × 181 cm (see fig. 86)
     Cathedral Treasury, Le Puy-en-Velay

68   André d'Ypres (Master of the Paris Parliament
     Crucifixion, Master of Dreux Budé)
     (before 1428–before 1479)
     Wings of a triptych of the Dreux Budé-
     Peschard family, c. 1454
     (1) *Arrest of Christ*. Panel, 48.8 × 30.5 cm.
     Collection Dr Heinrich Bisschoff, Bremen
     (2) *Resurrection*. Panel, 46 × 28 cm. Musée Fabre,
     Montpellier (see fig. 84)

This male portrait is one of the most enigmatic of the
Renaissance. The only firm piece of information is the
ornately rendered '1456' – the year in which it was
painted. It is not clear who is shown here or who was
responsible for this portrait executed on parchment.
Over the centuries, it has been attributed to painters
ranging from Mantegna through Burgkmair to
Fouquet, and to schools from Provence to Portugal.
The difficulty of placing it within the artistic
landscape is illustrative of the unusual position that
this portrait occupies in fifteenth-century painting.

The black-clad man is shown against a brown
background. His upper body is presented frontally,
his head is turned slightly and his eyes are fixed on the
viewer. The balustrade creates a feeling of distance
between the sitter and the onlooker. The composition,
the painstaking execution of the physiognomic details
and the lighting all reveal an intimate knowledge of
Early Netherlandish portraits, particularly those
of Jan van Eyck. Yet by emphasizing the frontal
character of the image, the painter achieves a
monumentality not found in Flemish portraiture,
which, despite the fundamental difference in means,
is reminiscent of Fouquet (cat. 70).

The Vaduz painting has been considered the work
of a Portuguese forerunner of Gonçalves on account
of its relationship with a portrait in the Louvre (fig. 11)
to which it has often been compared. However, the
stylistic differences between the two paintings tend to
refute this hypothesis. While the Paris portrait might
be linked with the Catalan art centring on Huguet, the
1456 portrait is rooted firmly in the Flemish tradition.

Hulin de Loo (1904) suspected that the artist might
have been a Fleming working in the south of France,
possibly the Master of the Aix Annunciation, who is
now widely identified as Barthélemy d'Eyck, court
painter to René of Anjou. Thiébaut (New York 1984)
offered detailed evidence to support the portrait's
attribution to d'Eyck, an exceptional artist who was
also active as a manuscript illuminator.

It was Bloch (1963) who first linked this large image of
the Holy Family, painted in tempera on canvas, with
the workshop of the Master of Flémalle or Robert
Campin. The figures, with their heavy drapery, and
the details of the simply rendered interior do, indeed,
recall that master's compositions. Moreover, the
closed-off fireplace with candleholders attached and a
bench positioned in front of it are also motifs that crop
up in the various panels grouped around the
Annunciation scene in the Flémallesque 'Merode
altarpiece' (The Cloisters, New York). The clothed
figure of the Christ Child, too, is closely linked to
the Virgin and Child paintings of both Campin and
Van der Weyden.

There are, however, striking differences in terms
of colour and painting technique, even if these to some
extent reflect the use of tempera. This prompted Eisler
(1963) to suggest that the canvas was painted by a
Netherlandish artist in the early sixteenth century
and that it thus harks back to earlier models – a not
untypical approach for the time. Châtelet (1996)
returned to the issue, concluding that the painting
from the Clarissan Convent at Le Puy-en-Velay was
the work of the Brussels painter Colyn de Coter, who
frequently reworked compositions by Campin and
Van der Weyden.

Nicole Reynaud (1989), by contrast, pointed to a
series of stylistic similarities between the *Holy Family*
and miniatures by Barthélemy d'Eyck, the 'Master of
the Aix Annunciation', and convincingly attributed it
to that artist. D'Eyck's *Annunciation* altarpiece, painted
between 1442 and 1445, is also connected to Campin's
painting by a number of motifs, while its still life
(cat. 65) is intimately linked to the image of the Holy
Family. According to Reynaud, the *Holy Family* in
Le Puy-en-Velay was commissioned by the local
Clarissan Order to mark the convent's foundation
in 1432. Accordingly, she placed the painting at the
beginning of Barthélemy d'Eyck's career – sometime
around 1435. König (1996), although strongly
supporting the attribution of the painting to René of
Anjou's court artist, believed it was produced during
d'Eyck's final phase.

These panels originally formed the wings of a triptych
whose centre panel, featuring the Crucifixion,
Carrying of the Cross and the Descent into Limbo,
is now in the J. Paul Getty Museum, Los Angeles.
Fredericksen (1983), who published the reconstruction,
noted close stylistic similarities with the *Crucifixion*
altarpiece of the Parliament of Paris (c. 1453–56; fig. 81),
painted by an artist who was deeply influenced by
Rogier van der Weyden. The links between the two
works and the French origins of the triptych were
confirmed when Sterling succeeded in identifying the
donor portraits. The left wing shows Dreux Budé, his
son Jean and Saint Christopher, the right wing features
Budé's wife, Jeanne Peschard, her daughters Jacquette
and Catherine and Saint Catherine.

Dreux Budé, who belonged to a family of
merchants, was adviser and secretary to Charles VII
and Louis XI, and was also acquainted with Fouquet's
patron, Etienne Chevalier (cat. 70). He was a
particular devotee of Saint Christopher – the family
chapel he endowed at the parish church of Saint-
Gervais in 1454 was also dedicated to that saint.
The triptych was probably commissioned for the
altar in the same chapel.

Sterling (1990) disputed the identification of the
Master of Dreux Budé with the Master of the
Parliament of Paris, linking the former with Conrad
de Vulcop, the Utrecht-born *peintre ordinaire* of King
Charles VII, and the latter with the Tournai-trained
Louis le Duc, who was later active in Paris. However,
Reynaud (Avril and Reynaud 1993) and most recently
Lorentz (1998) have attributed both works to André
d'Ypres on stylistic grounds.

Documentary evidence has recently emerged
confirming that the Amiens-born painter André
d'Ypres became an independent master in Tournai in
1428, and that he trained in the city at the same time
as Rogier van der Weyden. It is possible, therefore,
that André d'Ypres came into contact with Rogier's
pictorial inventions at an early stage and that he was
able to draw on them for his Paris Crucifixion scenes
around 1450.

Provenance: Before 1677, Johann Spillenberger, Vienna.
References: Laclotte and Thiébaut 1983; New York 1984; Schaefer 1990;
Thiébaut 1993.

Provenance: Convent of the Poor Clares, Le Puy-en-Velay.
References: Bloch 1963; Reynaud 1989, pp. 22–25; Châtelet 1996; König 1996;
Kemperdick 1997.

Provenance: Chapel of the Dreux Budé-Peschard family,
Saint-Gervais, Paris.
References: Fredericksen 1983; Sterling 1990; Avril and Reynaud 1993;
Leuven 1998; Lorentz 1998a; Lorentz 1998b.

69   Nicolas Dipre (active 1495–*c.* 1532)
Fragments of the *Altarpiece of the Virgin* for
Saint-Siffrein, Carpentras (?), 1499–1500
(1) *Joachim and Anne*. Panel, 26.5 × 51 cm.
Musée du Louvre, Paris (inv. RF 1986–3)
(2) *Birth of the Virgin*. Panel, 29.5 × 51 cm.
Musée du Louvre, Paris (inv. RF 1986–4)
(3) *Presentation of the Virgin*. Panel, 32 × 50 cm.
Musée du Louvre, Paris (inv. RF 1972–37)
(4) *Marriage of the Virgin*. Panel (transferred),
27 × 35 cm. Denver Art Museum (Acc. 1961.181)
(5) *Adoration of the Shepherds*. Panel, 29 × 48 cm.
Fine Arts Museums of San Francisco
(inv. 61.44.29)
(6) *Adoration of the Magi*. Panel, 28 × 47 cm.
Musée départemental d'Art sacré, Pont-
Saint-Esprit
(7) *Crucifixion*. Panel, 29.2 × 44.3 cm.
Detroit Institute of Arts (inv. 50.57)
(see figs 37–42)

Nicolas Dipre was the grandson of the Picard artist
André d'Ypres, who, despite his surname, came from
Amiens. The grandfather was active in Tournai in the
1420s, at the same time as Rogier van der Weyden and
Jacques Daret. Some time before the middle of the
century, he moved his workshop to Paris, where he
has been identified by art historians alternately as the
Master of the Crucifixion of the Paris Parliament and
the Master of Dreux Budé (see cat. 68). Nicolas Dipre
thus belonged to a respected and important family
of painters. He is likely to have learned his craft in its
Paris workshop, under his father Colin d'Amiens,
who may have been the Master of Coëtivy (see
Lorentz 1998a and 1998b) and who was praised
by Jean Lemaire de Belges, among others.
   There is little trace in the works attributed to Nicolas
Dipre of the intimate knowledge of Early Netherlandish
painting that his grandfather built up in Tournai, and
which evidently remained important to his father,
Colin d'Amiens. They are much more indebted to
the paintings of Enguerrand Quarton and above
all Barthélemy d'Eyck, who continued to exert
a significant influence on southern French art around
1500. Dipre appears to have left Paris shortly after
completing his training to settle in the papal city
of Avignon, where he contributed in 1495 to the
decorations to accompany the triumphal entrance
of Cardinal Giuliano della Rovere – the later Julius II.
Between 1495 and 1511, Dipre produced banners, shields
and theatrical decorations for the papal authorities. He
painted coats of arms and frescoes, and polychromed
sculptures. In 1508, he married the daughter of the
woodcarver Jean Bigle, with whom he collaborated
on a series of compound altarpieces (with carved centre
and painted wings) for churches and monasteries in
Avignon and the surrounding area. Four apprentices

were employed at this period in his workshop, which
appears to have been highly productive. Yet no trace has
survived of the many documented works that Dipre
produced throughout his career for various locations,
including the chapel of the Town Hall and the Church
of Saint-Rémy in Avignon.
   The sole exception is a fragment in the museum
at Carpentras, featuring the meeting of Joachim and
Anne at the Golden Gate in Jerusalem. Sterling (1941)
was able to attribute this to Nicolas Dipre, as the scene
is mentioned in a contract (published by Chobaut
1940), in which the painter agrees to produce a large
altarpiece devoted to the Virgin Mary on behalf of the
'*Confraternité de la conception de la Vierge*' in Carpentras,
for the Church of Saint-Siffrein. The painting was
ordered in 1499 and the painter undertook to deliver
it within a year. According to the contract, it was to
feature the Virgin Mary in the centre panel and two
pairs of scenes on either side, including *Joachim and
Anne* and the *Birth of the Virgin*. The altarpiece was to
be surmounted with an *Assumption*, flanked by two
prophets, and to stand on a predella containing five
scenes, the iconography of which was not specified
in the contract.
   The fragment in Carpentras formed the basis for
Sterling's (1942) proposed attribution of one of the
panels shown here – the *Marriage of the Virgin* – to
Dipre, which he identified as part of the predella of the
Carpentras altarpiece. Further scenes were identified
shortly afterwards, in the shape of the *Presentation of the
Virgin*, the *Adoration of the Shepherds*, the *Adoration of the
Magi* and the *Crucifixion* – whose composition derives
indirectly from a painting of the same theme by
Antonello da Messina. Undoubtedly produced in
the same workshop, the predella scenes clearly match,
given both their size and the characteristic ogee shape
of the original painted surface. Eisler (1977) offered
a preliminary reconstruction of the Carpentras
altarpiece and its predella, suggesting that the
Crucifixion was originally flanked by the two scenes
from the Life of the Virgin and the two Adorations.
   In the mid-1980s, however, two further panels
were connected with it, which cast doubt on this
reconstruction. Although the images of *Joachim and Anne*
and the *Birth of the Virgin* (now in the Louvre, Paris) are
closely related to the aforementioned panels in stylistic
terms, they increase the number of predella scenes
associated with the Carpentras altarpiece to seven,
whereas the 1499 contract specifies only five. It also
identifies Joachim and Anne and the Birth of the Virgin
as themes for the wings of the altarpiece proper. It is
possible, therefore, that the scenes attributed to Nicolas
Dipre actually come from different altarpieces.

70   Jean Fouquet (*c.* 1420–*c.* 1480)
Virgin and Child
(right wing of the 'Melun diptych'), *c.* 1450
Panel, 91.3 × 83.3 cm (see fig. 46)
Koninklijk Museum voor Schone Kunsten,
Antwerp (inv. 132)

The Virgin Mary is shown with the Christ Child
on her lap on a throne decorated with precious stones
and onyx. She wears an ermine cloak and a crown,
designating her as the Queen of Heaven. Her bodice
is open at the front, exposing her left breast. The red
seraphim surround the seemingly weightless throne,
with the blue cherubim approaching behind them.
It was their task to lead souls into heaven, to which
– as legend has it – they also bore the Virgin herself
following her death.
   The Madonna panel formed the right wing of a
diptych that Fouquet painted around 1450 for Etienne
Chevalier. It was intended to adorn the tomb of
Chevalier's wife, Catherine Budé, at the Collegiate
Church of Notre Dame in Melun. The donor wing
(Staatliche Museen, Berlin, inv. 1617) is set in
a monumental Renaissance portico, in which
Charles VII's *trésorier*, accompanied by Saint Stephen,
invokes the Virgin's intercession on behalf of his wife.
Early reports state that the diptych's now lost frame
was originally decorated with enamel medallions.
Fouquet proudly offers his own portrait in the only
surviving example (Louvre, Paris).
   The 'Melun diptych' is a high point in Fouquet's
painting, little of which has survived. He trained as a
manuscript illuminator and is likely to have come into
contact with the innovations of Early Netherlandish
art at an early date through his Paris colleagues. In the
1440s Fouquet moved to Italy, where he painted a
portrait of Pope Eugene IV in Rome, studied – so it
would seem – Fra Angelico's frescoes in the Vatican
and made the acquaintance of Filarete. Immediately
after his return, he painted the magnificent miniatures
in the *Hours of Etienne Chevalier* (Musée Condé,
Chantilly), in which he anticipated the
monumentality of the 'Melun diptych', painted shortly
afterwards. Art historians disagree on Fouquet's pre-
Italian work, but the Vienna portrait of the court fool
Gonella (fig. 129) appears to have been completed on
his arrival in Italy. Whereas the Eyckian realism
prevails in that portrait, it is blended with Italian
influences in the 'Melun diptych'.

Provenance: Saint-Siffrein, Carpentras (?).
References: Eisler 1977; Sterling 1981; Laclotte and Thiébaut 1983; Rosenberg
and Stewart 1987, pp. 21–23; Thiébaut 1989; Sterling 1990.

Provenance: Before 1775, Collegiate Church of Melun.
References: Reynaud 1983; Vandenbroeck 1985; Sterling 1988; Schaefer 1990;
Avril and Reynaud 1993.

71 Nicolas Froment (active 1461–1484)
René of Anjou and Jeanne de Laval
('Matheron diptych'), *c.* 1475–80
Panel, 17.7 × 13.4 cm each (see fig. 195)
Musée du Louvre, Paris (inv. 665)

72 Jean Hey (Master of Moulins?)
(active *c.* 1480–*c.* 1500)
Saint Victor (or Maurice?) and a Donor, c. 1480–85
Panel, 58.4 × 49.5 cm (see fig. 51)
Kelvingrove Art Gallery and Museum,
Glasgow (inv. 203)

73 Jean Hey (Master of Moulins?)
(active *c.* 1480–*c.* 1500)
Margaret of Austria, 1490
Panel, 32 × 23 cm (see fig. 214)
The Metropolitan Museum of Art, New York.
Robert Lehman Collection (inv. 1975.1.130)

Froment, who was a generation younger than Enguerrand Quarton (cat. 83) and Barthélemy d'Eyck (cats 65–67), was one of the most important painters in southern France in the third quarter of the fifteenth century. He was born in the border region between Flanders and Picardy, which is where he probably received his painter's training. He lived in Uzès in Languedoc between 1465 and 1467. Before that, he appears to have worked for a brief period in his native region. His triptych with the *Raising of Lazarus*, commissioned by Francesco Coppini, dates from 1461 and was probably painted during the chapter meeting of the Golden Fleece in Saint-Omer.

Froment received his most important commission from René of Anjou in 1475. His monumental *Triptych of the Burning Bush* in the Cathedral of Aix-en-Provence (fig. 48) is obviously the work of a painter rooted in the Van der Weyden tradition and influenced by Dieric Bouts, while traces of an early contact with the work of Barthélemy d'Eyck are also detectable in it.

The diminutive portrait diptych in the Louvre – the original red velvet case for which has survived – depends directly on the life-sized donors' portraits in the Aix work for its likenesses of the elderly King and his second wife, Jeanne de Laval. It was presumably based on the same portrait studies and executed around the same time. In the diptych, however, René and his Breton consort are not portrayed in all their royal grandeur – only the chain of the Order of Saint Michael around the King's neck refers to the sitters' rank. The closed diptych, which still has its original frame, features a white lily surmounted by a crown (René held the title of 'King of Jerusalem'). The motto '*Ditat-servata-fides*' appears both in the banderole wrapped around the stem of the lily and on the frame. The Paris diptych belonged to Jean de Matheron, who served as René's envoy, and may well have been a gift from King René to reward a faithful servant. It remained in the possession of the Matheron family until 1872.

This imposing donor panel from Glasgow was initially viewed as a fifteenth-century Netherlandish painting, and was exhibited in Bruges in 1902 as the work of Hugo van der Goes. It has since been identified as the work of a French artist, allowing its attribution to the Master of Moulins, who was named for the Marian triptych in Moulins Cathedral. The discovery that a painter of a similar calibre to Van der Goes had been active in France was seen by Max J. Friedländer (1903), the great authority on Early Netherlandish art, as the key finding to emerge from the Bruges exhibition devoted to 'Les Primitifs Flamands'.

This donor wing of a diptych is probably more closely related to Flemish painting than any other of the works ascribed to the Master of Moulins, who is nowadays widely identified as Jean Hey and considered as a pupil of Hugo van der Goes. While it also shows echoes of the triptych with the *Martyrdom of Saint Hippolytus* (cat. 7) which was left unfinished by Dieric Bouts, the painting illustrates the degree to which Jean Hey was indebted to Van der Goes' handling of landscape. Similarities with the Ghent master's work are also apparent in the facial details and the sense of monumentality, although there are differences in terms of both palette and technique. At the same time, the Glasgow donor's panel draws strongly on Bruges painting. The pattern of the splendid brocade hem on the robes of the donor – a high-ranking, though unidentified clergyman – derives, for instance, from paintings by Memling and Gerard David, while the reflection of the donor in the saint's breastplate harks back to the corresponding effect that Jan van Eyck used in the armour of Saint George in his 'Van der Paele Madonna' (cat. 22). It is possible, therefore, that the Glasgow painting is an early work of Jean Hey and that it was completed around the same time as the *Nativity* commissioned by Cardinal Jean Rolin in Burgundy (Autun).

This portrait, which was first attributed to the Master of Moulins at the 1904 exhibition 'Les Primitifs Français' in Paris, is one of the commissions that the painter, who is customarily identified with Jean Hey (see cats 72–75), carried out in the early 1490s in the immediate circle of the French royal court and that of the Bourbons. Other examples are the fragments of donor wings with the portraits of Madeleine of Burgundy and Pierre II of Bourbon (Louvre, Paris). Hulin de Loo (1932) suggested that the sitter of the New York portrait was Margaret of Austria, who was brought to Paris in 1483 as the bride-to-be of Charles VIII following Archduke Maximilian's defeat by the French. Margaret, who was still a minor at the time, remained in Paris until 1491, being groomed for her future role as Queen of France. She was, however, rejected by Charles at that point in favour of Princess Anne of Brittany, who had actually been promised to Maximilian, King of the Romans and Margaret's own father. This development unleashed a fierce propaganda war between Charles and Maximilian, who became Holy Roman Emperor shortly afterwards in 1493.

This portrait of Margaret, which was probably intended as the wing of a devotional diptych, shows her in a room in a tower, through the window of which a hilly landscape can be seen in the distance. In her hands, she holds a rosary made of pearls, which alludes both to her piety and to her name – *margarita* is Latin for 'pearl'.

The headdress, interwoven with gold thread, the red velvet gown, with its ermine cuffs, the gold chain around her neck, with links containing the initials *C* and *M* (*Charles* and *Marguerite*) and the splendid *fleur-de-lis*, set with precious stones, are all mentioned in the 1493 inventory of the Princess' possessions and may have been bridal gifts from Charles VIII. Obviously, Margaret is presented here in the guise of the future Queen of France (Eichberger 2000).

Since Margaret and her royal fiancé visited Moulins in the spring of 1490, it is likely that the portrait was painted on that occasion at the Bourbon court. In any case, it must have been done before she returned to the Low Countries in 1491/92.

Provenance: Jean de Matheron; until 1872, Matheron family through descent.
References: Spears Grayson 1976; Laclotte and Thiébaut 1983, no. 72; Robin 1983, p. 211; Dülberg 1990, nos 174–75.

Provenance: Before 1851, Archibald McLellan, Glasgow.
References: Hulin de Loo 1932; Huillet d'Istria 1961; Lorentz and Regond 1990; Reynolds 1996; Châtelet 2001.

Provenance: Don Sebastián Gabriel de Beaujeu, Braganza y Borbón, Infante of Spain and Portugal.
References: Sterling and Ainsworth 1990, no. 3; New York 1998; Châtelet 2001; Eichberger 2001.

74   Jean Hey (Master of Moulins?)
      (active *c.* 1480–*c.* 1500)
      Ecce Homo, 1494
      Panel, 39 × 30 cm (see fig. 90)
      Musées Royaux des Beaux-Arts de Belgique,
      Brussels (inv. 4497)

The *Imago Pietatis* – a half-length figure of Christ as the
Man of Sorrows – developed in Western Europe from
Byzantine miraculous images. It became an extremely
popular devotional image with a wide range of
variations (see cats 37, 81, 84, 99), the evolution
of which paralleled the growing importance of lay
religious movements in the fifteenth century.
The pictorial type illustrated here arose in the same
context. It shows the *Ostentatio Christi* – the public
display of the scourged Jesus prior to his crucifixion –
as a theme for private devotion. The type, which was
found widely in the Low Countries and on the Iberian
peninsula around 1500 (see cat. 120), differs from the
traditional Passion cycle in that it is stripped of any
narrative elements – Pilate's words *'ecce homo'* are the
only reference to the biblical context.

In this example, the opened curtains subtly
underscore the idea of Christ's public *Ostentatio*.
We know from an early Latin inscription on
the reverse of the painting that Jean Cueillette
commissioned it from Jean Hey in 1494. That
makes the work – which is directly influenced by
Netherlandish models, especially Hugo van der Goes
– the only securely attributable painting of this master,
who was mentioned by the poet Jean Lemaire de
Belges in the early sixteenth century in the same breath
as Perugino, Leonardo, Bellini and Jean Perréal. Jean
Hey seems to have come from the Low Countries –
the inscription refers to *'m*[agister] *Jo*[hannem] *Hey
teutonicu*[m] *pictorem egregium'* ('Master Johannes, the
outstanding German painter') – before making his
career in France.

The patron, Jean Cueillette, was active in Moulins
in 1494 as treasurer to Duke Pierre II of Bourbon,
before he became secretary to King Charles VIII of
France (Reynaud 1968). That means that Jean Hey
could have been working at the Bourbon residence in
1494 and that he might therefore be identified with the
artist known as the Master of Moulins, who was active
there at the time (Sterling 1968; Reynaud 1968;
Lorentz 1990).

Provenance: Piégard collection, Chécy (Loiret).
References: Huillet d'Istria 1961; Reynaud 1968; Lorentz and Regond 1990;
Reynolds 1996; Châtelet 2001.

75   Jean Hey (Master of Moulins?)
      (active *c.* 1480–*c.* 1500)
      The Virgin and Child Surrounded by Angels, *c.* 1500
      Panel, 38.5 × 29.5 cm (see fig. 77)
      Musées Royaux des Beaux-Arts de Belgique,
      Brussels (inv. 411)

This panel, which shows the Virgin praying to the
Christ Child, probably formed the centre panel of
a triptych or the left wing of a diptych. The
supernatural effect created by the golden background
is further heightened by the four angels who watch the
heavenly scene, two on either side. Their facial
expressions and gestures range from wonder and joy
to amazement and solicitude, revealing the painter as
a master in the rendering of human emotion. Equally
brilliant is the contrast between the quiet adoration
of Mary and the alertness of the Infant Christ, which
betrays the influence of the Ghent artist Hugo van
der Goes.

It is believed that this painter, who also owes an
unmistakable stylistic debt to Hugo van der Goes, was
indeed a pupil of the Ghent master. Named after a
monumental Virgin and Child triptych in Moulins,
commissioned by Duke Pierre II of Bourbon around
1498, the Master of Moulins must have left Ghent
around 1480 for Burgundy, where he painted an
Adoration of the Shepherds (Autun) for Cardinal Jean
Rolin (d. 1483) – a work that also derives from Hugo's
motifs. The celebrated Ghent artist continued to
influence the young painter throughout his career,
the remainder of which was pursued in France. The
grisaille Annunciation in the late *Virgin and Child
Enthroned with Saints* in Moulins, for instance, is based
on the 'Portinari altarpiece' (fig. 107). The Master of
Moulins came into contact with French painting
during his period of activity for the French royal court
and the House of Bourbon, and may also have been
familiar with Fouquet's work. In addition to portraits,
devotional paintings and altarpieces, he worked
as an illuminator, in which capacity he contributed
to the ordinances of the Order of Saint Michael
(Bibliothèque Nationale, Paris, Ms. fr. 14363),
which was presented to Charles VIII in 1493/94.

Various attempts have been made to identify the
master. Durrieu, Hulin and Sterling (1941) thought he
might be Jean Perréal, while Châtelet (most recently
in 2001) is more inclined towards Perréal's pupil, Jean
Prévost. However, since Sterling and Reynaud (1968)
published their research, the balance has shifted in
favour of Jean Hey, whose authorship of the *Ecce
Homo* (cat. 74) appears to be supported by an early
inscription.

Provenance: R. H. Benson.
References: Huillet d'Istria 1961; Reynaud 1968; Lorentz and Regond 1990;
Reynolds 1996; Châtelet 2001.

76   Josse Lieferinx (active 1470–1535)
      Abraham and the Three Angels, *c.* 1495–1500
      Panel, 45.9 × 66.6 cm (see fig. 52)
      Denver Art Museum (Acc. 1961.158)

This much repaired and restored panel – a fragment
of a composition that originally continued to the left –
illustrates the Old Testament story of Abraham and
the Three Angels, who prophesy that his long-held
wish for a child will be granted (Genesis 18:1–16).
Abraham is shown kneeling before the divine
apparition in front of his ramshackle house, in which
we make out his elderly wife Sarah. The painting owes
its idyllic character to genre-like details such as the
fleeces placed on the roof to dry, and the varied
landscape – a weird rock formation in the centre and a
river valley that runs away into the distance on the left.

There is a clear relationship between this work and
a small panel showing the same scene that has been
attributed to the young Antonello da Messina (cat. 86).
Antonello's painting is also a fragment, having been
cut down to the right of the angel. Nevertheless, it
shows the left-hand part of the composition that is
missing in Lieferinx's work. Even though the
presentation of the angels matches in the two
paintings down to the drapery, and there are
corresponding landscape motifs, too, it is open to
question whether the panel reproduced here derives
from Antonello's work. It is also possible that both
paintings stem from a common model, which, in view
of the strongly Flemish character of Antonello's
landscape, might hypothetically be placed in the
Netherlands, in the circle of Jan van Eyck and Petrus
Christus. Equally, Lieferinx might have based himself
on a copy after Antonello – a copy of the painting in
question can, indeed, be seen at Forza d'Agro in Sicily.

This panel was, in fact, first attributed to a northern
Italian follower of Antonello, before Sterling identified
its author as Josse Lieferinx. The latter, who was
probably born in the Hainaut town of Enghien, is first
recorded in Marseilles in 1493. He was commissioned
in 1498 to paint the *Saint Sebastian* altarpiece, together
with the Piedmontese artist Bernardino Simondi, who
died that same year. In 1503, he married one of the
daughters of the Burgundian painter Jean Changenet,
who had settled in Avignon. His nephew and heir,
Hans Clemer, was active in Saluzzo.

Provenance: Vicomte Bernard d'Hendecourt.
References: Haverkamp-Begemann 1958, pp. 18–28; Sterling 1964;
Eisler 1977; Laclotte and Thiébaut 1983, no. 85; Thiébaut 1993.

77   **Josse Lieferinx** (active 1470–1535)
Pilgrims at the Tomb of Saint Sebastian, 1498
Panel, 82 × 55 cm
Galleria Nazionale di Palazzo Barberini, Rome
(inv. 1590)

Josse Lieferinx is recorded in 1493 as the *serviteur* of the painter Philippon Mauroux. It is not clear whether he previously trained as an artist in the Netherlands or Picardy. Lieferinx was probably employed for several years in Mauroux's workshop before setting up on his own in Marseilles no later than 1497. Together with Bernardino Simondi from Venasca (Piedmont), he received a commission in that year to decorate the chapel of the Confraternity of Saint Sebastian at Notre-Dame-des-Accoules in Marseilles and to furnish it with an altarpiece. The Confraternity confirmed the commission after Simondi's death in 1498, finally paying Lieferinx 500 florins for the work, which was almost double the original price. The contract, which has been published by Albanés, specified eight scenes from the Life of Saint Sebastian, including his martyrdom. The predella was to feature a Pietà.

The latter, which can now be seen in Antwerp, is clearly rooted in the Netherlandish pictorial tradition. At the beginning of the twentieth century, Hulin de Loo, amongst others, attributed the predella panel and seven of the altarpiece's eight original panels (now in Philadelphia, Baltimore, St Petersburg and Rome) to an anonymous painter, dubbed the 'Master of Saint Sebastian'. Sterling linked the altarpiece fragments to the commission from the Confraternity of Saint Sebastian, enabling the anonymous master to be identified. The artist's work displays unmistakable links with Flemish painting, while it also stands out for its specifically Provençal style, all of which matches the profile of Josse Lieferinx emerging from contemporary sources as that of an artist with northern roots.

It was also Sterling who connected this image of crippled and injured people before the shrine of a saint with the *Saint Sebastian* altarpiece. Lieferinx successfully combines the accurate perspective of a Renaissance church interior with the hard-hitting representation of human suffering and hope. The composition was later taken up by the Spanish painter Juan de Nalda, who joined the workshop of Lieferinx's father-in-law – the Burgundian artist Jean Changenet.

78   **Antoine de Lonhy** (Master of the Trinity of Turin) (active c. 1446–1480/90)
Nativity, c. 1460–70
Panel, 107 × 59.7 cm (see fig. 133)
Museum Mayer van den Bergh, Antwerp
(inv. 127)

Sterling (1972) was the first to link this painting with the workshop of the Master of the Trinity of Turin, who was active in Piedmont in the second half of the fifteenth century. This painter, whom Sterling believed to have originated in France, played a key role in the dissemination of Franco-Flemish pictorial inventions in the Duchy of Savoy-Piedmont. Romano (1977 and 1989) has performed a detailed study of those of the master's paintings that remain in Piedmont. In the latter author's view, the Antwerp *Nativity* originally belonged to a lost triptych, together with a number of other surviving panels. Avril (1989) showed that the anonymous painter was also active as an illuminator, identifying him as the 'Master of the Saluzzo Hours' (British Library, London, Ms. Add. 27696), who is named for the Book of Hours that he completed for the Marquis of Saluzzo, following the death (in 1452) of Perronet Lamy, the artist who had begun it.

This sensational discovery enabled Avril to identify the master in question as Antoine de Lonhy – most likely a native of Burgundy, who worked for Nicolas Rolin in Autun in 1446, was active in Barcelona and Toulouse in the 1450s, and settled some time after 1462 in Savoy, where he performed a commission for Amedeo IX in Chambéry in 1466. Lonhy not only painted panels and illuminated manuscripts, he was also a muralist, he designed the stained-glass windows for Santa Maria del Mar in Barcelona, and he influenced the subsequent generation of Piedmontese artists, including painters such as Gian Martino Spanzotti and Defendente de Ferrari.

The physical features in the Antwerp *Nativity* display stylistic characteristics also found in Lonhy's miniatures and murals. The stocky figures recall images from the Flémalle group, which must have exerted at least an indirect influence on both the figures and the handling of the drapery. While the prominent inclusion of architecture is characteristic of Lonhy's oeuvre, the complex rendering of the roof timbers in this work is particularly interesting. This feature, uncommon in Flemish painting, is designed to enhance the spatial effect and, like the size of the figures, contributes significantly to the monumental impact of the painting.

79   **Antoine de Lonhy** (Master of the Trinity of Turin) (active c. 1446–1480/90)
Holy Trinity, c. 1470–80
Canvas (transferred), 172 × 82 cm (see fig. 138)
Museo Civico d'Arte Antica, Palazzo Madama, Turin (inv. 470/D)

The Duchy of Savoy nominally belonged to the Holy Roman Empire. It was bordered to the north by Burgundy and the Swiss Federation and to the west by the Kingdom of France, the Marquisate of Saluzzo and Provence. It shared its eastern border with the Duchy of Milan, the County of Asti, the Marquisate of Monferrato and the city-state of Genoa. This complex geographical position made the region a transit point for itinerant artists and created an artistic landscape in which different influences had long come together and intermingled.

The large-scale fragment of the *Holy Trinity* in Turin – a key painting of the Savoy-Piedmont school in the final decades of the fifteenth century – is an outstanding example of this interaction. To begin with, the artist drew on Early Netherlandish models from before 1450, in particular the *Holy Trinity* in Leuven, attributed to Jacques Daret, the Flémallesque *Trinity* wing of the Saint Petersburg diptych and Rogier van der Weyden's *Lamentation* panels. The impressive Renaissance architecture in the background, by contrast, refers to contemporary buildings designed by northern Italian, and more specifically Lombard, architects.

It was long suspected that the artist known initially as the 'Master of the Trinity of Turin', who produced altarpieces in Turin and Novalese and strongly influenced painting in Piedmont around 1500, was not a native of Savoy. Castelnuovo suggested that he came from Provence, while Sterling was more inclined towards a painter trained in Burgundy, which would have sufficiently acquainted him with the Flemish *ars nova*. Thanks to Avril (1989; see cat. 78), however, the master has been securely identified as the Burgundian illuminator and panel painter Antoine de Lonhy, whose career – reconstructed from both documentary sources and surviving work – was that of a versatile, itinerant artist. He worked initially in Burgundy, before moving successively to Toulouse, Barcelona, Piedmont (Turin) and finally Chambéry, where he entered the service of the Duke of Savoy.

Even though the size of Lonhy's oeuvre prompts questions regarding the use of assistants and workshop organization, the master's figural style stands out for its astonishing consistency, irrespective of the particular mode in which he happened to be working.

Provenance: House of Savoy collection.
References: Haverkamp-Begemann 1958; Sterling 1964; Laclotte and Thiébaut 1983.

Provenance: Purchased by Frits Mayer van den Bergh before 1902.
References: Sterling 1972, p. 13; Avril 1989; Romano 1989, pp. 35–44.

Provenance: Leone Fontana.
References: Sterling 1972; Castelfranchi Vegas 1984; Avril 1989; Romano 1989; Romano 1996; Madrid and Valencia 2001.

80	**Antoine de Lonhy (Master of the Trinity of Turin)** (active *c.* 1446–1480/90) *Presentation in the Temple, c.* 1480–90? Canvas (transferred), 135.5 × 130 cm (see fig. 128) Bob Jones University Museum & Gallery, Greenville (inv. P. 58.118)
81	**Workshop of Simon Marmion (?)** (*c.* 1420–1489) *Mater Dolorosa; Christ as the Man of Sorrows* (diptych), *c.* 1480 Panel, 44 × 30.5 cm each (see fig. 70) Stedelijke Musea, Groeningemuseum, Bruges (inv. 0.201–202)
82	**Master of Saint-Jean-de-Luze** (active 1460–1470) *Hugues de Rabutin, Seigneur d'Epiry (?)* (left wing of a diptych), *c.* 1470 Panel, 60.5 × 49.4 cm (see fig. 80) Musée des Beaux-Arts, Dijon (inv. D 1986–1–P)

80 Antoine de Lonhy (Master of the Trinity of Turin) (active *c.* 1446–1480/90)
Presentation in the Temple, c. 1480–90?
Canvas (transferred), 135.5 × 130 cm (see fig. 128)
Bob Jones University Museum & Gallery, Greenville (inv. P. 58.118)

A group of women, three of whom are marked out by haloes, follow the Holy Family in procession to the Temple. During the 'Purification' of the Virgin in the Temple in Jerusalem, the elderly Simeon, who is shown here with two assistants and wearing the robes of a Jewish high priest, recognized the Christ Child as the Messiah and took him from his mother's arms to the altar. Joseph, who is attired in unusual splendour, approaches the Temple behind Mary, carrying two sacrificial doves as symbols of the Old and the New Covenant. There are two striking aspects of the composition which have yet to be fully explained. The first is the strict isocephaly of the figure group – in other words, the fact that the heads of all the figures are shown at nearly the same level in a frieze-like arrangement. The other is the classicizing architecture of the Temple, which sets the painting apart from Netherlandish depictions of the same subject every bit as much as does the archaic golden ground.

The *Presentation in the Temple* originally belonged to a lost Marian altarpiece, which probably adorned the altar of a church in Piedmont. Another element of that same polyptych was the *Death of the Virgin* that once belonged to the collection of Balbo Bertone in Turin. The large, almost square painting was initially attributed to a Spanish painter, before Sterling (1972) and Romano (1977) persuasively ascribed it to the Master of the Trinity of Turin. That master has since been identified as Antoine de Lonhy, who entered the service of Amedeo IX of Savoy's court in Chambéry in 1466 (see cats 78, 79). Lonhy was briefly active in Barcelona before 1462, and the links between this composition and the work of Jaume Huguet are worthy of closer study. Romano (1989) places the painting's execution towards the end of Lonhy's career, together with the *Virgin and Child with Saint Anne* in the sacristy of Turin Cathedral.

The year '1490' appears lower left, together with the monogram CVE (Gillis van den Erborne?; see Sterling 1972). Avril (1989) has challenged the authenticity of this as an artist's signature, even though it does appear to be part of the original paint substance.

81 Workshop of Simon Marmion (?) (*c.* 1420–1489)
Mater Dolorosa; Christ as the Man of Sorrows (diptych), *c.* 1480
Panel, 44 × 30.5 cm each (see fig. 70)
Stedelijke Musea, Groeningemuseum, Bruges (inv. 0.201–202)

Simon Marmion, who was active in Valenciennes, was unquestionably one of the most important artists belonging to the generation of Hugo van der Goes and Hans Memling. This is despite the fact that his surviving work consists primarily of miniatures – indeed, Marmion was described by Jean Lemaire de Belges in the early sixteenth century as the 'prince among the illuminators'. He collaborated with the Mansel Master on the miniatures for the sumptuous *Fleur des histoires* codex that belonged to the Burgundian ducal library (Bibliothèque Royale, Brussels, Ms. 9231–33) and was commissioned by Guillaume Fillastre, Bishop of Tournai, to illustrate the *Grandes Chroniques de France* (Saltikov Library, Saint Petersburg, Ms. fr. 88). His miniatures in Margaret of York's *Visions de Tondal* manuscript (J. Paul Getty Museum, Los Angeles) and in the *Flora Hours* (Biblioteca Reale, Naples, Ms. IB 51) are among the most innovative cycles of illustrations in late fifteenth-century Franco-Flemish manuscripts.

As a panel painter, however, Marmion has proved a rather elusive figure. The painted wings of the compound altarpiece from the Abbey of Saint-Omer, which contain *Scenes from the Life of Saint Bertin* (fig. 78), are closely related in stylistic terms to the dedicatory miniature of the *Grandes Chroniques*. They form the undisputed core of an otherwise stylistically heterogeneous body of work. Grosshans (1992) and Ainsworth (1992) have recently shown through a comparative study of the underdrawings that several artists were actually responsible for the panels hitherto attributed to Marmion. His workshop in Valenciennes did, however, produce at least one important panel painter – Jan Provoost (see cats 54–55) – whose influence on Netherlandish art in the early sixteenth century is only gradually beginning to be acknowledged.

The Bruges diptych shows the grieving Virgin Mary on the left and the dead Christ on the right, both half-length and against a golden ground. There are, however, certain objections to its identification as a workshop copy after Marmion, as the composition might also derive from a lost devotional diptych by Rogier van der Weyden.

82 Master of Saint-Jean-de-Luze (active 1460–1470)
Hugues de Rabutin, Seigneur d'Epiry (?) (left wing of a diptych), *c.* 1470
Panel, 60.5 × 49.4 cm (see fig. 80)
Musée des Beaux-Arts, Dijon (inv. D 1986–1–P)

The portrait shows a middle-aged man, turned to the left, against a neutral green background, which appears to represent part of an interior. The sitter wears a fur-trimmed, red jacket and a high cap over his close-cropped hair. His hands are folded in prayer. His attention is focused on a stone statuette of the Madonna standing on a console in the wall beneath a stone baldachin. The words of his invocation are set out in three lines of golden letters. The panel is the left wing of a diptych rated among the masterpieces of Burgundian painting in the second half of the fifteenth century. The right wing contains a portrait of the sitter's wife before a statuette of Saint John the Evangelist (fig. 80). The stone sculptures – the style of which is deliberately archaic – no doubt represent the couple's patron saints.

The painting originated at the castle of Epiry in the Duchy of Burgundy, close to the parish of Saint-Emiland, which used to be known as Saint-Jean-de-Luze, from which the anonymous master derives his identifying name. The diptych probably shows the former chatelain, Hugues de Rabutin, Lord of Epiry and Balon, and his wife Jeanne – an illegitimate daughter of the Montaigu family, which was also related to the House of Burgundy (identification opposed by Vaivre 1987).

The diptych is the only work attributed to the Master of Saint-Jean-de-Luze. Although it is plainly influenced by Early Netherlandish examples, it does not reach their technical brilliance or intensity of colour. The hints of shadow in the background, which create the impression of candlelight, are certainly rooted in Flemish painting, as are the imitation sculptures – possibly influenced by earlier Burgundian court sculpture in Dijon. The rendering of the flesh parts and fabrics, by contrast, is more reminiscent of Provençal painting. Although this very ambivalence makes the two portraits typical of Burgundian art after 1450, stylistically speaking they appear to be isolated pieces. It is possible, therefore, that the anonymous artist who painted them was only temporarily active in Burgundy.

Provenance: Julius Weitzner.
References: Sterling 1972; Avril 1989; Romano 1989.

Provenance: Private collection, Belgium.
References: Hoffman 1969; Hoffman 1973; Hindman 1977; De Vos 1979, pp. 136–37; Ainsworth 1992; Grosshans 1992.

Provenance: Château of Epiry, near Saint-Emiland (Burgundy).
References: Bacri 1937, pp. 24–28; Ring 1949, no. 235; Vaivre 1987, pp. 356–68.

83 Enguerrand Quarton (c. 1416–1466)
Virgin and Child with Angels; Saint John the Baptist;
The Prophets Isaiah and Jeremiah (reconstruction
of a diptych), c. 1450
Panel, 30.3 × 20.3 cm; 30.2 × 20.5 cm (see fig. 85)
Staatliches Lindenau-Museum, Altenburg;
Musei Vaticani, Vatican City (Prophets)
(inv. 183 and 184)

Together with Barthélemy d'Eyck (cats 65–67),
Enguerrand Quarton, who came from the Diocese
of Laon, was the most important Provençal painter
in the mid-fifteenth century. His influence continued
to dominate southern French art until around 1500.
Quarton probably trained in Picardy or the
Netherlands around 1430, at which point he will have
come into contact with the Flemish *ars nova* – an
influence that was to remain apparent throughout his
career. Quarton appears to have moved to southern
France in the 1440s – possibly accompanying
Barthélemy d'Eyck, with whom he is first documented
in Aix-en-Provence in 1444. He was active in Avignon
by 1447, making his career as both a manuscript
illuminator and panel painter. In addition to the
monumental *Pietà* of Villeneuve-lès-Avignon (now
Louvre, Paris) and the immense *Coronation of the Virgin*
(1453) for the Charterhouse at the same location,
Quarton and his assistant Pierre Vilatte painted the
Virgin of Mercy for Jean Cadard and his wife (Musée
Condé, Chantilly) and, around 1465, the miniatures
for the *Missal of Jean de Martins* (Bibliothèque
Nationale, Paris, N.a.lat. 2661).

 This small diptych was long viewed as a workshop
piece, not least because of its poor state of
preservation. The images it contains are actually closer
to Quarton's miniatures than his panel paintings.
The composition with angels surrounding the Virgin
and Child draws on images produced by Campin's
workshop, while that of the Baptist sitting in a
landscape – the straightforward majesty of which is
intimately linked with the figure of God the Father in
the Paris Missal – displays surprising parallels with
Hans Memling's interpretation of the same subject in
the 'Floreins triptych' (cat. 50) and the 'Bembo diptych'
(Munich and Washington). The characteristic motif
of a row of trees in the background is also found in
Memling's Munich panel, suggesting that the two
works might draw on a common Flemish model.
It was recently discovered (Romano 1995) that the
diptych was originally surmounted with two prophets'
figures in lunettes, which derive directly from the
Ghent altarpiece (fig. 4) and will have lent the work
a more distinctly Netherlandish character.

Provenance: Before 1756, Museo Sacro di Biblioteca Apostolica, Rome;
from 1848, Baron Lindenau.
References: Sterling 1983; Laclotte and Thiébaut 1983; Romano 1994;
Paris 1999, Madrid and Valencia 2001.

84 Fra Angelico (Guido di Piero di Gino)
(c. 1395/1400–1455)
Holy Face, c. 1440–50
Panel, 55 × 39 cm (see fig. 99)
Museo Civico Giovanni Fattori, Livorno.
On loan from Santa Maria del Soccorso,
Livorno

This is undoubtedly one of the most moving images
painted by the Florentine master Fra Angelico. Christ,
wearing the crown of thorns, is shown frontally and
from the chest up against a neutral background. His
head is surrounded by a nimbus, inscribed with the
words 'IH[ESU]S XP[ISTU]S SAN[CTU]S', while the
golden hem of the red robe bears the inscription 'REX
REGVM ET D[OMI]NANTI[UM]'. The image directly
confronts the viewer with the Passion of Christ, not
least through the harsh and dramatic detail of Jesus'
bloodshot eyes. The theme and size of the painting,
which dates from between 1440 and 1450, suggest that
it was intended for private devotion.

 The strict frontality recalls Van Eyck's *Holy Face*
images, painted in Bruges in 1438 and 1440, which
have only survived in the form of copies (see cat. 37).
Although it would be misleading to compare the
Florentine work directly with Van Eyck's invention –
there are fundamental differences in terms of
iconography and hence also meaning – the contrast
between the Italian's expressive empathy and the cool,
intellectual approach of his Netherlandish counterpart
speaks volumes about the difference in mentality
between the two artists.

 It is not surprising that Rogier van der Weyden,
whose Passion pictures were quick to impress
contemporaries with their powerful expression of
emotion, should have based his *Entombment* (fig. 97)
on a work by Fra Angelico – more specifically, the
predella of the San Marco altarpiece (fig. 96). The
Florentine master also had a significant influence
on Jean Fouquet. In the Hours of Etienne Chevalier,
which he illustrated immediately after returning from
Italy, Fouquet drew repeatedly on compositions from
Fra Angelico's Vatican frescoes in the Capilla
Niccolina and, probably, on his murals – since
destroyed – in the *studiolo* of Pope Nicholas V. At the
very least, he will have had access to the preparatory
drawings for the *studiolo* frescoes.

Provenance: 1837, donated by S. Silvestri to the Cappella Addolorata
in Santa Maria del Soccorso, Livorno.
References: Baldini 1970, no. 45; Spike 1997, no. 83.

85 Anonymous copy (Veneto) after Jan van Eyck
(c. 1390–1441)
Crucifixion, c. 1460–70
Panel, 45 × 30 cm (see fig. 20)
Museo d'Arte Medievale e Moderna, Padua
(inv. 541)

This *Crucifixion* is attributed to an anonymous Paduan
artist and dated to the second half of the fifteenth
century. It is a partially unfinished copy after a
composition of Van Eyck, a variation on which
appears in the miniature that his workshop produced
for the Turin-Milan Hours (fig. 18). The mere fact
of its existence confirms the theory that an Eyckian
Crucifixion must have been present in the Veneto
region in the middle of the fifteenth century, the
composition of which was drawn on by, among
others, Mantegna for his *Crucifixion* in the San Zeno
altarpiece (fig. 102), and by Nicola di Maestro Antonio
d'Ancona and the circle of Squarcione in paintings in
the Galleria dell'Accademia in Venice.

 The immediate model for these northern Italian
copyists was a *Crucifixion* attributed to a member of
Van Eyck's workshop, now in the Galleria Franchetti,
Venice (cat. 34). This reportedly belonged to a Paduan
collection prior to 1902 and corresponds in size with
the painting reproduced here. However, comparison
of the two works reveals minor differences between
them, which cannot be explained by the unfinished
state of the Paduan copy. It is also significant,
moreover, that the latter only features the *INRI*
symbol at the top of the cross, while the Eyckian panel
has a three-part inscription, containing both Hebrew
and Latin letters. As far as this detail is concerned,
the copy appears to be closer to the *Crucifixion* in the
Turin-Milan Hours than to the presumed model.

 On closer examination, the relationship between
copy and prototype is further complicated by the fact
that the anonymous artist appears to have emulated the
pictorial structure and technique of Flemish paintings.
The detailed underdrawing on a light ground and the
robes of Mary and John, apparently still awaiting the
application of coloured glazes, seem to correspond
with different phases in the painting process applied
by Flemish artists. On the other hand, Strehlke (2001)
pointed out that the copy was painted in tempera and
suggested the possibility that the anonymous artist
might have copied an unfinished painting.

 Yet, whatever the case may be, the anonymous
Crucifixion is, like the *Saint Jerome* panel in Bergamo
(cat. 103), one of the rare examples in which Italian
artists reproduced a Netherlandish composition *in toto*.

Provenance: Rossi collection, Padua.
References: Châtelet 1980; Belting and Eichberger 1983; Castelfranchi
Vegas 1984; Limentani Virdis 1997; Venice 1999; Madrid and Valencia 2001;
Strehlke 2001.

86 **Antonello da Messina** (*c.* 1430–1479) *Abraham and the Three Angels, c.* 1450–55 Panel, 21.4 × 29.3 cm (see fig. 53) Museo della Magna Grecia, Reggio di Calabria (inv. 2984 c)	87 **Antonello da Messina** (*c.* 1430–1479) *Portrait of a Man, c.* 1470 Panel, 27 × 20 cm (see fig. 233) Musei Civici, Pinacoteca Malaspina, Pavia (inv. 30)	88 **Antonello da Messina** (*c.* 1430–1479) *Portrait of a Man,* 1476 Panel, 36 × 28 cm (see fig. 225) Museo Civico d'Arte Antica, Palazzo Madama, Turin (inv. 353)

This miniature-like panel shows three white-clad angels in front of an unusual rock formation that falls away precipitously to the left. A round table and two beehives stand in front of a tree to the left of the composition. The viewer's eye is drawn to a river valley winding between the mountains. As Brunelli (1908) realized, this panel is a fragment from an image of the Old Testament story of Abraham and the Three Angels, which has been cut down on the right. The original composition survives in a painting by Josse Lieferinx, in which Abraham is shown kneeling before the angels in front of his wife Sarah's house (cat. 76). The angels have come to tell him that the couple's long-held desire for a child is to be fulfilled.

With its high viewpoint, the landscape recalls the shoreline visible in the background of the Bucharest *Crucifixion* (fig. 145) – the earliest known painting by Antonello, executed even before he left for Sicily. The landscape motifs, however, are rendered in much greater detail and variety. Antonello's pursuit of realistic detail is evident in the plants and the slug, whereas the drapery of the robes seems much more artificial. Details of this nature already testify to Antonello's close study of Flemish art, especially the paintings of Jan van Eyck, with which he probably came into contact in Naples, during his apprenticeship with Colantonio (see cat. 94). Closer links are apparent when we compare Antonello's panel with Van Eyck's *Stigmatization of Saint Francis* (cats 28–29). Although it is certainly possible that the young Antonello was influenced by that particular composition, he may also have drawn on a lost Flemish model, another painting by Van Eyck or perhaps by Petrus Christus.

A copy by a follower of Antonello in Forza d'Agro, suggests that the latter's image of *Abraham and the Angels* was originally destined for Sicily, too, and that it was painted after the artist's return to Messina – in other words, just before 1457 at the latest.

Tradition has it that the painting was acquired by Marchese Luigi Malaspina di Sannazaro from a family in Verona. Bequeathed to the museum in Pavia in 1834, it was stolen in 1970 and recovered in 1977. The portrait's fragile condition was not improved by the restorations carried out by Cavenaghi (1915) and Pellicioli (1935–40). Although the painting is generally attributed to Antonello, as implied by the written signature (*'Antonellus Messaneus Pinxit'*) on the parapet, it is rarely discussed in the literature because it is considered almost impossible to analyse. Of course, many problems would disappear if the painting could be restored to its former condition, but even in its present state several details seem more reminiscent of the donor of the Quarton *Pietà* now in the Louvre (but originally in Avignon) than of any prototype by Van Eyck or Petrus Christus. Even the jacket worn by the man portrayed, with its collar meeting in a point behind the shoulders, bears more similarity to the jackets worn by some of the spectators in the background of Barthélemy d'Eyck's *Annunciation* in Aix-en-Provence (fig. 142) than it does to Italian costume. The use of the parapet, here possibly appearing for the first time in Antonello's painting, with his signature incised into the stone rather than written on a *cartellino* attached to the painting, recalls the so-called *'Timotheus'* by Jan van Eyck (fig. 223). The young man's pose, contrasting with the turn of his head, occurs in no other portrait by the artist. Antonello seems to be beginning to experiment here with the expressive possibilities of the way the man occupies space, thereby increasing the psychological insight inherent in the painting.

Zappia's proposed date (1981) of shortly before 1470, i.e. almost the same moment as the *Ecce Homo* in the Metropolitan Museum, New York, has more or less replaced the date of 1473 which, until 1981, was never disputed.

An engraving in Rosini's 1848 *Storia dell'Arte* reveals that the painting was in the Rinuccini collection in Florence at that time. In about 1850 it passed into the Trivulzio collection in Milan. It was transferred to Turin in 1935.

This is one of Antonello's most famous paintings, as much for the psychological quality of the characterization as for his ability to visualize ideas and emotions. The sitter's air of assured superiority (appearing almost like a direct challenge), combined with the eyes with their half-lowered lids and the enigmatic smile on the man's face, have made this an unforgettable image, part of our collective imagery.

Guided by the inscription on the *cartellino* ('1476 *Antonellus messaneus Pinxit'*), a number of art historians, in particular Lionello Venturi (1907) and Van Marle (1934), have suggested that the work belongs to Antonello's Milanese period. Yet, although the exact duration of his visit to Milan is not known, there seems to have been little scope for painting portraits. In addition, this hypothesis conflicts with the fact that the sitter is wearing a typical Venetian robe, complete with chaperon. Nevertheless, Sricchia Santoro (1986) detects in the portrait certain links with Bramante's early paintings done in Lombardy (at the time, however, he was living in Bergamo, in the Veneto). Other scholars have suggested that the unusual wording of the inscription (*'pinxit'*, rather than *'me pinxit'*) indicates that what we are looking at is a self-portrait.

Antonello's obvious attempt at rigour and formal abstraction, the clear perspective he achieves by systemizing the volumes into solid, ideal blocks (from which the extraordinary eyebrows swerve forth), constitute a step forwards in a basically Eyckian scheme, with the space defined by the parapet and the *cartellino*, artlessly fixed to it with spots of sealing wax. Here the Flemish adherence to reproducing every single item has been abandoned and, in the words of Longhi (1914), the artist creates a 'complex of realism and profound idealism', communicating thereby 'the feeling of a human monument'.

Provenance: Rota collection (?).
References: Jolly 1976; Laclotte and Thiébaut 1983; Sricchia Santorno 1986; Arbace 1993; Thiébaut 1993; Savettieri 1998.

Provenance: Verona (?).
References: Arbace 1983; Sricchia Santoro 1986; Thiébaut 1993; Barbera 1998; Savettieri 1998.

Provenance: Before 1848, Rinuccini collection, Florence (?).
References: Sricchia Santoro 1986; Lucco 1990; Arbace 1993; Thiébaut 1993; Barbera 1998; Savettieri 1998; Venice 1999.

89 Donato de' Bardi (active 1426–1451)
Crucifixion, c. 1435–40?
Canvas, 238 × 165 cm (see fig. 124)
Pinacoteca Civica, Savona

90 Giovanni Bellini (c. 1430–1516)
Portrait of a Man
Panel, 29 × 22 cm (see fig. 110)
Nivaagaards Malerisamling, Nivå (inv. 5)

91 Ludovico Brea (active 1470–1523)
Saint Peter, 1481–90
Panel, 76.5 × 42.5 cm (see fig. 119)
Galleria di Palazzo Bianco, Genoa (inv. B 300)

Genoa, which enjoyed close trading relations with Flanders from the thirteenth century onwards, showed itself to be extremely receptive to the influence of Flemish painting early in the fifteenth century. Jan van Eyck painted an *Annunciation* triptych for the city's Lomellini family that became very famous in Italy. It found its way from Genoa to Naples in as early as the 1440s. This monumental *Crucifixion*, which came to the museum at Savona from the Ospedale di San Paolo, though this was not its original destination, might well be one of the earliest surviving examples of the indirect influence that Early Netherlandish painting exerted in northern Italy. The very fact that it is executed on a textile support seems to reflect the importation of Flemish paintings on canvas (*Tüchlein*) – including some by Van Eyck – into Liguria. Recent evidence that part of the *Crucifixion* was done in oil paint and the inscription running around the frame are also indicative of a more than superficial knowledge of paintings by Jan van Eyck and other Early Netherlandish masters.

Identified as the work of Donato de' Bardi in a *cartellino* at the feet of Saint John, the *Crucifixion* relates extremely closely to Van Eyck's work in terms of the expressive gestures and physiognomies, and the barren, rocky landscape in the background. It is possible that Donato de' Bardi was able to draw on Eyckian models produced in the years prior to the completion of the Ghent altarpiece.

De' Bardi was an impoverished nobleman from Pavia, where he may also have trained. His presence in Genoa is first documented in 1426. He may have come into contact with the work of the Angevin court artists in nearby Provence in the 1440s, but this is not clear. As a painter known to have been active on the Ligurian coast and in Lombardy (Milan), De' Bardi's role as a conduit for Netherlandish formal innovation ought certainly not to be underestimated.

This painting was acquired by Johannes Hage at the end of the nineteenth century from the Haro collection in Paris, probably on the advice of Gustavo Frizzoni, who was the first to promote it (1910) as the work of Giovanni Bellini. Owing to its out-of-the-way location, very few scholars have made the trip to examine it; also to its disadvantage has been the slightly ambiguous public status of the Hage collection. At any rate, it has been accepted as an autograph work by Gronau (1930), Berenson (1957), Heinemann (1962) and Pignatti (1969); doubtful of its authenticity is Gamba (1937), while Tempestini (2000) considers that it belongs to the 'Venetian school'.

Although the portrait is still covered by a nineteenth-century sugary varnish, visible particularly in the eyes and on part of the sky, it has all the requirements to make it convincingly the work of Bellini, produced in about 1500; nearly all the scholars who have examined it share this opinion. This is one of the first works in which the artist shows the sitter against the sky, instead of the familiar dark background. It was probably painted a couple of years before the landscape made its appearance as background in the so-called *Pietro Bembo* at Hampton Court. The structural manner in which the figure is introduced into the composition strongly recalls Memling's portraiture, widely known in Venice after about 1470.

The Nice-born painter Ludovico Brea might have trained under Jean Miarlieti in Montpellier, with whom he collaborated in 1473 on an altarpiece for the Church of Santa Maria della Misericordia in his native city. His early work is clearly influenced by Provençal painting and, at least indirectly, by Flemish art, too. His 1475 *Pietà* from Cimiez is closely related to Enguerrand Quarton's work. In the 1480s, Brea responded increasingly to the stimulus of Lombard art, which spread along the Ligurian coast through the work of painters like Donato de' Bardi and especially Giovanni Mazone. In 1490, he finished an altarpiece for Savona Cathedral that Vincenzo Foppa had begun. Brea's workshop expanded significantly after 1500, employing the artist's sons and nephews along with other assistants. It continued to disseminate Provençal ideas in Liguria until the 1520s, while also enabling Lombard influences to spread along the southern French coast.

The image of *Saint Peter*, a recurrent theme in later paintings produced by the Brea workshop, originally belonged to an altarpiece in the Church of San Bartolomeo degli Armeni in Genoa. The colouring and painting technique recall the work of Lieferinx and Dipre, while the rendering of the clouds refers back indirectly to Flemish models. Netherlandish influences – as mediated through De' Bardi and Mazone – can also be identified in the *Crucifixion* scene in Genoa that comes from the same altarpiece (fig. 118). Three further fragments of the painting showing Saint Vincent Ferrer, Saint Nicholas of Tolentino and a donor are now in the Národní Galerie, Prague. Whereas current art historians tend to date the painting to the early 1490s on stylistic grounds, which would make it later than the Foppa altarpiece that Brea completed, one of their seventeenth-century predecessors was much more precise. According to the artists' lives compiled by Soprani and published by Ratti in 1780, a certain Biagio de' Gradi commissioned the Genoa altarpiece in 1481.

Provenance: Before 1780, Ospedale di San Paolo, Savona.
References: Castelfranchi Vegas 1984; Algeri and De Floriani 1991; Strehlke 2001.

Provenance: Haro collection, Paris.
References: Pignatti 1969; Tempestini 2000.

Provenance: San Bartolomeo degli Armeni, Genoa.
References: Labande 1937; Algeri and De Floriani 1991.

92 **Ludovico Brea** (active 1470–1523)
Virgin and Child Enthroned, 1494
Panel, 164 × 76 cm (see fig. 117)
Göteborgs Konstmuseum (inv. GKM 1058)

The Virgin Mary is shown sitting on an imposing
golden throne with the Christ Child, dressed in a red
shirt, on her lap. She wears a gold dress with a brocade
pattern beneath a blue cloak that also covers her head.
Mary holds a book in her left hand and gazes into the
distance. Her melancholy expression and the covering
of her head, which is an iconographical reference to
grief, allude to the Passion that awaits her son.

Small angels stand on either arm of the throne.
The one on the right wearing a red robe plays a flute,
while the one in green on the left has a lute. The angels
perform their music in honour of the Son of God
– shown here suckling at his mother's breast – in a
manner that recalls the Madonna scenes of Memling
and Gerard David. Brea based the form of the angels'
robes on northern Italian models, however, and his
painting owes an overall debt to Vincenzo Foppa.
The structure and decoration of the throne, and the
marvellous Renaissance frame, also reflect the Nice-
born artist's knowledge of Foppa and of works by
northern Italian – primarily Lombard – painters,
which spread along the Ligurian coast in the latter
part of the fifteenth century. Brea only draws on
Netherlandish models in this mixed-technique
Madonna panel (the painter used both tempera and oil
binders) for details such as the reflections in the eyes.

The impact of the monumental composition is
heightened by the contrast between the golden throne
and the dark background, which lends the painting a
remarkably sculptural quality. This would not have
been possible without the influence of Vincenzo
Foppa, whose 'Della Rovere altarpiece' for Savona
Cathedral was finished by Ludovico Brea in 1490.
According to the inscription, Brea completed the
Virgin and Child Enthroned for Paolo di Serravalle in
1494. He returned to Savona a year later, where he
painted one of his key works – a polyptych devoted
to the *Assumption* – for the Church of San Giacomo.

93 **Bartolomeo Caporali** (*c.* 1442–1509)
Saint Jerome, *c.* 1490–1500
Panel, 41 × 23.5 cm
Museo Nazionale di Capodimonte, Naples
(inv. Q1930 N.938)

Bartolomeo Caporali, who worked in Perugia, was
one of the most productive members of the Umbrian
school, together with Benedetto Bonfigli and Fiorenzo
di Lorenzo. In the course of his career, he held a
number of official posts within Perugia's painters'
corporation. In his younger days, he worked as a
fresco and panel painter, whose style was heavily
influenced by two other Perugians, Benozzo Gozzoli
and Niccolò Alunno. He was chiefly active, however,
as a painter of coats of arms and banners.

This small panel showing the Church Father Saint
Jerome originally formed part of a larger altarpiece and
seems to draw – indirectly at least – on Jan van Eyck's
Saint Jerome in His Study, which must have been in
Florence around 1480 (see cat. 30). Although Caporali
shows the saint in a full-length, standing position, the
background, with its bookshelves, apparently reflects
the Netherlandish model. It is possible that Caporali
saw Van Eyck's *Saint Jerome* in the papal city of Perugia,
as it probably passed to another prominent member of
the Papal Curia after Albergati's death, before finding
its way into Lorenzo de' Medici's collection.

94 **Niccolò Colantonio** (active 1440–1460/70)
Saint Vincent Ferrer Preaching; *The Virgin
Appearing to Saint Vincent Ferrer* (two panels
from the *Altarpiece of Saint Vincent Ferrer*),
c. 1455–65
Panel, 60 × 40 cm; 60 × 48.7 cm (see fig. 141)
Museo Nazionale di Capodimonte, Naples.
On loan from San Pietro Martire, Naples

In his 1524 letter to Marcantonio Michiel, in which
he discussed the art of his native city, Pietro Summonte
stated that Colantonio had been Antonello's teacher
and the first in the region to master the Flemish
technique of oil painting. Colantonio had copied
several paintings by Van Eyck and managed to imitate
them perfectly. Summonte's account enables us to
identify three of Colantonio's works. The first is his
Saint Francis altarpiece, the predella of which includes
an image of *Saint Jerome in His Study* (fig. 148), probably
based directly on Van Eyck. The other two paintings
are the San Lorenzo *Descent from the Cross* and the *Saint
Vincent Ferrer* altarpiece (fig. 141). All three are directly
linked to Aragonese rule in Naples and clearly testify to
Colantonio's role as a conduit for Early Netherlandish
painting in the Kingdom of Naples.

The influence of Van Eyck in particular on the
Neapolitan painter and his workshop is especially
plain in the scenes from the life of the Dominican
saint, Vincent Ferrer. The craggy landscape in which
Saint Vincent Ferrer Preaching is set, for instance, recalls
the background of the Ghent altarpiece (fig. 4) and
Van Eyck's *Saint Francis* pictures (cats 28, 29), while the
figures also appear to have been influenced by Flemish
models. The relationship with Van Eyck is even plainer
in Colantonio's *Rescue of a Ship in a Storm* – one of the
earliest autonomous landscapes anywhere – which
derives indirectly from Van Eyck's *Crossing of Saint
Julian and Saint Martha* in the Turin-Milan Hours.
In its detailed rendering of the scholar's study,
The Virgin Appearing to Saint Vincent Ferrer refers
to Van Eyck's lost 'Lomellini triptych', which
was shortly to inspire Antonello, too (fig. 111).

The altarpiece was commissioned by Isabella
Chiaromonte – the wife of Ferrante I of Aragon, who
appears in the predella with her children – following
the canonization of Vincent Ferrer by Pope Calixtus
III in 1455. The Queen, who died in 1465 and was
buried in the chapel at San Pietro Martire in which
the altarpiece was duly installed, had campaigned in
favour of the Valencia-born Dominican's sainthood.

Provenance: Faerber and Katzenstein collection.
Reference: Algeri and De Floriani 1991.

Reference: Leone de Castris 1999.

Provenance: Chapel of Saint Vincent Ferrer, San Pietro Martire, Naples.
References: Jolly 1976; Sricchia Santoro 1986; Naples 1997; Madrid and
Valencia 2001; Limentani Virdis and Pietrogiovanna 2001; Naples 2001.

95   Workshop or circle of Niccolò Colantonio
(active 1440–1460/70)
Prophet (?), *c.*1460–70
Panel, 60 × 45.4 cm (see fig. 144)
The Cleveland Museum of Art (inv. 1916.811)

A variety of attributions has been suggested for
this painting, which is generally considered to be a
portrait. Berenson argued at the turn of the twentieth
century that the painting, which had initially been
ascribed to Verrocchio's Florentine pupil Ghirlandaio
(see cat. 99), might in fact be the work of Justus of
Ghent (Joos van Wassenhove). He pointed to the
Netherlandish character of the painting and its
typological links with the *Uomini famosi* cycle at
Federico da Montefeltro's palace in Urbino, which has
since been securely attributed to Joos van Wassenhove
and Pedro Berruguete.

    Similarities with the *Saint Jerome* (fig. 148) that had
recently been reattributed to Colantonio prompted
Venturi (1930) to conclude that this painting, too,
must have been Colantonio's work. In support of this
view, he cited its affinities with both Flemish painting
and the portraits of Antonello da Messina. This
interpretation, which is rendered even more
persuasive by the still life in the background, was
shared by Desmonts (1931), although he continued
to identify the Neapolitan with the author of the
Aix *Annunciation* (see fig. 142 and cat. 65).

    The latter, which is now usually ascribed to
Barthélemy d'Eyck, and Colantonio's *Saint Jerome*
form the context within which this panel is currently
regarded alternatively as a product of the Neapolitan
or the Provençal school. This makes it a rather typical
example of the stylistic mixture that existed in the
western Mediterranean after 1450, in which
Netherlandish, Provençal, Spanish and southern Italian
influences combined to form a complex synthesis.

    The painting is not only problematic in terms of its
geographical origin – its original context and function
are also unclear. It seems improbable, to begin with, that
it really is an autonomous portrait. It is more plausible
that the painting belonged to a gallery of 'famous men'
or that it actually represents an Old Testament prophet
in a manner similar to the Aix triptych.

96   Workshop of Niccolò Colantonio
(active 1440–1460/70)
The Three Marys at the Tomb and the Resurrection,
*c.*1470?
Panel, 40.6 × 24.1 cm (see fig. 143)
Collection of Alexander Acevedo, New York

Two separate events related in the New Testament after
Christ's Crucifixion are linked here in a single image.
The painting shows the visit of the Holy Women to the
empty tomb together with the Resurrection. The two
scenes are incompatible both with the Gospel text and
with pictorial tradition, as the Resurrection had
already occurred by the time the Magdalen and her two
companions found only an angel in attendance at the
empty sepulchre. The unusual iconography probably
reflects the fact that the artist based his composition on
unfamiliar pictorial inventions.

    The Three Marys and the figure of the angel are
a detailed reprise of the Rotterdam *Three Marys at*
the Tomb (fig. 6), which is widely considered to be an
early work by Jan van Eyck. Van Eyck's diagonally
structured composition, which appears to have had
surprisingly little influence on Early Netherlandish
painting, is transformed here into an upright format,
as a result of which the sarcophagus, which in the
original is positioned horizontally, is now rendered
diagonally. The figure of the resurrected Christ, for
which numerous Netherlandish precursors can be
cited, is somewhat out of place in this composition
and is thus likely to have reflected the iconographical
scheme of a larger altarpiece.

    A noteworthy feature is the hilly landscape in the
distance, seen from above, with its prominent view of
a fortified city. This only appears to reflect the Eyckian
model in structural terms and is probably an original
addition by the artist. It is precisely in this respect that
the painting recalls the work of the Neapolitan artist
Niccolò Colantonio, for instance the landscapes in the
background of the altarpiece of *Saint Vincent Ferrer*
(cat. 94) and the *Descent from the Cross* in San Domenico
Maggiore, Naples. In Colantonio's limited surviving
oeuvre there are also parallels for the physiognomies
of the Three Marys and of the angel. It is plausible,
therefore, that this painting is the work of the
Neapolitan artist or his workshop, although it is not
clear how Van Eyck's composition came to exert such
an influence in Italy.

97   Piero di Cosimo (Piero di Lorenzo)
(*c.*1462–1521)
Giuliano da Sangallo and Francesco Giamberti
(pendant portraits), after 1480
Panel, 47.5 × 33.5 cm each (see fig. 226)
Rijksmuseum, Amsterdam (inv. C 1367
and C 1368). On loan from Mauritshuis,
The Hague

It was around 1480 that the Florentine painter Piero di
Lorenzo entered the workshop of Cosimo Rosselini,
whose name he was later to adopt as his own. He and
his master were employed in 1481–82 at the Vatican,
where they worked on the frescoes of the Sistine
Chapel at the same time as Sandro Botticelli,
Domenico Ghirlandaio and Pietro Perugino. The
primary influences discernible in the early work of
Piero di Cosimo, whose oeuvre has been
reconstructed entirely on the basis of a single painting
attributed to him by Vasari, are those of Ghirlandaio
and Filippino Lippi. His skills as a colourist, unusual
for a Florentine artist of his time, were, however,
directly stimulated by Hugo van der Goes' 'Portinari
altarpiece', which had been in Santa Maria Nuova
since 1483 (fig. 107). The landscape backgrounds of his
characteristic mythological scenes also frequently refer
to Netherlandish models. The double portrait of
Francesco Giamberti and his son, Giuliano da
Sangallo, is something of an exception in Piero's work,
possibly reflecting the unusual circumstances in which
it was commissioned. The pendant portraits
ultimately belong to the tradition of the medieval
master-builder's portrait, which enjoyed something of
a rebirth in fifteenth-century painting – especially in
the North. Both sitters had been trained as joiners and
masons. Francesco Giamberti and his son worked in
the circle of Michelozzo, among others, which
remained firmly rooted in the tradition of Gothic
masons' workshops ('lodges'), despite the innovations
of contemporary Renaissance architectural theory.
Giuliano, who became one of the leading architects
of his time, also remained true to that tradition.
It is logical, therefore, that the painter should have
adopted a northern portrait type for their likenesses.
The motif of a landscape stretching across both
panels, established through paintings produced in
Ghirlandaio's and other workshops, had ceased to be
innovatory in Florentine portraiture by the time these
portraits were painted (after 1480).

Provenance: Before 1912, A. A. Komarovsky, St Petersburg.
References: Weale 1909, pp. 20–21; Friedländer I (1967).

Provenance: Commissioned by Giuliano da Sangallo;
British Royal Collection.
References: Van Thiel *et al.* 1976, C1367–68; Castelfranchi Vegas 1984.

References: Ring 1949; Jolly 1976; Sricchia Santoro 1986; Arbace 1993.

98   **Antonio da Fabriano** (active *c.*1447–1489)
Saint Jerome in His Study, 1451
Panel, 88.4 × 52.8 cm (see fig. 114)
The Walters Art Museum, Baltimore
(inv. 37.439)

At the beginning of the nineteenth century this painting was in the collection of Don Luigi Faustini in Fabriano (Ricci 1834); it then passed into the hands of Romualdo Fornari, also in Fabriano (Marcoaldi 1867). It was acquired in about 1910 from Fornari's heirs by the dealer Drey, of Munich, who sold it in 1911–12 to Henry Walters.

Antonio's painting, signed and dated 1451, cannot be compared with that of any other contemporary painter from the Marches; an explanation for this paradoxical situation was furnished by Zeri (1948), who suggested that he must have received his training in Naples, in very close proximity to Colantonio. This was accepted until recently, when definitive proof was provided that Antonio da Fabriano is the same person as the painter Antonello da Fabriano, who was in Genoa in 1447–48. Antonio did not train in Naples, therefore, but in Genoa which, as we know, maintained close commercial links with Bruges and housed a number of paintings by Jan van Eyck. The continual exchanges, commercial and cultural, between the ports of Genoa, Naples and Valencia produced a kind of common language, with local variations of idiom, throughout the Mediterranean; this painting by Antonio da Fabriano is part of this phenomenon. It has a strong Hispano-Flemish, rather than purely Flemish, character, producing a family relationship with the work of the young Huguet, of Jacomart, of Lluis Dalmau and of the 'Master of Pere Roig de Corella'. In addition to the space collapsing as it comes nearer to the spectator (as in Dalmau), there are Jerome's face, similar to the faces in the work of Jacomart and the Roig de Corella Master; the bookshelf with books as in Barthélemy d'Eyck and in Colantonio; and, finally, the idea of the suite of rooms, as in Petrus Christus. The exquisite rendering of the gnarled, arthritic hands of the saint also reveals an indirect link with Flemish culture, through the intermediary this time of the work of Fra Diamante.

99   **Domenico Ghirlandaio** (Domenico Bigordi)
(1449–1494)
Christ Crowned with Thorns, *c.*1480
Panel, 54.3 × 33.7 cm (see fig. 62)
Philadelphia Museum of Art. The John
G. Johnson Collection (inv. j.1176a)

Although the panel was attributed to Memling in the early twentieth century, discrepancies in the painting technique show it to be the work of an Italian artist copying one of his Flemish counterpart's pictorial inventions. The panel's model was almost certainly Memling's *Christ as the Man of Sorrows*, which ended up in Genoa via a Florentine collection (cat. 51). The original work was once the left wing of a diptych for private devotion, whose companion piece – the grieving Virgin Mary – was recently identified, allowing the diptych to be reconstructed here for the first time (cat. 52).

This copy differs only slightly from Memling's Christ, with the exception of the iconographically important whipping-post inserted on the left-hand edge. Like the crown of thorns, the whipping-post refers to a specific moment in the Passion, even though Christ is pictured, as he is in the Flemish model, displaying wounds that were not inflicted until later.

Despite the fact that a variety of authors has linked the copy to the Florentine workshop of Domenico Ghirlandaio (Christiansen 1998), it appears to be an autograph work of that master (Fahy). The Florentine artist, who was influenced by Baldovinetti, Pollaiuolo and, above all, by Verrocchio, also showed himself in a number of paintings to be very open to Flemish influences. Landscape backgrounds of the kind found in portraits produced by his workshop draw on the works of Early Netherlandish artists such as Memling and Van der Goes, which found their way to Florence in that period. None the less, this image of Christ is the only example so far identified in which the Florentine copied a Netherlandish model so faithfully. Ghirlandaio's copy also indicates that Memling's original was probably sent to Italy immediately on completion.

100   **Jacobello di Antonello** (*c.*1455–1490?)
Virgin and Child, 1480
Panel, 67 × 45 cm (see fig. 103)
Pinacoteca dell'Accademia Carrara, Bergamo
(inv. 184)

Although this *Virgin and Child* had been listed as the work of Jacobello di Antonello in the bequest of Count Giacomo Carrara in 1796, the inscription on the *cartellino* – '1480 XIII Ind. Mēsis Decēbris/Jacobus Anto.lli filiu nō/humani pictoris me fecit' – was misinterpreted in the mid-nineteenth century, and the painting was ascribed to a certain 'Giacomo Comolli'. Toesca (1911) deserves the credit for having interpreted the signature correctly and for realizing that the date should be read as 1480 (rather than 1490). The unusual inscription thus begins to make sense. It alludes to the extraordinary skills as a painter of the artist's father, Antonello, who died the previous year.

Because this is the only signed work by the son of Antonello da Messina, and because it gives such striking evidence of his filial devotion, critical acclaim for it has grown over the years. Jacobello is now considered to have been a very close collaborator of his father in his later years, and to have achieved a quality only slightly less impressive than that of his father. This perhaps explains the hypothesis, advanced by Giovanni Previtali (1980) and now quite widely accepted, that the present painting, like the 'Benson Madonna' in Washington, was begun by Antonello and brought fairly near to completion by him, with Jacobello only providing the final touches. However, if this were the case, it would be hard to understand why Jacobello should have taken all the credit for the work, particularly as he was thus comparing himself with a painter of almost superhuman ability.

The reconstruction of Jacobello's activity on the basis of this one secure painting is only now beginning. Moreover, there is great confusion over his biographical details. Some authors think that he spent most of his life in Venice; others are convinced that he died young, before 1488. What is indisputable is that he assumed the tragic expressiveness used by his father in his final paintings, revealing even more clearly his links with Provençal (rather than northern European) taste, and particularly with Josse Lieferinx.

Provenance: Faustini collection, Fabriano (nineteenth century).
References: Zeri 1976; Cleri 1997; Natale 2001.

Provenance: 1913, purchased by John G. Johnson.
References: Friedländer VI; Christiansen 1998; Fahy (forthcoming).

Provenance: 1796, Count of Carrara collection.
References: Arbace 1983; Sricchia Santoro 1986; Savettieri 1998.

101　Fra Filippo Lippi (*c.* 1406–1469)
Saint Jerome, c. 1430–35
Panel, 54 × 37 cm (see fig. 168)
Staatliches Lindenau-Museum, Altenburg
(inv. 96)

This little panel is one of the earliest known examples of Italian Quattrocento painting in which Saint Jerome is shown as a penitent. It can probably be dated to the first half of the 1430s. The iconography is based on the saint's *Vita*, according to which he wrote his theological treatises in Bethlehem and Rome, before withdrawing to the Syrian desert to live in isolation and pursue a purer faith.

Filippo Lippi places the saint in the wilderness before an imposing, plateau-like rock formation, reminiscent of the landscapes of the northern Italian Trecento. A church can be made out beyond this simplified, craggy landscape, symbolizing distant civilization. The Church Father kneels on the ground. He has opened his penitent's robe to reveal his chest, which he beats with a rock. The skull serves as a symbol of mortality, while the crucifix in his left hand offers him hope and strength. A monk appears in the foreground, where he is about to remove the thorn from the paw of Jerome's emblematic lion.

Comparison with the landscape backgrounds that appear in Flemish painting around the same time – especially in Van Eyck's work – shows why northern models that found their way to Italy had such an impact on local painters. Piero della Francesca's painting of the same theme (Staatliche Museen, Berlin) dates from the following decade, yet already appears to have assimilated some of the innovations of Netherlandish art, while the influence of Flemish landscapes on Bellini's images of Saint Jerome is plain. Filippo Lippi himself is likely to have come directly into contact with Early Netherlandish painting shortly after completing this work. Around the mid-1430s, his images of the Virgin and Child enthroned begin to display a clearly modified spatial conception, apparently reflecting his intensive study of Jan van Eyck's art. His 1437 'Tarquinia Madonna' (fig. 104) is an early highlight in this respect.

102　Lorenzo Lotto (1480–1556/57)
The Penitent Saint Jerome, c. 1512–13
Panel, 55.8 × 40 cm (see fig. 134)
Muzeul National de Artă al României,
Bucharest (inv. 8002/36)

In spite of the presence of the signature – '*Laurent. Lotus*' on a rock at the lower left – the painting was not recognized as a work by Lotto until Frimmel (1894) identified it as the '*quadretto de S. Gieronimo*' quoted in about 1525 by Marcantonio Michiel. Basing his argument on Frimmel's description, Berenson (1895) dated the work to a few years after 1515, and this judgment was unanimously endorsed until Mariani Canova (1975) suggested that the painting might have been executed in 1544–46. Few scholars shared this opinion and it is now unanimously agreed that the painting dates from a short while after the artist's stay in Rome, in about 1512–13.

The depiction of the saint as a penitent in the desert, rather than as a scholar (the formula preferred by Van Eyck in the fifteenth century), had already been used by the artist, but with a different meditative slant, in his *Saint Jerome* in Castel Sant'Angelo in Rome. The much more dynamic pose in this painting imbues the character with a strong emotional emphasis, a kind of tragic, passionate madness. The huge grasshopper in the foreground, exactly parallel to the picture plane, seems to be perched on the picture's frame; this is quite consistent with Lotto's original approach to the problems and vagaries of pictorial representation. Like most of the northern painters, Lotto considered the purpose of painting to be to make a record of the unpredictable nature of life, beyond the virtual window represented by the frame – rather than rationalizing, or at least harmonizing, the facts of nature via his artistic vision. This is why his landscapes look more 'real' than those of almost any of his contemporaries in Italy. The admirable clarity of the distances (which has its source in Flemish painting) is mingled with an unmistakable echo of the styles of Dürer and Altdorfer in the definition of the branches of the trees and also of the various botanical species, represented here with extreme precision.

103　Anonymous (Northern Italy) (*c.* 1460–80)
Saint Jerome
Canvas mounted on panel, 53 × 36 cm
(see fig. 50)
Pinacoteca dell'Accademia Carrara,
Bergamo (inv. 729)

Saint Jerome is shown dressed as a cardinal in a barren, rocky landscape, in which he tends to a wounded lion. The artist subtly links the legend in which Jerome removes a thorn from the lion's paw – to which the Church Father owes his attribute – with the iconography of Jerome as a penitent in the wilderness, which was especially popular in Italy. This lends a special significance to the altar in the background. A city can be made out on the plain to the right of the rocks.

It was recognized at an early stage that the painting is based on a Netherlandish model from the workshop of Rogier van der Weyden, the monochrome *Saint Jerome* on the reverse of the left wing of the 'Sforza triptych' (see cat. 59), rendered as an illusionistic stone carving. The Italian painting follows the figures and rock formations in its Netherlandish model down to the smallest details. Only the colouring and the plain appear to be the painter's own invention.

The direct dependence on the Rogierian 'Sforza triptych' has prompted some authors to ascribe the painting to Zanetto Bugatto, the Milan court painter who was dispatched to the workshop of the Brussels town artist in 1461. This hypothesis is undermined by the fact that the 'Sforza triptych' was not painted for the Milan Sforzas, but for the Pesaro branch of the family. It also seems improbable for technical reasons that the work was done by a master like Bugatto, who was familiar with the Netherlandish painting technique. It is much more likely to have been painted by a northern Italian master who studied the triptych produced by Rogier's workshop in Pesaro.

Provenance: Probably identical with the *Saint Jerome* by Filippo Lippi listed in the 1492 Medici inventory.
References: Oertel 1942; Ruda 1997.

Provenance: Purchased between 1777 and 1787 by Baron Samuel von Brukenthal, Hermannstadt (now Sibiu, Romania).
Reference: Washington, Bergamo and Paris 1997–99.

Provenance: Before 1850, Guglielmo Lochis, Bergamo.
References: Cavalieri 1990; Madrid and Valencia 2001.

104　Pietro Perugino (Pietro Vannucci) (1446–1524)
Francesco delle Opere, 1494
Panel, 52 × 43 cm (see fig. 228)
Galleria degli Uffizi, Florence (inv. 1700)

Panofsky (1953) and Pope-Hennessy (1966) still argued that the portraits of Hans Memling were crucially influenced by Italian painting. Both scholars believed that Memling's innovative landscape backgrounds would not have been possible had the German-born artist not enjoyed a direct knowledge of the landscapes of Perugino, in particular.

In recent decades, however, art historians have fundamentally reassessed the relationship in question, revealing the importance of Memling's influence on Quattrocento portraiture in general and the Florentine school in particular. Many Venetian and Florentine merchants based in Bruges commissioned altarpieces and portraits from Memling, considerable numbers of which found their way to Italy, where artists like Bellini and Jacometto, and various Florentine painters saw them in Venice. In Florence itself, it was chiefly painters associated with Verrocchio's workshop who were the first to assimilate Memling's portrait types, with their landscape backgrounds. Apart from Domenico Ghirlandaio and Fra Bartolommeo, the most notable figure in this respect is the Umbrian-born Perugino, who worked in Verrocchio's workshop some time before 1472 – more or less at the same time as Leonardo da Vinci. It is possible that Perugino was already familiar with Netherlandish landscapes and with the work of Piero della Francesca from his time in Umbria – his landscape painting certainly shows signs of Memling's influence, not only in his portraits but also down to his rendering of foliage and similar details. Raphael's teacher even based the composition of his *Self-portrait* (fig. 237) on Memling's *Portrait of a Young Man* (cat. 49). The 1494 portrait of *Francesco delle Opere* also displays the profound influence that Flemish portrait painting exerted on Perugino. At the same time, however, the painting is a largely autonomous further development of its putative Flemish models, not least in terms of the rhetoricization of the sitter's gestures.

105　Alvise Vivarini (*c.* 1445/46–1503/5)
Crucifixion, *c.* 1470–75
Panel (rounded at the top), 73 × 51 cm
(see fig. 123)
Musei Civici, Pesaro. Pinacoteca
(inv. Gen. Polidori, 3914)

In the nineteenth century this painting was considered to be the work of Andrea Mantegna. In 1894 Berenson tentatively ascribed it to Giovanni Bellini. This attribution was widely accepted for about a century, although other names have been proposed, including Francesco Squarcione (Vaccaj 1909) or his workshop (Serra 1920), Marco Zoppo (Huse 1972) and a 'Master of the Pesaro Crucifixion' (Heinemann 1962), the author of a series of paintings, most of which have disappeared. The attribution to the young Alvise Vivarini in about 1470–75 was suggested independently by Conti (1987) and by Lucco (1990); Tempestini (1992 and 2000) is tempted to accept the attribution, but prefers to leave the question open for the time being.

What is undeniable is that the painting is strongly influenced by Giovanni Bellini, whose work was still marked at the time by the style of his brother-in-law Andrea Mantegna. Nevertheless, the more angular forms, the tendency for the volumes to twist and turn like green wood in a fire, the poses and even the expressions on the faces of the figures are comparable to early paintings by Alvise – for example the polyptych in the Galleria Nazionale delle Marche in Urbino, painted in 1476.

There is a distant echo of Flemish painting in the tragic demeanour of the Virgin Mary, reminiscent of the work of Rogier van der Weyden, and also in the position of the Magdalen's shoulders. Although these seem to recall Rogier's painting in the Uffizi, Florence (fig. 97), it is impossible to be specific on how this might have come about. At the same time the distances in the landscape background, seen against the rosy light of dawn and the blue of the sky, intensifying near the top of the painting, certainly remind us of the polyptych (on canvas) by Dieric Bouts, now dispersed between London, Brussels, Pasadena and Los Angeles but formerly in Venice, which acted as a model for Giovanni Bellini as well.

106　Louis Allyncbrood (Luis Alincbrot)
(*c.* 1410–before 1463)
Scenes from the Childhood and Passion of Christ
(triptych), *c.* 1445
Panel, 78 × 134 cm (see fig. 161)
Museo Nacional del Prado, Madrid (inv. 2538)

In 1427 Philip the Good dispatched Jan van Eyck to Aragon as part of a Burgundian diplomatic mission. The artist's itinerary included Barcelona and Valencia, and he met King Alfonso V, to whom he presented his portrait of the Duke of Burgundy. Alfonso was destined to become one of the keenest patrons and collectors of Flemish art. Together with the traditionally close trading links between Flanders and Valencia, he must have played a significant role in the early assimilation of the Flemish *ars nova* in local painting.

Allyncbrood's triptych, which is first documented at the Carmelite Monasterio de la Sanctissima Encarnación in Valencia – a sixteenth-century foundation – is a key work in any consideration of the influence exerted by Early Netherlandish painting in the Kingdom of Aragon prior to 1450. The coat of arms featured on the original frame indicates that the triptych, which dates from around 1445, was painted for a member of the prominent Valencian Ruiz de Corella family, who were lords of Cocentania. The composition, colouring and narrative structure of the triptych are all Netherlandish in character and display the artist's intimate knowledge of Flemish art. For that reason, it was suspected from an early date that the painter, whom Post (1943) first referred to as the 'Master of the Encarnación', might have been Netherlandish. The artist, to whom a *Crucifixion* in upright format (fig. 33) is also attributed, thus came to be identified with Luis Alincbrot or Allyncbrood. The latter was enrolled as a master in the Bruges painters' corporation, for which he served as *vinder* or arbitrator in 1432/33 and 1436/37. His presence in Valencia is recorded between 1439 and around 1463.

The triptych has a grisaille *Annunciation* on the closed wings, while the inside shows (partly simultaneous) scenes from the Childhood and Passion of Christ. It appears to have been less influenced by Van Eyck, however, than by works from the circle of the Master of Flémalle, especially those of Jacques Daret.

Provenance: 1494, commissioned by Francesco delle Opere.
Reference: Scarpellini 1991; Becherer 1997.

Provenance: Hercolani collection, Bologna.
References: Conti 1987; Lucco 1990; Lucco 1993; Tempestini 1999.

Provenance: Convento de la Encarnación, Valencia.
References: Bermejo 1980; Madrid and Valencia 2001, no. 36; Valencia 2001.

107 Spanish (?) copy after Dieric Bouts
(c. 1410–1475)
Triptych of the Passion, c. 1500?
Panel, 59.7 × 47.8 cm (centre); 59.7 × 21 cm
(wings) (see fig. 177)
Museo del Patriarca, Valencia

We know from surviving documents that this triptych
has been in Valencia since at least the end of the
sixteenth century. Its central panel features a *Descent
from the Cross* and is flanked by scenes of the *Crucifixion*
(left) and *Resurrection of Christ* (right). Originally
thought to be the original, the small, winged
altarpiece is now viewed as a copy of Dieric Bouts'
triptych in the Capilla Real in Granada. The Capilla
was founded by Queen Isabella the Catholic and her
husband, Ferdinand of Aragon, to serve as the royal
mausoleum for the House of Tastamara at Granada
Cathedral. A number of paintings from the Queen's
collection, including the altarpiece by the Leuven
town artist, were installed in the chapel, where they
remain to this day.

We are not certain, however, when and how Bouts'
paintings found their way to Spain. It is not impossible
that they were actually commissioned from Bouts for
the Castilian court through Spanish merchants
residing in Bruges. Bouts included illusionistic portal
sculptures that narratively extend the themes of the
principal scenes. A similar device is found in Rogier
van der Weyden's *Triptych of the Virgin*, which was
commissioned for the Charterhouse at Miraflores
by John II of Castile in 1445 (fig. 131). A copy of that
triptych was also installed at the Capilla Real. Bouts
might have included the motif at the express request
of his patron. He returned to it on one more occasion –
his *Life of the Virgin* in Madrid, which may also have
been commissioned by the Castilian royal court.

The copy in the Museo del Patriarca is a reduced
replica of Bouts' original by a Spanish painter.
Whether or not it is a contemporary copy is difficult
to decide, for the phenomenon of Spanish copies after
Early Netherlandish works has not yet received the
scholarly attention it deserves. The issue could be
settled by analysis of the painting technique and the
identification and dating of the wooden support.

108 Bartolomé Bermejo (Bartolomé de Cárdenas)
(c. 1440–1500)
Pietà with Angels, c. 1465–66
Panel, 94.8 × 61.9 cm (see fig. 163)
Mateu Collection, Palacio de Perelada, Gerona

Bartolomé Bermejo is rightly considered one of the
most important painters active in Aragon in the
second half of the fifteenth century. He was probably
born in Córdoba around 1440. We know from
surviving records that he chiefly worked in Valencia,
Saragossa and Barcelona. His earliest documented
work is a *Saint Michael* in the National Gallery,
London. Bermejo's art is indebted both to the Italian
Renaissance and to Netherlandish painting. The
influence of artists such as Colantonio, Ghirlandaio
and Botticelli can be clearly identified in his work,
alongside that of Van Eyck, Bouts, Van der Goes
and Christus. Since Bermejo will have had plenty of
opportunity to study Italian and Flemish art during
his time at the Aragonese court, the presence of these
influences does not tell us anything about possible
visits to Flanders or Naples. Allyncbrood's workshop
in Valencia might also have played an important role
in this respect. Bermejo is recorded in 1474 as having
been present in Daroca (Saragossa), where he worked
on the *Altarpiece of Santo Domingo de Silos* (fig. 152). He
spent the period 1477–81 in Saragossa. He probably
painted the Acqui Terme triptych (fig. 160) during a
second period in Valencia. He was in Barcelona in 1486
and died in Catalonia in 1495.

This *Pietà* clearly illustrates Bermejo's interest in
the realistic rendering of objects and fabrics. The finest
example of this is, perhaps, the goblet in the right
foreground. The two angels are more reminiscent
of the workshops of Campin and Van der Weyden
than of Van Eyck.

109 Bartolomé Bermejo (Bartolomé de Cárdenas)
(c. 1440–1500)
A Saint in His Study, c. 1474–77
Panel, 48.3 × 26 cm (see fig. 159)
The Art Institute of Chicago (inv. 1947.393)

Bartolomé Bermejo was one of the most important
painters active in Aragon in the second half of the
fifteenth century. His art was subject to both Flemish
and Italian influences – plentiful examples of which
were accessible to him at the Aragonese court. His
presence in Daroca (Saragossa) is documented around
1474. He was employed there on the *Altarpiece of Santo
Domingo de Silos* (Saint Dominic of Silos), the centre
panel of which is now in the Prado in Madrid (fig. 152).
The detailed contract that Bermejo signed to this end
with the parish of Daroca has been preserved. The
centre panel appears to have been completed by 1477,
but not so several other elements of the altarpiece,
including, perhaps, this *Saint in His Study*, whose small
size suggests that it may have been part of the predella.
The image of the saint with his mitre and halo is
closely related to that of Saint Dominic in the centre
panel. A number of other elements, including the lamp
and the floor-tiles, recall the *Death of the Virgin* (cat. 110).

The painting displays the artist's familiarity with
similar images of saints in Flemish and Italian art. His
knowledge of the lost *Saint Jerome* from Jan van Eyck's
'Lomellini triptych' might be attributable to a visit
to Naples, where it belonged at the time to the
Aragonese royal collection. Colantonio's *Saint Jerome*
(fig. 148) is another possible point of comparison.

Provenance: Colegio del Patriarca, Valencia.
References: Schöne 1938; Van Schoute 1963; Bermejo 1982.

Provenance: Private collection, Madrid.
References: De Young 1975; Berg Sobré 1998.

Provenance: Daroca, Sarragossa.
References: De Young 1975; Berg Sobré 1998.

110   **Bartolomé Bermejo** (Bartolomé de Cárdenas)
(*c.* 1440–1500)
Death of the Virgin, c. 1460–65
Panel, 63 × 41 cm (see fig. 58)
Staatliche Museen zu Berlin, Preussischer
Kulturbesitz. Gemäldegalerie (inv. 552)

The death of the Virgin Mary was a popular theme in
the late-medieval art of northern Europe. The scene is
typically set in a sober bedchamber, in which Christ's
mother lies on her deathbed, surrounded by the
apostles. Recurring details include a canopy or
curtains around the bed, and a candle that the dying
Mary holds in her hands or that is held out to her.
Almost without exception, Saint Peter, dressed as
a contemporary priest, bishop or even pope, stands
next to the bed, as if to administer the last rites.

The composition, iconography and realistic
apostles' portraits in Bermejo's panel in Berlin
undeniably draw on Early Netherlandish paintings.
It is believed that a lost prototype by Robert Campin
– known only through replicas and copies – served
as an important model in this respect. There are also
similarities, however, with Petrus Christus' painting
in San Diego (cat. 13). Although a good deal of
confusion remains regarding Bermejo's life, work and
chronology, the *Death of the Virgin* is widely viewed as
one of his earliest works. Probably dating from the
1460s, the painting is one of the first witnesses to the
influence of Netherlandish painting in Spain. This
would firmly rule out the frequently proposed yet
visually unconvincing link between this work and
Hugo van der Goes' Bruges panel, which dates from
the period 1477–82 (cat. 39).

Bermejo strikingly combines the Virgin's death
with her later Assumption – a highly unusual linkage
in the northern tradition. Whereas in Van der Goes'
case, for instance, it is Christ who receives his
mother's soul, Bermejo has God himself raise Mary's
body from the dead – an idea stressed by the glimpse
of a landscape in which an angel presents the risen
Mary's girdle to Doubting Thomas.

111   **Martín Bernat** (active *c.* 1469–1497)
Saint Blaise, c. 1480–90
Panel, 192 × 93 cm (see fig. 180)
López de Aragón collection, Madrid

Martín Bernat is viewed as an important follower of
Bartolomé Bermejo in Aragon, where he collaborated
with Miguel Jiménez – another Bermejo follower –
and the important Castilian artist Hernando del
Rincón among others. Bernat's life and work are
documented in some detail between 1469 and 1497.
He is cited in the first of those years when he took on
an apprentice, indicating that he must already have
established himself as a master for some time. A
contract survives from 1477, meanwhile, in which
Bernat agrees to finish several panels for the parish
of Daroca. These were elements of Bermejo's Daroca
altarpiece (see cat. 152), confirming that Bernat was
familiar with the older painter's most influential
composition and that he had the opportunity to study
its execution in detail.

It is plain that Bernat's *Saint Blaise* is directly based
on Bermejo's panel in terms of composition, technique
and iconography. The saint, who is enthroned at the
centre, is accompanied by two members of the clergy.
Blaise's robes are decorated with images of Old
Testament characters. Towards the bottom, for
instance, we make out a prophet, whose face is
concealed by one of the folds. Together with other
works by this master, Bernat's *Saint Blaise* testifies to
the immense influence of Bermejo's monumental
representation of an enthroned Saint (fig. 152), which
might in turn have derived indirectly from Van Eyck's
figure of God the Father in the Ghent altarpiece.
The composition spread well beyond the Iberian
peninsula, and echoes can even be detected in
Bruges painting prior to 1500 (cat. 46).

112   **Pedro Berruguete** (*c.* 1450–1503)
Virgin and Child, c. 1500
Panel, 61 × 44 cm (see fig. 166)
Museo Municipal, Madrid (inv. 35350)

Pedro Berruguete was born around 1450 in the
Castilian town of Paredes de Nava. He probably
trained in his native region, which was significantly
influenced by Flemish painting.

In addition to this Netherlandish element, the
artist was also inspired by a wide range of Italian
artists. We know from several sources that he travelled
to Italy (1473?–1482?), where he entered Duke Federico
da Montefeltro's court in Urbino and collaborated
with Justus of Ghent on the *Uomini famosi* cycle of
portraits for the *condottiere*'s *studiolo*. Having returned
from Italy, he worked until his death in 1503 in Castile,
where his patrons included the Catholic Kings.

This *Virgin and Child* in the Museo Municipal
testifies in the first instance to the immense influence
that the Flemish Primitives exerted on Berruguete's
work. It refers directly to the theme of the Madonna
Enthroned as it emerged in fifteenth-century Bruges
in the paintings of Jan van Eyck (cats 21–23), Petrus
Christus and Hans Memling. Post (1953) noted the
similarity with the youthful Rogier van der Weyden's
Thyssen *Virgin and Child* (Madrid), while Silva Maroto
(1998) linked the painting to Van Eyck's 'Lucca
Madonna' (fig. 21). The latter also commented,
however, on the persistent difficulty of identifying
direct models for Berruguete's work.

Details like the statuettes of Adam and Eve on
the throne derive directly from the Ghent altarpiece
(fig. 4). Their function is to symbolize the role played
by the Virgin and Child in the story of the Salvation.
Two other versions of this work are known: one in the
Cathedral at Palencia and one in a private collection
in Madrid.

Provenance: Before 1821, Solly collection.
References: De Young 1975; Berg Sobré 1998.

Provenance: Parcent collection, Madrid.
Reference: Post VIII.

References: Brussels 1985; Silva Maroto 1998.

SPAIN

113   Lluis Dalmau (documented 1428–1460)
        Saint Baudelius, 1448–50
        Panel, 255 × 161 cm (see fig. 158)
        Parish Church of Sant Baldiri, Sant Boí
        de Llobregat

114   Fernando Gallego (1440–1507)
        Adoration of the Magi, c. 1480–90
        Panel, 135.2 × 105 cm (see fig. 173)
        Museu Nacional d'Art de Catalunya, Barcelona
        (inv. 64084)

115   Fernando Gallego (1440–1507)
        Adoration of the Magi, c. 1495–1505
        Panel, 131 × 100 cm (see fig. 170)
        Museo de Bellas Artes de Asturias, Oviedo.
        On loan from the Pedro Masaveu collection

The Catalan artist Lluis Dalmau was court painter to King Alfonso v of Aragon in Valencia. In 1431, the court paid him for a visit he made to the Low Countries. He came into direct contact with Jan van Eyck's work in Bruges, and may also have seen paintings by Rogier van der Weyden in Brussels.

Having returned to Spain, he was commissioned by the City Council (*consellers*) of Barcelona to paint the *Altarpiece of the Consellers* for the chapel in the Town Hall (fig. 153). This painting, which we know from the surviving contract to date from around 1445, is one of the earliest works outside the Netherlands to assimilate elements of the Ghent altarpiece. Through Dalmau, Early Netherlandish painting exerted a lasting influence in Valencia and Catalonia, as witnessed by the work of artists such as Jaume Huguet (cat. 118).

Apart from the *Consellers* altarpiece, few works can be attributed to Dalmau. We know that he painted the monumental *Saint Baudelius* thanks to a surviving contract commissioning him to paint an altarpiece for the parish church of Sant Baldiri in Sant Boí de Llobregat. The *Saint Baudelius*, the altarpiece's centre panel, is all that survives of it. The saint, a former deacon of Nîmes, is shown wearing a dalmatic and holding an open book in his left hand and a martyr's palm in his right.

The image incorporates elements, such as the tile floor, that are typical of the Valencian school, but which are handled more naturalistically. While the saint's face recalls the figures in the *Consellers* retable, his features are also reminiscent of the portraits of Van Eyck and especially Van der Weyden. Similarities with Neapolitan painters, such as Colantonio, are accounted for by the fact that Naples was ruled at this time by King Alfonso v of Aragon.

Three signed works by Fernando Gallego are known – the *Pietà* in the Prado, the Marian triptych in the Diocesan Museum in Salamanca and the *Altarpiece of Cardinal Mella* in Zamora Cathedral. Gallego signed himself as 'Fernandus Galecus', referring to the Spanish province of Galicia. He was, however, active in Castile and was in all likelihood based in Salamanca. Virtually nothing is known about his training. Art historians disagree as to whether he undertook a study trip to the Netherlands, and while it is true that no documents survive testifying to any such visit to the North, his profound knowledge of the Flemish *ars nova* is convincing evidence of close contacts with northern art or artists.

Gallego painted more than one *Adoration of the Magi* – other versions are in the Museum of Art in Toledo, Ohio; Salamanca Cathedral; the Church of Santa María de Trujillo in San Lorenzo de Toro; and in the collection of Pedro Masaveu (see cat. 115). The Barcelona painting is certainly the most monumental and impressive in the series. In spite of the various influences it betrays, ranging from Rogier van der Weyden, Petrus Christus and Dieric Bouts to Conrad Witz and the Master of Uttenheim, it is an original composition thanks to the eccentric position of the main characters and the characteristically elongated figures.

Fernando Gallego painted several versions of the *Adoration of the Magi* (see cat. 114). In the Barcelona painting, he moves away from the centralized presentation of the figures. The group consisting of the Virgin, the Christ Child and Saint Joseph is shifted to the right, while the inclusion of the red curtain creates a distinctly theatrical feeling. In contrast to what we often find in contemporary scenes of this nature, Gallego shows little interest in luxurious and opulent details. On the contrary, he offers a fairly austere Adoration, in which the emphasis is on the restrained facial expressions. The Barcelona painting is an early work by Gallego that continues the approach adopted in the *Altarpiece of Cardinal Mella* in Zamora Cathedral.

In the Oviedo composition, the Holy Family occupies centre stage, with one of the Kings kneeling to the Virgin's left. The scene is located within a striking architectural construction, comprising a combination of wooden beams and stone. A glimpse of landscape is offered in the Flemish manner on both the left and right. The artist reused the figure of the curious boy looking through the window on a number of occasions. Interestingly, this is the only Gallego *Adoration* in which the black King appears; his presence is evidence of a later, northern influence, which suggests that this is the latest of Gallego's surviving *Adorations*.

Provenance: Sant Baldiri, Sant Boi de Llobregat.
References: Barcelona 1980; Madrid 1997.

Provenance: Montula collection.
Reference: Barcelona 2000.

References: Silva Maroto 1989; Barcelona 2000.

116 **Juan de Flandes** (active in Spain 1496–1519)
Scenes from the Life of Saint John the Baptist
('Miraflores altarpiece'), 1496–99
(1) *Birth and Naming of Saint John*. Panel,
88.4 × 49.9 cm. Cleveland Museum of Art
(inv. 1975.3)
(2, centre) *Baptism of Christ*. Panel, 186 × 110 cm.
Private collection, Madrid
(3) *Beheading of Saint John*. Panel, 106 × 66.5 cm
(with frame). Musée d'Art et d'Histoire de
Genève, Geneva (inv. CR 365)
(4) *Banquet of Herod*. Panel, 75 × 50.4 cm.
Museum Mayer van den Bergh, Antwerp
(inv. 124) (see fig. 245)

117 **Juan de Flandes and workshop**
(active in Spain 1496–1519)
Five panels from the *Altarpiece of Isabella
the Catholic, c.* 1496–1504
(1) *Raising of Lazarus*; (2) *Feeding of the Five
Thousand*; (3) *Christ and the Canaanite Woman*;
(4) *Arrest of Christ*; (5) *Nailing to the Cross*
Panel, 21–21.5 × 15.5–16.5 cm
(1–4) Patrimonio Nacional, Palacio Real,
Madrid (inv. 10002019, 10002021, 10002022
and 10002025)
(5) Kunsthistorisches Museum, Vienna.
Gemäldegalerie (inv. 6276)
(see figs 175, 215–218)

Juan de Flandes is first recorded as court painter to
Isabella of Castile in 1496 in connection with his
activities at the Miraflores Monastery in Burgos,
where he worked on an altarpiece with *Scenes from
the Life of John the Baptist*. Jozef de Coo and Nicole
Reynaud convincingly demonstrated in 1979 that
the artist referred to in the records of the Carthusian
monastery as '*Juan Flamenco*', is indeed Juan de Flandes.

Ponz praised the great beauty of the altarpiece in
his *Viaje de España* (1780). The work, which is believed
to have been painted during the early years of Juan's
employment at Isabella the Catholic's court, originally
comprised five panels, one of which has since been lost.
The Queen herself was present in Burgos in 1496 and
undoubtedly left her personal mark on the execution
of the retable. De Flandes quickly began to look for
ways to introduce Spanish elements into his art.

The four surviving panels provide a clear idea of
the early style that de Flandes pursued after arriving
in Castile. It is somewhat dreamy and meditative, and
the protagonists are placed firmly in the foreground.
The 'peaceful' atmosphere is further emphasized by the
upright format of the panels and by the strong verticals
within the compositions themselves. The meditative
aspect clearly refers to the work of Hans Memling
and Gerard David, while certain motifs, such as the
reflection of the burning city in the convex mirror
in the *Birth and Naming*, also draw on Jan van Eyck.

The panels have a powerfully symbolic strand,
whereby the presence of everyday objects and
creatures takes on a special meaning. The pheasant in
the *Beheading*, for instance, is undoubtedly intended as
an allusion to Herod's pride, while the gold chain held
by the King in the *Banquet* and the knife in Herodias'
hand symbolize their complicity in Saint John's death.
The *Baptism of Christ* refers directly to fifteenth-
century models – chiefly the corresponding scene in
Van der Weyden's *Saint John* triptych in Berlin – while
also displaying brilliant parallels with later Bruges
painting (cat. 17). Technical examination of the panel
indicates that Christ's loincloth is a later addition.

The lost fifth panel of the 'Miraflores altarpiece'

showed *Saint John Preaching to the Multitude* (see fig. 245).
Urbach recently discovered a photograph of the
missing painting at the Szepmüvészeti Múzeum in
Budapest and was able to confirm the original link
between the lost panel and the triptych. It once
belonged to the museum at Debrecen in eastern
Hungary.

Juan de Flandes is first recorded in 1496 in the accounts
of Isabella of Castile in connection with his activities at
the Monastery of Miraflores in Burgos, where he
worked on an altarpiece with *Scenes from the Life of John
the Baptist* (see cat. 116). There can be no doubt, however,
that he trained in the Low Countries prior to 1496 –
possibly in the circle of Hans Memling in Bruges.

The court painter remained in the service of
Isabella the Catholic until her death in 1504. He has
been linked on stylistic grounds to a polyptych
belonging to the Queen, which consisted of 47 panels
illustrating the Life of Christ. Following Isabella's
death, the painting was listed in an inventory drawn
up for the sale of the contents of the castle at Toro.
Diego Flores bought 32 of the 47 panels on 13 March
1505. These subsequently turn up in the 1516 inventory
of Margaret of Austria's collection in Mechelen. Two
of the 32 panels are explicitly linked in that document
to another of Isabella's court painters, namely Michel
Sittow (see cats 56, 57): 'Thirty small paintings out of
a total of 32, on pinewood and all the same size, of the
Life and Passion of Our Lord; the [other] two, an
Ascension [of Christ] and an *Assumption* [of the Virgin],
were the work of Michiel [Sittow] and were used to
make a diptych …'. There is some disagreement as to
the precise interpretation of this passage and Michel
Sittow's role in the execution of the altarpiece.
Some authors infer from the text that only the two
specifically attributed paintings – the *Ascension* and
the *Assumption* – are Sittow's work. Nicole Reynaud,
by contrast, has argued that the other thirty panels
also include some by the same artist. Sittow and de
Flandes might have been acquainted with one another
in Bruges and they will certainly have worked together
at Isabella of Castile's court. As early as 1929 Sanchez
Cantón suggested that a third artist besides de
Flandes and Sittow might have worked on the
Queen's polyptych. A plausible candidate would be
Felipe Morras, who entered Isabella's service as an
illuminator and painter in 1499 and who, on account
of his Picard origin, is very likely to have trained in
the Low Countries. He was highly regarded at the

Provenance: Charterhouse of Santa Maria de Miraflores, Burgos.
References: Lurie 1976; Martens 2000; Urbach 2001; Mund and Stroo 2002.

118 Jaume Huguet (*c.* 1412–1492)
Ordination of Saint Vincent by Bishop Valerius,
c. 1460–90
Panel, 176.7 × 98.2 cm (see fig. 157)
Museu Nacional d'Art de Catalunya, Barcelona
(inv. 15866)

119 Master of the Catholic Kings
(Diego de la Cruz?) (active *c.* 1485–1500)
Adoration of the Magi, *c.* 1496–97
Panel, 154 × 94 cm (see fig. 176)
Denver Art Museum (Acc. 1961.177)

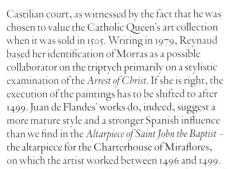

Castilian court, as witnessed by the fact that he was chosen to value the Catholic Queen's art collection when it was sold in 1505. Writing in 1979, Reynaud based her identification of Morras as a possible collaborator on the triptych primarily on a stylistic examination of the *Arrest of Christ*. If she is right, the execution of the paintings has to be shifted to after 1499. Juan de Flandes' works do, indeed, suggest a more mature style and a stronger Spanish influence than we find in the *Altarpiece of Saint John the Baptist* – the altarpiece for the Charterhouse of Miraflores, on which the artist worked between 1496 and 1499.

During the reign of Charles V, fifteen of the panels from Margaret of Austria's collection returned to Spain. They are now in the Palacio Real in Madrid and form the largest single group of panels from the original polyptych. The Vienna *Nailing to the Cross* was sold to the Marquesa of Denya in 1505. The other identified panels – 26 of them in total – now belong to a variety of museums and collections, including the Metropolitan Museum in New York, the Louvre in Paris, the Kunsthistorisches Museum in Vienna and the National Gallery in London.

Jaume Huguet was born around 1412 in Valls and was orphaned in 1419. Pere Huguet, Jaume's uncle and guardian, worked as an artist in Tarragona and from around 1433 in Barcelona, where he contributed to the decoration of the Cathedral. Jaume probably accompanied him to Barcelona, where he was strongly influenced by Bernat Martorell and Lluís Dalmau. The first document referring to Jaume as an artist – the cancellation of a contract for an altarpiece in Tarragona – dates from 1448. Huguet continued to work in Barcelona from that date until his death at the age of 80. Numerous surviving documents attest to his activities and to those of his many assistants. The primary conduit for the northern influence evident in Huguet's painting is likely to have been the work of Lluís Dalmau, including his *Altarpiece of the Consellers* (fig. 153) and above all his *Saint Baudelius* (cat. 113).

The panel with the *Ordination of Saint Vincent* belongs to a series of nine paintings from an altarpiece in the Church of Sant Vicenç de Sarriá near Barcelona, which were shown as anonymous works at the 1902 old masters exhibition in Barcelona. Five of the nine have since been attributed to Huguet or his workshop, including the panel shown here. It is difficult to date the *Saint Vincent* altarpiece. Correspondence between Huguet's widow and the parish of Sarriá suggests that the altarpiece was unfinished at the time of the painter's death in 1492. Huguet's skill as a portraitist is the panel's most obvious feature. The clergymen's faces have strongly individualized features and reveal a solid knowledge of Netherlandish portraiture.

The *Adoration of the Magi* belonged to an altarpiece devoted to the Life of Christ. The other seven panels – showing the *Annunciation*, *Visitation*, *Nativity*, *Circumcision*, *Presentation in the Temple*, *Christ Among the Doctors* and the *Marriage at Cana* – are now spread across a number of US collections. The altarpiece, which is considered to be one of the greatest achievements of the 'Hispano-Flemish' style, originally came from Valladolid and displays close links with the schools of Palencia and Burgos. Post identified the anonymous artists who worked on it with the common name of the 'Master of the Catholic Kings'. Art historians disagree as to the identity of the different painters. Gudiol (1955) attributed four of the panels to a master of French origin and the other four to Diego de la Cruz.

The name 'Master of the Catholic Kings' refers to the fact that the altarpiece was painted to mark the double marriage of the children of King Ferdinand and Queen Isabella – the 'Catholic Kings' – to the heirs of the Houses of Habsburg-Burgundy (1496/97). The new alliances are alluded to in the different panels, which are abundantly decorated with the coats of arms of Flanders, Brabant, Castile and the double-headed Habsburg eagle.

The painter of the *Adoration* clearly drew on Netherlandish models and may have deliberately quoted Rogier van der Weyden's famous 'Columba altarpiece' (Alte Pinakothek, Munich). Although the Three Kings are rather wooden, the artist took exceptional care in his execution of the middleground figures and, as was customary in images of this kind, lavished a great deal of attention on the rendering of the brilliant costumes.

Provenance: Collection of Isabella the Catholic.
Reference: Ishikawa 1989.

Provenance: Sant Vicenç de Sarriá, Barcelona.
References: Sureda i Pons 1994; Rome 1999.

Provenance: Valladolid (?).
References: Post IV–2; Gudiol 1966; Eisler 1977; Brown and Mann 1990.

120   Master of Osma
(active *c*.1470/80–1500)
Christ Crowned with Thorns (Ecce Homo), *c*.1500
Panel, 73.3 × 62.2 cm (see fig. 67)
Los Angeles County Museum of Art. Gift
of Dr and Mrs Herbert T. Kalmus (inv. 53.52)

The Master of (Burgo de) Osma was active in Soria,
Valladolid and Burgos. According to Silva Maroto,
he trained in the latter city in the circle of the painter
Diego de la Cruz. The master, who owes his name to
the Cathedral of Burgo de Osma in the province of
Soria, produced a body of work that is now spread
across museums all over the world. Four of his
paintings, however, remain in the Cathedral museum
– two with images of saints and two featuring
Marian themes.

The master's *Ecce Homo* is an interesting example
of the way northern and Italian compositional
schemes were applied in devotional works in late-
fifteenth-century Spain. Painters such as Diego de la
Cruz and the Osma Master were responding with
smaller panels of this kind, showing Christ and the
Virgin Mary, to growing Spanish demand for
devotional paintings.

This intensifying demand appears to have reflected
the reformation of the Spanish Catholic Church
following the fall of Granada and the unification of the
kingdoms of Aragon and Castile – events that were
accompanied by a burgeoning religious movement
throughout the Iberian peninsula. This small panel
clearly draws on devotional paintings by Antonello
da Messina (fig. 101) and Jean Hey (the Master of
Moulins?); it is especially close to the latter's 1494
Ecce Homo (cat. 74).

121   Master of Porciúncula
(active second half fifteenth century)
Stigmatization of Saint Francis, *c*.1470
Panel, 149 × 98 cm (see fig. 156)
Convento de Capuchinas, Castellón

This work was rescued from oblivion thanks to the
exhibition 'La clave Flamenca en Los Primitivos
Valencianos' in Valencia (2001). It was linked on that
occasion with Jan van Eyck's depiction of the same
theme, of which two versions have survived – one
in Turin and the other in Philadelphia (cats 28, 29).
A copy by the Master of Hoogstraten is in the Prado,
Madrid (cat. 45). The theme of Saint Francis receiving
the stigmata was particularly popular on the Iberian
peninsula and in Italy. The Franciscan Order was,
moreover, especially important to Aragon.

In 1444 in Valencia the merchant Juan Gregori is
recorded to have bought a painting of Saint George by
'Mestre Johannes' in Bruges, and then shipped it by way
of Valencia to Alfonso v's court in Naples. The 1448
will of the painter Juan Reixach (published by Cervero
Gomis) refers to an oil painting by '*Johannes*' showing
Saint Francis receiving the stigmata. A number of
elements, including the reference to the use of oil paint
and the great importance that Reixach attached to
the work, indicate that the author of the work was
Jan van Eyck.

A number of differences are apparent between
the Eyckian models in Turin and Philadelphia and
the Castellón painting, ascribed to the Master of
Porciúncula. Although the latter has retained the main
elements of the landscape, he shows the saint with a
halo, his hands held out towards the crucified Christ.
Several elements have also been moved, such as the
tree, which appears on the left in Van Eyck's versions
and on the right in the Valencian *Saint Francis*. The
open book, meanwhile, does not appear in Van Eyck's
original composition.

122   Master of Portillo
(active second half fifteenth century)
Saint John the Baptist Enthroned
Panel, 137 × 82.2 cm (see fig. 179)
Private collection, Madrid

The Master of Portillo, who probably came from
Picardy, was active in Palencia and Valladolid (Castile)
in the second half of the fifteenth century. The panel
formed the centre of an altarpiece in the Church of
San Juan del Pino in Valladolid. It displays similarities
with contemporary Bruges paintings such as the *Saint
Nicholas* by the Master of the Saint Lucy Legend
(possibly Jean Hervey; cat. 46), who was influenced in
this instance by Bermejo's monumental *Santo Domingo
de Silos* (cat. 152). If the Lucy Master's *Saint Nicholas*
was painted for a Spanish wool trader residing in
Bruges – as is suggested by the painting's style and
provenance – the brilliant view of the city in the
distance will have enabled the patron to allude in a
subtle manner to the time he had spent in Bruges.

The Master of Portillo also incorporated a city
view in his *Saint John the Baptist Enthroned*. Technical
examination has revealed that the left and right sides
of the cityscape were switched during the painting
process, indicating the importance attached to this
element by the artist and – presumably – by the
patron, who may have explicitly instructed him to
include this charming *veduta*.

Provenance: Collection of Dr and Mrs Herbert T. Kalmus.
Reference: Post IX (1949).

Provenance: Convento de Capuchinas, Castellón.
Reference: Valencia 2001.

Provenance: San Juan del Pino, Valladolid.
Reference: Post IX (1949).

123   **Master of Urgel** (active *c.* 1480/90–1500/10)
Saint Jerome, c. 1490
Panel, 188 × 101 cm (see fig. 169)
Museu Nacional d'Art de Catalunya, Barcelona
(inv. 15821)

124   **Anonymous (Portugal?)**
King João I of Portugal, c. 1435–40
Panel, 41 × 32 cm (see fig. 185)
Museu Nacional de Arte Antiga, Lisbon
(inv. 2006 Pint)

125   **Frey Carlos (?)** (active 1517–*c.* 1530)
Crucifixion, c. 1500?
Panel, 121 × 62 cm (see fig. 36)
Stedelijke Musea, Groeningemuseum, Bruges
(inv. 89.1)

This *Saint Jerome* might originally have belonged with the *Annunciation* in the same museum. Both works have been linked with the Master of (the Seo de) Urgel, who was active in Catalonia towards the end of the fifteenth century. There are two principal strands within the iconography of Saint Jerome – one showing the saint in his study and the other as a penitent in the wilderness. Hans Memling presented Jerome in the latter mode, kneeling before the cross and chastising himself with a stone, in a panel dating from around 1485 (Kunstmuseum, Basle). It is one of the earliest scenes of its kind in the North and, although no clear prototype has been identified, was probably inspired by Italian models, for example Piero and Filippo Lippi (fig. 168). A variety of similar works was produced in Bruges in this period, most likely prompted by Memling's example.

The Master of Urgel also presents Saint Jerome as a penitent, placing him in a naturalistic landscape that is unusual for Catalan art at that time. The only point of comparison is the rendering of the landscape in Bermejo's *Pietà of Canon Luis Desplá* (fig. 155). The use of oil paint increased the artist's scope for a realistic presentation of the surroundings in the manner of the Flemish *ars nova*.

The saint is shown kneeling before a crucifix, holding the stone with which he chastised himself. The image relates to the episode when, prior to writing his theological treatises in Rome and Bethlehem, Jerome withdrew for a number of years to the Syrian desert. The Master of Urgel characterizes not only Saint Jerome as a penitent, but, by alluding to his status as a cardinal and his literary activities, as a scholar, too.

According to the inscription on the frame, this is a posthumous memorial portrait of King João I of Portugal. *'Hec est vera digne ac venerabilis memorie Domini Joannis defucti qoun*[dam] *Portugalie nobilissimi et illustrissimi Regis ymago quippe qui du viveret de Juberot victoria est potentissimus'* ('This is the true likeness of his late majesty João, to his worthy and honoured memory, until recently the most noble and illustrious and, by reason of the victory of Aljubarrota [the decisive battle in the war between João and the King of Castile over the Portuguese succession in 1385], most powerful King of Portugal').

The portrait of the late ruler, presumably the right wing of a diptych in which the King will have been placed under the protective gaze of Christ or the Virgin Mary, is most probably the work of a Portuguese court artist. According to the inscription, it must have been completed shortly after the King's death. It may be the only – and therefore crucially important – witness to the immediate impact of Jan van Eyck's visit to Portugal in 1428. The Burgundian court artist travelled to Lisbon on that occasion as part of an official diplomatic mission from Philip the Good to arrange the Duke's marriage to Princess Isabella of Portugal, João I's daughter. Van Eyck painted two portraits of Isabella, one of which was dispatched to the Duke of Burgundy by land and the other by sea, to ensure the image's safe arrival. He probably took one of his own likenesses of Philip the Good with him, thereby introducing the prevailing Netherlandish mode of portraiture to Portugal.

In any case, the three-quarter bust portrait, which will have been painted between 1435 and 1440, follows Flemish examples, although the image of the late King is set against a brocade cloth of honour, rather than a neutral background. The rendering of the hands and the realistic execution of the fabric reflect at least a basic knowledge of Eyckian painting.

A number of questions are prompted by this upright *Crucifixion*. The composition and the way it is cropped are enough in themselves to make it unusual for Bruges painting, but the artist also placed the group around the Virgin Mary, grieving over her son's death, on a hill that ascends to the right. As a result, the composition is divided diagonally from the figure of the Magdalen kneeling to the left of the cross to the woman located on the right edge of the picture. This creates a powerful flow towards the right, so much so that there can be no doubt that the Bruges *Crucifixion* was originally the left wing of a triptych. The centre panel probably featured a Descent from the Cross, as was previously the case with Dieric Bouts (see cat. 107).

Judging by the colour scheme, the landscape and the rendering of the figures, this cannot be the work of a Bruges workshop around 1500. Admittedly, the use of colour does display certain similarities with Jan Provoost's *Crucifixion* (cat. 54), which has induced some scholars to place the panel in the circle of that artist. However, there are also parallels in that respect to the Bruges Master of San Lorenzo della Costa, who painted a triptych with the *Martyrdom of Saint Andrew* (fig. 116) for Andrea della Costa of Genoa in 1499.

Weniger (1999) recently argued that the painter of the altarpiece may have been an itinerant artist who influenced Portuguese painting around Francisco Henriques. He also found parallels for the upright format of the *Crucifixion* in Portuguese art around 1520 – more specifically, with the work of the Flemish artist who entered the Hieronymite Monastery of Évora as Frey (Brother) Carlos in 1517. The idea that the Bruges *Crucifixion* might be an early work by Frey Carlos certainly seems plausible, given the stylistic similarities. The figures have the same disproportionate hands and feet, for instance, as Frey Carlos' image of *John the Baptist* (cat. 126).

Provenance: Santo Doménec de Puigcerdà (Cerdaña) (?).
Reference: Madrid 1997.

Provenance: Kunsthistorisches Museum, Vienna.
References: Markl 1983; Porfirio 1991; Bonn 1999, no. 33.

Provenance: Until 1989 in a private chapel, Gingelom (Limburg).
References: De Vos 1998; Weniger 1999b.

126   **Frey Carlos** (active 1517–*c*. 1530)
John the Baptist, *c*. 1520
Panel, 100 × 65 cm (see fig. 191)
Museu Nacional de Arte Antiga, Lisbon
(inv. 1 Pint)

This Baptist panel is one of the paintings from the
Hieronymite Monastery in Évora attributed to the
institution's own workshop, which was headed from
1517 onwards by the Flemish artist Frey Carlos.

The saint is shown in a tiled room bounded to
the rear by a balustrade. Dressed in a claret cloak, he
appears with the lamb in his arms in front of a brocade
cloth of honour. A hilly landscape can be made out in
the background on either side of the cloth. The
painting, popularly known as 'The Good Shepherd'
because of the resemblance of its subject matter to the
biblical parable, recalls the manner in which Memling
and other Bruges painters represented the Baptist in
the second half of the fifteenth century – models on
which the Portuguese workshop must have drawn
at least indirectly.

As far as the colour scheme and the saint's
seemingly oversized limbs are concerned, there are
clear differences with the 1523 *Annunciation* (cat. 127)
that was also produced in Frey Carlos' workshop, with
its comparatively ethereal repertoire of figures. The
colouring of the flesh parts using white glazes that
have become transparent over the centuries is
reminiscent – especially in the saint's face – of panels
attributed to Francisco Henriques' workshop. The
supposition that Frey Carlos may have been employed
in that workshop before entering the monastery in 1517
is borne out by further stylistic observations. We do
not know the identities of any other painters who were
active in the Hieronymite workshop at Évora, whose
size and organization remain matters of conjecture.
The only thing of which we can be sure is that the
works produced there resemble the Portuguese-
Flemish painting personified by Henriques more
closely than they do the purely Portuguese works
of King Manuel I's court painter, Jorge Afonso.

127   **Frey Carlos** (active 1517–*c*. 1530)
Annunciation, 1523
Panel, 197.5 × 198 cm (see fig. 186)
Museu Nacional de Arte Antiga, Lisbon
(inv. 677 Pint)

This monumental *Annunciation*, inscribed with
the date 1523, came from a polyptych belonging to
the Hieronymite Monastery of Nossa Senhora do
Espinheiro in Évora. It was produced by the
institution's own workshop, first recorded in 1517.
The workshop, which created both altarpieces and,
in particular, a series of smaller devotional paintings,
appears to have been dominated by an artist from
Flanders, who entered the monastery at Évora in 1517
under the name of Frey (Brother) Carlos.

In spite of the complex interior, reminiscent of
Italian Renaissance architecture, the artist's handling
of perspective remains primarily empirical. The colour
scheme and rendering of the principal figures suggest
an intimate knowledge of the late work of Hugo van
der Goes. The figure of the Archangel Gabriel in
particular, who approaches seemingly weightlessly, is
hard to imagine without the immediate example of the
Ghent master, whereas the motif of the musician
angels, who are shown in the open on the left-hand
edge of the image, is remotely related to the work of
Gerard David. Unlike other members of the so-called
Portuguese-Flemish school, there is no doubt as to this
painter's Netherlandish origins.

All the evidence suggests that Frey Carlos was not
directly influenced by Antwerp painting, but that his
roots lay in Ghent or, likelier still, in Bruges. This
interpretation is supported by other works attributed
to him (cat. 125, 126). Frey Carlos probably came to
Portugal around 1500 with Francisco Henriques (see
cat. 129) and possibly spent some time in the latter's
Lisbon workshop. A *Crucifixion* in the Groeningemuseum in Bruges, which was mistakenly attributed
to Jan Provoost (cat. 125), seems to anticipate some of
the stylistic peculiarities of Frey Carlos' work and
might therefore actually be an early painting by the
Hieronymite artist, as Weniger (1999) suggested.

128   **Workshop of Nuno Gonçalves**
(active 1440–1471)
Saint Francis (?), *c*. 1460–70
Panel, 117.9 × 90.3 cm (see fig. 182)
Museu Nacional de Arte Antiga, Lisbon
(inv. 1345 Pint)

Saint Francis (?) sits in front of a green, patterned
background on a simple wooden bench. He is turned
to the left. Dressed in the robes of the Order he
founded, the saint points towards an image of Christ
on the Cross, bleeding from his wounds. The painting
once belonged to a large altarpiece, now broken up,
the precise structure of which is not known. It did,
however, also include images of Saints Paul, Peter and
possibly Augustine. The suggestion that these may
originally have been predella panels cannot be decided
one way or the other.

The strikingly realistic rendering of the portrait-
like face of Saint Francis, together with the structure
and technical execution of the drapery, is clearly
linked to the *Saint Vincent* altarpiece, the key work
of the Portuguese court painter Nuno Gonçalves
(fig. 188). Close stylistic similarities also exist with the
monks and fishermen in that polyptych, which is
customarily dated to 1469. These were probably done
by the same workshop assistants as were responsible
for *Saint Francis*. It would seem reasonable, therefore,
to date the panel to around the time of the completion
of the *Saint Vincent* altarpiece.

The latter work – a large structure originally
installed in Lisbon Cathedral – is without a doubt the
most important work of fifteenth-century Portuguese
art. In his 1549 treatise *Da pintura antiga*, Francisco
de Holanda states that it was the work of Nuno
Gonçalves, court painter to Afonso V of Portugal.
The altarpiece – one of the earliest and most
impressive group portraits in the history of European
art – is notable not only for its precise rendering of
fabrics and armour, but also for the astonishing
realism of its portraits, entirely unprecedented in
Portuguese art. This prompted some historians to
suggest links with Jan van Eyck, who travelled to
Portugal in 1428. The surviving body of paintings
from the Gonçalves workshop does not, however,
provide the evidence to verify such a claim. There are,
however, contemporary parallels with Gonçalves in
the shape of certain works by the Catalan painter
Jaume Huguet (fig. 149), who was an outstanding
portraitist, and of two paintings produced around
1450, one of which has been attributed to Barthélemy
d'Eyck (cat. 66).

Provenance: Monastery of Nossa Senhora do Espinheiro, Évora.
References: De Figueiredo 1924; Reis-Santos 1940; Couto 1943;
Bordeaux 1954, no. 120; Porfírio 1991.

Provenance: Monastery of Nossa Senhora do Espinheiro, Évora.
References: De Figueiredo 1924; Porfírio 1991; Dacos 1991; Carvalho 1994;
Bonn 1999, no. 45; Weniger 1999a; Weniger 1999b.

Provenance: Episcopal palace, São Vicente de Fora.
References: De Figueiredo 1910; Gusmão 1957; Dacos 1991; Porfírio 1991;
Abrantes and Vandevivere 1994.

129   **Francisco Henriques and workshop**
(active 1503–1518)
Visitation, c. 1505
Panel, 134.4 × 82.5 cm (see fig. 192)
Museu de Grão Vasco, Viseu (inv. 2143)

The thirteen panels making up the high altarpiece
of Viseu Cathedral were long attributed to the
Portuguese artist Fernando Vasco, following
Manuel Ribeiro Botelho Pereira's attribution of all
the building's paintings to 'Grão Vasco' in his 1630
Diálogos Morais Históricos e Políticos. It was only recently
recognized that the altarpiece was actually the work
of a Portuguese-Flemish workshop active several decades
earlier. The latter was probably headed by a Flemish
master who trained in the circle of Gerard David
or in an Antwerp workshop around 1500.

Rodrigues (1995) has drawn attention to a letter
written in September 1500, in which the Bishop of
Viseu states his intention to import a high altarpiece
for the cathedral from Flanders. He had not decided
at that point whether to opt for a painted or a carved
retable. Importing the altarpiece was not necessary,
however, as a number of Flemish painters had actually
settled in King Manuel I's Portugal. The foreign-born
– most likely Flemish – painter Francisco Henriques
was the first important representative of a Portuguese
strand of painting with a clearly Netherlandish
orientation, which flourished in the early decades of
the sixteenth century alongside a purely Portuguese
school. A number of Portuguese and Netherlandish
artists – or painters trained in Flanders – probably
worked on the Viseu panels under the Lisbon-based
Henriques. The artist himself, who is likely to have
produced the designs for the altarpiece, married the
sister of the Portuguese court painter Jorge Afonso.

The *Visitation* panel is an example of the work
produced by the Viseu workshop after Flemish
models. The composition derives from Van der
Weyden, whose pictorial formula proved successful in
the Low Countries and beyond. Colour scheme and
landscape, by contrast, look more towards Antwerp
painting around 1500.

130   **Master of Évora** (Southern Netherlands, c. 1510)
Two panels from the *Altarpiece of the Life
of the Virgin* in Évora Cathedral, c. 1510?
(1) *Virgin and Child Enthroned*. Panel,
277 × 133 cm
(2) *Death of the Virgin*. Panel, 188 × 110 cm
(see fig. 130)
Museu de Évora (inv. ME 1501 and 1513)

The altarpiece with the *Life of the Virgin* in Évora
Cathedral is made up of thirteen individual panels
and is one of the largest surviving Early Netherlandish
paintings in the world. Attribution, dating and the
precise circumstances leading up to this monumental
commission for the cathedral of Portugal's second
most important royal city remain unclear or are
at best disputed.

What we do know is that the work was
commissioned Dom Afonso, who served as Bishop
of Évora from 1485 until his death in 1522. The
altarpiece appears to have been destined for the Lady
Chapel – the *capela-mor* – in the Cathedral.

Following the example of the Bishop of Viseu,
who wanted to import a painting from Flanders for
his cathedral's high altar in 1500 (see cat. 129), the 1510
commission for the Évora altarpiece also appears to
have gone to a Netherlandish painter. The panels
making up the altarpiece might have been painted in
Flanders and shipped to Portugal separately, before
being installed in the Cathedral. Equally,
Netherlandish painters may have been brought to
Portugal to execute the altarpiece in situ, possibly
assisted by local artists. Whatever the case, the precise
Netherlandish origins of the Évora *Life of the Virgin* and
the tradition from which the principal master sprang
cannot be identified. Stylistic differences suggest that
several assistants were employed.

The *Virgin and Child Enthroned*, originally the centre
scene of the altarpiece, derives ultimately from Bruges
painting around 1500. Martens (1995) saw in it the hand
of the Master of the André Madonna, who belonged
to the circle of Gerard David, whereas Weniger
(1999a) believed it to be the work of the same assistant
from David's workshop who contributed to the *Saint
Anne* altarpiece in Washington. Most problematic of
all is the attribution of the narrative scenes from the
Life of the Virgin, which display the impact of the
Ghent, Bruges *and* Antwerp schools and whose
influence is also directly apparent in the Viseu
altarpiece.

131   **Master of Lourinhã** (active 1510–1525)
Death of Saint James the Greater, c. 1510–20
Panel, 128 × 84 cm (see fig. 184)
Museu Nacional de Arte Antiga, Lisbon
(inv. 21 Pint)

The Master of Lourinhã owes his name to two
paintings located in that town in Estremadura. The
works in question were produced in Portugal during
the reign of King Manuel I within the broad circle of
Francisco Henriques (cat. 129) and the Hieronymite
workshop of Frey Carlos (see cats 125–27). Some
authors have suggested that the master originated in
the Northern Netherlands, but it is more likely that he
– or they, for his name may conceals several artists,
each with his own workshop – was of Portuguese
descent.

The *Death of Saint James the Greater* originally
formed part of a polyptych with scenes from the saint's
life. The rendering of the landscape undoubtedly
reflects Netherlandish models, although the
composition is chiefly indebted to tapestry art. The
tapestries produced in Flemish manufactories were
among the Low Countries' most important export
goods and were avidly collected by the Portuguese
royal court.

Provenance: Cathedral, Viseu.
References: Reis-Santos 1946; Rodrigues 1995; Évora 1997, no. 27;
Weniger 1999a.

Provenance: Cathedral, Évora.
References: Dacos 1991; Martens 1995; Rodrigues 1995; Weniger 1999b.

Provenance: Convento de Palmeda (?).
References: Porfirio 1991; Weniger 1999a.

Lenders to the exhibition

Aix-en-Provence, Musée Granet: cat. 8
Aix-en-Provence, Sainte-Marie-Madeleine: cat. 65
Altenburg, Staatliches Lindenau-Museum: cats 83, 101
Amsterdam, Rijksmuseum: cat. 65
Amsterdam, Rijksmuseum. On loan from
    Mauritshuis, The Hague: cat. 97
Antwerp, Museum Mayer van den Bergh: cats 78, 116
Antwerp, Koninklijk Museum voor Schone Kunsten:
    cats 26, 48, 70

Baltimore, The Walters Art Museum: cat. 98
Barcelona, Museu Nacional d'Art de Catalunya:
    cats 114, 118, 123
Barcelona, Parish Church of Sant Baldiri, Sant Boí
    de Llobregat: cat. 113
Bergamo, Pinacoteca dell'Accademia Carrara:
    cats 100, 103
Berlin, Staatliche Museen zu Berlin, Preussischer
    Kulturbesitz. Gemäldegalerie: cats 35, 110
Birmingham, Birmingham Museums and Art Gallery:
    cat. 10
Bremen, Dr Heinrich Bisschoff: cat. 68
Bruges, Stedelijke Musea, Groeningemuseum: cats 5,
    15, 17, 22, 25, 37, 39, 43, 46, 53, 54, 61, 62, 81, 125;
    Depot Sint-Salvator: cat. 1, 7
Bruges, Stedelijke Musea, Memlingmuseum: cat. 50
Brussels, Musées Royaux des Beaux-Arts de Belgique:
    cats 59, 65, 74, 75
Bucharest, Muzeul National de Artă al României:
    cats 18, 102

Cambridge, Mass., Fogg Art Museum, Harvard
    University Art Museums. Francis H. Burr,
    Louise Haskell Daly, Alphaeus Hyatt and William
    M. Prichard Funds: cat. 36; The John Witt Randall
    Fund: cat. 44
Castellón de la Plana, Convento de Capuchinas:
    cat. 121
Chicago, The Art Institute of Chicago: cat. 109
Cincinnati, Estate Fred Ziv: cat. 47
Cleveland, The Cleveland Museum of Art: cats 95, 116;
    Leonard C. Hanna Jr. Bequest: cat. 9
Copenhagen, Statens Museum for Kunst: cats 11, 57

Denver, Denver Art Museum: cats 69, 76, 119
Detroit, Detroit Institute of Arts: cats 30, 69
Dijon, Musée des Beaux-Arts: cat. 82

Essen, Gallinat-Bank AG: cats 2, 60
Évora, Museu de Évora: cat. 130

Florence, Galleria degli Uffizi: cat. 104
Frankfurt, Städelsches Kunstinstitut und Städtische
    Galerie: cat. 21

Geneva, Musée d'Art et d'Histoire: cat. 116
Genoa, Galleria di Palazzo Bianco: cats 51, 91
Gerona, Palacio de Perelada, Mateu Collection:
    cat. 108

Glasgow, Kelvingrove Art Gallery and Museum:
    cats 63, 72
Göteborg, Göteborgs Konstmuseum: cat. 92
Granada, Capilla Real: cat. 6
Greenville, Bob Jones University Museum & Gallery:
    cat. 80

Le Puy-en-Velay, Cathedral Treasury: cat. 67
Lisbon, Museu Nacional do Azulejo: cat. 3
Lisbon, Museu Nacional de Arte Antiga: cats 38, 41, 55,
    124, 126, 127, 128, 131
Livorno, Museo Civico Giovanni Fattori. On loan
    from Santa Maria del Soccorso: cat. 84
Los Angeles, Los Angeles County Museum of Art.
    Mr and Mrs Allan Balch Collection: cat. 14;
    Gift of Dr and Mrs Herbert T. Kalmus: cat. 120

Maastricht, Bonnefantenmuseum. On loan from
    Rijksmuseum, Amsterdam: cat. 64
Madrid, López de Aragón collection: cat. 111
Madrid, Museo Municipal: cat. 112
Madrid, Museo Nacional del Prado: cats 32, 45, 106
Madrid, Museo Thyssen-Bornemisza: cat. 20
Madrid, Patrimonio Nacional, Palacio Real: cat. 117
Madrid, Private collections: cats 116, 122
Melbourne, National Gallery of Victoria: cat. 31
Montpellier, Musée Fabre: cat. 68

Naples, Museo Nazionale di Capodimonte: cat. 93;
    On loan from San Pietro Martire: cat. 94
New York, Alexander Acevedo: cat. 96
New York, The Metropolitan Museum of Art.
    Robert Lehman Collection: cats 49, 73
Nivå, Nivaagaards Malerisamling: cat. 90

Oviedo, Museo de Bellas Artes de Asturias. On loan
    from the Pedro Masaveu collection: cat. 115

Padua, Museo d'Arte Medievale e Moderna: cat. 85
Paris, Musée du Louvre: cats 33, 69, 71
Pavia, Musei Civici, Pinacoteca Malaspina: cat. 87
Pesaro, Musei Civici. Pinacoteca: cat. 105
Philadelphia, Philadelphia Museum of Art, The John
    G. Johnson Collection: cats 29, 99
Prague, Prague Castle Collection: cat. 40
Private collection: cat. 58

Reggio di Calabria, Museo della Magna Grecia: cat. 86
Rome, Galleria Nazionale di Palazzo Barberini: cat. 77
Rotterdam, Museum Boijmans Van Beuningen:
    cat. 65

San Diego, Timken Art Gallery. Putnam Foundation:
    cat. 13
San Francisco, Fine Arts Museums of San Francisco:
    cats 4, 69
Savona, Pinacoteca Civica: cat. 89

The Hague, Koninklijk Kabinet van Schilderijen
    'Mauritshuis': cat. 56; On loan from Noortman BV,
    Maastricht: cat. 27
Turin, Galleria Sabauda: cat. 28
Turin, Museo Civico d'Arte Antica, Palazzo Madama:
    cats 79, 88

United Kingdom, Private collection: cat. 52

Vaduz, Sammlungen des Fürsten von Liechtenstein,
    Schloss Vaduz: cat. 66
Valencia, Museo del Patriarca: cat. 107
Venice, Galleria Giorgio Franchetti alla Ca' d'Oro:
    cat. 34
Vienna, Kunsthistorisches Museum. Gemäldegalerie:
    cats 24, 117
Viseu, Museo de Grão Vasco: cat. 129

Washington DC, Dumbarton Oaks Research Library
    and Collections. House Collection: cat. 16
Washington DC, National Gallery of Art. Samuel
    H. Kress Collection: cat. 12; Andrew W. Mellon
    Collection: cat. 19
Worcester, Mass., Worcester Art Museum: cat. 41

Bibliography

Abbreviations

AB	*The Art Bulletin*
BM	*The Burlington Magazine*
DoA	J. Turner (ed.), *The Dictionary of Art*, 34 vols, New York 1996
GdBA	*Gazette des Beaux-Arts*
JBKMSKA	*Jaarboek Koninklijk Museum voor Schone Kunsten Antwerpen*
JPKS	*Jahrbuch der Preußischen Kunstsammlungen*
JKSK	*Jahrbuch der kunsthistorischen Sammlungen des allerhöchsten Kaiserhauses, Wien*
JWCI	*Journal of the Warburg and Courtauld Institutes*
RdA	*Revue de l'Art*
ZfKG	*Zeitschrift für Kunstgeschichte*

Abrantes and Vandevivere 1994 – A. Abrantes and I. Vandevivere (eds), *Nuno Gonçalves, novos documentos. Estudo da pintura portuguesa de século XV*, Lisbon 1994.

Ainsworth 1992 – M. W. Ainsworth, 'New Observations on the Working Technnique in Simon Marmion's Panel Painting', in Kren 1992.

Ainsworth 1995 – M. W. Ainsworth (ed.), *Petrus Christus in Renaissance Bruges*, Turnhout 1995.

Ainsworth 1998 – M. W. Ainsworth, *Gerard David. Purity of Vision in an Age of Transition*, New York 1998.

Ainsworth and Martens 1994 – M. W. Ainsworth and M. P. J. Martens, *Petrus Christus. Renaissance Master of Bruges*, New York 1994.

Aix-en-Provence 1981 – *Le Roi René et son temps*, exh. cat. Aix-en-Provence 1981.

Algeri 1998 – G. Algeri, 'Testimonianze e presenze fiamminghe nella pittura del Quattrocento', in Boccardo and Di Fabio 1997.

Algeri and De Floriani 1991 – G. Algeri and A. de Floriani, *La Pittura in Liguria: il Quattrocento*, Genoa 1991.

Alizieri 1873 – F. Alizieri, *Notizie dei professori del disegno dalle origini al secolo XVI*, II, Genoa 1873.

Almeida and Barroso de Albuquerque 2000 – J. F. de Almeida and M. M. Barroso de Albuquerque, *Os paneis de Nuno Gonçalves*, Lisbon and São Paulo 2000.

Altringer 1998 – L. Altringer, 'Hadrian VI.', *Hochrenaissance im Vatikan*, exh. cat. Bonn 1998.

Alvarez 1998 – M. T. Alvarez, 'Artistic Enterprise and Spanish Patronage: The Art Market during the Reign of Isabel of Castile (1474–1594)', in North and Ormrod 1998.

Ames-Lewis 1979 – F. Ames-Lewis, 'Fra Filippo Lippi and Flanders', *ZfKG*, 42 (1979).

Ames-Lewis 1993a – F. Ames-Lewis, 'Painters in Padua and Netherlandish Art, 1435–1455', in Poeschke 1993.

Ames-Lewis 1993b – F. Ames-Lewis, 'Princes, Court Painters, and Netherlandish Art', in *Mantegna and 15th-century Court Culture*, London 1993.

Antwerp 1991 – *Flandre et Portugal: Au conflit de deux cultures. Europalia Portugal 1991*, exh. cat. Antwerp 1991.

Antwerp 1995 – *Vlaanderen en Castilla y León*, Antwerp 1995.

Anzelewsky 1985 – F. Anzelewsky, 'Towards an Identification of the Vienna Portrait by Jan van Eyck', in *Tribute to Lotte Brand Philipp*, New York 1985.

Appuhn 1979 – H. Appuhn, *Der Triumphzug Kaiser Maximilians I. 1516–1518*, Dortmund 1979.

Arbace 1993 – L. Arbace, *Antonello da Messina*, Florence 1993.

Aronberg Lavin 1967 – M. Aronberg Lavin, 'The Altar of Corpus Domini in Urbino: Paolo Uccello, Joos van Ghent, Piero della Francesca', *AB*, 49 (1967).

Arras 1999 – *Fragments d'une splendeur. Arras à la fin du Moyen Âge*, exh. cat. Arras 1999.

Avril 1989 – F. Avril, 'Le Maître des Heures de Saluces: Antoine de Lonhy', *RdA*, 85 (1989).

Avril 2001 – F. Avril, 'La iluminación francesa del siglo XV y el mundo mediterráneo', in Madrid and Valencia 2001.

Avril and Reynaud 1993 – F. Avril and N. Reynaud, *Les manuscrits à peintures en France. 1440–1520*, exh. cat. Paris 1993.

Backmann 1997 – S. Backmann, 'Kunstagenten oder Kaufleute? Die Firma Ott im Kunsthandel zwischen Oberdeutschland und Venedig (1550–1650)', in K. Bergdolt and J. Brüning (eds), *Kunst und ihre Auftraggeber im 16. Jahrbundert. Venedig und Augsburg im Vergleich*, Berlin 1997.

Bähr 1997 – I. Bähr, 'Bilderfindungen der frühen niederländischen Malerei im Spiegel der Tafeln des Meisters von Sopetrán', *Pantheon*, 55, 1997.

Baldass 1952 – L. von Baldass, *Van Eyck*, London and New York 1952.

Baldini 1970 – U. Baldini, *L'Opera completa dell'Angelico*, Milan 1970.

Barbera 1998 – G. Barbera, *Antonello da Messina*, Milan 1998.

Barcelona 1980 – *Barcelona restaura*, exh. cat. Barcelona 1980.

Barcelona 2000 – *El arte en Cataluña y los reinos hispanos en tiempos de Carlos I*, exh. cat. Barcelona 2000.

Barocchi 1971 – P. Barocchi (ed.), *Scritti d'arte del Cinquecento*, I, Milan and Naples 1971.

Barocchi 1979 – P. Barocchi, *Ristori*, IV, Milan 1979.

Barolsky 1991 – P. Barolsky, *Why Mona Lisa Smiles and Other Tales by Vasari*, University Park and London 1991.

Barolsky 1992 – P. Barolsky, *Giotto's Father and the Family of Vasari's Lives*, University Park and London 1992.

Bauch 1961 – K. Bauch, 'Bildnisse des Jan van Eyck', *Jahreshefte der Heidelberger Akademie der Wissenschaften*, 1961–62.

Bauman 1986 – G. C. Bauman, 'Early Flemish Portraits, 1425–1525', *Metropolitan Museum of Art Bulletin*, 43 (1986).

Baxandall 1963 – M. Baxandall, 'A dialogue on art from the court of Leonello d'Este: Angelo Decembrio's "De politia literaria"', *JWCI*, 26 (1963).

Baxandall 1964 – M. Baxandall, 'Bartolomaeus Facius On Painting', *JWCI*, 27 (1964).

Baxandall 1971 – M. Baxandall, *Giotto and the Orators*, Oxford 1971.

Baxandall 1985 – French edition of Baxandall 1971.

Bazin 1952 – G. Bazin, 'Petrus Christus et les rapports entre l'Italie et la Flandre au milieu du XVe siècle', *Revue des Arts* 1952.

Beaune 1991 – C. Beaune, *Naissance de la nation France*, Paris 1991.

Becherer 1997 – J. A. Becherer (ed.), *Pietro Perugino*, exh. cat. Grand Rapid Falls, N.Y., 1997.

Belting and Eichberger 1983 – H. Belting and D. Eichberger, *Jan van Eyck als Erzähler. Frühe Tafelbilder im Umkreis des New Yorker Diptychons*, Worms 1983.

Belting and Kruse 1994 – H. Belting and C. Kruse, *Die Erfindung des Gemäldes. Das erste Jahrhundert der niederländischen Malerei*, Munich 1994.

Berg Sobré 1989 – J. Berg Sobré, *Behind the Altar Table. The Development of the Painted Retable in Spain, 1350–1500*, Columbia 1989.

Berg Sobré 1998 – J. Berg Sobré, *Bartolomé de Cárdenas 'El Bermejo'. Itinerant Painter in the Crown of Aragon*, San Francisco 1998.

Bermejo 1980 – E. Bermejo, *La pintura de los primitivos flamencos en España*, I, Madrid 1980.

Bermejo 1982 – E. Bermejo, *La pintura de los primitivos flamencos en España*, II, Madrid 1982.

Bermejo Martínez – See Bermejo.

Beyer 2000 – A. Beyer, *Parthenope. Neapel und der Süden der Renaissance*, Munich and Berlin 2000.

Bloch 1963 – V. Bloch, 'An unknown composition by the Master of Flémalle', *BM*, 105 (1963).

Blockmans 1995 – W. Blockmans, 'The Creative Environment: Incentives to and Functions of Bruges Art Production', in Ainsworth 1995.

Blockmans 1996 – W. Blockmans, 'The Burgundian Court and the Urban Milieu as Patrons in 15th Century Bruges', in Michael North (ed.), *Economic History and the Arts*, Cologne, Weimar and Vienna 1996.

Blockmans and Prevenier 1998 – W. Blockmans and W. Prevenier, 'The second Flowering 1492–1530', in *The Promised Lands. The Low Countries under Burgundian Rule, 1369–1530*, Philadelphia 1998.

Boccardo and Di Fabio 1994 – P. Boccardo and C. Di Fabio, *Ritorno a Palazzo. Dipinti e arazzi nell'appartamento del Doge*, exh. cat. Genoa 1994.

Boccardo and Di Fabio 1997 – P. Boccardo and C. Di Fabio (eds), *Pittura Fiamminga in Liguria secoli XIV–XVIII*, Cinisello Balsamo 1998.

Bologna 1954 – F. Bologna, 'Un "San Gerolamo" lombardo del Quattrocento', *Paragone*, 49 (1954).

Bologna 1977 – F. Bologna, *Napoli e le rotte mediterranee della pittura da Alfonso il Magnanimo a Ferdinando il Cattolico*, Naples 1977.

Bonn 1999 – *Die großen Sammlungen VIII: Museu Nacional de Arte Antiga Lissabon*, exh. cat. Bonn 1999.

Bonn and Vienna 2000 – *Kaiser Karl V. 1500–1558. Macht und Ohnmacht in Europa*, exh. cat. Bonn and Vienna 2000.

Borchert 1995 – 'Memling's Antwerp "God the Father with Music Making Angels"', *Colloque* X, Louvain-la-Neuve 1995.

Borchert 1997 – 'Rogier's St. Luke: The Case for Corporate Identification', in Purtle 1997.

Borchert 2000 – T. H. Borchert, *L'homme au chaperon bleu de Jan van Eyck*, Metz 2000.

Boskovits 1987 – M. Boskovits, 'Niccolò Corso e gli altri. Spigolature di pittura lombardo-ligure di secondo Quattrocento', *Arte Cristiana*, 75 (1987).

Bosshard 1992 – E. Bosshard, 'Revealing van Eyck: The Examination of the Thyssen-Bornemisza "Annunciation"', *Apollo*, 1992.

Brans 1952 – J. V. L. Brans, *Isabel la Católica y el arte hispanoflamenco*, Madrid 1952.

Boon 1965 – K. G. Boon, 'Gossaert en de Renaissance in de Nederlanden', in *Jan Gossaert genaamd Mabuse*, exh. cat. Rotterdam and Bruges 1965.

Bossuyt 1994 – I. Bossuyt, *De Vlaamse polyfonie*, Leuven 1994.

Bouchot 1904 – H. Bouchot, *Les Primitifs français, 1292–1500. Complément documentaire au catalogue officiel de l'exposition*, Paris 1904.

Briels 1980 – J. Briels, 'Amator Pictoriae Artis. De Antwerpse kunstverzamelaar Peeter Stevens (1590–1668) en zijn Constkamer', *JBKMSKA*, 1980.

Brinkman 1993 – P. Brinkman, *Het Geheim van Van Eyck*, Zwolle 1993.

Brinkmann 1996 – B. Brinkmann, 'Master of the Older Prayerbook of Maximilian', in *DoA*.

Brown and Mann 1990 – J. Brown and R. G. Mann, *Spanish Paintings of the Fifteenth through Nineteenth Centuries. The Collections of the National Gallery of Art Systematic Catalogue*, Washington (DC), 1990.

Bruges 1902 – *Les Primitifs Flamands*, exh. cat. Bruges 1902.

Bruges 1962 – *Toison d'Or*, exh. cat. Bruges 1962.

Bruges 1994 – *Hans Memling*, Bruges 1994.

Bruges 1998 – *Bruges and the Renaissance*, 2 vols, exh. cat. Bruges 1998.

Brussels 1979 – *Rogier van der Weyden – Rogier de la Pasture*, exh. cat. Brussels 1979.

Brussels 1985 – *Splendours of Spain. Europalia Spain 1985*, exh. cat. Brussels 1985.

Bruyn 1957 – J. Bruyn, *Van Eyck Problemen*, Utrecht 1957.

Bruyn 1963 – J. Bruyn, 'The Master of Moulins and Hugo van der Goes', *BM* (1963).

Bruyn 1982 – J. Bruyn, 'Antonello en de Nederlanden', *Oud Holland*, 96 (1982).

Buck 1995 – S. Buck, 'Petrus Christus' Berlin Wings and the Metropolitan Museum's Eyckian Diptych', in Ainsworth 1995.

Buck 2000 – S. Buck, 'An Approach to Looking at Eyckian Drawings', in Foister, Jones and Cool 2000.

Büttner 2000 – N. Büttner, *Die Erfindung der Landschaft: Kosmographie und Landschaftskunst im Zeitalter Bruegels*, Göttingen 2000.

Buijsen 1996 – E. Buijsen, 'A Rediscovered Wing of a Diptych by Hans Memling (*c.* 1440–1494)', *Oud Holland*, 110 (1996).

Burke 1984 – P. Burke, *Die Renaissance in Italien. Sozialgeschichte einer Kunst zwischen Tradition und Erfindung*, Berlin 1984.

Burke 1999 – P. Burke, 'Re-Presenting Charles V', in *Charles V and his Time 1500–1558*, Antwerp 1999.

Busch 1973 – R. von Busch, *Studien zu deutschen Antikensammlungen des 16. Jahrhunderts*, Diss. Tübingen 1973.

Cabrera and Garrido 1981 – J. M. Cabrera and C. Garrido, 'Dibujos subyacentes en las obras de Fernando Gallego', *Boletín del Museo del Prado*, 4 (1981).

Cabrera and Garrido 1982 – J. M. Cabrera and C. Garrido, 'El dibujo subyacente y otros aspectos técnicos de las tablas de Sopetrán', *Boletín del Museo del Prado*, 7 (1982).

Caldera (forthcoming) – M. Caldera, *Donato de' Bardi* (forthcoming).

Campbell 1974 – L. Campbell, 'Robert Campin, the Master of Flémalle and the Master of Mérode', *BM*, 116 (1974).

Campbell 1979 – L. Campbell, 'L'art du portrait dans l'œuvre de van der Weyden', Brussels 1979.

Campbell 1976 – L. Campbell, 'The Art Market in the Southern Netherlands in the Fifteenth Century', *The Burlington Magazine*, 118 (1976).

Campbell 1981a – L. Campbell, 'The Early Netherlandish Painters and their Workshops', *Colloque III*, Louvain-la-Neuve 1981.

Campbell 1981b – L. Campbell, 'Netherlandish Pictures in the Veneto in the fifteenth and sixteenth centuries', *BM* (1981).

Campbell 1983 – L. Campbell, 'Memling and the followers of Verrocchio', *BM* (1983).

Campbell 1990 – L. Campbell, *Renaissance Portraits*, London and New Haven 1990.

Campbell 1991 – L. Campbell, 'Review of *Gerard David* by Hans J. van Miegroet', *BM*, 133 (1991).

Campbell 1993 – L. Campbell, 'Rogier van der Weyden and his Workshop', *Proceedings of the British Academy*, 84 (1993).

Campbell 1996 – L. Campbell, 'Campin's Portraits', in Foister and Nash 1996.

Campbell 1998 – L. Campbell, *National Gallery Catalogues: The Fifteenth Century Netherlandish Schools*, London 1998.

Campbell, Foister and Roy 1997 – L. Campbell, S. Foister and A. Roy (eds), 'Methods and Materials of Northern European Painting', *National Gallery Technical Bulletin*, 19 (1997).

Campori 1870 – G. Campori, *Raccolte di cataloghi ed inventarii inediti*, Modena 1870.

Canfield 1995 – G. B. Canfield, 'The Reception of Flemish Art in Renaissance Florence and Naples', in Ainsworth 1995.

Carvalho 1994 – J. A. S. Carvalho, 'Pintura luso-flamenga em Évora no início do século XVI. O Mestre da Lamentação do Espinheiro', *A Cidade de Évora*, 71–76 (1988–94).

Castelfranchi Vegas 1983 – L. Castelfranchi Vegas, *Italia e Fiandra nella pittura del Quattrocento*, Milan 1983.

Castelfranchi Vegas 1984 – L. Castelfranchi Vegas, *Italien und Flandern*, Stuttgart and Zürich 1984.

Castelnovi 1987 – E. Castelnovi, *Il Quattrocento e il primo Cinquecento* (La Pittura a Genova e in Liguria, I), Genoa 1987.

Cavalieri 1990 – F. Cavalieri, 'Echi fiamminghi in Italia: una tavoletta del '400', *Osservatori delle Arti*, 4 (1990).

Cavelli 1997 – C. Cavelli Traverso, 'Da Provost a Massys', in Boccardo and Di Fabio 1997.

Champion 1969 – P. Champion, *Vie de Charles d'Orléans (1394–1465)*, Paris 1969 (2nd edition).

Chapuis 1995 – J. Chapuis, *Duitse en Franse schilderijen, vijftiende en zestiende eeuw. Rotterdam Museum Boijmans Van Beuningen*, Rotterdam 1995.

Châtelet 1964 – A. Châtelet, 'Le retable du Parlement de Paris', *Art de France*, 4, 1964.

Châtelet 1980 – A. Châtelet, 'Un collaborateur de Van Eyck en Italie', in *Relations artistiques entre les Pays-Bas et l'Italie à la Renaissance*, Brussels and Rome 1980.

Châtelet 1981 – A. Châtelet, *Les Primitifs Hollandais*, Lausanne 1981.

Châtelet 1993 – A. Châtelet, *Jean van Eyck Enlumineur. Les Heures de Turin et de Turin-Milan*, Strasbourg 1993.

Châtelet 1995 – A. Châtelet, 'Petrus Christus: A propos de l'exposition de New York', *Belgisch Tijdschrift voor Oudheidkunde en Kunstgeschiedenis*, 64 (1995).

Châtelet 1996 – A. Châtelet, *Robert Campin, Le Maître de Flémalle*, Antwerp 1996.

Châtelet 1998 – A. Châtelet, 'Pour en finir avec Barthélemy d'Eyck', *GdBA*, 140 (1998).

Châtelet 2000 – A. Châtelet, 'Jan van Eyck entre l'Italie et la France', *Journal des Savants* (2000).

Châtelet 2001 – A. Châtelet, *Jean Prévost. Le Maître de Moulins*, Paris 2001.

Chiavari Cattaneo Della Volta 1997 – E. Chiavari Cattaneo Della Volta, *Adorno / Adornes*, Genoa 1997.

Christiansen 1998 – K. Christiansen, 'The View from Italy', in New York 1998.

Ciardi 1965 – P. R. Ciardi, *La Raccolta Gagnola, dipinti e sculture*, Milan 1965.

Clancy 1998 – S. Clancy, 'Die Werkstatt Jean Fouquets', *Künstlerwerkstätten der Renaissance*, Zurich and Düsseldorf 1998.

Cleri 1997 – B. Cleri, *Antonio da Fabriano*, Cinisello Balsamo (MI) 1997.

Collar de Cáceres 1986 – F. Collar de Cáceres, 'El Maestro de los Luna y el retablo de El Muyo', *Boletín del Seminario de Arte y Arqueología de Valladolid*, 52 (1986).

Collier 1983 – J. M. Collier, 'Perspective in the Arnolfini Portrait', *AB*, 65 (1983).

Collobi Ragghianti 1990 – L. Collobi Ragghianti, *Dipinti fiamminghi in Italia 1420–1570*, Bologna 1990.

Cologne 1993 – *Stefan Lochner. Werk und Wirkung*, exh. cat. Cologne 1993.

Comblen-Sonkes and Lorentz 1995 – M. Comblen-Sonkes and P. Lorentz, *Le Musée du Louvre, II* (Les Primitifs flamands, Corpus), Brussels 1995.
Comblen-Sonkes and Lorentz 2002 – M. Comblen-Sonkes and P. Lorentz, *Le Musée du Louvre, III* (Les Primitifs flamands, Corpus), Brussels 2002.
Company 1987 – X. Company, *La pintura valenciana de Jacomart a Pao de Sant Leocadi*, Barcelona 1987.
Company 1990 – X. Company, *La pintura hispanoflamenca*, Valencia 1990.
Coo and Reynaud 1979 – J. de Coo and N. Reynaud, 'Origen del retablo de san Juan Bautista atribuido a Juan de Flandes', *Archivo Español de Arte y Arqueología* (1979).
Coremans 1953 – P. Coremans *et al.*, *L'Agneau mystique au laboratoire. Examen et traitement*, Brussels 1953.
Couto 1943 – J. Couto, *A pintura flamenga em Évora no sécolo XVI. Variedade de estilos e de técnicas na obra atribuída a Frey Carlos*, Évora 1943.
Crowe and Cavalcaselle 1875 – J. A. Crowe and G. B. Cavalcaselle, *The Early Flemish Painters: Notices of their Lifes and Works*, London 1879; French edition, Brussels 1862–63; German edition Leipzig 1875.
Curvelo 1999 – A. Curvelo, 'Königin Eleonore, 1458–1525', in Bonn 1999.
Cuttler 1968 – C. Cuttler, *From Pucelle to Bruegel*, London *et al.* 1968.
Dacos 1991 – N. Dacos, 'Les artistes flamands et leur influence au Portugal', in Antwerp 1991.
Dacos 1995 – N. Dacos, 'Pour voir et pour apprendre', in *Fiammingbi a Roma 1508–1608*, exh. cat. Brussels 1995.
D'Ancona and Aeschliemann 1951 – P. d'Ancona and E. Aeschliemann (eds), *Vespasiano da Bisticci, Vite di uomini illustri del secolo XV*, Milan 1951.
Davies 1972 – M. Davies, *Rogier van der Weyden*, London 1972.
Debae 1995 – M. Debae, *La Bibliothèque de Marguerite d'Autriche*, Leuven 1995.
De Figueiredo 1910 – J. De Figueiredo, *O Pintor Nuno Gonçalves*, Lisbon 1910.
De Figueiredo 1924 – J. De Figueiredo, 'Pintura primitiva portuguesa. Frey Carlos', *Lusitânia*, 1, Lisbon 1924.
Del Treppo 1994 – M. Del Treppo, 'Le avventure storiografiche della tavola Strozzi', in *Fra Storia e Storiografia. Scritti in onore di Pasquale Villani*, Bologna 1994.
Demus, Klauner and Schütz 1981 – K. Demus, F. Klauner and K. Schütz, *Kunsthistorisches Museum Wien. Katalog der Gemäldegalerie. Flämische Malerei von Jan van Eyck bis Pieter Bruegel d.Ä.*, Vienna 1981.
De Roover 1963 – R. De Roover, *The Rise and Decline of the Medici Bank 1397–1494*, Cambridge (Mass.) 1963.
Deswarte-Rosa 1997 – S. Deswarte-Rosa, 'Si dipinge col cervello et non con le mani', *Bollettino D'Arte* 1997.
Devliegher 1964 – L. Devliegher, 'De Blijde Inkomst van Karel de Stoute en Margaretha van York te Damme in 1468', *Handelingen van het Genootschap voor Geschiedenis, Société d'Emulation*, 101 (1964).
De Vos 1979 – D. De Vos, *Stedelijke Musea Brugge. Catalogus Schilderijen 15de en 16de eeuw*, Bruges 1979.
De Vos 1989 – D. De Vos, *Groeningemuseum Brugge*, Ghent 1989.
De Vos 1992 – D. De Vos, 'Bruges and the Flemish Primitives in Europe', in *Bruges and Europe*, Antwerp 1992.
De Vos 1994 – D. De Vos, *Hans Memling. The Complete Works*, London and New York 1994.
De Vos 1999 – D. De Vos, *Rogier van der Weyden The Complete Works*, London and New York, 1999.
De Vrij 1999 – M. R. de Vrij, 'A Portrait of King Christian the Second of Denmark in the Chrysler Museum Norfolk', *Konsthistorisk Tidskrift – revy för konst och konstkorkning*, 68 (1999).
Dhanens 1965 – E. Dhanens, *Het retabel van het Lam Gods in de Sint-Baafskathedraal te Gent*, Ghent 1965.
Dhanens 1980 – E. Dhanens, *Hubert en Jan van Eyck*, Antwerp 1980.
Dhanens 1984 – E. Dhanens, 'De Heilige Antonius met geknielde stichter te Kopenhagen', *Academia Analecta*, 45 (1984).
Dhanens 1995 – E. Dhanens, 'Rogier van der Weyden. Revisie van de documenten', *Verhandelingen van de Koninklijke Academie voor Wetenschappen, Letteren en Schone Kunsten van België*, 57, no. 19 (1995).
Dhanens 1998 – E. Dhanens, *Hugo van der Goes*, Antwerp 1998.
Dijkstra 1990 – J. Dijkstra, *Origineel en kopie. Een onderzoek naar de navolging van de Meester van Flémalle en Rogier van der Weyden*, Amsterdam 1990.
Dijkstra 1997 – J. Dijkstra, 'Enkele opmerkingen over het *Retable du Parlement de Paris*', in *Album Discipulorum J. R. J. van Asperen de Boer*, Zwolle 1997.
Doering 1896 – O. Doering, *Des Augsburger Patriciers Philipp Hainhofer Beziehungen zum Herzog Philipp II. von Pommern-Stettin. Correspondenzen aus den Jahren 1610–1619*, Vienna 1896.
Domínguez Casas 1993 – R. Domínguez Casas, *Arte y etiqueta de los Reyes Católicos*, Valladolid 1993.
Doutrepont 1906 – G. Doutrepont, *Inventaire de la 'Librairie' de Philippe le Bon (1420)*, Brussels 1906.
Dülberg 1990 – A. Dülberg, *Privatporträts. Geschichte und Ikonologie einer Gattung im 15. und 16. Jahrhundert*, Berlin 1990.
Dunkerton 1999 – J. Dunkerton, 'North and South: Painting Techniques in Renaissance Venice', in Venice 1999.
Durrieu 1902 – A. Châtelet (ed.), *P. Durrieu: Heures de Turin*, Turin 1967.
Durrieu 1903 – P. Durrieu, 'Les débuts des Van Eyck', *GdBA*, 30 (1903).
Durrieu 1906a – P. Durrieu, 'Le maître des Heures du Maréchal de Boucicaut', *Revue de l'art ancien et moderne*, 19 (1906).
Durrieu 1906b – P. Durrieu, 'Le maître des Heures du Maréchal de Boucicaut', *Revue de l'art ancien et moderne*, 20 (1906).
Duverger 1928 – J. Duverger, 'De Werken van "Johannes" in de Verzamelingen van Margareta van Oostenrijk', *Oud Holland*, 45 (1928).
Duverger 1930 – J. Duverger, 'Gerard Horenbault (1465–1530) hofschilder van Margareta van Oostenrijk', *Kunst. Maandblad voor oude en jonge kunst*, 4 (1930).
Duverger 1936 – J. Duverger, 'Jan van Eyck voor 1422. Nieuwe gegevens en hypothesen', *Handelingen van het 3de Congres voor Algemene Kunstgeschiedenis*, Ghent 1936.
Duverger 1969 – J. Duverger, 'Hofschilder Lieven van Lathem (ca. 1430–1493)', *JBKMSKA*, 1969.
Duverger 1971 – J. Duverger, 'Jan Mostaert, ereschilder van Margareta van Oostenrijk', *Aachener Kunstblätter*, 41 (1971).
Duverger 1977 – J. Duverger, 'Jan van Eyck as Court Painter', *Connoisseur*, 194 (1977).
Dvořák 1903 – M. Dvořák, 'Das Rätsel der Kunst der Brüder van Eyck', *Jahrbuch der kunsthistorischen Sammlungen...* (1903), reprint Munich 1925.
Eichberger 1992 – D. Eichberger, 'Burgundian Tapestries – Art for Export and for Pleasure', *Australian Journal of Art*, 10 (1992).
Eichberger 1996 – D. Eichberger, 'Female Patronage in the Light of Dynastic Ambitions and Artistic Quality', *Renaissance Studies*, 10 (1996).
Eichberger 1998 – D. Eichberger, 'Devotional Objects in Book Format: Diptychs in the Collection of Margaret of Austria and her Family', in *The Art of the Book. Its Place in Medieval Worship*, Exeter 1998.
Eichberger 2000a – D. Eichberger, 'A Noble Residence for a Female Regent. Margaret of Austria and the Construction of the *Court of Savoy* in Mechelen', in *Gender, Architecture and Power in Early Modern Europe*, Aldershot 2000.
Eichberger 2000b – D. Eichberger, *Leben mit Kunst – Wirken durch Kunst. Sammelwesen und Hofkunst unter Margarete von Österreich, Regentin der Niederlande*, Turnhout and London 2000.
Eichberger 2001 – D. Eichberger, 'A Renaissance Princess Named Margaret. Fashioning a Public Image in a Courtly Society', *Melbourne Art Journal*, 4 (2001).
Eichberger and Beaven 1995 – D. Eichberger and L. Beaven, 'Family Members and Political Allies: The Portrait Collection of Margaret of Austria', *Art Bulletin*, 77 (1995).
Eisler 1977 – C. T. Eisler, *Paintings from the Samuel H. Kress Collection: European Schools Excluding Italian*, Oxford 1977.
Eisler 1989 – C. T. Eisler, *Early Netherlandish Painting. The Thyssen-Bornemisza Collection*, London 1989.
Elkins 1991 – J. Elkins, 'On the Arnolfini Portrait and the Lucca Madonna: Did Jan van Eyck Have a Perspectival System?', *AB*, 73 (1991).
Elsig 1998 – F. Elsig, 'Notes sur la peinture en Savoie autour de 1450', *Nuovi Studi*, 5 (1998).
Elsig 2001 – See Madrid and Valencia 2001.
Erbe 1993 – M. Erbe, *Belgien. Niederlande. Luxemburg. Geschichte des niederländischen Raums*, Stuttgart 1993.
Evans 1993 – M. L. Evans, '"Uno maestro solenne" Joos van Wassenhove in Italy', *Nederlands Kunsthistorisch Jaarboek*, 44 (1993).
Évora 1997 – *A Painter in Évora. Francisco Henriques During the Age of King Manuel I*, exh. cat. Évora 1997.
Faggin 1968 – G. T. Faggin, *L'Opera completa dei Van Eyck*, Milan 1968.
Faries 1996 – M. Faries, 'Jan van Scorel', in *DoA*.
Faries 1997 – M. Faries, 'The Underdrawing of Memling's Last Judgment Altarpiece', *Memling Studies 1994*, Leuven 1997.
Faries 1999 – M. Faries, 'The Underdrawing in Jan van Eyck's Dresden Triptych', *Colloque XII*, Leuven 1999.
Favaretto 1990 – I. Favaretto, *Arte antica e cultura antiquaria nelle collezioni Venete al tempo della Serenissima*, Rome 1990.
Filarete (Von Oettingen ed.) – W. von Oettingen, *Filaretes Tractat über die Baukunst*, Vienna 1890.
Filarete (Spencer ed.) – J. R. Spencer, *Filarete, Treatise on Architecture*, 2 vols, New Haven 1965.
Filangieri 1891 – G. Filangieri, *Documenti per la storia, le arti, le industrie delle provincie napoletane*, Naples 1891.
Finoli and Grassi 1972 – M. Finoli and L. Grassi (eds), *Filarete, Trattato d'Architettura*, 2 vols, Milan 1972.
Finot 1895 – J. Finot, *Inventaire sommaire des Archives départementales antérieures à 1790*, VIII, Lille 1895.
Fletcher 1981 – J. Fletcher, 'Marcantonio Michiel: His Friends and Collection', *BM* (1981).
Fletcher 1989 – J. Fletcher, 'Bernardo Bembo and Leonardo's portrait of Ginevra de' Benci', *BM* (1989).
Focillon 1936 – H. Focillon, 'Le style monumental dans l'art de Jean Fouquet', *GdBA* (1936).
Foister, Jones and Cool 2000 – S. Foister, S. Jones and D. Cool (eds), *Investigating Jan van Eyck*, Turnhout 2000.
Foister and Nash 1996 – S. Foister and S. Nash (eds), *Robert Campin. New Directions in Scholarship*, Turnhout 1996.
Fontaine (forthcoming) – M. Fontaine, 'Antiquaires et rites funéraires', in *Les Funérailles à la Renaissance* (Actes du XIIe colloque international de la Société Française d'Etudes du Seizième Siècle, Bar-le-Duc, 2–5 décembre 1999), Geneva (forthcoming).
Fontana Amoretti 1996 – M. Fontana Amoretti, *I misteri delle tavole fiamminghe*, exh. cat. Genoa 1996.
Fontana Amoretti 1998 – M. Fontana Amoretti *et al.*, *Liguria, Repertori of Dutch and Flemish Paintings in Italian Public Collections*, 1, Florence 1998.
Fredericksen 1983 – B. Fredericksen, 'A Parisian Triptych Reconstituted', *The J. Paul Getty Museum Journal*, 11 (1983).
Friedländer 1903 – M. J. Friedländer, 'Die Brügger Leihausstellung von 1902', *Repertorium für Kunstwissenschaft*, 26 (1903).
Friedländer 1924–37 – M. J. Friedländer, *Die Altniederländische Malerei*, 13 vols, Berlin and Leiden 1924–37.
Friedländer 1967 – M. J. Friedländer, *Early Netherlandish Painting*, Brussels and Leiden 1967.
Frimmel 1888 – T. Frimmel, *Der Anonimo Morelli. Marcantonio Michiel's Notizia d'opere del disegno*, Vienna 1888.
Fronek 1995 – J. Fronek, 'Painting Techniques, Their Effects and Changes in the Los Angeles Portrait of a Man by Christus', in Ainsworth 1995.
Garrido 1995 – C. Garrido, 'Le processus créatif chez Juan de Flandes', *Colloque X*, Louvain-la-Neuve 1995.
Gaya Nuño 1958 – Juan Antonio Gaya Nuño, *Fernando Gallego*, Madrid 1958.
Galassi 1989 – M. C. Galassi, 'Il disegno sottostante del "Cristo benedicente" di Palazzo Bianco: contributo dell'analisi riflettografica al problema attributivo', *Bollettino de Musei Civici Genovesi* (1989).
Galassi 1997 – M. C. Galassi, 'A Technical Approach to a Presumed Memling Diptych: Original Work and Some Italian Copies', in *Memling Studies 1994*, Leuven 1997.
Garzelli 1984 – A. Garzelli, 'Sulla fortuna del "Gerolamo" mediceo del van Eyck nell'arte fiorentina del quattrocento', in *Scritti di Storia dell'arte in onore di Roberto Salvini*, Florence 1984.
Geirnaert 2000 – N. Geirnaert, 'Anselm Adornes and his Daughters: Owners of Two Paintings of Saint Francis by Jan van Eyck?', in Foister, Jones and Cool 2000.
Gellman 1995 – L. B. Gellman, 'Two Lost Portraits by Petrus Christus', in Ainsworth 1995.
Gibson 1989 – W. S. Gibson, *Mirror of the Earth: The World Landscape Tradition in Sixteenth-Century Flemish Painting*, Princeton 1989.
Gifford 1999 – M. Gifford, 'Van Eyck's Washington Annunciation: Technical Evidence for Iconographic Development', *AB*, 81 (1999).
Gifford 2000 – M. Gifford, 'Assessing the Evolution of van Eyck's Iconography through Technical Study of the Washington Annunciation, I', in Foister, Jones and Cool 2000.
Ginzburg 1996 – C. Ginzburg, 'Le peintre et le bouffon: le "Portrait de Gonella" de Jean Fouquet', *RdA*, 3 (1996).
Gobiet 1984 – R. Gobiet, *Der Briefwechsel zwischen Philipp Hainhofer und Herzog August d. J. von Braunschweig-Lüneburg*, Munich 1984.
Goffen 1999 – R. Goffen, 'Crossing the Alps: Portraiture in Renaissance Venice', in Venice 1999.
Goldthwaite 1993 – R. Goldthwaite, *Wealth and Demand for Art in Italy, 1300–1600*, Baltimore 1993.
Gombrich 1976 – E. H. Gombrich, 'Light, Form and Texture in 15th-century painting North and South of the Alps', in *The Heritage of Apelles*, London 1976.
Gonzalez Palencia 1929 – C. Gonzalez Palencia, 'La capilla de don Álvaro de Luna en la catedral de Toledo', *Archivo Español de Arte y Arqueología*, 5 (1929).
Grodecki 1996 – C. Grodecki, 'Le "maître Nicolas d'Amiens" et la mise au tombeau de Malesherbes', *Bulletin monumental* (1996).
Grosshans 1992 – R. Grosshans, 'Simon Marion and the Saint Bertin Altarpiece: Notes on the Genesis of the Painting', in Kren 1992.
Guasti 1877 – C. Guasti (ed.), *Alessandra Macingbi negli Strozzi: Lettera di una gentildonna fiorentina del secolo XV ai figliuoli esuli*, Florence 1877.
Gudiol 1955 – J. Gudiol, *Pintura gótica*, Madrid 1955.
Gudiol 1966 – J. Gudiol, 'El pintor Diego de la Cruz', *Goya* (1966).
Gudiol and Alcolea i Blanch 1989 – J. Gudiol and S. Alcolea i Blanch, *La pintura gótica catalana*, Barcelona 1989.
Guiffrey 1894–96 – J. Guiffrey, *Inventaires de Jean Duc de Berry, 1401–1416*, Paris 1894–96.
Gusmão 1957 – A. de Gusmão, *Nuno Gonçalves*, Lisbon 1957.
Hall 1998 – E. Hall, 'The Detroit Saint Jerome in Search of its painter', *Bulletin of the Detroit Institute of Arts*, 72 (1998).
Hand 1978 – J. O. Hand, *Joos van Cleve: the Early and Mature Paintings*, Ph.D. Diss., Princeton University 1978.
Hand 1996 – J. O. Hand, 'Joos van Cleve', in *DoA*.
Hand and Wolff 1986 – J. O. Hand and M. Wolff, *Early Netherlandish Painting: The Collection of the National Gallery of Art. Systematic Catalogue*, Washington 1986.
Harbison 1990 – C. Harbison, *Jan van Eyck. The Play of Realism*, London 1990.
Harfield Strens 1968 – B. Harfield Strens, 'L'arrivo del trittico Portinari a Firenze', in *Commentari*, XIX, 1968.
Haverkamp-Begemann 1958 – E. Haverkamp-Begemann, 'Een onbekend werk van de Meester van de Hl. Sebastiaan', *Bulletin des Musées Royaux des Beaux-Arts de Belgique*, 7 (1958).
Heers 1978 – J. Heers, *Itinéraire d'Anselme Adorno*, Paris 1978.
Heers 1983 – J. Heers, *Genova nel Quattrocento*, Milan 1983.
Heers 1989 – J. Heers, 'Concorterie et Alberghi à Gênes: la ville et la campagne', in *Storia dei genovesi*, IX, 1989.
Heller and Studolski 1995 – B. Heller and L. Studolski, 'Recent Scientific Investigation of the Detroit Saint Jerome', in Ainsworth 1995.
Heller and Studolski 1998, 'Saint Jerome in the Laboratory: Scientific Evidence and the Enigmas of an Eyckian Panel', *Bulletin of the Detroit Institute of Arts*, 72 (1998).
Hendrikman 2001 – L. I. Hendrikman, 'Christiaan II als Scandinavische Constantijn', *Millennium*, 15, no. 1 (2001).
Hertlein 1977 – E. Hertlein, 'Das Grabmonument Kaiser Friedrichs III. (1415–1493) als habsburgisches Denkmal', *Pantheon*, 35 (1977).
Herzner 1995 – V. Herzner, *Jan van Eyck und der Genter Altar*, Worms 1995.
Heinritz 1993 – U. Heinritz, 'Eine Überlegung zu Jacques Coene', *ZfKG*, 56 (1993).
Hindman 1977 – S. Hindman, 'The Case of Simon Marmion: Attributions and Documents', *ZfKG*, 40 (1977).
Hockney 2002 – D. Hockney, *The Secret Knowledge. Rediscovering the Lost Technique of the Old Masters*, London 2002.
Hoff and Davies 1971 – U. Hoff and M. Davies, *The National Gallery of Victoria, Melbourne* (Les Primitifs Flamands, Corpus), Brussels 1971.
Hoffman 1969 – E. W. Hoffman, 'Simon Marmion Re-considered', *Scriptorium*, 23 (1969).
Hoffman 1973 – E. W. Hoffman, 'Simon Marmion or The Master of the Altarpiece of Saint-Bertin: A Problem in Attribution', *Scriptorium*, 27 (1973).
Hood 1993 – W. Hood, *Fra Angelico at San Marco*, New Haven 1993.
Hulin de Loo 1902 – G. Hulin de Loo, *Bruges 1902. Expositions de tableaux flamands des XIVe, XVe, et XVIe siècles, Catalogue critique*, Ghent 1902.

Hulin de Loo 1904 – G. Hulin de Loo, *L'exposition des Primitifs français au point de vue de l'influence des frères Van Eyck sur la peinture française et provençale*, Brussels and Paris 1904.
Hulin de Loo 1911 – G. Hulin de Loo, *Heures de Milan*, Brussels and Paris 1911.
Hulin de Loo 1932 – G. Hulin de Loo, 'L'Exposition d'art français, à Londres, en 1932. Notes sur quelques tableaux du xve siècle', *Académie royale de Belgique. Bulletin de la Classe des Beaux-Arts*, 14 (1932).
Huillet d'Istria 1961 – M. Huillet d'Istria, *La Peinture française de la fin du Moyen Âge. Le Maître de Moulins*, Paris 1961.
Huillet d'Istria 1964 – M. Huillet d'Istria, 'The Problem of the Master of Moulins', *BM* (1964).
Hunter 1993 – J. Hunter, 'Who is Jan van Eyck's "Cardinal Albergati"?', *AB*, 75 (1993).
Huvenne 1984 – P. Huvenne, *Pieter Pourbus*, exh. cat. Bruges 1984.
Hyde 1997 – H. Hyde, 'Gerard David's Cervara Altarpiece. An Examination of the Commission for the Monastery of San Girolamo della Cervara', *Arte Cristiana* 1997.
Innsbruck 1992 – *Hispania–Austria*, exh. cat. Innsbruck 1992.
Ishikawa 1989 – C. L. Ishikawa, 'The "Retablo de la Reina Católica" by Juan de Flandes and Michel Sittow', Ph.D. Diss., Philadelphia, Bryn Mawr College, 1989 (to be published Turnhout 2003).
Jacobs 1989 – L. Jacobs, 'The Marketing and Standardization of South Netherlandish Carved Altarpieces. Limits on the Role of the Patron', *AB*, 71 (1989).
Janssen 1988 – D. Janssen, *Similitudo. Untersuchungen zu den Bildnissen Jan van Eycks*, Cologne 1988.
Janssens de Bisthoven 1981 – A. Janssens de Bisthoven *et al.*, *Museum voor Schone Kunsten (Groeningemuseum) Brugge* (Les Primitifs Flamands, Corpus), Brussels 1981.
Jolly 1976 – P. H. Jolly, *Jan van Eyck and St. Jerome: A Study of Eyckian Influence in Colantonio and Antonello da Messina in Quattrocento Naples*, Ph.D. Diss., University of Pennsylvania 1976.
Jolly 1981 – P. H. Jolly, 'Rogier van der Weyden's Escorial and Philadelphia *Crucifixions* and their relation to Fra Angelico at San Marco', *Oud Holland*, 95 (1981).
Jolly 1998 – P. H. Jolly, 'Jan van Eyck's Italian Pilgrimage. A miraculous Florentine Annunciation and the Ghent Altarpiece', *ZfKG*, 61 (1998).
Jones 1995 – S. Jones, 'The "Virgin of Nicolas van Maelbeke" and the Followers of Jan van Eyck', in Ainsworth 1995.
Jones 2000 – S. Jones, 'The Use of Workshop Drawings by Jan van Eyck and his Followers', in Foister, Jones and Cool 2000.
Kapp 1987 – M. Kapp, *Musikalische Handschriften des burgundischen Hofes in Mechelen und Brüssel ca. 1495–1530. Studien zur Entwicklung Gerard Horenbouts und seiner Werkstatt*, Ph.D. Diss., Julius-Maximilians-Universität, Würzburg 1987.
Kantorowicz 1939–40 – E. Kantorowicz, 'The Este Portrait by Roger van der Weyden', *JWCI*, 3 (1939).
Kemperdick 1997 – S. Kemperdick, *Der Meister von Flémalle. Die Werkstatt Robert Campins und Rogier van der Weyden*, Turnhout 1997.
Knapp 1917 – F. Knapp, 'Hugo van der Goes' Portinari-Altar und sein Einfluß auf Lionardo da Vinci, Botticelli, Filippino Lippi, Piero di Cosimo u.a.', *Mitteilungen des Kunsthistorischen Instituts in Florenz*, 2 (1917).
König 1982 – E. König, *Französische Buchmalerei um 1450. Der Jouvenel Maler, der Maler des Genfer Boccaccio und die Anfänge Jean Fouquets*, Berlin 1982.
König 1994 – E. König *et al.*, *Die Blätter im Louvre und das verlorene Turiner Gebetbuch. RF 2022–2025 Département des Arts graphiques Musée du Louvre, Paris, und Handschrift K.IV.29, Biblioteca Nazionale Universitaria, Torino; Kommentar zum Faksimile*, Lucerne 1994.
König 1996 – E. König, *Das liebentbrannte Herz: der Wiener Codex und der Maler Barthélemy d'Eyck*, Graz 1996.
König 1998 – E. König *et al.*, *Das Berliner Stundenbuch der Maria von Burgund und Kaiser Maximilians*, Berlin 1998.
Koerner 1993 – J. L. Koerner, *Moment of Self Portraiture in German Renaissance Art*, Chicago and London 1993.
Koster 2000 – M. L. Koster, *Hugo van der Goes's Portinari Altarpiece: Northern Invention and Florentine Reception*, Ph.D. Diss., Columbia University.
Koster 2001 – M. L. Koster, review of Venice 1999 and Madrid and Valencia 2001, *Simiolus*, 28 (2001).
Kren 1992 – T. Kren (ed.), *Margaret of York, Simon Marion and The Visions of Tondal*, Malibu 1992.
Kris and Kurz 1980 – E. Kris and O. Kurz, *Die Legende vom Künstler*, Frankfurt 1980.
Kristeller 1965 – P. O. Kristeller, 'The Humanist Bartolomeo Facio and his Unknown Correspondance', in *From Renaissance to Counterreformation: Essays in Honor of Garrett Mattingly*, New York 1965.
Labande 1937 – L.-H. Labande, *Les Bréa. Peintres niçois des xve et xvie siècles en Provence et en Ligurie*, Nice 1937.
Laclotte 1994 – *Hommage à Michel Laclotte. Etudes sur la peinture du Moyen-Age et de la Renaissance*, Milan and Paris 1994.
Laclotte and Thiébaut 1983 – M. Laclotte and D. Thiébaut, *L'école d'Avignon*, Paris 1983.
Lammertse 1994 – F. Lammertse (ed.), *Van Eyck to Bruegel. 1400–1550. Dutch and Flemish Painting in the collection of the Museum Boymans-van Beuningen*, Rotterdam 1994.
Lane 1971 – B. G. Lane, 'Petrus Christus: A Reconstructed Triptych with an Italian Motif', *AB*, 52 (1971).
Lavalleye 1936 – J. Lavalleye, *Juste de Gand*, Brussels and Rome 1936.
Lemaire 1994 – J. Lemaire, *Les Visions de la vie de cour dans la littérature française de la fin du Moyen Age*, Brussels and Paris 1994.
Lemaire and Rouzet 1991 – M. H. Lemaire and A. Rouzet, *Isabelle de Portugal. Duchesse de Bourgogne, 1397–1471*, Brussels 1991.
Leone de Castris 1997 – See Naples 1997.
Leone de Castris 1999 – P. Leone de Castris *et al.*, *Museo e Gallerie Nazionali di Capodimonte. Dipinti dal XIII al XVI secolo: le collezioni borboniche e post unitarie*, Naples 1999.
Lessing 1974 – G. E. Lessing, *Werke in 6 Bänden*, H. Göpfert (ed.), vi, Munich 1974.
Lestocquoy 1979 – J. Lestocquoy, *Deux siècles d'histoire de la tapisserie (1300–1500). Paris, Arras, Lille, Tournai, Bruxelles*, Arras 1979.
Leuven 1998 – *Dieric Bouts*, exh. cat. Leuven 1998.
Lieb 1958 – N. Lieb, *Die Fugger und die Kunst im Zeitalter der hohen Renaissance*, Munich 1958.
Lieb 1980 – N. Lieb, *Octavian Secundus Fugger (1549–1600) und die Kunst*, Tübingen 1980.
Lievens de Waegh 1991 – M.-L. Lievens de Waegh, *Le Musée national d'art ancien et le Musée national des carreaux de faïence de Lisbonne* (Les Primitifs Flamands, Corpus), Brussels 1991.
Limentani Virdis 1997 – C. Limentani Virdis (ed.), *La pittura fiamminga nel Veneto e nell'Emilia*, Verona 1997.
Limentani Virdis and Pietrogiovanna 2001 – C. Limentani Virdis and M. Pietrogiovanna, *Retables: L'âge gothique de la Renaissance*, Paris 2001.
Lisbon 1959 – *A Rainha D. Leonor*, exh. cat. Lisbon 1959.
Lorentz 1994 – P. Lorentz, 'Le Cardinal Rolin et Jean Hey', in *La bonne étoile de Rolin. Mécénat et efflorescence artistique dans la Bourgogne du xve siècle*, Autun 1994.
Lorentz 1998a – P. Lorentz, 'A propos du "réalisme" flamand: la Crucifixion du Parlement de Paris et la porte du beau roi Philippe au Palais de la Cité', *Cahiers de la Rotonde*, 20 (1998).
Lorentz 1998b – P. Lorentz, 'Le retable du Parlement de Paris et son peintre: trois hypothèses récentes', *Bulletin Monumental*, 156 (1998).
Lorentz 1999 – P. Lorentz, 'Les Rolin et les "Primitifs flamands"', in *La Splendeur des Rolin. Un mécénat privé à la cour de Bourgogne*, Paris 1999.
Lorentz 1999 – P. Lorentz, 'Maistre Jaques Daret, pantre, pour lors demourant à Arras', in Arras 1999.
Lorentz and Regond 1990 – P. Lorentz and A. Regond, *Jean Hey: le Maître de Moulins*, Moulins 1990.
Lorentz and Reynaud 1994 – P. Lorentz and N. Reynaud, 'Un ange de Hans Memling, v. 1435–1494 au Louvre', *Revue du Louvre et des Musées de France*, 44 (1994).
Luber 1998 – K. C. Luber, 'Recognizing Van Eyck', *Bulletin Philadelphia Museum of Art* (1998).
Lucco 1990 – M. Lucco (ed.), *La pittura a Venezia nel primo Cinquecento*, 2 vols, Milan 1989–90.
Lucco 1993 – M. Lucco, 'Marco Zoppo nella pittura veneziana', in B. Giovannucci Vigi (ed.), *Marco Zoppo, Cento 1433–1478 Venezia. Atti del Convegno Internazionale di Studi sulla pittura del Quattrocento Padano, Cento, 8–9 ottobre 1993*, Milan 1993.
Lurie 1976 – A. T. Lurie, 'Birth and Naming of St. John the Baptist Attributed to Juan de Flandes. A Newly Discovered Panel from a Hypothetical Altarpiece', *Bulletin of the Cleveland Museum of Art*, 63 (1976).
Lurie 1981 – A. T. Lurie, 'A Newly Discovered Eyckian St. John the Baptist in a Landscape', *Bulletin of the Cleveland Museum of Art*, 67 (1981).
MacBeth and Spronk 1997 – R. MacBeth and R. Spronk, 'A Material History of Rogier's St. Luke Drawing the Virgin: Conservation Treatment and Findings from Technical Examinations', in Purtle 1997.
Madrid 1993 – *Los Reyes Católicos. Paisaje artístico de una monarquía*, Madrid 1993.
Madrid 1997 – *Cathalonia: Arte Gótico en los siglos XIV–XV*, exh. cat. Madrid 1997.
Madrid and Valencia 2001 – *El Renacimiento Mediterráneo. Viajes de artistas e itinerarios de obras entre Italia, Francia y España en el siglo XV*, exh. cat. Madrid and Valencia 2001.
Malaguzzi Valeri 1902 – F. Malaguzzi Valeri, *Pittori Lombardi del Quattrocento*, Milan 1902.
Maquet-Tombu 1951 – J. Maquet-Tombu, 'Roger van der Weyden, pèlerin de l'année sainte 1450', *Les Arts plastiques* (1951).
Marijnissen 1978 – R. H. Marijnissen, 'On Scholarship: Some Reflections on the Study of Early Netherlandish Painting', *Mededelingen van de Koninklijke Academie voor Wetenschappen, Letteren en Schone Kunsten* (1978).
Marinesco 1959 – C. Marinesco, 'Les affaires commerciales en Flandre d'Alphonse v d'Aragon, roi de Naples (1416–1458)', *Revue historique*, 221 (1959).
Markl 1983 – D. Markl, 'Mestre Jácome, pintor italiano e o retrato de D. João i do Museu Nacional de Arte Antiga', in *Poetas e Trovadores*, Lisbon 1983.
Markl 1988 – D. Markl, *O retábulo de S. Vincente da Sé de Lisboa e os documentos*, Lisbon 1988.
Marrow 1968 – J. H. Marrow, 'Review *Heures de Turin*', *AB*, 50, 1968.
Marrow 1997 – J. H. Marrow, 'Artistic Identity in Early Netherlandish Painting; The Place of Rogier van der Weyden's St. Luke Drawing the Virgin', in Purtle 1997.
Marshall White 1997 – E. Marshall White, 'Rogier van der Weyden, Hugo van der Goes, and the Making of the Netherlandish St. Luke Tradition', in Purtle 1997.
Martens 1992a – M. P. J. Martens, *Artistic Patronage in Bruges Institutions*, Ph.D. Diss. University of California at Santa Barbara 1992.
Martens 1992b – M. P. J. Martens, *Lodewijk van Gruuthuse*, exh. cat. Bruges 1992.
Martens 1995a – M. P. J. Martens, 'Discussion', in Ainsworth 1995.
Martens 1995b – D. Martens, 'La Vierge en majesté de l'ancien retable de la Sé d'Évora', *GdBA*, 126 (1995).
Martens 1998a – M. P. J. Martens, 'Some Aspects of the Origins of the Art Market in 15th Century Bruges', in North and Ormrod 1998.
Martens 1998b – D. Martens, 'Metamorfosis hispánicas de una composición de Dieric Bouts', *Goya* (1998).
Martens 2000 – D. Martens, 'Identification du *Tableau de l'adoration des Mages* flamand, anciennement à la Chartreuse de Miraflores', *Annales d'histoire de l'art et d'archéologie*, 23 (2000).
Martens 2001 – D. Martens, 'Diego de la Cruz, cuarente años después de su redescubrimiento: balance de las investigaciones y nuevas propuestas', *Goya* (2001).
Medica 1991 – M. Medica, 'Rogier van der Weyden', in *Le Muse e il Principe. Arte di corte nel Rinascimento padano*, exh. cat. Modena 1991.
Meiss 1961 – M. Meiss, '"Highland" in the Lowlands; Jan van Eyck, the Master of Flémalle, and the Franco-Italian Tradition', *GdBA*, 57 (1961).
Meiss 1963 – M. Meiss, 'French and Italian Variations on an Early Fifteenth-Century Theme: St. Jerome in his Study', *GdBA*, 62 (1963).
Meiss 1967 – M. Meiss, *French Painting in the Time of Jean de Berry. The late XIVth Century and the Patronage of the Duke*, London and New York 1967.
Meiss 1969 – M. Meiss, *French Painting in the Time of Jean de Berry. The Boucicaut Master*, London and New York 1969.
Meiss 1974 – M. Meiss, *French Painting in the Time of Jean de Berry. The Limbourgs and their Contemporaries*, New York 1974.
Meiss 1976 – M. Meiss, 'Jan van Eyck and the Italian Renaissance', in *The Painter's Choice. Problems in the Interpretation of Renaissance Art*, New York 1976.
Menz 1959 – H. Menz, 'Zur Freilegung einer Inschrift auf dem Eyck-Altar der Dresdner Gemäldegalerie', *Jahrbuch der Staatlichen Kunstsammlungen Dresden*, 1959.
Mérindol 1987 – C. de Mérindol, *Le roi René et la seconde maison d'Anjou*, Paris 1987.
Messina 1981 – *Antonello da Messina*, exh. cat. Messina 1981–82.
Michelant 1871 – M. Michelant, 'Inventaire des vaisselles, joyaux, peintures, manuscrits etc., de Marguerite d'Autriche, régente et gouvernante des Pays-Bas, dressé en son palais de Malines, le 9 juillet 1523', *Compte rendu des séances de la Commission royale d'histoire. Académie royale des Sciences, des Lettres et des Beaux-Arts de Belgique (Bruxelles)*, 12 (1871).
Miglio 1975 – M. Miglio, *Storiografia pontificia del Quattrocento*, Bologna 1975.
Montias 1982 – J. M. Montias, *Artists and Artisans in Delft. A Socio-Economic Study of the Seventeenth Century*, Princeton 1982.
Montias 1987 – J. M. Montias, 'Cost and Value in Seventeenth-Century Dutch Art', *Art History*, 10 (1987).
Montias 1988 – J. M. Montias, 'Art Dealers in the Seventeenth-Century Netherlands', *Simiolus*, 18 (1988).
Montias 1990 – J. M. Montias, 'Estimates of the Number of Dutch Master-Painters, their Earnings and their Output in 1650', *Leidschrift* 6 (1990), p. 70.
Montias 1991 – J. M. Montias, 'Works of Art in Seventeenth-Century Amsterdam. An Analysis of Subjects and Attributions', in D. Freedberg and J. de Vries (eds), *Art in History, History in Art. Studies in Seventeenth-Century Dutch Culture*, Los Angeles 1991.
Montias 1993 – J. M. Montias, 'Le marché de l'art aux Pays-Bas, xve et xvie siècles', in *Annales, Economies, Sociétés, Civilisations*, 1993.
Morel 1908 – P. Morel, *Les Lombards dans la Flandre française et le Hainaut*, Lille 1908.
Mund and Stroo 2002 – H. Mund and C. Stroo, *Museum Mayer Van den Bergh, Antwerpen* (Les Primitifs Flamands, Corpus), Brussels 2002.
Müntz 1888 – H. Müntz, *Les Collections des Médicis au xve siècle*, Paris and London 1888.
Müntz 1895 – H. Müntz, 'Rogier van der Weyden à Milan et à Florence. Ses portraits de Sforza et des Medicis. Avec des notes sur les artistes flamands ou allemands ayant travaillé en Italie au xve siècle', *Revue de l'art chrétien*, 37 (1895).
Mulazzani 1971 – G. Mulazzani, 'Observations on the Sforza Triptych in the Brussels Museum', *BM*, 113 (1971).
Naples 1997 – *Quattrocento aragonese. La pittura a Napoli al tempo di Alfonso e Ferrant d'Aragona*, exh. cat. Naples 1997.
Naples 2001 – *Colantonio – Antonello*, exh. cat. Naples 2001.
Natale 1991 – M. Natale, 'Lo studiolo di Belfiore: un cantiere ancora aperto', in *Le Muse e il principe. Arte di corte nel Rinascimento paduano*, exh. cat. Milan 1991.
Natale 1999 – M. Natale, *La Raccolta Cagnola*, Milan 1999.
Natale 2001 – M. Natale, 'El Mediterráneo que nos une', in Madrid and Valencia 2001.
Neidhardt and Schölzel 2000 – H.J. Neidhardt and C. Schölzel, 'Jan van Eyck's Dresden Triptych', in Foister, Jones and Cool 2000.
Nepi Sciré 1999 – See Venice 1999.
New York 1984 – *Liechtenstein. The Princely Collection*, exh. cat. New York 1984.
New York 1998 – *From Van Eyck to Bruegel*, exh. cat. New York 1998.
Nicolini 1925 – F. Nicolini, *L'arte napoletana del Rinascimento e la lettera di P. Summonte a M. A. Michiel*, Naples 1925.
Nordman 1998 – D. Nordman, *Frontières de France. De l'espace au territoire, xvie–xixe siècle*, Paris 1998.
North 1992 – M. North, *Kunst und Kommerz im Goldenen Zeitalter. Zur Sozialgeschichte der niederländischen Malerei des 17. Jahrhunderts*, Cologne, Weimar and Vienna 1992.
North 1995 – M. North, 'Art and Commerce in the Dutch Republic', in K. Davids and J. Lucassen (eds), *A Miracle Mirrored. The Dutch Republic in European Perspective*, Cambridge 1995.
North 1996 – M. North (ed.), *Economic History and the Arts*, Cologne, Vienna and Weimar 1996.
North 1998 – M. North, 'Kunst und Bürgerliche Repräsentation in der Frühen Neuzeit', *Historische Zeitschrift*, 267 (1998).
North 2001 – M. North, *Das Goldene Zeitalter. Kunst und Kommerz in der niederländischen Malerei des 17. Jahrhunderts*, Cologne, Weimar and Vienna 2001.
North 2002a – M. North, *Kunstsammeln und Geschmack im 18. Jahrhundert*, Berlin 2002.
North 2002b – M. North, *The Long Way of Professionalisation in the Early Modern German Art Trade*, in S. Cavaciocchi (ed.), *Economia e arte Secc. XIII–XVIII*, Prato 2002 (forthcoming).
North and Ormrod 1998 – M. North and D. Ormrod (eds), *Markets for Art, 1400–1800*, Aldershot 1998.
Nuremberg 1971 – *Albrecht Dürer 1471–1971*, exh. cat. Nuremberg 1971.
Nuttall 1992 – P. Nuttall, 'Decorum, Devotion and Dramatic Expression: Early Netherlandish Painting in Renaissance Italy', in *Decorum in Renaissance Narrative Art*, London 1992.
Nuttall 1996 – P. Nuttall, 'Domenico Ghirlandaio and Northern Art', *Apollo*, 143 (1996).
Nuttall 2000 – P. Nuttall, 'Jan van Eyck's Paintings in Italy', in Foister, Jones and Cool 2000.

Nuttall (forthcoming) – P. Nuttall, *From Flanders to Florence: The Impact of Netherlandish Painting, 1430–1500*, New Haven and London (forthcoming).

Oertel 1942 – R. Oertel, *Fra Filippo Lippi*, Vienna 1942.

Ohler 2000 – N. Ohler, *Pilgerstab und Jakobsmuschel*, Düsseldorf 2000.

Origo 1985 – I. Origo, *'Im Namen Gottes und des Geschäfts'. Lebensbild eines toskanischen Kaufmanns der Frührenaissance. Francesco di Marco Datini 1335–1410*, Munich 1985.

Otto 1964 – G. Otto, *Bernard Strigel*, Munich and Berlin 1964.

Pächt 1959 – O. Pächt, 'Rezension J. Bruyn, Van Eyck problemen', *Kunstchronik*, 12 (1959).

Pächt 1974 – O. Pächt, 'Die Autorschaft des Gonella-Bildnisses', *JKSK*, 70 (1974).

Pächt 1989 – O. Pächt, *Van Eyck. Die Begründer der altniederländischen Malerei*, Munich 1989.

Pane 1975 – R. Pane, *Il Rinascimento nell'Italia meridionale*, I, Milan 1975.

Panera Cuevas 1995 – F. J. Panera Cuevas, *El retablo de la catedral y la pintura gótica internacional en Salamanca*, Salamanca 1995.

Panhans 1974 – G. Panhans, 'Florentiner Maler verarbeiten ein Eyckisches Bild', *Wiener Jahrbuch für Kunstgeschichte*, 27 (1974).

Panhans-Bühler 1978 – U. Panhans-Bühler, *Eklektizismus und Originalität im Werk des Petrus Christus*, Vienna 1978.

Panofsky 1953 – E. Panofsky, *Early Netherlandish Painting. Its Origins and Character*, Cambridge (Mass.) 1953.

Panofsky 1954 – E. Panofsky, 'A Letter to Saint Jerome. A Note on the Relationship between Petrus Christus and Jan van Eyck', in *Studies in Art and Literature for Belle da Costa Greene*, Princeton 1954.

Panofsky 1977 – E. Panofsky, *Albrecht Dürer*, Hamburg 1977.

Papini and Lanciano 1914 – G. Papini and Lanciano (eds), *Alessandra Macinghi Strozzi: Lettere e figlioli*, Florence 1914.

Paravicini 2001 – W. Paravicini, 'Die zwölf "Magnificences" Karls des Kühnen', *Vorträge und Forschungen*, 51 (2001).

Paris 1999 – *Avignon. Musée du Petit Palais. Peintures et sculptures*, exh. cat. Paris 1999.

Parma 1999a – E. Parma (ed.), *La pittura in Liguria. Il Cinquecento*, Genoa and Recco 1999.

Parma 1999b – E. Parma, 'Genoa–Bruges: The Art Market and Cultural Exchange in the Fifteenth Century', in *Italy and the Low Countries – Artistic Relations. The Fifteenth Century*, Florence 1999.

Passoni 1988 – R. Passoni, 'Opere fiamminghe a Chieri', in M. Di Macco and G. Romano, *Arte del Quattrocento a Chieri. Per i restauri nel Battistero*, Turin 1988.

Pauwels 1998 – A. and H. Pauwels, 'Dirk Bouts' Laatste Avondmaal, een belangrijk keerpunt in de evolutie van de perspectief in de schilderkunst van de Nederlanden', in Leuven 1998.

Paviot 1990 – J. Paviot, 'La vie de Jan van Eyck selon des documents écrits', *Revue des archéologues et historiens d'art de Louvain*, 23 (1990).

Paviot 1991 – J. Paviot, 'La Mappemonde attribuée à Jan van Eyck par Facio: une pièce à retirer de son œuvre', *Revue des archéologues et historiens de l'art de Louvain*, 24 (1991).

Paviot 1995 – J. Paviot (ed.) *Portugal et Bourgogne au XVe siècle*, Lisbon and Paris 1995.

Paviot 1999 – J. Paviot, 'Les Honneurs de la cour d'Eléonore de Poitiers', in *Autour de Marguerite d'Ecosse. Reines, princesses et dames du XVe siècle*, Paris 1999.

Paviot 2000a – J. Paviot, 'Etude préliminaire', in *Les Chevaliers de l'Ordre de la Toison d'or au XVe siècle*, Frankfurt 2000.

Paviot 2000b – J. Paviot, 'Jacques de Luxembourg. Politique et culture chez un grand seigneur du XVe siècle', in *Penser le pouvoir au Moyen Age (VIIIe–XVe siècle). Etudes d'histoire et de littérature offertes à Françoise Autrand*, Paris 2000.

Pemán y Pemartín 1969 – C. Pemán y Pemartín, *Juan van Eyck y España*, Cádiz 1969.

Pettenati 1996 – S. Pettenati, 'How the Heures de Milan became the Heures de Turin-Milan', in Van Buren 1996.

Petti-Balbi 1996 – G. Petti-Balbi, *Mercanti e nationes nelle Fiandre: i genovesi in età bassomedievale*, Pisa 1996.

Philadelphia 1997 – *Jan van Eyck: Two Paintings of Saint Francis Receiving the Stigmata*, Philadelphia 1997.

Pierce 1928 – C. W. Pierce, 'The Sforza Triptych', *Art Studies*, 6 (1928).

Pignatti 1969 – T. Pignatti, *L'Opera completa di Giovanni Bellini*, Milan 1969.

Poeschke 1993 – J. Poeschke (ed.), *Italienische Frührenaissance und Nordeuropäisches Mittelalter*, Munich 1993.

Pontano 1965 – G. Pontano, *I Trattati delle virtù sociali*, Rome 1965.

Ponz 1788 – A. Ponz, *Viaje de España*, Madrid 1788.

Pope-Hennessy 1966 – J. Pope-Hennessy, *The Portrait in the Renaissance*, Princeton 1966.

Pope-Hennessy and Christiansen 1980 – J. Pope-Hennessy and K. Christiansen, 'Secular Painting in Fifteenth-Century Tuscany: Birth Trays, Cassone Panels and Portraits', *Metropolitan Museum of Art Bulletin*, 38 (1980).

Porfírio 1991 – J. L. Porfírio, *Pintura Portugesa – Museu Nacional de Arte Antiga*, Lisbon 1991.

Post I–XII – R. C. Post, *A History of Spanish Painting*, 12 vols, Cambridge (Mass.) 1930–59.

Post 1943 – R. C. Post, 'The Master of the Encarnation', *GdBA* (1943).

Preimesberger 1991 – R. Preimesberger, 'Zu Jan van Eycks Diptychon der Sammlung Thyssen-Bornemisza', *ZfKG*, 54 (1991).

Preimesberger 1992 – R. Preimesberger, 'Ein "Prüfstein der Malerei" bei Jan van Eyck', in *Der Künstler über sich in seinem Werk*, Berlin 1992.

Purtle 1982 – C. Purtle, *The Marian Paintings of Jan van Eyck*, Princeton 1982.

Purtle 1997 – C. Purtle (ed.), *Rogier van der Weyden. St. Luke Drawing the Virgin* (Selected Essays in Context), Turnhout 1997.

Purtle 1999 – C. Purtle, 'Van Eyck's Washington Annunciation: Narrative Time and Metaphoric Tradition', *AB*, 81 (1999).

Purtle 2000 – C. Purtle, 'Assessing the Evolution of Van Eyck's Iconography through Technical Study of the Washington Annunciation, II: New Light on the Development of Van Eyck's Architectural Narrative', in Foister, Jones and Cool 2000.

Quaini 1991 – M. Quaini, 'L'immaginario geografico medievale, il viaggio di scoperta e l'universo concettuale del grande viaggio di Colombo', in *Relazioni di viaggio e conoscenza del mondo fra Medioevo e Umanesimo*, Genoa 1991.

Rebora, Rovera and Bocchiotti 1987 – G. Rebora, G, Rovera and G. Bocchiotti, *Bartolomé Bermejo e il Trittico di Acqui*, Acqui Terme 1987.

Reis-Santos 1940 – L. Reis-Santos, *Frei Carlos*, Lisbon 1940.

Reis-Santos 1946 – L. Reis Santos, *Vasco Fernandes e os Pintores de Viseu do Século XVI*, Lisbon 1946.

Renders 1933 – E. Renders, *Hubert van Eyck. Personnage de légende*, Paris and Brussels 1933.

Reynaud 1968 – N. Reynaud, 'Jean Hey, peintre de Moulins et son client Jean Cueillette', *RdA*, I (1968).

Reynaud 1981 – N. Reynaud, *Jean Fouquet*, Paris 1981.

Reynaud 1983 – N. Reynaud, 'La radiographie du portrait de Charles VII par Fouquet', *La Revue du Louvre et des Musées de France*, 1983.

Reynaud 1988 – N. Reynaud, 'Barthélemy d'Eyck avant 1450', *RdA* 1988.

Reynaud and Resort 1991 – N. Reynaud and C. Resort, 'Les portraits d'hommes illustres du studiolo d'Urbin au Louvre par Juste de Gand et Pedro Berruguete', *Revue du Louvre et des Musées de France*, 41 (1991).

Reynolds 1996 – C. Reynolds, 'The Master of Moulins', in *DoA*.

Reynolds 2000 – C. Reynolds, 'The King of Painters', in Foister, Jones and Cool 2000.

Ridderbos 1991 – See Van Asperen de Boer, Ridderbos and Zeldenrust 1991.

Ridderbos 1993 – B. Ridderbos, 'In de suizende stilte van de binnenkamer. Interpretaties van het Arnolfini-portret', *Nederlands Kunsthistorisch Jaarboek*, 44 (1993).

Ring 1949 – G. Ring, *A Century of French Painting. 1400–1500*, London 1949.

Riquer 1967 – M. de Riquer, *Caballeros andantes españoles*, Madrid 1967.

Riquer 1979 – M. de Riquer, *Cavelleria fra realtà e letteratura nel quattrocento*, Bari 1979.

Roberts 1987 – A. Roberts, 'Review of Paolo Torresan, *Il Dipingere di Fiandra*', *AB* (1987).

Robin 1985 – F. Robin, *La cour d'Anjou-Provence. La vie artistique sous le règne de René*, Paris 1985.

Rodger 1993 – R. Rodger (ed.), *European Urban History*, Leicester and London 1993.

Rodrigues 1995 – D. Rodrigues, 'Pintura: o ciclo renascentista. A prevalência do gosto e o classicismo efémero', in P. Pereira, *Historia da Arte Portuguesa*, 2 vols, Lisbon 1995.

Roeck 1991 – B. Roeck, *Lebenswelt und Kultur des Bürgertums in der Frühen Neuzeit*, Munich 1991.

Roeck 1999 – B. Roeck, 'Venice and Germany: Commercial Contacts and Intellectual Inspirations', in Venice 1999.

Rohlmann 1993 – M. Rohlmann, 'Zitate flämischer Landschaftsmotive in Florentiner Quattrocentomalerei', in Poeschke 1993.

Rohlmann 1994 – M. Rohlmann, *Auftragskunst und Sammlerbild. Altniederländische Tafelmalerei im Florenz des Quattrocento*, Alfter 1994.

Rohlmann 1997 – M. Rohlmann, 'Memling und Italien: Flämische Malerei für die bologneser Familie Loiani', in *Memling Studies 1994*, Leuven 1997.

Rome 1999 – *Bagliori del medioevo. Arte romanica e gotica dal Museu Nacional d'art de Catalunya*, exh. cat. Rome 1999.

Romano 1989 – G. Romano, 'Sur Antoine de Lonhy en Piémont', *RdA*, 85 (1989).

Romano 1994 – G. Romano, 'Tra la Francia e l'Italia: note su Giacomo Jaquerio e una proposta per Enguerrand Quarton', in Laclotte 1994.

Romano 1996 – G. Romano (ed.), *Primitivi piemontesi nei musei di Torino*, Turin 1996.

Romano (forthcoming) – S. Romano, 'Naples from the Anjou to Spain: Patrons and Paintings', in *Naples. Italian Center of the Renaissance*, New Haven and London (forthcoming).

Rosenauer 1993 – A. Rosenauer, 'Van Eyck und Italien', in Poeschke 1993.

Rosenberg 1997 – C. M. Rosenberg, *The Este Monuments and Urban Development in Renaissance Ferrara*, Cambridge 1997.

Rowlands 1962 – J. Rowlands, 'A Man of Sorrows by Petrus Christus', *BM*, 104 (1962).

Roy 2000 – A. Roy, 'Van Eyck's Technique. The Myth and the Reality, I', in Foister, Jones and Cool 2000.

Ruda 1984 – J. Ruda, 'Flemish Painting and the Early Renaissance in Florence: Questions of Influence', *ZfKG*, 47 (1984).

Ruda 1993 – J. Ruda, *Fra Filippo Lippi, Life and Work, with a Complete Catalogue*, New York 1993.

Ruda 1997 – J. Ruda, *Fra Filippo Lippi*, London 1997.

Ryder 1990 – A. Ryder, *Alfonso the Magnanimous, King of Aragon, Naples and Sicily*, Oxford 1990.

Salmi 1922 – M. Salmi, 'Ugo van der Goes nel trittico della cappella Portinari sede della compagnia dei pittori fiorentini', in *L'Italia e l'arte straniera: atti del X congresso internazionale di storia dell'arte in Roma*, Rome 1922.

Salmon 1855 – A. Salmon, 'Description de la ville de Tours sous le règne de Louis X. Par F. Florio', *Mémoires de la Société archéologique de Touraine*, 7 (1855).

Sánchez Cantón 1917 – F. J. Sánchez Cantón, 'Maestro Jorge Inglés, pintor y miniaturista del marqués de Santillana', *Boletín de la Sociedad Española de Excursiones*, 1917.

Sánchez Cantón 1950 – F. J. Sánchez Cantón, *Libros, tapices y cuadros que coleccionó Isabel la Católica*, Madrid 1950.

Sánchez Cantón 1964 – F. J. Sánchez Cantón, *Mestre Nicolas Frances*, Madrid 1964.

Sander 1992 – J. Sander, *Hugo van der Goes. Stilentwicklung und Chronologie*, Mainz 1992.

Sander 1993 – J. Sander, *Katalog der Gemälde im Städelschen Kunstinstitut Frankfurt am Main. Niederländische Gemälde im Städel, 1400–1550*, Mainz 1993.

Savettieri 1998 – C. Savettieri, *Antonello da Messina*, Palermo 1998.

Scailliérez 1991 – C. Scailliérez, *Joos van Cleve au Louvre*, exh. cat. Paris 1991.

Scailliérez 1997 – C. Scailliérez, 'Joos van Cleve e Genova', in Boccardo and Di Fabio 1997.

Scarpellini 1991 – P. Scarpellini, *Pietro Perugino*, New York 1991.

Schabacker 1974 – P. Schabacker, *Petrus Christus*, Utrecht 1974.

Schabacker 1974–76 – P. Schabacker, 'Jan van Eyck's Woman at her Toilet. Proposals Concerning its Subject and Context', *Fogg Art Museum Annual Report*, 1974–76.

Schaefer 1994 – C. Schaefer, *Jean Fouquet*, Dresden 1994.

Schauder 1991 – M. Schauder, 'Konrad Witz und die Utrechter Buchmalerei', in *Masters and Miniatures*, Doornspijk 1991.

Schauder 1993 – M. Schauder, 'War Jan van Eyck in Santiago de Compostela?', in *Pielgrzymki w kulture sredniowiecznej Europy*, Poznán 1993.

Scheller 1999 – R. W. Scheller, 'L'union des princes: Louis XII, his allies and the Venetian campaign 1509', *Oud Holland*, 27 (1999).

Schmid 1991 – W. Schmid, *Kölner Renaissancekultur im Spiegel der Aufzeichnungen des Hermann Weinsberg (1518–1597)*, Cologne 1991, chap. 3.

Schmid 1996 – W. Schmid, 'Dürer's Enterprise. Market Area, Market Potential, Product Range', in M. North (ed.), *Economic History and the Arts*, Cologne, Weimar and Vienna 1996.

Schöne 1937 – W. Schöne, 'Über einige altniederländische Bilder vor allem in Spanien', *JPKS*, 58 (1937).

Schöne 1938 – W. Schöne, *Dieric Bouts und seine Schule*, Berlin and Leipzig 1938.

Schreurs 2000 – E. Schreurs (ed.), *De schatkamer van Alamire. Muziek en miniaturen uit Keizer Karels Tijd (1500–1535)*, Leuven 2000.

Sciolla and Volpi 2001 – G. C. Sciolla and C. Volpi, *Da van Eyck a Bruegbel. Scritti sulle arti di Domenico Lampsonio*, Turin 2001.

Seidel 1993 – L. Seidel, *Jan van Eyck's Arnolfini Portrait. Stories of an Icon*, Cambridge and New York 1993.

Shearman 1992 – J. Shearman, *Only Connect …*, Princeton 1992.

Silva Maroto 1989 – P. Silva Maroto, 'Fernando Gallego *Adoración de los Magos*', in *Obras maestras de la colección Masaveu*, exh. cat. Madrid 1989.

Silva Maroto 1990 – P. Silva Maroto, *Pintura hispanoflamenca: Burgos y Palencia*, 3 vols, Valladolid 1990.

Silva Maroto 1993 – P. Silva Maroto, *Pintura hispanoflamenca*, Madrid 1993.

Silva Maroto 1994 – P. Silva Maroto, 'Juan de Flandes', in Van Schoute 1994.

Silva Maroto 1998 – P. Silva Maroto, *Pedro Berruguete*, Salamanca 1998.

Silva Maroto 1999 – P. Silva Maroto, 'La pintura castellana en tiempos de Siloe', *Gil de Siloe. Congreso Internacional, Burgos* (forthcoming).

Silva Maroto 2001 – P. Silva Maroto, 'El Arte en España en la época del primer Marqués de Santillana (1398–1459)', in *El Marqués de Santillana*, exh. cat. Santillana 2001.

Silva Maroto and Garrido 1991 – P. Silva Maroto and C. Garrido, 'Contribution du dessin sous-jacent à l'identification et à la connaissance des peintres hispano-flamands castillans', *Colloque IX*, Leuven 1993.

Silver 1983 – L. Silver, 'Fountain and Source: A Rediscovered Eyckian Icon', *Pantheon*, 41 (1983).

Silver 1984 – L. Silver, *The Paintings of Quentin Massys with Catalogue Raisonné*, Montclair (NJ) 1984.

Simonetti 2000 – F. Simonetti, *Ecce Homo. Antonello da Messina, Genova e Piacenza: due versioni a confronto*, exh. cat. Genoa 2000.

Simonson Fuchs 1982 – A. Simonson Fuchs, 'The Virgin of the Councillors by Luis Dalmau (1443–1445): the contract and its Eyckian execution', *GdBA*, 99 (1982).

Skelton 1972 – R. A. Skelton, *Maps. A Historical Survey of Their Study and Collecting*, Chicago 1972.

Smeyers 1997 – M. Smeyers, 'The Philadelphia-Turin Paintings and the Turin-Milan Hours', in Philadelphia 1997.

Smeyers and Stroo 1994 – M. Smeyers and C. Stroo, 'Hubert en Jan van Eyck', in Van Schoute 1994.

Smit 1999 – H. Smit, '"Un si bello et onorato mistero". Flemish weavers employed by the city government of Siena (1438–1480)', in *Italy and the Low Countries – Artistic Relations. The Fifteenth Century*, Florence 1999.

Smith 1979 – J. C. Smith, *The Artistic Patronage of Philip the Good, Duke of Burgundy (1416–1467)*, Ph.D. Diss., Columbia University (1979).

Snyder 1973 – J. Snyder, 'The Chronology of Jan van Eyck's Paintings', in *Album Amicorum J. G. van Gelder*, The Hague 1973.

Spallanzani and Gaeta Bertelà 1992 – M. Spallanzani and G. Gaeta Bertelà, *Libro d'inventario dei beni di Lorenzo il Magnifico*, Florence 1992.

Spears Grayson 1976 – M. Spears Grayson, 'The Northern Origins of Nicolas Froment's Resurrection of Lazarus Altarpiece in the Uffizi Gallery', *AB*, 58 (1976).

Spike 1997 – J. T. Spike, *Fra Angelico*, Milan 1997.

Spronk 1995 – R. Spronk, 'More than meets the eye: An Introduction to Technical Examination of Early Netherlandish Painting at the Fogg Art Museum', *Harvard University Art Museums Bulletin*, 5 (1995).

Spronk 1998 – R. Spronk, 'Jan Provoost', in Bruges 1998.

Sricchia Santoro 1981 – F. Sricchia Santoro, 'L'Ambiente della formazione di Antonello; la cultura artistica a Napoli negli anni di Renato d'Angiò (1438–1442) e di Alfonso d'Aragona (1443–1458)', in Messina 1981.

Sricchia Santoro 1986 – F. Sricchia Santoro, *Antonello e l'Europa*, Milan 1986.

Sricchia Santoro 1990 – F. Sricchia Santoro, 'Una traccia per il tirocinio di Zanetto Bugatto in Fiandra', in *Scritti in onore di Giuliano Briganti*, Milan 1990.

Steenbock 1998 – F. Steenbock, 'Zur Überlieferungsgeschichte des Stundenbuches der Maria von Burgund und Kaiser Maximilians', in König 1998.

Stabel 1997 – P. Stabel, *Dwarfs among Giants. The Flemish Urban Network in the Late Middle Ages*, Leuven and Apeldoorn 1997.

STABEL 1999 – P. Stabel, 'Venice and the Low Countries: Commercial Contacts and Intellectual Inspirations', in Venice 1999.

STEPPE 1983 – J. K. Steppe, 'De Mappamonde geschilderd door Jan van Eyck voor Filips de Goede', *Academia Analecta*, 44 (1983).

STEPPE 1983b – J. K. Steppe, 'Lambert van Eyck en het portret van Jacoba van Beieren', *Academia Analecta*, 44 (1983).

STERLING 1941 – C. Sterling, *La Peinture française, les peintres du Moyen Age*, Paris 1941.

STERLING 1964 – C. Sterling, 'Josse Lieferinxe, peintre provençal', *La Revue du Louvre et des Musées de France*, 1 (1964).

STERLING 1968 – C. Sterling, 'Jean Hey, le Maître de Moulins', *RdA*, 1 (1968).

STERLING 1969 – C. Sterling, 'Etudes savoyardes I: Au temps du Duc Amédée', *L'Œil*, 1969.

STERLING 1971 – C. Sterling, 'Observations on Petrus Christus', *AB*, 53 (1971).

STERLING 1972 – C. Sterling, 'Etudes savoyardes II: Le Maître de la Trinité de Turin', *L'Œil*, 1972.

STERLING 1973 – C. Sterling, 'Pour Jean Changenet et Juan de Nalda', *L'Œil*, 1973.

STERLING 1976 – C. Sterling, 'Jan van Eyck avant 1432', *RdA* 33 (1976).

STERLING 1981 – C. Sterling, 'Nicolas Froment, peintre du nord de la France', *Etudes d'art médiéval offertes à Louis Grodecki*, Paris 1981.

STERLING 1983 – C. Sterling, *Enguerrand Quarton*, Paris 1983.

STERLING 1984 – C. Sterling, 'A la recherche des Œuvres de Zanetto Bugatto: une nouvelle piste', *Scritti di Storia dell'arte in onore di Federico Zeri*, Milan 1984.

STERLING 1986 – C. Sterling, 'L'influence de Conrad Witz en Savoie', *RdA*, 71 (1986).

STERLING 1988 – C. Sterling, 'Fouquet en Italie', *L'Œil*, 1988.

STERLING 1990 – C. Sterling, *La peinture médiévale à Paris, 1300–1500*, II, Paris 1990.

STERLING and AINSWORTH 1998 – C. Sterling and M. W. Ainsworth, 'France', in *The Robert Lehman Collection, II: Fifteenth- to Eighteenth-Century European Painting, France, Central Europe, the Netherlands, Spain, and Great Britain*, New York 1998.

STREHLKE 1997 – C. B. Strehlke, 'Jan van Eyck: Un artista per il Mediterraneo', in Turin 1997.

STREHLKE 2001 – C. B. Strehlke, review of Madrid and Valencia 2001, *BM* (2001).

STROO and SYFER-D'OLNE 1996 – C. Stroo and P. Syfer-d'Olne, *The Flemish Primitives I. The Master of Flémalle and Rogier van der Weyden Groups. Catalogue of Early Netherlandish Painting in the Royal Museums of Fine Arts of Belgium*, Turnhout 1996.

SUREDA I PONS 1994 – J. Sureda i Pons, *Un cert Jaume Huguet, el capvestre d'un somni*, Tarrasa 1994.

TAHON 1998 – E. Tahon, *Lancelot Blondeel*, Bruges 1998.

TEMPESTINI 1999 – A. Tempestini, *Giovanni Bellini*, New York 1999.

THIÉBAUT 1984 – D. Thiébaut, 'Portrait of a Man, dated 1456', in New York 1984.

THIÉBAUT 1989 – D. Thiébaut, 'Nicolas Dipre: deux nouveaux éléments de prédelle au Louvre', *La Revue du Louvre et des Musées de France*, 1989.

THIÉBAUT 1993 – D. Thiébaut, *Le Christ à la colonne d'Antonello da Messina*, Paris 1993.

THIÉBAUT 1999 – D. Thiébaut: 'Dal 1435 al 1500: il primato artistico dei pittori', in *La pittura francese*, Milan 1999.

THOMPSON and CAMPBELL 1974 – C. Thompson and L. Campbell, *Hugo van der Goes and the Trinity Panels in Edinburgh*, Edinburgh 1974.

THOSS 1987 – D. Thoss, *Flämische Buchmalerei. Handschriftenschätze aus dem Burgunderreich*, exh. cat. Graz 1987.

TOMASINI PIETRAMELLARA and TURCHINI 1985 – A. Tomasini Pietramellara and A. Turchini (eds), *Castel Sismondo e Sigismondo Pandolfo Malatesta – Le Signorie die Malatesti. Storia, società, cultura*, 1, Rimini 1985.

TORMO 1924 – E. Tormo, 'Las tablas Memlingianas del museo de Amberes. Su primitivo destino, fecha y autor', in *Mélanges Bertaux*, Paris 1924.

TOSCANO 2001 – G. Toscano, 'Nápoles y el Mediterráneo', in Madrid and Valencia 2001.

TORRESAN 1981 – P. Torresan, *Il dipingere di Fiandra. La pittura neerlandese nella letteratura artistica del Quattro- e Cinquecento*, Modena 1981.

TOURNAI 1967 – J. P. Asselberghs, *La tapisserie tournaisienne au XVe siècle*, exh. cat. Tournai 1967.

TOURNAI 1968 – J. P. Asselberghs, *La tapisserie tournaisienne au XVIe siècle*, exh. cat. Tournai 1968.

TRIZNA 1976 – J. Trizna, *Michel Sittow*, Brussels 1976.

TROESCHER 1966 – G. Troescher, *Burgundische Malerei. Maler und Malwerke um 1400 in Burgund, dem Berry mit der Auvergne und in Savoyen mit ihren Quellen und Ausstrahlungen*, Berlin 1966.

TROESCHER 1967 – G. Troescher, 'Die Pilgerfahrt des Robert Campin. Altniederländische und südwestdeutsche Maler in Südostfrankreich', *Jahrbuch der Berliner Museen*, 9 (1967).

TURIN 1997 – *Jan van Eyck, 1390–c. 1441. Opere a confronto*, exh. cat. Turin 1997.

UPTON 1975 – J. M. Upton, 'Devotional Imagery and Style in the Washington Nativity, by Petrus Christus', *Studies in the History of Art*, 7 (1975).

UPTON 1990 – J. M. Upton, *Petrus Christus: His Place in Fifteenth-Century Flemish Painting*, University Park and London 1990.

URBACH 2001 – S. Urbach, 'Tanulmányok. *Nyombiztosítás* bgy korai németalföldi kép egykor Magyar mgángyujteményben', *Müvészettörténeti Értesitö* (2001).

VAN ASPEREN DE BOER 1979 – J. R. J. van Asperen de Boer, 'A scientific re-examination of the Ghent Altarpiece', *Oud Holland*, 93 (1979).

VAN ASPEREN DE BOER 1992 – J. R. J. van Asperen de Boer *et al.*, 'Underdrawing in the Painting of the Rogier van der Weyden and Master of Flémalle Groups', *Nederlands Kunsthistorisch Jaarboek*, 41 (1990), Zwolle 1992.

VAN ASPEREN DE BOER 1997 – J. R. J. van Asperen de Boer, 'On the Underdrawing and Painting Technique of the Master of Aix', *Colloque XI*, Louvain-la-Neuve 1997.

VAN ASPEREN DE BOER, RIDDERBOS and ZELDENRUST 1991 – J. R. J. van Asperen de Boer, B. Ridderbos and M. Zeldenrust, 'Portrait of a Man with a Ring by Jan van Eyck', *Bulletin van het Rijksmuseum*, 39 (1991).

VAN BUREN 1991 – A. H. van Buren, 'Jan van Eyck in the Hours of Turin and Milan, approached through the Fashion in Dress', in *Masters and Miniatures*, Doornspijk 1991.

VAN BUREN 1996a – A. H. van Buren *et al.*, *Heures de Turin-Milan. Inv. No. 47, Museo Civico d'Arte Antica, Torino, Kommentar zum Faksimile*, Lucerne 1996.

VAN BUREN 1996b – A. H. van Buren, 'Van Eyck', in *DoA*.

VANDENBROECK 1985 – P. Vandenbroeck, *Koninklijk Museum voor Schone Kunsten Antwerpen. Catalogus schilderijen 14e en 15e eeuw*, Antwerp 1985.

VANDEVIVERE 1967 – I. Vandevivere, *La cathédrale de Palencia et l'église paroissiale de Cervera de Pisuerga* (Les Primitifs Flamands, Corpus), Brussels 1967.

VANDEVIVERE 1985 – I. Vandevivere, *Juan de Flandes. Europalia Spanje*, exh. cat. Bruges 1985.

VAN MIEGROET 1986 – H. van Miegroet, *De invloed van de vroege Nederlandse schilderkunst in de eerste helft van de 15de eeuw op Konrad Witz*, Brussels 1986.

VAN MIEGROET 1989 – H. van Miegroet, *Gerard David*, Antwerp 1989.

VAN SCHOUTE 1963 – R. van Schoute, *La Chapelle royale de Grenade* (Les Primitifs Flamands, Corpus), Brussels 1963.

VAN SCHOUTE 1994 – R. van Schoute *et al.*, *De Vlaamse Primitieven*, Leuven 1994.

VAN THIEL *et al.* 1976 – P. J. J. van Thiel *et al.*, *Alle schilderijen van het Rijksmuseum te Amsterdam*, Amsterdam and Haarlem 1976.

VANWIJNSBERGHE 2000 – D. Vanwijnsberghe, 'Du nouveau sur le peintre André d'Ypres, artiste du Nord installé à Paris', *Bulletin monumental* (2000).

VALENCIA 2001 – *La clave flamenca en los primitivos valencianos*, exh. cat. Valencia 2001.

VASARI (Bettarini ed.) – G. Vasari, *Le Vite de' più eccelenti architetti, pittori e scultori...*, Florence 1550, 2nd edition Florence 1568; R. Bettarini (ed.), Florence 1966.

VASARI (Milanesi ed.) – G. Vasari, *Le Vite de' più eccelenti architetti, pittori e scultori...*, Florence 1550, 2nd edition Florence 1568; G. Milanesi (ed.), 9 vols, Florence 1878–85.

VAUGHAN 1970 – R. Vaughan, *Philip the Good. The Apogee of Burgundy*, London and Harlow 1970.

VAUGHAN 1973 – R. Vaughan, *Charles the Bold. The Last Valois Duke of Burgundy*, London 1973.

VENICE 1999 – *Renaissance Venice and the North: Crosscurrents in the time of Bellini, Dürer and Titian*, exh. cat. Venice, London and Milan 1999.

VEROUGSTRAETE and VAN SCHOUTE 2000 – H. Verougstraete and R. van Schoute, 'Frames and Supports of some Eyckian Paintings', in Foister, Jones and Cool 2000.

VICINI, CARBONI and PEDEMONTE (forthcoming) – S. Vicini, F. Carboni and E. Pedemonte, 'Chemical Characterisation with Analytical Instruments of Pigments taken from the Saint Andrew Panel' (forthcoming).

VIENNA 2000 – *Maximilian I. Der Aufstieg eines Kaisers: von seiner Geburt bis zur Alleinherrschaft, 1459–1493*, exh. cat. Vienna 2000.

VILLADSEN 1998 – V. Villadsen, *Statens Museum for Kunst – 1827–1952*, Copenhagen 1998.

VOLK-KNÜTTEL 1980 – B. Volk-Knüttel, 'Maximilian I. von Bayern als Sammler und Auftraggeber. Seine Korrespondenz mit Philipp Hainhofer 1611–1615', in H. Glaser (ed.), *Quellen und Studien zur Kunstpolitik der Wittelsbacher vom 16. bis zum 18. Jahrhundert*, Munich 1980.

WALDMAN 2001 – L. A. Waldman, 'New documents for Memling's Portinari portraits in the Metropolitan Museum of Art', *Apollo*, 153 (2001).

WARBURG 1932 – A. Warburg, *Gesammelte Schriften*, I, Leipzig and Berlin 1932.

WARNKE 1996 – M. Warnke, *Hofkünstler. Zur Vorgeschichte des modernen Künstlers*, Cologne 1996.

WASHINGTON, BERGAMO and PARIS 1997–99 – *Lorenzo Lotto*, exh. cat. Washington, Bergamo and Paris 1997–99.

WEALE 1909 – W. H. J. Weale, 'Les Christus', *Annales de la Société d'Emulation de Bruges*, 59 (1909).

WEISS 1955 – R. Weiss, 'Jan van Eyck's Albergati Portrait', *BM*, 97 (1955).

WEISS 1956 – R. Weiss, 'Van Eyck and the Italians, I', *Italian Studies*, 11 (1956).

WEISS 1957 – R. Weiss, 'Van Eyck and the Italians, II,' *Italian Studies*, 12 (1957).

WENIGER 1996 – M. Weniger, *'En Flandes y en otra parte' – Michel Sittow, Juan de Flandes, Felipe Morros*, Ph.D. Diss. Freie Universität, Berlin 1996.

WENIGER 1999a – M. Weniger, 'Altportugiesische Maler', in Bonn 1999.

WENIGER 1999b – M. Weniger, 'Provoost and Portugal', *Colloque XII*, Leuven 1999.

WESCHER 1947 – P. Wescher, *Jean Fouquet und seine Zeit*, Basle 1947.

WHITE 2000 – R. White, 'Van Eyck's Technique. The Myth and the Reality, I', in Foister, Jones and Cool 2000.

WIESFLECKER 1971–86 – H. Wiesflecker, *Kaiser Maximilian I.*, 5 vols, Munich and Vienna 1971–86.

WILSON 1990 – J. C. Wilson, 'The Participation of Painters in the Bruges "Pandt" Market, 1512–1550', *BM*, 82 (1990).

WILSON 1998 – J. C. Wilson, *Painting in Bruges at the Close of the Middle Ages*, University Park 1998.

WINKLER 1913 – F. Winkler, *Der Meister von Flémalle und Rogier van der Weyden*, Strasbourg 1913.

WINKLER 1932 – F. Winkler, 'Der Meister von Moulins und Hugo van der Goes', *Pantheon*, 5 (1932).

WINKLER 1942 – F. Winkler, 'Neuentdeckte Altniederländer: Sanders Bening', *Pantheon*, 15 (1942).

WINKLER 1964 – F. Winkler, *Das Werk des Hugo van der Goes*, Berlin 1964.

WOLFF 1998 – M. Wolff, 'Flanders', in *The Robert Lehman Collection, II: Fifteenth- to Eighteenth-Century European Painting, France, Central Europe, the Netherlands, Spain, and Great Britain*, New York 1998.

WOLFTHAL 1989 – D. Wolfthal, *The Beginning of Netherlandish Canvas Painting: 1400–1530*, Cambridge and New York 1989.

WYMANS 1969 – G. Wymans, 'Sur un prétendu pèlerinage expiatoire de Robert Campin en Provence (1428–1430)', in *Annales de la Fédération archéologique et folklorique de Belgique*, Liège 1969.

YARZA LUACES 1991 – J. Yarza Luaces, 'Isabel la Católica promotora de las artes', *Reales Sitios*, 110 (1991).

YARZA LUACES 1992 – J. Yarza Luaces, 'Gusto y promotor en la época de los Reyes Católicos', *Ephialte. Lecturas de Historia del Arte* (1992).

YARZA LUACES 1993 – J. Yarza Luaces, 'El arte de los Países Bajos en la España de los Reyes Católicos', in *Reyes y Mecenas*, Toledo 1993.

YARZA LUACES 1995 – J. Yarza Luaces, 'La pittura spagnola del Medioevo: il mondo gotico', in *La pittura in Europa. La pittura spagnola*, I, Milan 1995.

YARZA LUACES 2001 – J. Yarza Luaces, 'La miniatura del Renacimiento', in Madrid and Valencia 2001.

YOUNG 1975 – E. Young, *Bartolomé Bermejo: The Great Hispano-Flemish Master*, London 1975.

ZEMAN 2002 – G. Zeman, 'Eine altniederländische Silberstiftzeichnung und ihre Bedeutung für van Eycks Dresdner Marienaltar', *ZfKG*, 65 (2002).

ZERI 1976 – F. Zeri, *Italian Paintings in the Walters Art Gallery*, Baltimore 1976.

ZIMERMAN and KREYCZI 1885 – H. Zimerman and F. Kreyczi, 'Regesten', *Jahrbuch des allerhöchsten Kaiserhauses*, 3 (1885).

Index of names

Acknowledgments

The authors would like to thank the many people who have contributed in one way or another to the exhibition and the catalogue. Special thanks are due to the following: Vincenzo Abbate; Maryan W. Ainsworth; Alexander Acevedo; Michele Ahern; Santiago Alcolea Blanch; Giuliana Algeri; Chiara Angelini; Marián Aparicio; Alberto Arainza; D'Artagnan; Paola Astrua; Adriana Augusti; Lut Ausloos; Colin Bailey; Davide Banzato; Jaime Barrachina; Anna Maria Bava; Evelyn Bavier; Graham Beal; Barbara Beel; Sarah Beel; Sylvain Bellenger; Stephanie Belt; Christiane Besson; Octavian Boiescu; Janine Bofill; Stephen Borys; José Luís Brera; Bettina van den Bremt; Peter van den Brink; Christopher Brown; Mar Boroubia; Helena Bussers; Paul van Calster; Enrique de Calderón; Luís Alonso Cámara; Antonio Cañizares; Beatrice Capaul; Edouard Carbonell; Franca Carboni; James Carder; Ricardo María Carlos; José A. S. Carvalho; Jos Casier; Simonetta Castronovo; Claude Chabanon; Alessandro Cecchi; Richard Celis; Fulvio Cervini; Rocío del Casar; Michel Ceuterick; Julien Chapuis; Richard Charlton-Jones; Fernando Checa Cremades; Keith Christiansen; Bruce Christman; Minora Collins; Denis Coutagne; Katherine Crawford; James Cuno; Margarita Cuyás i Robinson; Jean Pierre Cuzin; Brigit Daprà; Jan Denolf; Ann Depoorter; Ingmari Desaix; Liesbeth De Belie; Jan De Bock; Anna De Gennaro; Gigliola De Martini; Chris Dercon; Mariana Dragu; Karel De Sutter; Anne de Wallens; Jeff Dunn; Frits Duparc; Clario Di Fabio; Jane Farrington; Everett Fahy; Barbara Fegley; Larry Feinberg; Jan-Piet Filedt-Kok; Hal Fischer; Stephen Fliegel; Francine Flynn; Jordi Figuerola; Bart Fransen; Björn Fredlund; Elena Fucikova; Jaak Gabriëls; Guido Gandino; Ivan Gaskell; Francesca Giampaolo; Jeroen Giltaij; Ruth Gleisberg; Eric Gordon; Ted Gott; Michaela Gregor; Alexander van Grevenstein; Rainald Grosshans; John O. Hand; Anne d'Harnoncourt; Paulo Henriques; Martin Herda; Kristina Hermann Fiore; Michel Hilaire; Timothy Husband; Paul Huvenne; Guido Jansen; Erin Jones; Sue Jones; André Jordaan; Ieva Kanepe; Laurence B. Kanter; Jan Kelch; Edward Keenan; George Keyes; Richard Knight; Olaf Koester; Jos Koldeweij; Fritz Koreny; Thomas Kren; Cécile Krings; Friso Lammertse; Paul Lang; Elena Lattanzi; Ronald de Leeuw; Chantal Leplat; Bernd Lindemann; Iva Lisikewycz; Diego López; Susana López; Tomás Llorens; Philippe Lorentz; Nathalie van Looy; Mauro Lucco; Alexandru Lungu; Anne Luyckx; Mireille Madou; Ekkehard Mai; Rosa Manote; Patrice J. Marandel; Emilio Marcos; Werner Marks; Maria Teodora Marques; Didier Martens; Maximiliaan P. J. Martens; Santiago Martínez; Eliana Mattiauda; Sophia McAllister; Mirjam Meisen; Rona Millenaar; Claude Misson; Lorenza Mochi; Hanne Møller; Hélène Mund; Steven Nash; Marnix Neerman; Uta Neidhardt; Giovanna Nepi; Jan Nicolaisen; Hans Nieuwdorp; John Nolan; Rob Noortman; Mark O'Neill; Joaquim Oliveira; Lynn F. Orr; Nils Orht; Enrica Pagella; Elena Parma; Joaquín Pascual; Giovanna Patrignani; Chantal Pauwels; Leo Peeters; Marília Pereira; Franca Pellegrini; Jutta Penndorf; Michelle Peplin; Paolo Dal Poggetto; José Luís Porfirio; Domenico Portera; Tine van Poucke; Earl Powell; Carmen Priego; Productie vzw Brugge 2002; Carol Purtle; Miguel Ángel Recio; Katharine Reid; Mary Reilly; Manuel Reyes; Andrea Rich; Joe Rishel; Nuria Rivero; Dalilah Rodrigues; Josefina Rodriguez; Pierre Rosenberg; Francesco Rossi; Claudio Sabbione; Jochen Sander; Scott Schaefer; Liesbeth Schotsman; Karl Schütz; Gary Schwartz; Wilfried Seipel; Martha Sharma; Barb Sicko; Peter Sigmond; Pilar Silva; Elizabeth Smallwood; Valeria Sola; Carlenrica Spantigatti; Joneath Spicer; Nicolá Spinosa; Ron Spronk; Timothy Standring; Emmanuel Starcky; Angela Steinmetz; Karen Stewart; Marion C. Stewart; Cyriel Stroo; Mary Suzor; Nancy Swallow; Bernard Terlay; Roxana Theordorescu; Carl Brandon Strehlke; Bernard Terlay; Marianne Thys; Dominique Thiébaut; L. Van Thiel Cooveos; Stanton Thomas; Madalena Thomaz; José Antonio de Urbina; Susan Urbach; Rik Vandekonijnenburg; Ellen Vandenbulcke; Stephane Vandenberge; Roger Vangheluwe; George Vaughan; Giovanni Villa; Donata Vicini; Alvaro Fernandez Villaverde; Rosella Vodret; James Welu; Uwe Wieczorek; Eliane de Wilde; Jan Willems; Olivier Zeder; Fred Ziv (†); Miguel Zugaza; Jan van Zwam.

Photographic Credits

Every effort has been made to contact copyright-holders of photographs. Any copyright-holders we have been unable to reach or to whom inaccurate acknowledgment has been made are invited to contact the publisher: Ludion, Muinkkaai 42, B-9000 Gent; Herengracht 376, NL-1016 CH Amsterdam.

Abegg-Stiftung, Riggisberg: fig. 140. – Alexander Gallery, New York: fig. 143; cat. 96. – Fratelli Alinari I.D.E.A. spa: figs 105, 237. – The Allan Memorial Art Museum, Oberlin, Ohio: fig. 23. – Editrice L'Ancora di Acqui Terme: fig. 160. – The Art Institute of Chicago, Chicago: fig. 159; cat. 109. – Bayerische Staatsgemäldesammlungen, Alte Pinakothek und Kunstdia-Archiv Artothek, Peissenberg: fig. 96. – Former Collection of Rodríguez Bauzá, Madrid: fig. 33. – Bibliothèque nationale de France, Paris: fig. 194. – Bibliothèque Royale de Belgique, Brussels: fig. 206. – Bildarchiv Österreichische Nationalbibliothek, Vienna: fig. 205. – Birmingham Museums and Art Gallery, Birmingham: fig. 66; cat. 10. – Heinrich Bischoff, Bremen: fig. 84 (left wing). – Bob Jones University Museum & Gallery, Greenville: fig. 128; cat. 80. – Bonnefantenmuseum, Maastricht: fig. 88; cat. 64. – Bridgeman Art Library, London: figs 13, 91, 93, 102, 107, 111–12, 127, 142, 152–53, 172, 210, 228, 223, 240; cat. 104. – Capilla Real, Granada: fig. 171. – Castle Collection, Prague: fig. 43; cat. 40. – The Cleveland Museum of Art: figs 9, 144, 245; cats 9, 95. – Collegio Alberoni, Piacenza: fig. 101. – Conservation des Antiquités et Objets d'Art de la Haute-Loire (photo: Christiane Besson-Benoit): fig. 86; cat. 67. – Convento de Capuchinas, Castellón: fig. 156. – Denver Art Museum: figs 41, 52, 176; cats 69, 76, 119. – Detroit Institute of Arts: figs 37, 113; cats 30, 69. – Divisão de Documentaçao Fotográfica/Instituto Português de Museus (photos: Pedro Ferreira, Francisco Matias, Manuel Palma, Luis Pavão, José Pessoa): figs 34, 181–91, 249; cats 38, 41, 55, 124, 126–28, 130–31. – Dumbarton Oaks Research Library, Washington, DC. House Collection: fig. 47; cat. 16. – Collection Duque de Infantado, Madrid: fig. 32. – The Fine Art Museums of San Francisco: fig. 42; cat. 69. – Fogg Art Museum, Harvard University Art Museums, Cambridge (Mass.): figs 126, 251; cats 36, 44. – The Frick Collection, New York: fig. 22. – Galleria Borghese, Rome: fig. 224. – Galleria di Palazzo Bianco, Genoa (photo: Archivo Fotografico del Comune di Genova): figs 63, 118–20, 122; cats 51, 91. – Galleria degli Uffizi, Florence: fig. 97. – Galleria dell'Accademia, Turin: fig. 106. – Galleria Giorgio Franchetti alla Ca' d'Oro, Venice: fig. 21; cat. 34. – Galleria Nazionale di Palazzo Barberini, Rome: figs 55, 104; cat. 77. – Galleria Nazionale di Palazzo Ducale, Urbino: figs 135–36. – Galleria Regionale di Sicilia, Palazzo Abatellis, Palermo: fig. 248. – Galleria Sabauda, Turin: fig. 242; cat. 28. – Gallinat-Bank AG, Essen: figs 68, 71; cats 2, 60. – Göteborgs Konstmuseum: fig. 117; cat. 92. – Kelvingrove Art Gallery and Museum, Glasgow: figs 51, 54; cats 63, 72. – Koninklijk Kabinet van Schilderijen 'Mauritshuis', The Hague: figs 208, 236; cats 27, 56. – Koninklijk Museum voor Schone Kunsten, Antwerp: figs 1, 46, 98, 164, 204, 227; cats 26, 48, 70. – Kunsthistorisches Museum, Vienna. Gemäldegalerie: figs 7, 83, 129, 175; cats 24, 115. – López de Aragón, Madrid: fig. 180; cat. 111. – Los Angeles County Museum of Art (photo: Museum Associates/LACMA): figs 67, 232; cats 14, 120. – Hugo Maertens: figs 73, 76, 100, 178, 229; cats 7, 25, 37, 46. – Paul M.R. Maeyaert: fig. 4. – Collection Mateu, Palacio de Perelada, Gerona: fig. 163; cat. 108. – The Metropolitan Museum of Art, New York: figs 15, 16, 106, 108, 122, 130, 214, 238–39; cats 49, 73. – Musée d'Art et d'Histoire, Geneva (photo: Yves Siza): fig. 245. – Musée de l'Hôtel-Dieu, Beaune: figs 60, 61. – Musée départemental d'Art sacré, Pont-Saint-Esprit: fig. 42; cat. 69. – Musée des Beaux-Arts, Dijon (photo: François Jay): figs 80, 200; cat. 82. – Musée des Beaux-Arts, Lyon (photo: Studio Basset): fig. 59. – Musée du Louvre, Paris (photos: RMN, Arnaudet, Jean Schormans, Gérard Blot): figs 11, 25, 38–40, 81, 82, 122, 195; cats 33, 69, 71. – Musée Fabre, Montpellier (photo: Frédéric Jaulmes): fig. 84 (right wing). – Musée Granet, Aix-en-Provence (photo: Bernard Terlay): fig. 44; cat. 8. – Musée Grobet-Labadie, Marseille (photo: Yves Gallois): fig. 198. – Musées Royaux des Beaux-Arts de Belgique, Brussels: figs 69, 77, 139, 146–47 (photos: Speltdoorn), fig. 90 (photo: Cussac); cats 59, 77 (photo: Speltdoorn), cat. 74 (photo Cussac). – Musei Civici, Pesaro. Pinacoteca: fig. 123; cat. 105. – Musei Civici, Pinacoteca Malaspina, Pavia (photo: Fiorenzo Cantalupi): fig. 233; cat. 87. – Musei Vaticani, Vatican City: fig. 85. – Museo Civico d'Arte Antica, Turin: figs 18, 138, 225; cats 79, 88. – Museo Civico Giovanni Fattori, Livorno: fig. 99; cat. 84. – Museo d'Arte Medievale e Moderna, Padua: fig. 20; cat. 85. – Museo de Bellas Artes de Asturias, Oviedo: fig. 170; cat. 118. – Museo de Bellas Artes, Valencia: fig. 165. – Museo de la Colegiata de San Cosme y Damián, Covarrubias (Burgos): fig. 28; cat. 42. – Museo del Patriarca, Valencia: fig. 177; cat. 107. – Museo della Magna Grecia, Reggio di Calabria: fig. 53; cat. 86. – Museo Lázaro Galdiano, Madrid: figs 162, 167. – Museo Municipal, Madrid: fig. 166; cat. 112. – Museo Nacional del Prado, Madrid: figs 24, 161, 241; cats 32, 45, 106. – Museo Nazionale di Capodimonte, Naples (photo: Luciano Pedicini): figs 141, 148; cat. 94. – Museo Poldi-Pezzoli, Milan: fig. 235. – Museo Thyssen-Bornemisza, Madrid: figs 26, 234; cat. 20. – Museu Calouste Gulbenkian, Lisbon: fig. 72. – Museu de Grão Vasco, Viseu: fig. 192; cat. 129. – Museu Frederic Marès, Barcelona: fig. 154. – Museu Nacional d'Art de Catalunya, Barcelona: figs 149–50, 157, 169, 173; cats 116–17, 123. – Museu Nacional do Azulejo, Lisbon: fig. 193; cat. 3. – Museum Boijmans Van Beuningen, Rotterdam: figs 6, 146–47, 211; cat. 65. – Museum der Bildenden Künste, Leipzig: fig. 246. – Museum Mayer van den Bergh, Antwerp: figs 133, 245; cat. 78. – Muzeul National de Artă al României, Bucharest: figs 134, 145, 219; cat. 18, 102. – National Gallery, London: figs 10, 203, 207. – National Gallery of Art, Washington: figs 17, 125, 213, 230; cats 12, 19. – National Gallery of Victoria, Melbourne: fig. 27; cat. 31. – Nelson-Atkins Museum of Art, Kansas City (photo: Mel McLean): fig. 30. – Nivaagaards Malerisamling, Nivå: fig. 110; cat. 90. – Parish Church of Sant Baldiri, Sant Boí de Llobregat: fig. 158; cat. 113. – Patrimonio Nacional, Palacio Real, Madrid: figs 215–218; cat. 115. – J. Paul Getty Museum, Los Angeles: fig. 84 (centre). – Philadelphia Museum of Art, Philadelphia. The John G. Johnson Collection: figs 62, 82, 87, 243; cats 29, 99. – Pinacoteca Civica, Savona: fig. 124; cat. 89. – Pinacoteca dell'Accademia Carrara, Bergamo: figs 50, 65, 103, 222; cat. 103. – Pinacoteca di Brera, Milan: fig. 137. – Private collection, Madrid: fig. 179; cat. 122. – Rijksmuseum, Amsterdam: fig. 226; cat. 97. – Sammlungen des Fürsten von Liechtenstein, Schloss Vaduz: fig. 89; cat. 66. – Staatliche Kunstsammlungen, Dresden. Gemäldegalerie Alte Meister (photo: Klut, Dresden): fig. 115; cat. 23. – Staatliche Kunstsammlungen, Dresden. Kupferstich-Kabinett: fig. 12. – Staatliche Museen zu Berlin. Gemäldegalerie (photos: Jörg P. Anders): figs 14, 19, 58, 78, 131, 196, 247; cats 35, 110. – Staatliches Lindenau-Museum, Altenburg: figs 85, 168; cats 83, 101. – Städelsches Kunstinstitut und Städtische Galerie, Frankfurt: figs 12, 29, 94, 95, 132; cat. 21. – Statens Museum for Kunst, Copenhagen (photos: Hans Petersen): figs 8, 209; cats 11, 57. – Stedelijke Musea, Groeningemuseum, Bruges: figs 2, 3, 36, 56, 57, 70, 74, 92, 197, 199, 201, 244, 250, 252; cats 1, 5, 15, 17, 22, 39, 43, 53, 54, 61, 62, 81, 125. – Stedelijke Musea, Memlingmuseum, Bruges: figs 3, 75, 221; cat. 50. – The Sterling and Francine Clark Art Institute, Williamstown, Mass.: fig. 231. – Timken Art Gallery, San Diego. Putnam Foundation: fig. 45; cat. 13. – Villa Cagnola, Gazzada (Varese): fig. 121. – The Walters Art Museum, Baltimore: fig. 114; cat. 98. – The Worcester Art Museum, Worcester, Mass.: fig. 35; cat. 41.